W9-ALU-875

FROM
EVE
TO
DAWN

Other Books by Marilyn French

Fiction

The Women's Room (1977)

The Bleeding Heart (1980)

Her Mother's Daughter (1987)

Our Father (1994)

My Summer with George (1996)

In the Name of Friendship (2006)

Nonfiction

Beyond Power. On Women, Men and Morals (1988)

Women in India (1990)

The War Against Women (1992)

A Season in Hell. A Memoir (1998)

A HISTORY OF WOMEN

VOLUME 3:

INFERNOS AND PARADISES, THE TRIUMPH OF CAPITALISM IN THE 19TH CENTURY

MARILYN FRENCH

Foreword by
Margaret Atwood

The Feminist Press
at The City University of New York

Published in 2008 by The Feminist Press at The City University of New York
The Graduate Center
365 Fifth Avenue, Suite 5406
New York, NY 10016
www.feministpress.org

The Library of Congress provided the following Cataloguing-in-Publication Data for all four volumes of this series:

Library of Congress Cataloging-in-Publication Data

French, Marilyn, 1929–
From eve to dawn / Marilyn French ; foreword by Margaret Atwood.
p. cm.
Originally published: Toronto : McArthur, 2002.

ISBN 978-155861-583- 0 (trade paper)

1. Women—History. I. Title.
HQ1121.F74 2008
305.4209—dc22

2007033836

This publication was made possible, in part, by the Lawrence W. Levine Foundation, Inc., and by Florence Howe, Joanne Markell, and Eileen Bonnie Schaefer.

Cover design by Black Cat Design
Cover illustration by Carole Hoff

12 11 10 09 08 5 4 3 2 1

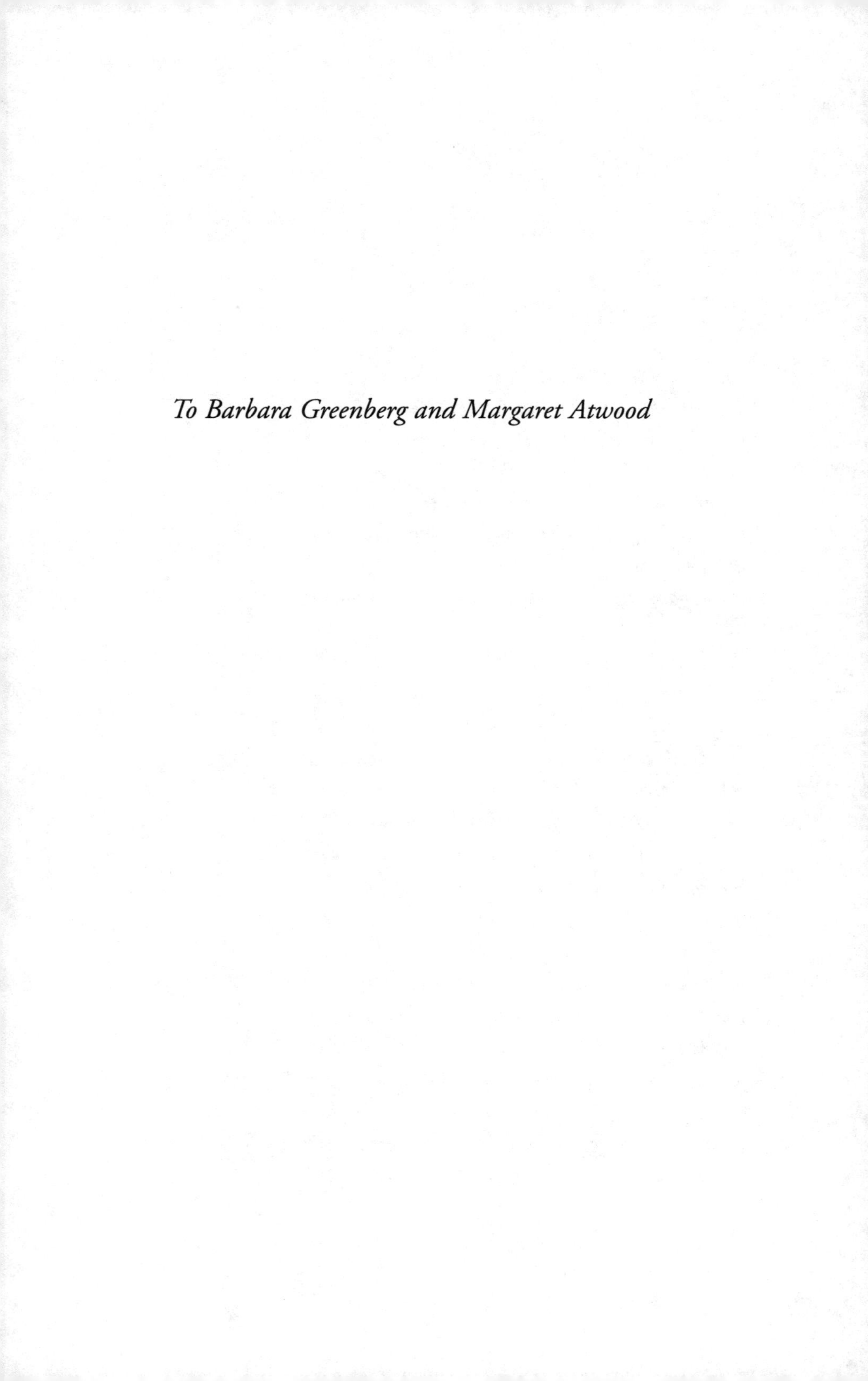

To Barbara Greenberg and Margaret Atwood

CHANGES OF NAME

Changes of name, style, faith, vocation, partner
occur so often among your friends that you
don't know now where you stand with them. You're tilling
what you believe to be the good old acreage
but the plains on which you live seem windier, and the bus
when it U-turns at the bend to take on passengers
isn't delivering any, or much except catalogs.
Most mornings you walk down and back unaltered.

Where did everyone go, where is everyone?
How come it's only you and the birds in the open
with rivers echoing Bach and skies by Turner
and rich steam from a kettle of soup left simmering
into the air, but where are the hands with their bowls?
Changes of mind, changes of diet and rhythm
have swept them leagues from you, even the elders,
even the youths for whom you sang and poured

so when the angel alights nearby, what pleasure
to welcome him, to see his wings descending
like black silk lingerie but perfectly solemn
and yet invitingly. As if from Eve to Dawn
your own name changes. Your intimate ghosts
veer off to sea the way old weather does, and something
is settled. Although the angel leaves without you
and without touching you, you know: it is settled.

—*Barbara Greenberg*

CONTENTS

FOREWORD

FROM EVE TO DAWN is Marilyn French's enormous four-volume, nearly two-thousand-page history of women. It runs from prehistory until the present, and is global in scope: the first volume alone covers Peru, Egypt, Sumer, China, India, Mexico, Greece, and Rome, as well as religions from Judaism to Christianity and Islam. It examines not only actions and laws, but also the thinking behind them. It's sometimes annoying, in the same way that Henry Fielding's *Amelia* is annoying—enough suffering!—and it's sometimes maddeningly reductionist; but it can't be dismissed. As a reference work it's invaluable: the bibliographies alone are worth the price. And as a warning about the appalling extremes of human behavior and male weirdness, it's indispensable.

Especially now. There was a moment in the 1990s when, it was believed, history was over and Utopia had arrived, looking very much like a shopping mall, and "feminist issues" were supposed dead. But that moment was brief. Islamic and American right-wing fundamentalists are on the rise, and one of the first aims of both is the suppression of women: their bodies, their minds, the results of their labors—women, it appears, do most of the work around this planet—and last but not least, their wardrobes.

From Eve to Dawn has a point of view, one that will be familiar to the readers of French's best-selling 1977 novel, *The Women's Room*. "The people who oppressed women were men," French claims. "Not all men oppressed women, but most benefited (or thought they benefited) from this domination, and most contributed to it, if only by doing nothing to stop or ease it."

Women who read this book will do so with horror and growing anger: *From Eve to Dawn* is to Simone de Beauvoir's *The Second Sex* as wolf is to poodle. Men who read it might be put off by the depiction of the collective male as brutal psychopath, or puzzled by French's idea that men should "take responsibility for what their sex has done." (How responsible can you be for Sumerian monarchs, Egyptian pharaohs, or Napoleon Bonaparte?) However, no one will be able to avoid the relentless piling up of detail and event—the bizarre customs, the woman-hating legal structures, the gynecological absurdities, the child abuse, the sanctioned violence, the sexual outrages—millennium after millennium. How to explain them? Are all men twisted? Are all women doomed? Is there hope? French is ambivalent about the twisted part, but, being a peculiarly American kind of activist, she insists on hope.

Her project started out as a sweeping television series. It would have made riveting viewing. Think of the visuals—witch-burnings, rapes, stonings-to-death, Jack the Ripper clones, bedizened courtesans, and martyrs from Joan of Arc to Rebecca Nurse. The television series fell off the rails, but French kept on, writing and researching with ferocious dedication, consulting hundreds of sources and dozens of specialists and scholars, although she was interrupted by a battle with cancer that almost killed her. The whole thing took her 20 years.

Her intention was to put together a narrative answer to a question that had bothered her for a long time: how had men ended up with all the power—specifically, with all the power over women? Had it always been like that? If not, how was such power grasped and then enforced? Nothing she had read had addressed this issue directly. In most conventional histories, women simply aren't there. Or they're there as footnotes. Their absence is like the shadowy corner in a painting where there's something going on that you can't quite see.

French aimed to throw some light into that corner. Her first volume—*Origins*—is the shortest. It starts with speculations about the kind of egalitarian hunter-gatherer societies also described by Jared Diamond in his classic, *Guns, Germs and Steel.* No society, says French, has ever been a matriarchy—that is, a society in which women are all-powerful and do dastardly things to men. But societies were once matrilineal: that is, children were thought to descend from the mother, not the father. Many have wondered why that state of affairs changed, but change it did; and as agriculture took over, and patriarchy set in, women and children came to be viewed as property—men's property, to be bought, sold, traded, stolen, or killed.

As psychologists have told us, the more you mistreat people, the more pressing your need to explain why your victims deserve their fate. A great deal has been written about the "natural" inferiority of women, much of it by the philosophers and religionmakers whose ideas underpin Western society. Much of this thinking was grounded in what French calls, with wondrous understatement, "men's insistent concern with female reproduction." Male self-esteem, it seemed, depended on men not being women. All the more necessary that women should be forced to be as "female" as possible, even when—especially when—the male-created definition of "female" included the power to pollute, seduce, and weaken men.

With the advent of larger kingdoms and complex and structured religions, the costumes and interior decoration got better, but things got worse for women. Priests—having arguably displaced priestesses—came up with decrees from the gods who had arguably replaced goddesses, and kings obliged with legal codes and penalties. There were conflicts between spiritual and temporal power brokers, but the main tendency of both was the same: men good, women bad, by definition. Some of French's information boggles the mind: the "horse sacrifice" of ancient India, for instance, during which the priests forced the raja's wife to copulate with a dead horse. The account of the creation of Islam is particularly fascinating: like Christianity, it was woman-friendly at the start, and supported and spread by women. But not for long.

The Masculine Mystique (Volume Two) is no more cheerful. Two kinds of feudalism are briskly dealt with: the European and the Japanese. Then it's on to the appropriations by Europeans of Africa, of Latin America, of North America, and thence to the American enslavement of blacks, with women at the bottom of the heap in all cases. You'd think the Enlightenment would have loosened things up, at least theoretically, but at the salons run by educated and intelligent women the philosophers were still debating—while hoovering up the refreshments—whether women had souls, or were just a kind of more advanced animal. In the 18th century, however, women were beginning to find their voices. Also they took to writing, a habit they have not yet given up.

Then came the French Revolution. At first, women as a caste were crushed by the Jacobins despite the key role they had played in the aristocracy-toppling action. As far as the male revolutionaries were concerned, "Revolution was possible only if women were utterly excluded from power."

Liberty, equality, and fraternity did not include sorority. When Napoleon got control "he reversed every right women had won." Yet after this point, says French, "women were never again silent." Having participated in the overthrow of the old order, they wanted a few rights of their own.

Infernos and Paradises, the third volume, and *Revolution and the Struggles for Justice*, the fourth volume, take us through the growing movement for the emancipation of women in the 19th and 20th centuries, with the gains and reverses, the triumphs and the backlashes, played out against a background of imperialism, capitalism, and world wars. The Russian Revolution is particularly gripping—women were essential to its success—and particularly dispiriting as to the results. "Sexual freedom meant liberty for men and maternity for women," says French. "Wanting sex without responsibility, men charged women who rejected them with 'bourgeois prudery.' . . . To treat women as men's equals without reference to women's reproduction . . . is to place women in the impossible situation of being expected to do everything men do, and to reproduce society and maintain it, all at the same time and alone."

It's in the final three chapters of the fourth volume that French comes into her home territory, the realm of her most personal knowledge and her deepest enthusiasms. "The History of Feminism," "The Political Is Personal, The Personal Is Political," and "The Future of Feminism" make up the promised "dawn" of the general title. These sections are thorough and thoughtful. In them, French covers the contemporary ground, including the views of antifeminist and conservative women—who, she argues, see the world much as feminists do—one half of humanity acting as predators on the other half—but differ in the degree of their idealism or hope. (If gender differences are "natural," nothing to be done but to manipulate the morally inferior male with your feminine wiles, if any.) But almost all women, she believes—feminist or not—are "moving in the same direction along different paths."

Whether you share this optimism or not will depend on whether you believe Earth Titanic is already sinking. A fair chance and a fun time on the dance floor for all would be nice, in theory. In practice, it may be a scramble for the lifeboats. But whatever you think of French's conclusions, the issues she raises cannot be ignored. Women, it seems, are not a footnote after all: they are the necessary center around which the wheel of power revolves; or, seen another way, they are the broad base of the triangle that sustains a few oligarchs at the top. No history you will read, post-French, will ever look the same again.

Margaret Atwood
Canada
August 2004

INTRODUCTION

FROM *EVE TO DAWN* was first published in Canada in 2002–2003, but it was written over a decade earlier. Publishers bought it, but procrastinated, intimidated by its length. Each one finally declined to print. The book, which took me more than fifteen years to research and write, was 10,000 pages long. Initially I refused the publishers' pleas to cut it, but eventually, I had to do so. Removing so much material harmed the book. For instance, in recounting women's battle for education, I described the awesome daily schedule of the first young women in England to attend college. I provided the onerous schedules of the first young women to study nursing with Florence Nightingale. In removing detail like this, I diminished the richness of the story, and the reader's admiration for these women. Unfortunately, I did not keep careful records of these removals, and can no longer retrieve them. The information can still be found, but only in my sources, the books or articles from which I gleaned my material.

The world has changed since I finished writing the book, but none of the changes alters the history of women very much. For instance, I had predicted that Serbia, in rabid Christian zeal, would mount military action against the other Yugoslavian states. But I had to remove this bit, since, by the time the book was published in 2002, the wars in Yugoslavia, initiated by Serbia, had not only begun but ended. Originally, I predicted that "fundamentalist" Islamic movements in the Middle East would grow; by the time the book was published, this forecast was a fait accompli.

The major change affecting women during the last three decades is this proliferation of fundamentalisms. These religious movements are widespread, occurring within every world religion: Christianity (the born-again Christian movement in the United States, the drive to criminalize abortion centered in the Catholic Church); Islam (militant brotherhoods like the Taliban in most Muslim states), and even Judaism (e.g., Gush Emunim in Israel) and Hinduism, which are both historically nonproselytizing. The politics of these movements are not new, but the emotions of the men involved in them intensified to the point of fanaticism after the1970s. Thus, whatever their claims, they were not only responses to Western colonization or industrialization, but a backlash against spreading feminism.

Another major change that occurred during this period was the demise of the USSR and the shift from socialism to a kind of capitalism in Russia and its satellite states, without in most cases much movement toward democratization. China too has shifted in the direction of capitalism without moderating its dictatorial government. It has also experienced considerable industrialization and Westernization. Economic changes like these, globalization, and the emergence of "free trade" thinking, have increased the gap between the very rich and everyone else, and affect women and men similarly. Economic changes hit the most vulnerable people hardest, and everywhere in the world, women and children are the most vulnerable. Women and children make up four-fifths of the poorest people on earth. One consequence of these economic developments is a huge increase in slavery, trade in human beings, which particularly affects women, who are nowadays bought and sold across the globe for use as prostitutes and slave laborers—and in China, as slave-wives. Unlike earlier forms of slavery, this form is illegal, yet thrives everywhere.

But women continue to fight for egalitarian treatment: despite the double standards, women in Iran (a religious dictatorship) and Egypt (a secular dictatorship) try to work within the law. The Iranian government frequently imprisons, whips, and even kills women who challenge its standards; Egypt imprisons them. Government does not get involved in Pakistan, Afghanistan, or the former Soviet republics, where women who appear to deviate from the oppressive moral code are punished and killed by their own families—their fathers or brothers—or their village councils. Yet women go on protesting.

Men involved in fundamentalist movements see feminism as a threat. Feminism is simply the belief that women are human beings with human rights. Human rights are not radical claims, but merely basic rights—the right to walk around in the world at will, to breathe the air and drink water and eat food sufficient to maintain life, to speak at will and control one's own body and its movements, including its sexuality. Fundamentalists deny women this status, treating them as if they were nonhuman beings created by a deity to serve men, who own them. Fundamentalist movements thrust the history of women into a tragic new phase. Across the globe, men who see feminism as a threat to their dominance are clamping down with religious fervor on women in order to maintain their dominance.

Control over a woman is the only form of dominance most men possess, for most men are merely subjects of more powerful men. But so unanimous is the drive for dominance in male cultures that men can abuse women across the board with impunity. A man in India who burns his wife to death in a dowry dispute has no trouble obtaining a second wife from another family that allegedly loves its daughter.[1] Latin American and Muslim men who kill their wives under the guise of an "honor" killing have no trouble finding replacements.

Misogyny is not an adequate term for this behavior. It is rooted not in hatred of women, but in a belief that women are not human beings, but animals designed to serve men and men's ends, with no other purpose in life. Men in such cultures see women who resist such service as perverse, godless creatures who deny the purpose for which they were created. In light of the ubiquity and self-righteousness of such men, we need to consider the origins of their beliefs.

In the original Preface to this book I said, "I wrote this history because I needed a story to make sense of what I knew of the past and what I saw in the present." In fact, I began with a vision. The first time I had the vision, it was a dream, but it recurred many times over my lifetime, and in its later reincarnations I was awake when I saw it—although always in bed, on the verge of sleep. I never consciously summoned this vision. In it, I am tortured by not-knowing, and one day I awaken to find an angel sitting on the side of my bed. It is a male angel, and gold from head to toe, like an Oscar—although the first time I had it, I was a young girl and knew nothing about Oscars. I welcome the angel and plead my case: please, please explain to me how things got to be the way they are, I say. Things make no sense. I don't understand how they came about. The angel agrees, and proceeds to explain. He talks for a long time and at the end I understand everything. It all makes sense. I am filled with gratitude. Yes, the angel says, but now that you know, you are not permitted to live. You must die. Okay, I say. I don't mind. He embraces me and together we magically ascend to heaven. I am in bliss because I understand everything.

This dream, or vision, is what drove me throughout the years of work. I did not start with a belief; the story emerged from the material as I did the research, especially after I started work on Africa, where the process of patriarchic organization was still occurring when Arab traders arrived there. I let the explanation filter into the text as I discovered it. The argument is thus threaded through the text, and is not readily abstracted from it. I am taking the opportunity in this new Introduction to offer the explanation separately.

Humans of some form have lived on the planet for almost four million years, although our own species, homo sapiens sapiens, is only about 100,000 years old. We do not know how earlier hominids lived, but we can study our nearest relatives, chimpanzees, to get some idea. Chimpanzees live in heterosocial groups, males and females, young and old, together. (Other animals do not live this way. Many mammals—lions, and elephants, for instance, live in homosocial groups—related females together, along with their young, and males in isolation.) Dominance hierarchies are also unisexual: those among males affect only males; those among females affect only females. Moreover, dominance has a narrow meaning for animals: a dominant male has first dibs over food and sexual access to females. Inferior males are expected to defer to the alpha male in disputes over food or sex. But his dominance can be and regularly is challenged or evaded; it also shifts from one animal to another. In no animal species do dominant males or females dictate the behavior of other animals. They do not rule each other, as humans try to do. An animal may have authority because of her status in the group, but does not possess the right to command other animals to do or not do anything.

But females regularly intervene in male affairs. Within chimpanzee society, a particular animal may be loved or respected, usually because she has offered others comfort, grooming, or care. This gives her the authority to intervene when males are fighting among themselves, or picking on a particular animal. Her authority resides solely in the willingness of the other animals to hearken to her.

Females regularly disregard male status, having sex with whom they choose, often with low-status chimps.[2]

Chimpanzees live in family groups of 20 to 30 in the forest. Females migrate to other groups to mate, but may return to their natal group afterward. Females take total responsibility for socializing the young. A mother teaches her child what is good as food and medicine, to make a bed each night, to make and use tools, and to communicate with other chimps through calls and expressive sound. She feeds her baby until it is five years old, but chimps usually remain with their mothers for a decade. If a mother dies, her baby often dies of grief, unless other family members take care of it. Fatherhood is of course unknown—as is the case with most animals—but males are heavily involved in tending the young.[3]

Chimpanzees often display empathetic behavior, even for beings of different species.[4] Their ability to feel empathy leads them occasionally to perform seemingly altruistic acts, in what is the foundation of a moral sense. Because chimp young, like human babies, require years of parental care to survive, they have a need to be loved. From the mother-child bond of love arises the bond unifying the chimpanzee community.

Scientists assume that early hominids lived in much the same way, in groups made up of sisters and brothers, the women's children, and their mates. This form of society is called matricentry. It is important to distinguish this from matriarchy, a term many people use in error. Matriarchy means "ruled by mothers." There has never been a matriarchal state, so far as we know, although there may be matriarchal families. Matricentry means centered around the mother, a form found in most families.

Female chimpanzees produce only about three infants in a lifetime, one every five or six years. Hominids may have done the same. Fatherhood was unknown and remained so during most of the three-plus millennia of human existence. For hundreds of years, people lived by gathering fruits, vegetables, and grains, which was done almost entirely by females. Males gather, when they do, only for themselves; females feed the entire clan. Both sexes hunted small animals with their hands. Around 10,000 BCE, people—probably women—started to plant crops, perhaps wheat. The move to horticulture caused a major change in human life because it entailed living in settled communities.

Women being central in the group, and being the ones who fed the group, were also the ones considered to have rights in the land. All early societies in Africa and North America believed land could not be owned, but that those who settled it had the right to use it. In prehistory, women had rights to use the land, which passed to their daughters. This system was still pervasive when foreigners penetrated indigenous societies. Women remained on the land they inherited, and men migrated from other clans to mate with them. Children belonged to the mother, the only known parent, and were named for her. If a mating was unhappy, a man could leave his wife but could not take the children, who were part of her matriline. All babies were accepted in their mother's clan from birth. There was no such thing as illegitimacy. Nor, in such societies, could men abuse their wives, who were surrounded by family members who would protect them.

Anthropologists who studied the remaining matrilineal groups in earlier decades reported that they were harmonious. They are now usually male-dominant, although men derive their importance from their sisters. Children inherit from their uncles. In hunting-gathering societies, men remain at the village when the women go to gather; they gamble, they play, and they watch the children. Only occasionally do they hunt. Male-female groups may hunt together with nets and spears.[5] When a clan discovered weaving or pottery-making, it was usually women who did this work too. But men's sociability and playfulness gave them an advantage when politics—negotiations among different clans—began. The women, who gathered singly although they went out together, were more bound to their own family units because they took responsibility for them.

Hominids and early humans lived this way for nearly four million years. They lived in peace; there are no signs of weapons until about 10,000 years ago. Some communities left traces behind, like Catal Hüyük in Turkey. This Anatolian community thrived from about 10,000 BCE until 8,000 BCE—surviving longer than ancient Greece or Sumer or any European nation. Its people lived in connected houses entered from the top by a ladder. (Houses of early periods were often shaped like internal female organs: they had a vaginal passage leading to a room shaped like the uterus—like igloos). In Catal Hüyük, many houses had shrines attached to them. Their wall paintings showed that they were devoted to animals and hunting. Later, when the supply of animals had dwindled, they were devoted to goddesses. The people of Catal Hüyük traveled far—their middens contained jewels, mirrors, stones, and woods from thousands of miles away. They had a rich and varied diet including alcoholic drinks; they had weaving and pottery and painting and made female figurines.[6] Their paintings depict a dangerous game played by young men and women: leaping the bull, and showed both sexes in lovely, sexy clothes.[7]

The ruins of Knossos are even more impressive, containing paved streets, houses with roof gardens, gutters, toilets, and baths. It seems to have been an egalitarian society with writing, a very high standard of living and a love of art. In their paintings, women sit in the front and men in the rear at public events. Women are depicted as hunters, farmers, merchants, chariot drivers; one is even commander of a ship. The city was probably destroyed by a volcano.

Not only these towns but this entire political structure perished. People went on living in matricentric, matrilineal clans—they still exist in Africa—but some clans changed their political structure. The first states arose in Egypt and Sumer, toward the end of the fourth millennium. The beginnings of a move toward patriarchy are reflected in Egyptian art, which depicts human beings of equal size until the end of the fourth millennium, when artists began to paint one man taller amid a crowd of others of normal height. This change reflects a political change in African societies that was occurring when the first Arab merchants infiltrated it and observed the process. It is the shift to patriarchy.

Patriarchy was the result of a revolution, the world's first. It occurred after men had realized they had a part in procreation, knowledge that triggered their discontent. They may have wanted to own the young they fathered, in order to control their labor, but it appears their main objective was to obtain more power over women. They raided villages to obtain captive women. (Many societies—like Rome, for instance—have founding myths based on men's rape of women.) Once removed from their clan, women had no claim to land or labor in their home villages, and were freed of their obligation to their families. Having no rights, they were essentially slaves.[8] Men mated with them, keeping them under surveillance, but because they were unsure how long it took for a fetus to mature, or how to prove fatherhood, they killed the firstborn child. Murder of firstborn children is a regular mark of patrilineal groups.

Men kept these women under surveillance in their villages to assure their paternity, and began to make rules that applied only to women. Thus, the first criminals were women. Men declared it a crime (adultery) for women to have sex with anyone but their owners, and for women to abort children, although men had the right in every ancient society, to murder their own children (infanticide). Men declared that children belonged to their fathers and named them for the fathers. Children whose fathers were unknown were decreed illegitimate, bastards.

Women, kidnapped from various villages, often could not speak the language of their captors, nor those spoken by other women in the village. Forever alien, they were probably unhappy. Most patrilineal groups allowed them to leave, but forbade their taking the children with them, so few women left. Children belonged to their patriliny, which disposed of them as it chose. Doubtless women's unhappiness communicated itself to the men, because in most patrilinies, men do not live with women. In past and present patrilinies, men use women for sex and require women to feed them, but live in separate men's houses. Some require great subservience, bowing and other forms of obeisance, from the enslaved women.

The society in men's houses, according to anthropologists who have studied them, is miserable—contentious and bickering. Women live with their children in women's houses until boys are taken from them at adolescence. Girls remain until they are grown enough to be used as barter to other clans in a search for wives. It is in these clans that the most cruel male puberty rites occur, when boys are taken from their mothers and introduced into the men's houses. Many of these clans have myths referring to a time when women had powers that they have lost—sometimes symbolized by flutes or other instruments. The message of puberty rites is the same whether a boy is being initiated by the Chaka, by British public (private) schools, or by the Catholic Church: the first birth, through women, is merely nature, a lowly state. To become a human being, a boy must be born again through men. Many puberty rites force boys to simulate crawling through the birth canal, and inflict pain supposedly caused by birth. Sometimes the penis is cut to draw blood, simulating women's menstruation. A boy learns through this process that the important parent is the father, whom he must obey. He learns the power structure he must live within and he learns to reject his mother as an inferior being, and emotion as an unworthy state. He learns to bear pain stoically and to isolate himself emotionally.

Matrilineal and patrilineal clans coexisted for thousands of years—indeed, they still do. The clans found in many Arab, Asian, and African states and in South America are descendants of these ancient clans. Some people consider clans egalitarian, because all the clans are equal in importance. But they are not egalitarian, they are male-dominant. Few matrilineal clans still exist, and even they have become male-dominant.

During the fourth millennium, in certain places, however, men grew ambitious and built a larger structure, the state. A state is a property ruled by a particular government. States are supposed to be bound by fixed geographical features, are supposed to contain people related by genetic background and the same language, but none of these is actually the case. What we call the state arose first in Sumer and Egypt, and soon afterward, in China. It arose because certain men, not satisfied with dominance over women, wanted to dominate men. To this end, they introduced the two major instruments of patriarchy: war and religion.

A different form of religion had long existed everywhere, as is attested to by the ubiquity of female figurines. People implored the female principle, a goddess, for corn and oil and babies. If a goddess did not come through, her adherents turned their backs on her. She was powerful but not fearsome. Her main worshippers were priestesses, who also guarded the communal granary. (In American Indian groups like the Iroquois, women controlled stored food. Thus, the clan could not go to war without female approval.)

Myths of many peoples describe the long struggle by a particular male god to unseat a goddess. The god uses various methods of attack, but invariably fails. The goddess is invincible. Then one day he discovers weapons. When he attacks the goddess with weapons, he is able to overthrow her. He becomes supreme and immediately names subsidiary gods (and sometimes, a few goddesses): hierarchy is born. In some societies, myths describe a time when women owned the flutes—or other magical instruments—until men found a way to trick them out of them, or to steal them. We can deduce the shift from clan structure to a state, and the shift from matricentry, matrilinearity, and matrilocal marriage to patriarchy.

Unlike the goddesses, male gods made decrees: they dictated

rules and punishments for breaking the rules. All present world religions are patriarchal and male-dominant, and willfully deny godhead to women, from the early and very harsh Laws of Manu, which form Hindu law, to the Jewish man's daily prayer thanking god for not making him a woman, to the founding mystery of the Catholic Church, a Trinity made up of a father who alone creates a son, who together with him creates the Holy Ghost. Mohammed, who started out treating women as almost equal to men, himself changed as he aged, and the Hadith, the books commenting on the Koran, present a long record of Muslim leaders increasingly confining women and denying their humanity.[9]

From a largely anarchic world, humankind moved to patriarchy, authoritarian rule by the fathers. Early states were formed by one warrior who set himself up as king, general (leader in war), and head priest. The ruler and his entire family claimed to be humanly superior to all others by virtue of their relationship to deity. This was the beginning of a class system. Some early class systems may have been related to color. Caste, the Indian word for class, means color in Portuguese.

In the beginning, upper-class women may not have been bound by rules binding other women. Egyptian women were governed by the fairly egalitarian laws of their own land until Alexander ushered in a Greek dynasty that followed Greek law (which was extremely discriminating against women). There are records of women pharaohs (although they have been partly erased): women were rulers and military generals in China, empresses in Japan, and the heads of households in Egypt. But over time, as the goddesses were demoted into barmaids and prostitutes, women were all treated as servants, whatever their class—consider Athena, waiting on Achilles in *The Odessey*.

Early states were ruled by men who filled the position of chief general, head of state, and head priest. Sargon, for example, who lived around 2,350 BCE, was a warrior said to make rivers run red with blood. A Semite from Akkad, as a general, he ruled a unified Sumer and Akkad, and named himself head priest. His daughter, Enheduanna, head priestess of Inanna, was also a great poet (the first poet we know about), and a philosopher. Her work celebrates her father's connection to the goddess Ishtar/Inanna. For millennia, Chinese and Japanese emperors maintained that they were related to deity or received their power from a deity. Witness the "divine right" of European kings. In early periods, humans might be sacrificed when such a ruler died, even if the group still worshipped a goddess.

Increasingly, rulers required the supremacy of a male god. The people demurred, they liked their goddesses and would not switch. As late as the Roman Empire, governments tried various stratagems to displace goddesses. The conflict is apparent in inadvertent slips in the sacred books—in the Vedas, the Old Testament, and Persian history. These volumes of women's history trace this movement in many societies. There are local variations, and some heroines along the way, but the picture is similar throughout history. I urge you to read a chapter at a time, pausing between them. Reading the books will alert you to the many ways women can be—and have been—constricted, and on what grounds. The great moment comes in the twentieth century, when women joined together to end this oppression.

Since there is a concerted movement worldwide to retract the progress women have made in the last three or four decades, it is essential that we be aware of what can happen—what has happened—and what is happening now. Women have made progress but only in certain geographical areas, and only in some classes. That is, women in the West who are educated have won great battles for rights. Yet even educated Western women continue to suffer from double standards, and there is much remaining to be done even here. But our sisters in the East require the most help. The American government claimed, when we first invaded Afghanistan, that part of the purpose was to liberate Afghan women—just as the British claimed, when they invaded India, that their purpose was to end the practice of suttee. In fact, the British did not give a damn about Indian women, just as the American government doesn't give a damn about Afghan women. A fine book by Ann Jones presents Afghan women as they live today.[10]

We are facing a long battle. Many of us are unaware that the war is even engaged, but if you watch television, or pay attention to the way the sexes are depicted in any medium, if you pay attention to history, and know what has happened in the past, you will realize that the rights we have so arduously won in the United States slowly but surely can be rescinded by a right-wing Supreme Court combined with a right-wing government. And are.

Acknowledgments

Although only I bear responsibility for the statements and point of view of this book, as well as the errors it must contain, I have not written it alone. Tens of scholars helped me, with essays summarizing the important points about their periods, bibliographies, and in some cases, articles or books. They helped me generously, even when they disagreed with my approach to historiography or disapproved of using anthropological information in a history. I thank them all.

First, I thank Claudia Koonz, who helped organize the subject matter and found most of the historian contributors. Jo Ann McNamara gave me information about Europe over an amazing period—from the Roman Empire all the way through to the late Christian period; Marcia Wright and Susan Hall patiently guided me through the thicket of Africa, the history of a continent. In addition, I thank Françoise Basch, Jon-Christian Billigmeier, Charlotte Bunch, Rebecca Cann, Blanche Cook, Elizabeth Croll, Ann Farnsworth, Kirsten Fischer, Jean Franco, Martha Gimenez,

Karen Gottshang, Carol Hochstedler, Anne Holmes, Nikki Keddie, Renate Klein, Johanna Lessinger, Susan Mann, Marjorie Mbilinyi, John Mencher, Carol Meyers, Marysa Navarro, Karen Nussbaum, Veena Oldenburg, Leslie Peirce, Cathy Rakowski, Nan Rothschild, Kumkum Roy, Karen Rubinson, Irene Silverblatt, and Stephanie Urdang. Help was also given by Alice Kessler-Harris, Catherine Pellissier, Carroll Smith-Rosenberg, Ann Snitow, Amy Swerdlow, Romila Thapur, and Alice Valentine. Researchers included Judith Byfield, Binnur Ercen, Tikva Frymer-Kensky, Rivka Harris, Kathi Kern, Stella Maloof, Linda Mitchell, Lisa Norling, Claire Potter, Gisela Shue, Temma Kaplan, and Tracey Weis. Other notable assistance came from Fadwa al Guindi, Beatrice Campbell, Donna Haraway, Barbara Lesko, Lynn Mally, Rayna Rapp, Judith Tucker, and Ann Volks. My incalculably important assistants over this fifteen-year period were Betsy Chalfin, Isabelle de Cordier, Hana Elwell, and Judi Silverman.

Marilyn French
New York, New York
June 2007

CAPITALISM TRIUMPHANT

THE NINETEENTH CENTURY ROILED WITH CONTRADICTION. It was the lowest point in women's history: a male historian has pointed out that nineteenth-century British women had fewer rights than Babylonian women possessed when Hammurabi's Code was written.[1] Moreover, British women were no worse off than women in other Western countries, and perhaps better off than women in Eastern societies.

But the nineteenth century was also the period in which women as a caste for the first time stood up en masse and demanded an end to subjugation. Hard-earned victories gradually won them the right to acquire advanced education, to learn a profession and actually practice it, and to own their personal property. From the perspective of this book, it is the most cheering period in female history, the moment the tide began to turn.

It was just such a period for workers, too (many of whom were now women); they also began to stand up and protest wages that were inadequate to maintain life, as well as inhumane working conditions and hours. Middle-class people, including many women, sided with the workers, arguing also that tiny children should not be working in factories, tied to machines, and that all children should be decently fed, healed, and educated.

But of course, such arguments would not have been necessary if the actual conditions of life were not so hellish. Cities were overcrowded, filthy, and unhealthy; factories were unsanitary and unhygienic, and workers were treated worse than animals. Yet even so, agricultural workers often found factory work preferable to work on the farm, which was brutally hard and demeaning.

To complete the picture of this age of contrasts, it was also a period when socialists (and others) began to envision better ways of living, inventing utopian schemes for living and working in harmony with nature and the machine. Some of these schemes were realized, in towns that still stand (as ruins) in England and the United States. But none of them were successful, largely because men continued to exploit women.

The industrial hells wrought in northern cities were paralleled by imperialist expansion in the south and east, in Africa and Asia. The horrors described in Joseph Conrad's great novella "Heart of Darkness" occurred in this period. The nineteenth century's cruel expropriation of Africa and Asia reverberates today, having created problems that still persist.

CHAPTER 1

IMPERIALISM IN AFRICA

Between about 1830 and the Second World War, two developments changed the human condition itself. One was the invention of power-driven machines that brought on the industrial revolution, changing not only the kind of work people did but also where, with whom, and under what conditions they worked and lived. The other was the emergence of a new vision of humanity, a new morality. Enlightenment ideas subverted the passive acceptance that characterizes much religious thinking. People burning with new conceptions of human nature and human rights envisioned new possibilities for living.

Power-driven machines gave humans greater control over matter and in some ways offered an easier life than they had imagined possible. But men's exploitation of this new power and of the people who worked the machines created infernos—working and living conditions more terrible than any large population had ever endured. Reacting to such conditions and armed with the new vision of humans as creatures with *rights*, people began to devise social and political arrangements that would foster human well-being and rebuild their societies. The resulting movements—abolitionism, socialism, feminism, utopian, social welfare, and labor movements—sometimes at odds with each other, sometimes overlapping, did create beneficial changes, but also some of the cruelest societies on earth.

For, everywhere, the new moral vision was ignored or co-opted by men with a newly intense and insatiable drive for power—domination through wealth or influence, and control through might or knowledge. These two tendencies, in opposition, intersection, and interconnection, gave the nineteenth century its character. Technology provided a means to ease the human lot, but it also created a dehumanizing hell on earth; at the same time, a new sense of power and right infused human images of alternative ways to live and attempts to realize heaven on earth. This chapter examines women's involvement in both sides of this dichotomy, their strategies for living and for changing their lives.

As the new ideas of freedom and equality that inspired revolutions in late eighteenth- and early nineteenth-century Europe affected Western attitudes toward Africa, humanitarian groups, especially in England and the United States, began to protest slavery. Slavery was finally abolished—if mainly for economic rather than humanitarian reasons. Individuals and groups may have been morally motivated but societies were not. Moralists' efforts to push through emancipatory legislation were supported by early capitalists because a free-wage labor system was cheaper than slavery. The capitalists' goal of exploiting the resources and markets of what we now call Third World countries militated against depleting those populations. Their own countries had plenty of workers who did not have to be kept.

Britain's economy did not depend on slave labor, so its abolition movement began earlier and was stronger than that in the United States, where in 1860 slave-produced cotton made up 60 percent of exports. Britain passed laws in 1807 barring British subjects from slave trading, and in 1833 abolished slavery and slave trade in

Canada and its Caribbean, Indian Ocean, and South African colonies (but not in India or other Eastern possessions). Thereafter, taking a high moral tone, Britain used influence and sometimes force to prevent other nations and their colonies from trafficking in and earning profits from the cheap labor of slaves English colonies were by then denied—although some Britons continued to trade slaves.

Of the other major slave-holding powers, France and Portugal, France was the first to prohibit slavery in its colonies. But this 1794 prohibition was a response to massive slave revolts in Martinique and St. Domingue the previous year. Napoleon later reinstituted slavery. After the English defeated Napoleon in 1818, the French, yielding to British pressure, outlawed slave trading, but barely enforced the ban. The 1848 French Revolution brought to power humanitarian thinkers who abolished slavery on French soil, including French colonies and possessions. Still, colonists had ways of deceiving governments, which themselves were not always averse to being deceived. Some of the cruelest instances of European viciousness to Africans occurred after abolition.

In Portugal slavery was merely whispered against until 1836, when the export of slaves from Portuguese territories was outlawed. Slave trade continued quite openly just the same. Portugal outlawed slavery in its territories in 1878, but slaves were shipped to French and Portuguese islands in the guise of contract labor well into the twentieth century. The Portuguese government impressed Africans to work in Portuguese mines until Mozambique became independent in 1975. Then labor became more "voluntary."

In the nineteenth century, European states expanded their power base in Africa simply by calling a region a "colony," subject to their law and power. They made deals with individual Africans to provide slaves and other commodities, using the age-old techniques of patriarchy—male supremacy, co-optation, and divisiveness—to undermine and destroy local solidarity. Africans devised strategies to survive, accommodate, resist, or oppose European power. Women used all tacks: they maintained their people, subverted foreign impositions, and led resistance movements. This section begins the discussion of women's experience in the nineteenth century by looking at the way the treatment of women in Africa was affected by predations of slave trading in the imperialist period.

Slavery's Destruction of African Societies

Slavery had a profound effect on all Africans, but it affected men and women differently. It treated men individually, women as a caste. Africans of both sexes were enslaved and transported; but of Africans involved in trading, only men profited. After the British and French governments abandoned the slave trade, it was taken over by Angolans, Brazilians, Americans, Dutch, English, and French commercial firms that insinuated themselves along the coast. Backed with capital from their lineage, African men ran these new commercial centers as merchant lords over all-male households. They charged Europeans customs fees, regulated local business, provided auxiliary services, and sent goods to the interior on credit. A successful man called his household his "town" and demonstrated status in the old way—collecting wives, clients, and slaves. He educated his sons and nephews, trained them in the business, and gave them a patrimony in slaves.

Some slaves remained slaves even after the decline of the "peculiar institution": they were "slaves of the church," agricultural and household slaves attached to missions. Missionaries required agricultural slaves to marry and live in clusters near the mission. All household slaves were male—boys and young men; women could not enter mission houses. After the missionaries left, the "slaves of the church" went on living in all-male enclaves. Both sexes were impressed to serve an overlord to work on his or her behalf; but owners valued women as providers—of food, sex, and children—and men as worker-sons being trained to take over an all-male institution.

Kongo

In dealings between Africans and Europeans, only formal political power counted; Europeans were comfortable dealing man-to-man with Africans but would not accept female African leaders. In dealings with Europeans, African men gained power—and cash. No longer dependent on women, they could buy food and goods that wives had formerly provided. Exposed to new languages and customs, they gained education and experience as merchants and brokers. In time, matrilineal inheritance faded and women's elite status crumbled; they became wives, not sisters, sequestered at home and segregated at public events.[2] Some merchants reportedly offered visiting European men sexual use of their wives or daughters. Territories like Kongo may have remained sexually integrated even after class stratification, but they were now transformed into patriarchal societies in which only men functioned publicly and women were relegated to back rooms. As social mobility increased for men, it decreased for women.

People in the interior still followed the old ways, but the foreclosure of women from coastal commerce kept women out of the new commercial world. Women found new markets for their crops, supplying the *barracoons* (pens for slaves awaiting export) near the coast. When slave trade ended, they sold foods like groundnuts to Europeans for cash. As commerce expanded, women offered more variety at local markets and opened roadside food stands to cater to commercial caravans. But barter was still the rule: few women had cash, needed to purchase European goods.

Aside from commerce, the only way to get rich was by tribute. The old tribute system had died; men now controlled roads and markets, and granted titles. On the coast almost every man, even a low-level worker, could afford a slave; slaves were in such demand that they could negotiate their working conditions. But female slaves could rise in status only through marriage and motherhood, and all wives—royal, free, or slave—did field work. No woman had leisure; rich men's wives had only the help of co-wives. Some scholars believe that women may perhaps have preferred polygyny because it lessened their workload. Some co-wives developed close bonds. There were virtually no women in politics; Kongo was now an outpost in a Western commercial network in which women had lost most of their power.

East Africa: Zanzibar

The city-states of east Africa, which had grown rich by controlling trade routes, were invaded and conquered by Portugal in the sixteenth century. Over the next 200 years, various New World, Asian, and north African states contested to control the rising demand for slaves. In 1840, after conquering the Mazrui rulers of Mombasa, the Sultan of Oman, Seyyid Said, moved his headquarters to Zanzibar and consolidated his control over the east African coast, neighboring islands, slave routes, and major trade centers and towns in the interior, creating the Zanzibar commercial empire. Zanzibari rulers set the conditions under which Asian and European merchants could reside and trade in the empire.[3]

As the Atlantic slave trade declined in the early nineteenth century, slave trading in east Africa expanded. After British, American, and Indian financiers wrested control of trade routes from Muslim Zanzibari rulers, the Arabs built huge coconut and clove plantations on Zanzibar. By 1850 they dominated the world clove market. African plantations were little worlds centered on a compound where owners lived with their family and servants. Until the mechanization of farming, plantation agriculture relied heavily on slave labor. Huge farms dedicated to few crops required enormous amounts of human labor and were most profitable when that labor was unpaid.

Basil Davidson writes that African slavery was not like that of the New World. In the Americas, slaves could not marry, testify in court, or own slaves; they were overworked, often punished, whipped, tortured, separated from their families, and killed. African slaves were more like European serfs or peasants.[4] An observer of the Ashanti (Asante) of west Africa, quoted by Howard Zinn, attested that slaves could marry, own property or slaves themselves, and swear oaths as competent witnesses. "An Ashanti slave, nine cases out of ten . . . became an adopted member of the family, and in time his descendants so merged and intermarried with the owner's kinsmen that only a few [knew] their origin." Africans tended to absorb slaves into their families to increase their lineage, and even made them their heirs. In Sierra Leone, slaves were never overworked and never punished so as to draw blood. Zinn quotes John Newton, slave trader turned anti-slavery leader: "The state of slavery, among these wild barbarous people, as we esteem them, is much milder than in our colonies. For as, on the one hand, they have no land in high cultivation, like our West India plantations, and therefore no call for that excessive, unintermitted labor, which exhausts our slaves: so, on the other hand, no man is permitted to draw blood even from a slave."[5]

But if conditions there were less excruciating than in the New World, they were still very abusive: slaves died young and did not reproduce. Plantation work did not *use* slaves, it *consumed* them. Over half of Zanzibar's slaves were women. Work was divided by sex: men picked cloves, women separated the buds from the stems, spread them on mats to dry, and supervised the drying, which took about a week. When slaves threatened slowdowns, wanting piecework wages and a five-day week, the Arabs gave them Thursday and Friday (the Muslim holy day). On these days, slaves could hire themselves out to carry loads, clean copra (coconut shells), do construction, tote water, or make products to sell, and keep their wages. Asians and Europeans, who were barred from owning slaves, hired slaves on their days off, directly or from their owners.

Owners established a hierarchy to keep slaves under control, writes Frederick Cooper.[6] Lowest in rank was the new unskilled plantation worker, *mtumwa mjinga* (stupid slave); then came those brought to the coast as children and socialized locally: *wakulia* ("people brought up here"). Above them were the locally born *wazalia*. The highest rank, except for concubines, were the skilled workers—carpenters, masons, metal workers, door carvers, and boat builders—solely male trades. Women could reach high rank only as seamstresses or concubines. Muslim law held that concubines could not be resold in an owner's lifetime and were to be freed at his death. Actually, they were freed at caprice by owners who were moved by a show of submissiveness. *Wazalia*, often freed with nothing after years of labor, ended up as serfs, *wahadimu*, still dependent on their former owners for land, shelter, and work. Some remained on the plantation as tenants or servants after their owner died, and, when the British took over east Africa, became their tenants, sharecroppers.

Women slaves worked in the fields, sold produce for the mistress in town markets, and carried goods outside the house in daylight. *Wazalia* were often house slaves; in the 1890s Mtoro bin Mwinyi Bakari outlined their work (*mzalia* is the singular of *wazalia*).

> The work of the [female] *mzalia* is to serve in the house, to wash vessels and plates or clothes or to be taught to cook, to plait mats, to sweep the house, to go to the well to draw water, to go to the shop to buy rice or meat; when food is ready, to dish it up for the master, to hold the basin for him to wash his hands . . . to wash his feet, and to oil him; but only if his wife approves. If the wife wants to go into the country or to a mourning or a wedding, she accompanies her, and if she has an umbrella, she carries it.[7]

In societies with huge disparities in wealth and power, the privileged, always fearful of rebellion, must justify their superiority. Their claims must contain enough seeming truth to be swallowed by the oppressed. Today, the rich justify their wealth on grounds of merit and hard work; they claim to be more talented or to work harder than others. Since some rich people do work hard and are talented, the claim seems real, and other grounds for privilege—inherited status, inherited wealth, willingness to exploit—melt into invisibility. For millennia, male superiority has been rationalized by the claim that it is based in nature. Legal and institutional leashes on women cast an aura of truth on the claim. Whites made precisely the same claims about blacks, claims that were "proven" true by similar leashes. Arab slaveholders, who at first did not hold the racist belief that dark skin denoted inferiority, justified black slavery by devising an ideology making Africans uncultured outsiders.[8]

Owners knew that to keep their slaves they had to control a huge class which might over generations become conscious of its solidarity and strength and rebel or resist. Slaves living within thinking distance of their homelands might flee. To reconcile them to subjection, the Arabs presented slavery as a reciprocal arrangement placing obligations on both slaves and owners. Although owners granted concessions under pressure, they presented them (like a five-day week) as generous benefits conferred by a superior people. Their major weapon was religion: the Arabs assimilated Africans to Islam, offering them religious instruction and encouraging them to spread it among themselves—to a degree. The problem was that Islam preaches equality. So owners concocted a two-tiered religion that accepted slaves as lower-level Muslims with fewer obligations. Muslims in the city of Lamu relegated slaves to one section of the mosque, barring them from certain rituals (as they did women). They invented a symbolism associating free Lamuans with light, heaven, and purity, and slaves with nature, beings too earthbound to understand more than the basic precepts of Islam. Close contact with slaves would contaminate free Lamuans; Arabs were better Muslims.

Arabs devised rituals to reinforce divisions among slaves, as well as between slaves and free people or owners. Each rank of slaves dressed differently: male plantation slaves could not wear caps, shoes, or *kanzus* (sophisticated coastal clothes). Female slaves, because they were forbidden to wear veils or headcloths, were probably harassed in street, field, and market. *Wazalia* were permitted to shake hands and eat with owners and free people. At special feasts, high-ranking male slaves could sit with free men (only concubines could sit with free women). The sexes were segregated. Slaves addressed their owners not by name but by "Mwinyi" or "Bwaba" (Master). In time, free Arab women were expected to call men of their own class "Master," reinforcing women's subordinate status.

Physical punishment was always the core of discipline on plantations, but Zanzibar lacked the armed force to back slave owners or intimidate the labor force, especially in remote agricultural districts. Harshly punished slaves often fled to establish Maroon villages or joined maverick potentates who challenged the sultan's authority. Once Christian missions became secure havens (in the 1870s), slaves took refuge with missionaries opposed to slavery.

Africans adopted Arab culture; they spoke Swahili, wore coastal dress, and converted to Islam, often with ardor. Some owners rewarded acculturation by giving slaves (especially *wazalia* who had learned to follow coastal ways) a greater role and more responsible positions in household rituals and social activities. But the situation was delicate: by adopting Islamic culture slaves undermined the owners' myth of slave inferiority. Owners had to grant slaves some rights, but to acknowledge them as Muslims or human beings equal to their owners would subvert the entire premise of enslavement. And since Muslims may not enslave other Muslims, the conversion of slaves to Islam created a tricky problem. In particular, slave women were never expected to follow Islamic sex and marriage laws decreeing adultery a crime; many slave women were *required* to perform "adulterous" acts.

Indeed concubines and their offspring presented plantation owners with their worst problems. In Islamic law an owner cannot sell a concubine after she bears him a child, and he must free her in his will. Concubines' children were legitimate and free, the juridical equals of wives' children. In some regions Muslims ignored these laws. East African Muslims, wanting to augment their kin-groups, obeyed them to a degree, but did not value the children of concubines equally with those of wives. Some Arabs made concubines' sons lesser kin to free sons, but daughters were always slaves. In Mombasa concubines' children were part of both worlds; in Malindi, most respected families accepted concubines' sons but not their daughters. The royal dynasty of Zanzibar imported expensive prestigious Caucasian and Ethiopian concubines, and *their* sons became princes. Racism had become a factor in the ranking of people.

All over east Africa, people wanted slave women for plantation and domestic work. Since they fetched higher prices than men, no woman not bound to a man was safe in the interior. Slaves could be resold, and free women could be sold. Widows whose husbands' lineage agreed were sold. Some gave themselves as slaves to a known man to escape sale. Marcia Wright describes such a woman from central Africa. Narwimba, whose husband had died, was afraid for herself and her children. She went to her husband's nephew, and begged him, "Take me to wife; so that we might be protected."[9] Some captured women committed suicide, leaping from dhows into the Indian Ocean. Fugitives were severely punished if they were caught. Missionary David Livingstone, for example, came upon a woman who had been tied by her neck to a tree to die slowly for this "crime." Slave raids into the interior multiplied, and rulers sold their own subjects to fight off the raiders for cash to buy guns and ammunition. Slave and ivory trade generated powerful chiefdoms and kingdoms as Arabs, Asians, and Swahili battled for control.

Shambala

After the 1830s, when the Kilindi had conquered the Shambala, they began trading with the Zanzibar commercial empire for slaves, ivory, imported cloth, and firearms. As the Zanzibar empire expanded and needed more slaves, slaves became the Kilindis' most important export "product." Over time, they had to travel farther and farther afield to find them, and they increasingly pulled men from farm work to go on slave raids or to defend villages and trade routes from raiders. Subject peoples disliked letting their homelands get run down, and resisted mainly by fleeing. The Kilindis' hold weakened. Chiefdom raided chiefdom, men sold children and wives or used them to pay fines for minor or invented crimes. Settlements unprotected by a state could not defend themselves.

It was a terrifying time, an old man remembered: "People simply seized and sold one another. If someone came across you and you weren't very strong he would just grab hold of you. Off to be sold you go." Women and children were most easily kidnapped, and women dared not leave their houses to work in the fields without armed guards: crops withered and people starved. Women killed their babies rather than see them starve or be enslaved. Traditionally, women whose husbands abused them, or whose kin failed to help them in need, had committed "cooking pot suicide": they would concoct an ancient poisonous herbal potion, and, cursing their kin—especially brothers and sons—would give it to their young children to drink and drink it themselves. Like desperate Chinese and Japanese women, they had no power but to die; and in Africa too, the act of cursing and suicide was seen as a pollution of the entire lineage. Since families wished to prevent this, the threat of suicide could sometimes work to women's advantage.

But in this period, suicide was not a strategy; enslaved women committed suicide and murdered their children in despair. Whole villages picked themselves up and moved to remote mountains to escape the raids. Subject peoples like the Bondei broke away from Kilindi rule, murdered as many Kilindi as possible, and re-established their old patrilineal groups. Late in the century, a Kilindi chief explained: "Every Kilindi needs to make war so he can capture slaves to sell for gun powder." Slavery created a vicious cycle: people needed guns to capture slaves to trade for guns to get more slaves. By the 1890s, east African agriculture declined to subsistence farming: the region was ruined.

The Cape

African societies that tried to maintain their traditional structure—like the peoples of the misnamed Cape of Good Hope in present-day South Africa—were cruelly pressured and often simply crushed. Moreover, whites acted secretively, blaming Africans. Since only whites kept written records, their false version of events was often enshrined as truth. Recent research has revealed the truth about a phenomenon called the *mfecane*, "the crushing," supposedly a progressive trampling of blacks by blacks in the period of the Zulu leader Shaka (1810–30).

The term *mfecane*, coined by a white, has no African root, writes Julian Cobbing; it describes a total fabrication.[10] In brief, two Britons, Moffat and Melville, claimed that Zulu aggression against other black societies had displaced a society, which then crushed the next society, continuing in a domino effect. The massacres supposedly left (African) women and children homeless and starving, and godly Christians took these refugees back to their settlements and tried to find work for them.

Moffat, a missionary, and Melville, a government commissioner, wrote from their base in Natal that revolutions in northern 'Nguni societies southwest of Delagoa Bay had brought a fierce insane Zulu chief, Shaka, to power in the early 1820s. (In fact, no people called 'Nguni existed.) Moffat and Melville described an 1823–25 Zulu rampage led by Shaka, whom they credited with inventing the *ibutho*, transforming battle tactics with short stabbing spears and "horns and chest" battle formations. Although Shaka was a real person, the weapons and formation had long predated him. But the British public believed the claims. Whites wanted to usurp African land and slave raids, but England had abolished slave trade, and the public would not support aggressive war. To justify military action, Moffat and Melville created a false history, writing that Shaka had made a treaty ceding Britain considerable land but was not fulfillling it (the Zulu knew nothing of this allegation until

1828) and was depopulating Natal. Histories still maintain that the expansionist Zulus overran other societies, precipitating a chain reaction as groups desperate for land fled inland, each overrunning the next society, with genocidal effect.

In fact, according to Cobbing, the Zulu were crushed between two white fronts. British relations with Shaka were utterly mendacious, and the British eventually arranged to have him murdered. British abolition of slave trade in 1807 meant that settlers in the Cape Colony could not *increase* their slaveholdings, although in 1823 they still owned slaves. (To abolish slave *trade* is not to abolish *slavery*.) British frontier policies were so cruel toward Africans that the English lived in fear of reprisal, and in terror banned all blacks but the Khoi (whom they called Hottentots) from working on Colony farms. From 1812 blacks could be shot if they were seen west of the Fish River; after 1819, if they stepped west of Keiskamma. Blacks who were dispossessed from their land could not travel for work.

Originally, the Khoi, Capetown herders, had welcomed and traded with the Dutch, the first whites to intrude on their land. But when British explorer Henry Stanley imported cattle with sleeping sickness, Khoi herds were decimated. In addition, smallpox brought by whites almost annihilated the Khoi, leaving so few that the British lost their fear of them and forced them into serfdom between 1809 and 1812. The San (Bushmen) might also have been pressed into serfdom if the British had not already genocidally exterminated them. When more settlers were sent out from Britain in 1820, a labor shortage threatened the colony's existence, so British traders and missionaries began raiding the Delagoa Bay region for slaves. The missionaries had co-opted the Griqua, a frontier people, and in 1827, 1832, and 1837 Boers joined British-led Griqua in attacks on the area.

Neither the British government nor the British public could be told that Britons were raiding for slaves, so Moffat and Melville concocted reports of battles at Dithakong and Mbolompo against a fictional tribe of Mantatees and an army 100,000 strong led by Mantatisi, mother of Sekonyela, the Tlokwa leader, whose name conveniently resembled "Mantatee." Calling Mantatisi (or Mmanthatisi) a fierce woman, they compiled an entire history of her leadership of her cannibalistic people in a sub-continental holocaust that wiped out nearly 2 million blacks. In reality, Mantatisi was a leader remembered by her people for saving them, not for leading them in a war that conveniently emptied the area so that Europeans could move in during the 1830s and 1840s.

Moffat and Melville's reports won support and sympathy in England by describing the actual refugees as marauding bands of semidemonic *cannibalistic* women and children who ravaged the countryside like locusts. They saw "bones littering the veld" after savage wars among blacks (the bones, real enough, came from their own slave raids) which left hordes of refugees wandering the countryside. What could Christian men do but take in these homeless, hungry folk with no place to go, weeping mothers searching for their kidnapped children? To help the missions deal with this misery, whites in London, Glasgow, Paris, and Boston poured money into mission societies.

But the battles waged against "savage" Africans to save "innocent" women and children were actually slave and cattle raids. The Griqua took cattle as their cut; the missionaries got cattle, women, and children. The British force killed as many men as possible because the Cape slave market wanted only women and boys. By 1824 they had brought several thousand new slaves into the colony. Slaves were given a tiny wage, almost nothing, to disguise their real state, which was that they were sold and bought and could not leave. White farmers sometimes accompanied the raiders, seizing a slave so as not to have to pay for her. In 1822–23 Moffat and Melville invented a second "horde," the "Fetcani" (a Tembu word for bandits used by the Boers to describe any people whose cattle *they* raided). When the British governor sent armies across the Kei to capture people for slaves under the pretext of a

Zulu invasion, the story was that the "Fetcani" had driven the Tembu from their land. In reality, an army directed by whites surrounded Ngwane villages before dawn and attacked, killing 70 people and plundering 25,000 cattle. In a second attack hundreds of Ngwane were killed, their cattle and over a hundred captives taken, mainly women and children.

Given such events, the Zulus were essentially forced to become militaristic: their choice lay between that and annihilation. But militaristic states always oppress women, and to this day, the Zulu remain male-dominated and militaristic. The men own the cattle exchanged as bride wealth; women are required to be subservient to husbands, husband's "mothers," "fathers" (men in a paternal relationship), and senior brothers, especially during their early probationary and childbearing years. After the 1870s white South Africans also encouraged male domination and delegated judicial authority in both the home and community to elder indigenous males. Wright states that even today the people of this region—the Zulu, Swazi, and Basoto—are extremely sexually stratified and nationalistic in a way that is utterly congenial with the doctrines of apartheid. This partially explains the conflict between the African National Congress and the Kwazulu that raged throughout the struggle against apartheid, and reverberates still today.

Accommodations to Slavery

Women Traders in West Africa

After the European invasion, resourceful independent west African women, like other African women, tried to use Europeans for their own ends. They succeeded for a time, but were finally crushed. Some west African women were coastal traders with a long history of economic independence and initiative. According to legend, queens ruled coastal Senegal, Gambia, and Upper Guinea; rich women ruled west African villages when the Portuguese arrived. The first Portuguese traders worked from ships, later settling in coastal and riverine villages. For commercial advantage, they formed relationships with the most influential women who would have them; in return for trading privileges, the women tended the men and taught them African customs.

George Brooks has studied these women, called *senoras, signares, senhara*, or *senhoras*. Most lived on the tiny islands of St. Louis and Gore, in Senegal, and had high social rank, great beauty—Brooks sounds quite in love with them—and style, wearing splendid brilliantly colored clothes and gold and silver jewelry.[11] These sharp businesswomen owned ships, houses, and large bands of slaves. They knew how to acquire wealth and also how to enjoy it: they built two story houses with large airy rooms opening onto verandas, and lived in luxury and comfort, giving balls at which their slaves entertained. These women never sold their slaves, many of whom were artisans, and treated them indulgently. The *signares* nursed the Europeans during their frequent illnesses. (Between a sixth and a fifth of Europeans died each year in the unfamiliar Senegalese climate. In the rainy season, July to October on St. Louis island, three of every ten Europeans died.) In the eighteenth and nineteenth centuries, long after the Dutch had displaced the Portuguese, to be in turn displaced by the French, men viewed these women with great respect, and integrated themselves into the women's lives. Until the British came. When they got to Senegal, they built a fort, described by the man sent to manage it as a "dismal heap of ruins [inhabited by] the most mutinous, drunken, abandoned fellows I ever met with." Brooks writes that they were racist "rootless" bachelors, reckless gamblers, and alcoholics who would not associate openly with African women.

Sierra Leone, like Liberia, was a colony founded by former slaves who could not return to their homelands. In 1792 the Sierra Leone Company established the colony with a thousand Nova Scotian and American slaves who had supported the British during the Revolution, writes E. Frances White.[12] They were joined in 1800 by Jamaican Maroons who had fought the British to an impasse and accepted relocation in settlement. As the British tried to end slave trading, their ships intercepted slave ships and took the captives to a British naval base in Freetown, where 50,000 west African recaptives eventually settled. The British tried to meld these people into a tribe called Krios. ("Creole" means krio-speaking in Africa.) Other fugitive slaves joined them and the people traded African palm products and kola nuts for imported European goods. The overwhelming majority of Sierra Leoneans were Yoruba, Ibo, or Popo, from today's Nigeria and Benin.

Most female recaptives in Sierra Leone were Yoruba. Since they shared a similar background and were often from the same ethnic group, the culture they created had a Yoruba character. The Yoruba reversed the common African division of labor: men farmed and women marketed the produce. This arrangement gave Yoruba women independence—freedom to travel long distances while trading and the freedom to divorce. They divorced to advance themselves economically and could do so because they were financially independent of their husbands. Also, they grew up in fairly urban economically developed areas and were not intimidated by Freetown. But by tradition, west African women did not trade until they were past forty: young wives, who were held responsible for feeding the family, were pressed into domestic and farm work. As they usually worked alone, they produced little surplus. Men tried to keep wives from earning money, fearing they would repay their bride price and divorce them. (Men realized they exploited women.) The British, trying to "civilize" the Africans, imposed monogamy, which would have undermined women traders if a large number of newly arrived recaptive women had not fallen into British hands. They "apprenticed" the newcomers to men who made them work in the fields or carry produce, so that older women could continue to trade.

By 1830 many Freetown women were prominent traders; some were famous, like the Hausa recaptive Betsy Carew, who married a Bambara butcher, Thomas, and supplied meat to the army.

Adorned in gold earrings and a coral necklace, she made formal calls on Europeans and sent one of her sons to London to school. The couple later expanded their business into retailing imported liquor. Another contractor for the British government, Elizabeth Coles, supplied the military with meat and vegetables from her large garden. Most traders worked on a small scale, but in 1838, thirty Sierra Leoneans ran factories; women, never as successful as men, ran factories on the rivers, reaching their peak of success in the 1870s.

Inland Africans resented traders, who tended to exploit or cheat them, and hated the English for offering their runaway slaves refuge in Freetown. Inland men didn't like their women to see Sierra Leonean women traders' freedom and autonomy. So they kidnapped, murdered, or enslaved women traders. Elizabeth Coles (not the woman above) was a twenty-five-year-old from a peninsula village who went inland to Senehu to trade in 1888, protected by her landlord, Madame Yoko, a pro-British chief. When Senehu was attacked, Coles and three other Sierra Leonean women were captured. The others, who made the mistake of speaking English, revealing their identity, were killed. Coles, enslaved, survived by acting ignorant of English. She was recognized by a Temne trader and rescued.

In 1895 England declared Sierra Leone a protectorate and imposed taxes. Interior groups—the Sus, Temne, Yoni Temne, and Masimerah—rebelled. But the British, perhaps strategically, blamed coastal peoples for the war and bypassed them to ally with hinterland chiefs and local elites, penetrating ever more deeply in order to appropriate inland territories. Unable to operate without British protection, the traders and their culture died out.

Resistance to Slavery: Male States, Female Leadership

Some Africans tried to resist European predation by building power bases of their own. Both women and men created such bases, but women generally made themselves powerful centers around which people gathered in loose organizations, while men built highly centralized military states. Women never ruled in such states but acted in them on every level, as slaves (women were the first to be enslaved, last to be freed), administrators, and slave owners.

The Yoruba and the Oyo Empire

Slave traders reached present-day southern Nigeria about 1650, and seized 1.5 million people along its coast from the late seventeenth to the early nineteenth century, writes Babatunde Agiri.[13] This region was home to the Yoruba, some of whom used profit from the slave trade to build a state, the Oyo Empire. They hoped to protect their own people from being transported by providing the Europeans with foreign slaves they had bought, captured, or coerced as tribute from other Yoruba groups or their neighbors, the Bariba, the Hausa, and the Nupe. To protect its own people, the Oyo Empire became itself a slave-state.

In the 1790s European wars disrupted slave trade in west Africa, breaking Oyo's connection to the Atlantic trade. With its economy disintegrating, the army rebelled in 1817; Dahomey stopped paying tribute and intervened. When uprisings shook the Muslim Ilorin Emirate, some fortified cities withdrew and merged with Dahomey into a new Yoruba state, the Oyo Empire. Built for resistance, the empire was militaristic: army chiefs maintained standing armies and ruled its cities, which did large-scale slave trading. Neighbors scurried to protect their people, often in vain. Historians believe that a state became necessary to defend people against European aggression.

An *alaafin* ruled the Oyo Empire; nobles in the *oyo mesi* (council of state) headed lineages with huge numbers of wives, slaves, and other dependents. The army was made up of slaves, some of whom were specialists in the care and use of horses. Since the cavalry was the backbone of the Oyo army, slaves were essential to sustaining the empire. Slaves managed provincial towns, collected caravan tolls and taxes, and acted as messengers, farmers, and household servants. Slavery was intrinsic to Yoruba thinking: the Yoruba religion emphasized the importance of one's kin-group and of *ori* (destiny, one's inner, spiritual head). People's well-being depended on their *ori* and on ritual sacrifices to the gods at Yoruba shrines. Ambitious people were told to be patient and prudent in order to develop a good character. Inequality was a given. The Yoruba metaphor for the social entity was a hand: as fingers of unequal length are all useful, so people of unequal status were useful in the community—even slaves who had slave parents or those who had lost the higher status of their natural families through misbehavior like theft or misfortune, capture in war, or kidnapping.

In a climate in which freedom was vulnerability, free men in need of protection attached themselves to lineage leaders as clients. Called "slaves" of the chief, they had to pay tribute at ceremonies and sometimes work on a chief's farm a number of days a week, but they were not bound and could switch allegiance easily. There were also "pawns," mainly females pledged as collateral for loans. Their bondage was often endless, as they had to pay off the loan *and* the interest on it. A child pawned by her father lived with and served his creditor, who fed her. Parents unable to feed their own children often pawned them to someone who could; if the parents could not redeem them, they remained in bondage their whole lives. If they ran away, debtors had to find or replace them. Adult pawns served a mutually agreed number of days a week.

Exposure to Western ideas led some Yoruba to abandon their traditions. Although transported Yoruba maintained their traditional religion in the New World, a new generation of African men adopted the Western value of individual achievement. Scorning the Yoruba idea that good behavior propitiated *ori*, they became war captains, aggressive and skilled at fighting, farming, and trade. To have their importance recognized in Africa, they had to own many other human beings. Anna Hinderer, a nineteenth-century Western observer, wrote: "There are no riches in [Yoruba land]; slaves and wives make a man great in this country."[14]

Doubts about the efficacy of the Yoruba gods drew many Yoruba to Islam or Christianity, neither of which justified slave revolt. Islam condoned slavery, and Catholic missionaries in Oyo in the 1840s were divided about it; some deplored slavery, and some bought slaves or assisted the slave trade. But both groups challenged Yoruba religion and social structure. The British too were equivocal. A decade after landing at Lagos in 1851, they decreed it a colony and themselves its rulers. As they moved further into the interior, they rarely protected black Christian communities from slave traders, but did send military excursions to stop slave exports, and in the 1880s and 1890s tried to stop them inland.

Methodists and the Church Missionary Society (CMS) opposed slave trade and slavery, and the CMS helped make Sierra Leone a haven for fugitive African slaves. But after Britain had emancipated slaves in its territories in 1833, the CMS *supported* domestic slavery. Missionaries wanted to convert Africans to Christianity, but the religion did not appeal to them. Sierra Leonean Yoruba Christian converts returned to Yorubaland to proselytize after their emancipation. The most prominent of them, Bishop Samuel Crowther, a leader in the antislavery campaign, would not have been able to convert African slave owners if he had opposed domestic slavery. So he supported it, claiming African slavery was humane. His group also insisted on compensating owners for freed slaves.

In 1879 the CMS forbade Christians to own slaves. A minister who tried to enforce the rule was confronted by a group of Egba converts led by prominent women trader slave owners who declared that people would rather go into the interior with their slaves than remain without them. Local mission workers warned the CMS that preaching against slavery could cause the widespread murder of white missionaries and the extirpation of Christianity in Africa. Ironically, of all African slave owners, both white and black, Christians treated their slaves most harshly and worked them hardest, insisting on the "Protestant ethic" of hard work.

The gradual defeat of the entire continent of Africa was probably inevitable, given the Europeans' superior arms and their intense drive for acquisition. No African of the colonial period permanently overcame the Europeans. Men built militaristic, hierarchical states to keep their people under control and oppose the Europeans. Women created networks that enabled their people to maintain some integrity and dignity, as well as helping African cultures survive. Both failed: women were killed, and states collapsed. Africa fell under Europe's heel. But the women's legacy of courage and unity fed a continuing resistance.

Nehanda of Zimbabwe

African women retained their ancient aura of spiritual power into the modern era. Some, like Nehanda of Zimbabwe, used it in overtly political ways. Nehanda Nyaksikana, a Shona religious leader and prophet, lived between 1863 and 1898. The Shona believed she incarnated the spirit of the original Nehanda of the Shona, who had lived in the fifteenth century. According to legend, when her father, the chief, died, it was the practice that a son had to commit incest with his sister in order to rule (females must still have inherited the right to rule). Discovering that one of her brothers was willing to do so, Nehanda was so dismayed that she disappeared into a cleft in a rock. The rock was then named after her, and her spirit was said to return to guard her people whenever they needed to resist.

Centuries later, in the late 1880s, the British invaded Mashonaland to exploit the people and their land: the invading expedition was financed by the British South Africa Company, which had major mining interests in South Africa. The guiding spirit of the enterprise was Cecil Rhodes, who became enormously rich from those interests. The Shona believed Nehanda Nyaksikana had taken on the original Nehanda's spirit to lead them in resisting.

Nehanda led the Shona in the Chimurenga war of resistance, from 1896 to 1897. Other peoples joined them, including the Ndebele. Nehanda's headquarters lay in the Musakain Mazoew district, an impregnable mountain fortress pierced by a network of caves, inaccessible except through treacherous narrow passages. It had plentiful water, grain storage, and cattle kraals. From this retreat, Nehanda chose targets: mines, trading posts, police stations, white settlers, and African collaborators. Her army won control of most rural areas and forced the British to ask for reinforcements to protect their settlers. A white settler wrote: "At the present moment Nianda [sic] is the most powerful wizard in Mashonaland and has the power of ordering all the people who rose lately and her orders would in every case be obeyed." (Nehanda was a general, but female, therefore a *wizard*.) The British made deals that divided the Ndebele and the Shona; they then made peace with the Ndebele and focused entirely on the Shona.

In December 1897 the British captured Nehanda and Kagubi, a male leader; contrary to all military protocol, they killed her—something they would not do to a white military opponent—hanging her on April 27, 1897. A white Catholic priest wrote:

> Everyone felt relieved after the execution as the very existence of the main actors in the horrors of the rebellion, though they were secured in prison, made one feel uncomfortable. With their deaths, it was universally felt the rebellion was finished, their bodies were buried in a secret place so no natives could take away their bodies and claim that their spirit had descended to any other prophetess or witchdoctor. The younger generation, it was hoped, now knew that the white Queen [Victoria] meant to reign.[15]

Yaa Asantewa and the Asante

After Ghana fell, its people went on living as they had for centuries. With its huge forests and plentiful water, Ghana was stable: homesteads and fields were occupied for generations by the same people, including the Akan clans, which grew into states. In the 1670s Osei Tutu tried to unite the Akan states, ostensibly to overthrow neighboring Denkyira but really to dominate the confederacy himself, writes David Sweetman.[16] With a priest, Osei invented the myth of the Golden Stool, a wooden stool decorated with gold that floated down from heaven during a ceremony. The stool became the symbol of Asante unification, and reigning rulers were said to be "on the stool." But no one sat on it; it was considered more exalted even than the ruler, and during ceremonies, sat on its own throne higher than the ruler's.

The Akan states retained many matricentric customs: chiefs had to be descended from a certain female line and inherited their status from their mothers. The queen mother and her advisers might rule themselves or choose a ruler (*asantehene*) from among her grandsons or great-grandsons. Women often led troops into battle, and they filled high offices and supervised women's affairs. The *asantehema*, the king's wife and co-ruler, had symbolic status but also participated in state councils. Princesses were involved in political power struggles. These facts suggest that women retained considerable power in Asante lineages.

By 1750 the Asante Empire almost reached the sea, but the Asante never assimilated those they conquered or dispersed their armies. So, whenever they seemed vulnerable, their subjects rebelled. Asante disputes over British efforts to end the slave trade led to wars in 1811 and 1816. An uneasy truce lasted until 1874, when the Asante attacked the British, who retaliated by invading the country. Reaching the Asante capital, Kumase, they declared it a colony, deposing the *asantehene*. But neither superior British arms nor the civil war over succession that mired the Asante for a decade could break the people. They were almost wholly destroyed and their king exiled when, in a final drive to repel the British from their land, the Asante made a woman their leader.

In 1884 Nana Afrane Kuma ruled Edweso, an Asante state, with his mother, Queen Yaa Asantewa. In a civil war, he sided with Prempeh I, of Yaa Asantewa's Oyoko clan. The British signed treaties with and offered protection to states that rebelled against the Asante.

Prempeh was "enstooled" in 1894; in 1896, when the British set up a protectorate at Kumase, they ordered Prempeh to pay for the expedition. When he refused, they exiled him and his supporters, including Nana Afrane Kuma and Prempeh's mother, also a major political figure.[17] Thinking they had finally won the war, the British established a residency in Kumase and built a fort for their administrators. When the new British governor paid a visit, he ignorantly and arrogantly demanded the golden stool to sit upon.

This electrified the people, and they silently left the ceremony. Three days later, war erupted—the Yaa Asantewa war, named for the woman who led it. In April, Yaa besieged Kumase, trapping the British in their fort. Their major ally, the king of Bekwai, was too frightened of Yaa to send reinforcements to help them, and he could barely keep his men from joining her. By mid-June, with thirty Britons a day dying inside the fort, the remaining men tried to escape. Yaa Asantewa let them go. In July British reinforcements with Maxim guns arrived in Kumase; they retook the city and set out to capture Yaa Asantewa. She and her soldiers resisted until the end of September, when the British surrounded the forest she was hiding in. She spat in the face of the officer who arrested her, but the strength of the Asante resistance had forced the British to respect her and they treated all their captives as prisoners of war—there were few executions. They exiled Yaa Asantewa and her son to the Seychelle Islands, where she lived another twenty years. Yaa was defeated but she had forced the English to recognize the Asante people. The Asante still sing about "Yaa Asantewa, the warrior woman who carries a gun and a sword of state in battle."

Resistance to Male Domination

East African Spirit Mediums

Most African societies had some degree of male domination before Europeans arrived, but the invaders increased it by generating war and militarism. Many Europeans dealt only with men, thereby nullifying women's power; they turned entire regions into predatory jungles where women were safe only if they were "owned" by a man. In the next phase of domination, the European states completed the patriarchization of the continent by imposing Western notions of property rights and law. But women continued to resist male supremacy, some through religion.

Africa has a long tradition of female spiritual leadership. Women like Nzinga of Angola, Amina of Hausaland, Beatrice of Kongo, and Nehanda of Zimbabwe were spiritual leaders who had military or political skills. Some women used spiritual power and the beliefs of their societies to improve their lives and those of other women. Such women, known as spirit mediums, were active in local spirit-possession religions. Iris Berger has studied this tradition among nineteenth-century east African women in southern and western Uganda, Rwanda, Burundi, and northwestern Tanzania, where local religions were often devoted to a legendary hero who was apotheosized—seen as a god. Among the leaders and their large followings were both females and males.[18]

In east Africa patrilineal clans farmed and herded in scattered settlements with a centralized political structure stratified by class and occasionally by ethnicity. Men were superior to women, but upper-class women were superior to lower-class men and a few upper-class women had wealth and authority. But only men had political power, legal rights—the right to inherit cattle and land and to act independently outside the home. Women were not supposed to speak in public or even look a man in the eyes; if questioned, a woman was expected to avoid answering, claiming ignorance. Most women were totally subservient to their husbands and fathers, who retained authority over them throughout life, even after marriage. Women who rose above their sex-based status did so by gaining the favor of a male superior, mainly by manipulation, lying, or flattery. Women had authority only over children, younger sisters, and their husbands' subordinates. Burundian men claimed women were stronger than men, and so more suited to physical labor, but inferior to men because they were clumsy, lacked agility, were unable to control their emotions, and were prone to jealousy. Although women's part in childbearing was passive—men planted "seed" in their "earth"—it was said to age them more quickly than men.

Women could be rainmakers (it was a hereditary profession and the chief rainmaker was famous), and they could be spirit mediums, who entered trances during which they were "possessed," inhabited by the spirit of a departed god who spoke through them to the living. Spirit mediums, called Bandwa, were members of religions; they dressed strikingly in animal skin or bark cloth and enjoyed considerable respect. A potential medium was sent a sign, perhaps a long illness, after which she was ritually initiated. Indeed, the approved cure for women who went into trances, grew ill, and cried was to join a religion. They became part of a secret society higher than ordinary society. Only a few were professionals; most lived ordinary lives between ceremonies during which they danced, made rhythmic music, spoke in an esoteric language, adorned themselves, and acted out roles.

All observers noted that women, the mainstay of the religions, were predominant. Most were childless women who had to worship the ancestors of their husbands' lineage, and whose husbands would approve their devotion to a religion that might help them get pregnant. But Berger and others believe that women often used religion to gain the authority and status their society denied them and to assert themselves in the face of male domination. Some religions gave a "possessed" wife control over her husband during trances: she might order a man to drive his other wives away, terrify him into ceasing to beat her, demand control over household goods, or order her husband to carry or hire someone to carry the heavy burdens he had laid on her. The subtext of religion seems to have been to impel husbands to treat their wives more fairly.

Some rituals allowed women to share men's prerogatives and status. In Busoga only men were allowed to sit on stools, but female mediums sat on skin seats during trances; in some ceremonies, women wore male ceremonial dress, sat on stools, carried spears, and judged trials. In others, possessed women could act like men, speak inconsiderately, and abuse parents or superiors without paying compensation afterward. Religion could alter women's oppression, and also give temporary relief. There were rituals that reversed class distinctions (most members were lower-class); men could reverse gender, dressing as women and insulting others during trances. The assumed status was held only during possession: after it, people reverted to their usual status. High-status men could allow women or lower-class men this liberty without risking their positions in the social order.

Some African priestesses and mediums became powerful and prestigious figures.[19] Only "great witches" and royal princesses could own or inherit property, but some mediums became rich. In Nkore the female diviner Nyabuzana owned land and a palace and had such high prestige that in ceremonial dress she could claim any cow she wanted. The role of spiritual outlaw—priestess, medium, or soothsayer—fits the cultural image of women and empowers dispossessed women in many cultures.

Despite government declarations abolishing slave trade and slavery, and some efforts to enforce them, African slavery lasted into the twentieth century—and still exists, mainly for young women. Europeans impoverished Africa, killed or exported its people, expropriated their land, and eroded its culture. The number of Africans enslaved may be as high as 250 million—between 1500 and 1800, 11 million were transported, almost 8 million across the Atlantic to Brazil and the Caribbean, and 3 million across the Sahara, Red Sea, and Indian Ocean. A healing fact that does not mitigate their tragedy or that of the people they left behind is that their descendants now enrich societies across the world. Africa and its traditions endured, largely because of African women's powerful resilient behavior in the face of patriarchy—in both its indigenous and imported forms.[20]

CHAPTER 2

INDUSTRIALIZATION

THE INDUSTRIAL REVOLUTION BEGAN AROUND 1780, when machines were invented to manufacture cloth faster than humans could. By 1800 water- and steam-driven machines were producing energy to make chemicals, iron, and pottery. By 1850 railroads were crossing continents.

The first country to industrialize was England, then the richest country in the world, with its many colonies and a navy huge enough to reach them, their resources, and their markets. For the British, as for all governments, national interest meant the interests of the ruling class, and Britain used its power over colonies to benefit British capitalists. By placing tariffs on foreign imports, it thwarted colonial industries and forced colonies to produce raw materials so that they had to buy British manufactures. A tariff on Indian cloth, for example, made India's major export prohibitively expensive in England, stimulated domestic cloth production, and left the Indian economy even more vulnerable to British demands. The capitalist system dictated the work of colonists, and industrial states thwarted the development of colonial industry. Capitalism revolutionized life globally.

Another reason the industrial revolution began in England was the availability of British workers. The overwhelming majority of Europeans lived on the land and grew their own food. In 1830, 60 percent of French and Italians, over 70 percent of Prussians, 90 percent of Spaniards, and 95 percent of Russians farmed. Most Britons worked on the land but few owned any: England had wiped out its peasant class. A few landlords with thousand-acre estates had appropriated *half* the country. Landowners leased land to tenant farmers, and hired the landless, or farmers with tiny plots, for day wages to grow crops mainly to sell. Some grazed sheep on their land, even enclosing village commons to prevent their pure-bred sheep from mixing with other varieties. In England, displaced peasants became a desperate labor force willing to work for a pittance, whereas France still had a sturdy lower middle class of very conservative peasant landowners, who rarely emigrated. Many Britons emigrated, and many Germans; in Germany, rich men freed their serfs in return for a third to half of their land.

Before British landowners ejected the peasantry from the land and industrialization began in Europe, most people had a place to live. They may have been bowed down by arduous work that did not always suffice to keep them from starving, but they were bound to that work and to their land. Industrial labor was actually *less* onerous than life on the land; industrial ills *seem* worse because they are more documented. Systematic studies of the conditions of workers' lives began in the nineteenth century. The impulse to make these studies arose from the new belief that conditions could be altered to make them more bearable, that life could be improved. It is important to bear in mind as we examine workers' conditions that peasants' lives may in some ways have been worse.

The industrial revolution transformed the nature of work by tapping new energy sources; and it also transformed the relations between classes. Peasants and nobles gradually became workers and owners. A new elite arose: men with capital. Capitalism revolutionized society by putting a new concept of human relations into practice. The feudal system was based on a notion of bonds of rights and obligations; the capitalist system is based in an ideology of freedom which claims that instead of being contracted by bondage to others or to land, a free person contracts with another free person to buy (or sell) labor. This formula—men buy labor, not people—separates production from reproduction; but its rhetoric of freedom (people cannot be bought) and individualism is accompanied by a profound indifference to the survival of masses of humans. Capitalist ideology claims that labor can be freely bought and sold. But in truth, unequal ownership of resources bars the majority from such freedom. For a huge dispossessed class utterly vulnerable to capital's demands, *freedom* means the freedom to starve or work for any wage offered. The wage that connects capital and labor is a constant cause of struggle; the workers' only sustenance, providing maintenance, renewal, and reproduction, is the capitalist's major item of budget savings.

Older traditions lingered after capitalism emerged: workers like domestic servants, farm or textile workers, and seamstresses were still housed and fed by their employers, families or mill owners who provided dormitories. Such workers remained bound—under surveillance, forced to obey their employer's orders—but employers also remained responsible for workers' safety, health, and diet. Increasingly, though, employer responsibility ended with the wage. Profits were staggering, yet wages were so low that workers could not live on them. Owners hired mainly women and children, paying them abominably. In 1833 a family of five needed at least 20 shillings a week to survive, but only 2000 of 12,000 Glasgow cotton mill workers averaged more than 11 shillings a week. Average wages in 131 Manchester mills were under 12 shillings. Nor could people avoid the factories; weavers, a large prosperous and skilled-labor force, were decimated by competition from machines. From 1795 to about 1834 weavers' wages fell by 83 percent: 500,000 weavers and their families starved to death.

As manufacture moved to factories, "putting-out" work (piecework done at home) declined, making it harder for artisan or peasant families with a little land to survive. Many became landless seekers of waged work: proletarians. Families swarmed to cities expecting to work together as they always had and at first were hired as families, including children over five or six. (Men soon separated themselves from women and children.)[1] At first, the factory system was the leading edge, not the dominant mode of production. Most work was still done traditionally, and most female workers were still domestic servants. Feeling they had to establish the upper hand over labor, factory owners created a highly regulated, heavily policed environment.

To force workers to show up, they held back their wages or tied them to contracts for twenty-one years. Discipline was harsh: the slightest infraction could mean instant dismissal, transfer to the worst job, or a fine. No one had any autonomy; discipline and work rhythms were imposed by others. People resisted factory discipline, not because they did not want to work but because they resented losing control of their labor. Factory work was regulated by bells or whistles: arriving ten minutes late could mean losing a whole morning's wages. Workers had to work fourteen to eighteen straight hours at the same task with only a short break—or none at all—to eat. Forbidden to talk or walk about or rest for a moment, they could only wait for the next bell or whistle. In some factories they had to gobble food down beside their machines. They were literally not given time or place to pee: toilets were scarce or nonexistent. Owners buying only labor ignored workers' bodies or minds—giving no thought to their fatigue, health, safety, morale, personal refreshment and renewal, or ability to produce healthy children.

Factory foremen were most savage to women and children, considering them mere property. Managers tied tiny children to machines to keep them awake and upright; like husbands in home workshops, they beat children and women and used women sexually, threatening punishment or dismissal for resistance. Parliamentary and official inquiries from 1800 on regularly record male supervisors molesting female workers, cuffing and strapping children, dragging them from sleep and weighting them with iron as punishment.

Factory conditions were appalling. Open machines had dangerous moving parts that could injure the children who cleaned under or around them. Over 50,000 children worked in mines hauling laden underground trams, often for twelve hours at a stretch. Women too hauled coal trams. Tiny children put in charge of the doors that ventilated the mines sometimes fell asleep, imperiling everyone in the mine. Trapped gas frequently exploded. Textile mills were unventilated and workers breathed in fibers that later caused fatal lung disease; the lead used in making glazed pottery poisoned workers. Underfed workers suffered spinal curvature and bone deformations from standing still for long hours.

After fourteen or more hours of numbing work, and a walk to and from the factory that might add an hour at each end, women, men, and children stumbled through smoggy, smoky cities to cramped basement rooms without windows or drains, or to cold dark hovels or corners of flats without water or toilets—the first slums. Crowded filthy cities lacked sewers or drains, garbage rotted in the streets, and gutters stank of excrement and urine. Factories, railways, and chimneys polluted the air. On the pittances they earned, people ate poorly; rickets was common. Epidemics swept the crowded slums, and thousands died of cholera, typhus, and tuberculosis. And during the frequent economic downturns, people lost their jobs and their small hold on life. In 1810 factory workers rioted, chanting "Bread or blood!" They stole to eat; from 1805 to 1833, larceny convictions in England rose 540 percent; over 25,000 people were hanged, most for petty theft. In 1842, one in eleven Britons was a pauper.

We have not yet seen the full consequences of the industrial revolution: we are still living them out. It made life less arduous for millions *and* it impoverished millions; it enriched life by introducing items once unavailable or nonexistent *and* it created more stress, pollution, noise, and ugliness. It changed the air we breathe, our diets, the pace of life, and the way we look at life. Its most serious immediate consequences were social; the rich used their wealth mainly to amass huge fortunes by exploiting workers. People newly imbued with the Enlightenment idea of human rights were outraged at the wretched lot of the mass of humanity. Protesting their misery in riots and strikes, the poor learned class consciousness, a revolutionary development. They became aware of themselves as a coherent group with a place in history, exploited by and struggling with another group. They learned to protest not as individuals or in informal groups but *collectively*. Their struggle triggered the political movements and revolutions that constitute the history of the modern age.

Working-Class Women

Industry operated initially on the same assumptions as the traditional family labor system. Eager to keep the price of labor low and the supply high, owners happily let men and women fight it out. The price of labor depended on organization; men organized in the precapitalist craft guild system used their solidarity to control wages and access to the labor supply. Men's insistence on patriarchal privilege infused the wage struggle, which was really a male war against women. Refusing to demand that women should earn the same as men, men battled to control the labor market *and* the family through wages. Very quickly, men's wages became the family wage. Owners were pleased to pay women less and keep them in low-level jobs.

Women who remained at home to maintain the family and raise children were still productive, but because capitalist thought excluded renewal and reproduction from productive labor (defined as production of surplus value, or profit), their work was considered valueless. (Recall that some simple societies define whatever women produce as worthless even when it sustains the group, and value only what men produce, or define women's work as nonwork.) Without wages, women had no voice in a family. As production moved to factories where jobs were sex-segregated, the two sexes were less likely to work together. In an agricultural society, most people worked at home, together; in industrialized society, people's jobs distanced them from home and from each other. Work became "homosocial," a word coined by Carroll Smith-Rosenberg to describe same-sex social affiliations.[2] Sexual segregation had always existed in institutions like the Catholic Church, universities, the military; in this century it became near-universal and gender roles rigidified.

Textile Workers

Most factory women worked in textiles. In 1835 almost half of English cotton-textile workers were female, and this number increased over the century. British factory women saw work as a contribution to their families, not as a means to economic independence. Françoise Basch describes the atrocious conditions in most mills.[3] Temperatures averaged 30°–35°C or higher, the unventilated air in carding workshops was permeated with fluff that lodged in the lungs, and the noise was deafening. Girls of eleven assigned to wet-spin linen stood barefoot in water; water flowing from the spindles soaked their clothes and saturated the air with steam twelve to fourteen hours a day. Workers lost limbs to machines, suffered vitamin deficiencies, exhaustion, blindness, ulcers, asthma, and—most often in textile work—tuberculosis.

What may have been the first textile mill in the United States opened in 1822 in Lowell, Massachusetts, with all elements of production under one roof. The Lowell system was designed to maintain tight control over workers, mainly daughters of local Yankee farmers drawn to the mills by the promise of their own wages. Most of them planned to work only until marriage and sent all or part of their wages home. The Lowell Manufacturing Company put them in dormitories with strict rules: "The Company will not continue to employ any person who shall smoke within the Company's premises, or be guilty of inebriety, or other improper conduct. . . .

The doors must be closed at ten o'clock in the evening, and no person admitted after that time without reasonable excuse." The girls did the same tasks as at home—weaving and spinning—but the work was mechanized and conditions were oppressive, as shown in a poem some of them composed: "Amidst the clashing noise and din/ Of the ever beating loom/ Stood a fair young girl with throbbing brow/ Working her way to the tomb."

Wherever industrialization occurred, the same pattern appears: all workers were overworked and underpaid, but women were given the most difficult, menial jobs, had no hope of advancing, and were paid less than men.[4] When Russia industrialized in the late nineteenth century, women filled the factories. By 1914, millions worked in industry, almost half a million in textiles alone, many under fourteen years old. In every trade, women were given the heaviest and hardest labor (this was still true in the Soviet Union). In wood depots and sawmills they lugged the heaviest loads. Any machines available were given to men, and women worked manually. Yet the minimum female wage was 17 rubles a month, the male, 21.

In the first textile mills in France and Italy, male owners, like the Lowell owners, acted *in loco parentis* for young female workers, decreeing rules of conduct to limit their mobility and freedom—they sometimes even tried to arrange marriages for them. Control over girls' lives served owners' interests: they guaranteed the workers' presence and reinforced control of their work. Families were content because daughters' wages were sent *directly to their parents.* In England, not until the 1890s could single working girls living at home keep some of their own wages; French and Italian servant girls went on sending money home even when they no longer expected to return to marry and live. Patriarchal controls over women were maintained in all circumstances.[5]

But industry offered young women opportunities they had not had since patriarchy began. Industrial capitalism had contradictory consequences for women. On the one hand, it exploited and damaged them by placing them in dangerous and unhealthy environments, forcing them to work inhumane hours at repetitive tasks for low wages. On the other, it offered single women the possibility of liberation from the oppressive patriarchal family. Work in the Lowell mill, for instance, gave young American women independence from their families. Family life was extremely oppressive for daughters, as other family members saw them as servants who were expected to do menial work, serve, nurse, and obey with little freedom. Working and living together away from home, young female American mill workers discovered sisterhood, solidarity, and class consciousness. Lowell women formed a literary club, writing and reading their work to each other, and producing a magazine, *The Lowell Offering*.[6] They formed deep bonds, so when owners increased hours (without extra pay) or ordered speed-ups (more production on faster machines without extra pay), their solidarity made them the first Americans to strike.

Thus capitalism, which elevated patriarchy by turning its major value, power, into the *only* value, also destabilized it by enabling women for the first time in history to become economically independent. Despite the patriarchal solidarity inherent in the deal the mill owners made with New England farmers— "Send us your daughters and we will guard them as you do and they will earn money for you"—the Lowell mill girls used their situation to develop the solidarity to resist both owners and family.

But the power that solidarity had given the Lowell mill women did not last. Women moved back and forth between mill and farm to help their families seasonally, despite rules that mill owners made to prevent this. In the 1840s a huge influx of Irish immigrants arrived seeking work. Competition made Yankee women fear giving up a job, and employers came to prefer the Irishwomen: fleeing famine and poverty, they were desperate enough to work for low wages and terrified enough to fear being organized. The patriarchal strategy of divide and conquer worked: Yankee and Irish competed in enmity, unable to unify in a common cause.

When unions began organizing northern workers, mills moved south and appealed to white women from rural areas. Having analyzed the family labor system, and knowing that women and children did the essential work on farms, owners presented factories as a refuge for impoverished countrywomen tenant farmers and their children. They lured families by offering mill-owned houses on condition that at least one person per room work in the mill.[7] Women especially were drawn: the first to apply for mill work were those who had worked hardest in commercial farming: female heads of household, widows, single women, and itinerant laborers. Once again, capitalism empowered women while exploiting them.

Home Workers

Some women worked at home, doing "piecework" or "sweated labor." Later, they worked in sweatshops: indeed, the industry of New York, London, and European cities was built on sweated labor, the low-priced labor of women and children.[8] At first, shoe-making wives and daughters did binding for male household heads, who were paid for the finished shoes. Later, shop bosses in shoe manufacturing centers like Lynn, Massachusetts, dealt directly with pieceworkers, hiring women to stitch and bind the uppers at home, while men worked together in shops. When the sewing machine was invented in 1855, men pushed women out of shoe manufacture entirely (until the end of the century). Thus isolated, women could not organize to resist. Women pieceworkers were paid appalling wages: a woman trying to supplement a man's inadequate pay by sewing might work as long and hard as he, but earn under $2 a week compared to his $10–$15.

Moreover, married women felt they had to conceal their labor. Charlotte Woodward, a glove sewer, one of the few paid workers at the women's rights convention in Seneca Falls in 1848, explained:

> We women work secretly in the seclusion of our bedchambers because all society was built on the theory that men,

> not women earned money and that men alone supported the family. . . . But I do not believe that there was any community in which the souls of some women were not beating their wings in rebellion. For my own obscure self I can say that every fiber of my being rebelled, although silently, all the hours that I sat and sewed gloves for a miserable pittance, which, as it was earned, could never be mine. I wanted to work, but I wanted to choose my task and I wanted to collect my wages. That was my form of rebellion against the life into which I was born.[9]

Piecework was not just poorly paid but risky: women returning bundles of finished work might be told they had done poor work and be paid less than the agreed price or nothing at all. If demand for a product waned or the economy contracted, they were given less work and they starved. But women with small children had little alternative to piecework. Factory owners, who always limited married women's opportunities, did so increasingly over the century, preferring young single women, believing them more malleable and reliable. Still, piecework earnings of women from cultures which forbade women to go out without a male guard could shift their families from starvation to survival.

Artisans' homes were also workshops. In weavers' households, small children carded and combed, older daughters and wives spun, and fathers wove. Without cooperation, weavers could earn little. Whole families did laundry in Parisian households, but women always did the soaping and ironing. Parents willed their shops to daughters as often as sons. Craftsmen's wives often helped them with tailoring, shoemaking, or baking, or kept the shop, selling goods and keeping accounts. In households where men did putting-out work at home for a manufacturer, wives often negotiated the terms of workloads and wages. Wives of Lyon and Saint-Etienne silk weavers transported raw materials and finished products back and forth. They were beasts of burden, carrying heavy loads over long distances, but as liaisons between their husbands and manufacturers, they got the pay for the finished work. Wives of English knife-makers performed similar functions. The practice was so common in some trades that when craftsmen started to work in factories, employers still gave their wages to their wives.[10]

Women in the Needle Trades

Sewing requires great skill, but seamstresses lived in great hardship. Four months of the year, they worked an average twelve- to thirteen-hour day; during the two London "seasons"—April to August, October to December—they often worked twenty hours straight. They averaged eighteen, sitting all day in tiny dark airless workshops either freezing or overheated. Fifty seamstresses worked in one large room sunlit by day, lamp-lit at night, rooms so hot and oppressive that young women sometimes fainted at their work. At night they slept crammed into cells, eighteen in a room with one window, or five in a single attic bed. They had ten minutes for breakfast, fifteen or twenty for tea or dinner after the working day. They sometimes simply lay down on the floor and curled up for a few hours without eating, then started work again.

Long sedentary hours severely impaired workers' health: while working, they drove themselves, and fainted when they finished. They had poor digestion, weak lungs, and pains in their sides, and the circulation in their hands and feet simply ceased from lack of exercise, "never seeing the outside of the door from Sunday to Sunday." All seamstresses' eyesight was damaged and all were ill by the end of the season. But since owners discharged sick women, they feared to complain and continued working, harming their health further. Most were "second hands" earning board, lodging, and £20 to £30 a year. Healthy youngsters from the country became so ill they had to leave the trade, most often to become ladies' maids.

Many seamstresses described their food as "insufficient and unwholesome." With poor food, and horrible work hours and working conditions, many had swollen ankles, spinal curvatures, tuberculosis, asthma, and blindness: many English needlewomen ended their lives in the North London Ophthalmic Institution. They were not paid enough to live. At a labor meeting, slopworkers, trousermakers and seamstresses compared notes: 151 had never slept in a bed; 508 had to borrow clothes to attend the meeting; four or five owned underwear; only five had earned over 5 shillings the week before.

Capitalism created this wretchedness but it also created the conditions to change it. People working together could organize: a rhetoric of freedom provided a basis for action. A group discussion in England at a labor meeting led women to form the Association for the Aid and Benefit of Milliners and Dressmakers in 1843. Asking employers to end Sunday work, respect the twelve-hour day, and pay a minimum weekly wage of 9 shillings, the association set up an employment office to find seamstresses jobs in shops that abided by these requests. It urged employers to add extra staff during peak periods instead of grossly overworking the regular staff, and offer medical supervision of workers (who often fainted or fell ill over their work). It encouraged owners to install some form of ventilation.

American needlewomen also founded unions. The United Tailoresses Society (UTS), a trade union, was founded in 1831; the Shirt Sewers' Cooperative Union formed between 1851 and 1853 to sell its products directly to the public; the Sewingwomen's Protective and Benevolent Union acted as a mutual aid society and trade union in 1864–65; and the Working Woman's Association (WWA) functioned in 1868–69 as trade union, debating society, and feminist pressure group.[11] The most militant, the UTS, was run by tailoresses themselves, who developed a coherent theory of economic exploitation—systematized class and sex oppression based in male dominance. With the solidarity conferred by preindustrial organizations, men fought for a "family" wage. They demanded higher wages on the grounds that they supported women and children. But most women and children worked, many men were not married, and married men with families often abandoned or barely supported them. Louise Mitchell of the UTS argued: "When we complained to our employers and others of the inequality of our wages with that of men, the excuse is, they have families to support from which females are exempt. Now this is either a sad mistake or a willful oversight. How many females are there who have families to support and how many single men who have none."

The WWA was founded by feminists Susan B. Anthony and Elizabeth Cady Stanton, who also founded the newspaper *Revolution*. If their main goal was to recruit women workers into the suffrage movement, they also wished to help them. Feminist analyses of oppression focused on sex struggle, and male exploitation of women. This generated conflicts based on fear of male judgments, as suggested in an 1868 *New York Times* piece on the WWA:

> A meeting of ladies was held at the *Revolution* offices for the purpose of organizing an association of working women who might act for the interests of its members in the same manner as the association of working men, regulating the wages, etc. of [members]. . . .Mrs. Stanton thought the name [of the new association] should be Working Woman's Suffrage Association. Miss Augusta Lewis said that woman's wrongs should be redressed before her rights were proclaimed and that the word "suffrage would couple the association . . . with short hair and bloomers and other vagaries."

The focus on sex struggle alienated working women who were less exploited by their men—who were also exploited—than by their employers. They felt class struggle was essential: the WWA lasted less than a year.

Even organized workers were overmatched by employers and money interests, and no strategy guaranteed success. Strategies that avoided the confrontation created by class theory produced only short-term benefits for a few; strategies based in economic analysis were also short-lived, although seeing economic oppression as man-made helped women develop the thinking and confidence they needed to counter notions of natural female inferiority. Needlewomen's organizations did not achieve their stated goals, but they succeeded by developing a political analysis.

Women, who in general welcomed industrial production, soon saw that it could make them independent or leave them destitute, and felt it necessary to reiterate a fact that still needs reiteration: many women do not have men to support them. Some people blamed women for this fact, refusing to acknowledge the injustice of an economic system that allowed only men a living wage. Women explained they had lost husbands or fathers in the Civil War, and received no recompense. But they did not want pensions and especially did not want charity: charitable institutions were wretched and humiliating and jobs created by charities lowered everyone's wages. Women wanted work. Despite the enormous wealth around them, they did not attack the rich, nor did large numbers of them follow advice to migrate west, where they knew no one. They attacked the system, becoming the first American workers to analyze class structure.[12]

Boston entrepreneurs mechanized the garment industry early, mainly because of a labor shortage. The Irish influx in the 1840s made cheap unskilled labor available and in 1846, Elias Howe of Cambridge invented the sewing machine. When Britain allied with the south during the Civil War, the north stopped importing British cloth, placing a greater demand on domestic producers. By 1865 Boston factory owners had created the "Boston system" of dividing mechanized tasks, a sewing assembly line: one person did only facings, another only buttonholes, and so on. By eliminating the need for multiple skills, manufacturers could hire unskilled workers for low wages, and throw accomplished seamstresses and tailors out of work.[13]

Women in Trades

Women seem to have been hired as telephone operators as soon as phones became available to the public in 1879, and they made up the great majority of telephone operators. Male operators worked mainly at night. Late in the century, women went to work in offices: the first British government department to hire women as clerks was the Post Office. A busy subculture of women worked on their own, market women, servicers like carters, petty traders, street hawkers, laundresses, and boardinghouse keepers, who swelled cities over the century. They also learned trades they were later excluded from, like mailmaking, brickmaking, and mining.

Much of what we know about working women comes from a Victorian gentleman, Arthur Munby. Obsessed with working women, mainly their dress and manners, he observed and interviewed them, and wrote a book that tingles with his titillation. He is constantly wondering if their work made them less "ladylike" or "feminine"; he is thrilled by women in "male" guise—trousered, dirty, swaggering, roughly dressed.[14] The middle class saw women doing manual labor as "degraded" because, unlike ladies, who always had chaperones, they were alone, vulnerable to sexual approach (the men who accosted them were *not* seen as degraded). In fact, laboring women were as sexually free as men in their culture and ended up married with families, just like ladies.

Brickmakers worked barefoot, legs bare to above the knee, in stained ragged clothes, with mud-stained faces and hair. Their foul mouths shocked Munby. Most were young. Munby noted that a thirteen-year-old would have been "pretty in face and form" if she were clean and healthy, but the flush in her cheeks was from exhaustion, not health. He watched her move weakly, unsteadily, raising a twenty-five-pound mass of clay on her head, balancing it as she squatted to pick up another twenty-five-pound mass which she held against her stomach. Lumbering six or seven yards with her burden, she lay it on a molding bench, repeating these actions for ten to twelve hours every working day.

Many women and children worked in mines doing very arduous and low-paid work. Deep in the mines everyone worked naked or half-naked. Women wore old trousers and a shirt—improper and undressed in a period when corsets and bustles and layers of petticoats were prescribed. Basch describes women bent double in water up to their knees lugging heavy loads of coal. Girls of six or seven went down first and came up last, working the doors for ventilation and to let corves (metal tubs or baskets used to haul coal) pass through. Women guided and pushed corves along the gallery rails, and in narrow seams, got down on hands and knees harnessed to a belt with a chain that passed between their legs to draw a sledge over considerable distances along sloping galleries. In unprofitable shafts, owners saved money by having women rather than rails or pit ponies convey heavy baskets of coal.[15]

Laws barring underground mine work by children and women were passed in the 1840s, impelled by Lord Ashley, who in 1842 published a report on child labor in mines, with illustrations and woodcuts for parliamentarians who did not care to read. He proposed new legislation in a two-hour speech that moved his audience to tears—and to the passage of an act forbidding female labor underground and the apprenticeship of children under eleven. These laws were modeled on an 1833 law barring the employment of young children in textile mills and establishing an eight-hour workday for children over nine—the first major industrial legislation enacted in England. In 1844 laws banned night work and fourteen to sixteen-hour days for women and children under eighteen, decreeing a maximum of twelve hours of labor and strengthening safety regulations and the powers of factory inspectors. In 1847 a ten-hour day was imposed on women and youths under eighteen; later laws decreed that their hours must fall between morning and 7 p.m., thereby ending night shifts.

Such laws seem humane, but real humanity would have included men under their terms. Lacking that, the laws injured those they were intended to help. Adherents of laissez-faire policy opposed such laws, warning that women in mining regions would be unemployed; mine owners argued that women had a right to choose their own work and that mothers' indefeasible rights over their children would be violated by state regulation of children's labor. The rhetoric of rights served the mine owners' desire for cheap labor; and they ignored mothers' rights when it came to child custody. Owners who used women in mines with seams too narrow for horses to haul coal would be ruined if they had to use men (who got higher wages) for this work, warned a millionaire colliery owner: they would shut the mines, forcing women and their families to starve.

But even people who perceived the needs of working-class families opposed laws barring child labor on the grounds that a child working in a textile mill could relieve a mother from work so she could tend younger children. In 1833 legislators opposed to child labor laws argued that limiting the working hours of infants would force "the mothers of families to work in mills; a consequence which is much deprecated as extremely mischievous." French inspectors supposed to enforce an 1841 child labor law frequently reported that families needed their children's wages.

In the 1830s and 1840s, England and France passed laws requiring manufacturers to educate child workers; this led to a marked decline in illiteracy, but not to universal education. An anguished schoolteacher in the industrial north wrote in 1861: "At ten, sometimes nine or eight, even the weakest children are stolen from us to be sent to ruin their bodies and lose their souls in the dust and disorder of workshops for a few sous a day."[16] In 1867 an inspector in Reims charged that children's education was sacrificed for "the material interest of the family"; in 1870 inspectors in Sommes reported that about six hundred children between seven and thirteen years received no schooling whatever. But some understood: "One of the principal causes of school nonattendance stems from poverty, from the need above all to satisfy those material interests which affect their very existence."

Even after the law made school compulsory, mere thousands of children attended English factory schools. Cities had inadequate facilities for public education, but there were even fewer in the countryside. Manchester children studied erratically between three and twelve years of age, but remained largely uneducated. They might go to school, but if the family was desperate, money was short, or jobs opened up, they were sent to work—selling matches, running errands, or working in tobacco shops.

Domestic Servants

Westerners derided the African style of exhibiting status—having a large entourage of dependents—but nineteenth-century middle-class Europeans used the same symbol. Social scientists studying status found its surest determinant to be the number of "deference givers," and accorded middle-class status only to families with at least one servant. Middle-class people surrounded themselves with "rituals of order," presenting themselves as public images, works of art freed from the realm of the necessary. Conventions that lower-ranked groups use back doors, deal only with servants, or use titles when addressing upper-ranked people enabled elites to appear free from realities like uncombed hair, unwashed faces or, as Edith Wharton's mother scornfully declared, untidy drawing-rooms. The drive to disassociate the self from necessity is unspoken and probably unconscious. Likely unaware of their own psychological dependence on servants, people did what they could to bind servants into economic and physical dependency on them.

Most waged workers were employed in agriculture or domestic service. In Milan, in 1881, 1901, and 1911 censuses, most waged women were domestic servants; the second largest group were needlewomen. In 1881 one out of every twenty-two Britishers was a servant; in London the proportion was one in fifteen. Until the end of the century, over a third of working Englishwomen were under twenty and a third of those between fifteen and twenty were servants: girls of nine or ten were in service. In 1911, 35 percent of working women were servants. People increasingly hired females, writes Leonore Davidoff, not just because men demanded higher wages but also because men were less amenable to control.[17] Girls, seen as property by their families, were used to supervision. A servant's life was determined by the household she worked in: in a big house with a staff of servants she might have some autonomy, a high standard of living, and considerable authority over others. But most were "slavies" in lower-middle-class suburban or artisan households or lodging houses. American James Fenimore Cooper wrote that the servant in his Southampton lodging house in the 1830s was "worse off than an Asiatic slave."

Yet many European women preferred domestic service to factory or shop work with their risky freedoms.[18] Families also preferred it and usually kept sons at home to work the farm, sending daughters out into service where they would be safe in a family environment, and guaranteed a room, food, and clothing. Wages were low, but they could save their wages for their marriages—domestic work gave them enough security to defer marriage until they found men who pleased them.

But not in the United States, where domestic service was the least desired work. American women wanted independence above all, and servants were on constant call and under constant surveillance. Before the Civil War, women considered domestic service "immigrant work" fit only for unskilled newcomers.[19] Black women, who made up a huge contingent of servants, preferred work in which they were not at the beck and call of a white family and had time to take care of their own families. Female domestic servants worked from before dawn until their employers went to bed, but were on call twenty-four hours a day. Employers closely supervised the morals (read "sex life") of female, not male, servants—yet male employers regularly sexually harassed or raped girls who had virtually no redress. Working alone, servants could not organize collectively or protest, and they depended on references. Factory work involved long but discrete hours, and when they ended, workers were free.

Servants were in an uneasy position because most women were

actually servants in their own homes. Work by a woman without a contract stipulating her wages was considered voluntary: dependent sisters, aunts, or cousins were really unpaid servants. Like female kin and wives, paid servants were confined to the home, responsible for chores and subject to the caprice of the master. Unlike wives, servants were paid for their work and not legally bound to provide sexual service. But wages were tiny, sex was often coerced or demanded, and, if a woman became pregnant by a master or his son, she was cast off and dishonored. Discussing the situation of servants and wives in nineteenth-century England, where law decreed "husband and wife are one and the husband is that one," Davidoff shows how arrangements bolstered male control.[20] For example, in European cities, maids from different households slept together on the top floor of blocks of flats. When London flats were built, this feature was deliberately omitted so that families would not lose control of their servants. Most English families lived in one-family houses with gardens that allowed easier surveillance and confinement of servants.

Domestic servants experienced domination intimately. Of the conflicts between masters and servants that reached the police courts, most concerned broken contracts (with servants charging masters four times more frequently than the reverse).[21] But many complained of physical or emotional abuse. It was no longer acceptable for employers to beat servants, but some pushed woman servants around or boxed their ears or scolded them humiliatingly, calling them "silly girl," "lazybones," or "blockhead." Young servants were most unhappy about being confined; some were daring enough to sneak out at night. Many employers felt they had the right to search servants' personal belongings or read their letters.

Male employers exposed themselves to servants, frightening some into bringing charges. But formal cases only hint at the rampancy of sexual harassment. Male employers regularly cuddled, kissed, or touched female servants' bodies. In the morality of the time, acts that caused no visible injury were harmless, and most servants suffered silently. But male employers and upper servants commonly raped or seduced young girls, making them pregnant. In such cases, not only was a servant girl alone dishonored and disgraced, but she alone had to face the consequences of an act she may not have been able to control. Some were discharged; others gave their babies to charities. However men rationalized such acts, they symbolized the real employer/servant relation of domination and powerlessness, class exploitation in the domestic sphere, imposed on women not just socially but also personally.

Shop Clerks and Prostitutes

To be a salesclerk in a fine shop was a prestigious position, but clerks worked very hard and even the highest paid earned pittances. In nineteenth-century France, shop girls worked thirteen- or fourteen-hour days, from about eight in the morning. They had to walk up and down stairs to fetch merchandise and were sent on errands, often climbing forty flights of stairs a day. In 1876 and even in 1901, British clerks often worked eighty-five hours a week. The time allotted for meals—thirty minutes at midday and fifteen to twenty minutes for afternoon tea—included the time to reach and return from an eating place. They suffered from digestive troubles and anemia and had to be on their feet constantly, even when not waiting on customers or tidying stock.[22] Shops were not affected by the newly passed laws covering factory workers, and were drafty and poorly ventilated, with glaring gaslight. Toilets were dank, small, and not sex-segregated; many small shops had none at all.

Reformers, especially Americans, deplored women working as shop clerks, considering department stores portals of prostitution: people were sure that poor young women exposed to luxuries they had never seen before and would never be able to afford would be turned to prostitution.[23] A 1915 study of department store saleswomen showing that the highest paid clerks most often turned to prostitution "proved" that rising expectations were the motivation. But perhaps the women were better paid *because* they were prostitutes, since the main prerequisite for working in a shop was dressing well and being attractive, and clothes were expensive. Women without proper dress were turned away; shop girls had to be stylish. French clerks might run up and down stairs all day, but they had to dress formally on wages of 1 franc a day, 3 to 12 in commissions.

Everything was stacked against them, and many women survived only by becoming prostitutes. Almost all prostitutes had another job, usually as servants or seamstresses. Needlewomen's wages were so low that many became whores to eke out a living. Female garment industry workers were paid starvation wages. Shop clerks had to dress well. Not only were women paid half as much as men for comparable work, but *in no occupation did women workers earn enough to support themselves independently*. Moreover, fair game for male employers—and often told to initiate the household sons sexually (some derived pride from the function)—servants gained sexual experience. A servant fired when *her* "crime" (sexual activity with the master class, seen as unfortunate but normal) became known often was driven to prostitution.

Prostitution could provide a living. Surveys of prostitutes show that most came from the working class and became whores to stay alive, and most had jobs that paid too little to live on. Many American prostitutes interviewed in the late nineteenth and early twentieth centuries were unskilled workers earning $4–$6 a week when they needed $9 a week to survive alone. In Italy most registered prostitutes were country-born peasants, single, and poor; they became prostitutes when they moved to the cities, in lieu of or along with other work: in 1875, 7 percent of them worked in the textile industry, 23 percent in garment making, and 28 percent as servants.[24]

By mid-century, prostitutes thronged every major city, military base, and even the countryside.[25] In England, every commission of inquiry into rural prostitution blamed starvation wages. W.R. Greg called them women "for whom there is no fall . . . for they stood already on the lowest level of existence."[26] Reports are filled with

women like a young unemployed milliner who went on the streets to feed her father, a docker who was ill and could not work, and workers who sold their bodies to feed their children. Most working-class women did not set out to be prostitutes, but entered "the life" gradually, after a seduction and betrayal, or as a temporary measure when they or their families were in economic difficulties.

Almost every city in the late nineteenth- and early twentieth-century United States had a thriving "red-light" district.[27] Patronage of bars and brothels was open, amounting to *de facto* legalization of prostitution. Brothels covered an economic gamut, catering to different classes of men and specific tastes. A few luxurious houses offered "special" services to the rich and highly placed, politicians and gentlemen, for $5 to $10 a trick. Some houses charged a dollar or two, drawing a middle-class clientele. Older, less attractive prostitutes charged 50 cents for a quickie in shabby tenement brothels called "cribs." Some walked the streets, although fewer than today. Prostitutes too had a pecking order and class snobbery: each rank considered those below them economically "trash" who cheapened the status of the profession.

But some women gained independence and a supportive female subculture through prostitution. As whores, they could profit from a sexual war in which women were usually victims. Some earned enough to live alone, which was impossible in waged work, domestic service, or marriage. Some earned enough to spend money on fun and luxuries, things other women could not afford. In the past, prostitutes were the only class of women living outside male control (even nuns had to obey priests and the church hierarchy), and prostitution was often the only paid profession men allowed women. To have women sexually available to all, men had to enable them to live outside the control of other men. Later, it was the only profession in which they let them earn a decent living.

Although prostitution is created by male demand, patriarchy lays the onus of sexuality on women: women, not men, are responsible for the sexual morality of society. Prostitutes violate the morality

that women are expected to uphold. Men keep women in a vise in patriarchies: demanding that women fulfill the function of sexual availability, they pay prostitutes enough to live but also label them criminal and place them beyond the protection of law; as wives, they were deprived of property or rights over themselves and their children.

Prostitutes have always been treated with contempt, and after the Protestant revolution, have been cast out from society as beneath consideration, undeserving of civil or political rights. During waves of reform, societies arrested, whipped, expelled, or transported prostitutes. Trying to check the spread of venereal disease in garrison towns and seaports, in 1864, 1866, and 1869, England passed the Contagious Diseases Acts, which transformed the prostitute into "a conduit of infection to respectable society."[28] The bearer of disease, the scapegoat carrying the sins of society in her genitals, she was an object of class guilt, "a powerful symbol of sexual and economic exploitation under industrial capitalism."[29]

Society's Attitudes Toward Working Women

Protective legislation ostensibly arises from compassion for women and children. Its adherents use a rhetoric of pity; those opposed to it use a rhetoric of freedom. In both cases, rhetoric masks real motivation. Those who opposed protective laws wanted a continued source of cheap labor; those in favor feared female independence. Neither cared about what the actual people wanted.

Protective laws often did not use the term *women*, including women in the category of "young persons" as if they were minors. Both Ashley's 1842 speech and Engels' *The Condition of the Working Class in England* in1844 stressed that women's labor led to the "dissolution of family ties," to social disintegration. Reports by factory inspectors, observers, and officials obsessed about the immorality of female factory workers, married or single, as demonstrated by increased illegitimacy, widespread promiscuity, prostitution, alcoholism, and delinquency. Whether women with families worked

like their husbands, supported the family when a husband was unemployed, or had no man to support them (40 percent of Englishwomen were unmarried in 1841) was irrelevant: women's working for wages destroyed the fabric of the family.

There *was* a serious increase in illegitimate births in many European cities from 1750 to 1850, not because of female immorality but because of a new male freedom. Rural sex had always been relatively free; couples usually deferred marriage until pregnancy proved a woman's fertility. In 1850 the London *Morning Chronicle* declared "co-habitation before marriage . . . almost universal" in rural areas. Country women could rely on men's promises of marriage: few men dared break them in villages, where the moral force of the entire community pressured them to accept their responsibility. Men needed mates to survive; children repaid their cost within a few years by work in household and farm. Marriages might be unhappy, husbands might abuse wives, but illegitimacy was rare.

Such customs could not be enforced in cities lacking community, and where mates and children were not economic necessities. Statistics then and now show that many men evaded responsibility for children. Young rural women who went on believing promises of marriage learned that country rules did not apply in cities. The requirement that domestic servants be single meant that women either went without sex and affection or had affairs. Many men broke their promises because they earned too little to support a family or had a chance to work elsewhere, but those who simply chose to ignore responsibility could not be forced to accept it. In such cases, a woman could either abandon her baby or struggle to feed it on wages insufficient to support even one of them.

Illegitimacy rates increased in this period even in the English countryside, perhaps because most men were landless and immune to community pressure. European birth rates were high because people were living longer and producing more children. Birth rates began to fall in France after 1820 when French peasants began to use contraception, probably *coitus interruptus*. Infant and child mortality also declined somewhat in the nineteenth century, but mortality rates varied greatly by economic class (as they do today in the United States). The wealthy in England and France enjoyed better health and lived longer than the rural or urban poor. Life expectancies were appallingly low and infant mortality rates high in the urban slums of industrial cities. Of babies born in 1850, half reached fifteen with two living parents; less than 10 percent reached fifteen with both parents and all siblings alive. Working-class people's health and longevity were also affected by their work: some occupations shortened lives.

Illegitimacy, alcoholism, prostitution, and "promiscuity" were no more common in women factory workers than among servants or farm women. The upper classes, men especially, had always enjoyed sexual freedom. Only the middle class inhibited sex, preferring emotion repressed. Adherents of protective laws declared that female immorality threatened the social fabric, but what they really feared was female independence. Paid work outside the home, especially if it freed women from the restraints of Victorian dress and manners, might inspire them to defy other restraints. Legislators argued that factory work kept women from devoting themselves exclusively to their families but feared the challenge to male dominance of a breadwinner wife and a husband who stayed home to tend children, clean, and cook (which of course few men did). Legislators cried that women who supported the family "virtually turned [their husbands] into eunuchs."[30]

Lord Ashley was shocked that women workers formed clubs and associations to "meet together to drink, sing and smoke" and "gradually [acquire] all those privileges which are held to be the proper portion of the male sex." Indeed, the idea of "privilege" underlay the entire controversy.[31] "Protection of women" was code, like "protection of the family" today, for preserving patriarchal customs. In mid-century England, of six million women over twenty, half worked in industry, and over a third supported themselves. People who earned wages instead of depending on inheritances could ignore their parents' dictates about marriage. In regions where waged work was available, more couples married and younger than before, following *their* desires, unconcerned about property or money. In some regions, couples did not bother to marry, but simply lived together in what their contemporaries called "concubinage" (compromising only the woman). Such unions had always been common but seem to have increased in nineteenth-century England and France. They were known to last, often happily, especially between workers in the same trade. Parents in these liaisons did not abandon their children.

Once children were forbidden to work, mothers with babies had to find work to feed them; laws "protecting" women from night work or heavy lifting kept them in the lowest-paid jobs. Later laws required employers to pay women giving birth and caring for newborns; these laws functioned to keep employers from hiring women at all. Women and children were driven from hardship to starvation. Nevertheless, arguments over protective laws continued throughout the century and into this one. The issue divided even feminists, who had no economic agenda beyond their concern for women's safety and health or their freedom and economic status. Protective legislation that applies only to one sex divides the labor force, injuring all its members. A similar problem resulted from men's insistence on dominating unions.

Moreover, protective laws did not confront the real problem: an economic and political structure that consigned reproduction to an invisible domestic realm, and treated it as a *nonproductive* activity requiring no support. By patronizing female reproduction as entirely women's concern, a trifle or luxury women chose for amusement, industry pushed women into a desperate situation.

Married Women

It is no exaggeration to call nineteenth-century working-class women's situation desperate: single women could not earn enough to live, married women could not get jobs, mothers with mates who could not or chose not to support their children watched them starve. A Frenchman of the period observed: "A single woman cannot earn a living in Paris. . . . A good half of young workers, if not the majority, find themselves with this alternative: to live in privation or to marry."[32] Patriarchies force women to marry, often through family pressure. Nineteenth-century Western women were forced into marriage by economic pressure. Women had to marry: single mothers married men who had not sired their children; servants married—usually men of higher status.

But married women could not get work, especially as industrialization increased. In agricultural France of the 1860s, 40 percent of married women worked family farms or ran family businesses; in 1896, 52 percent of single and 38 percent of married women worked outside the home. But in industrial England in 1851 only 25 percent of married women had paid work; by 1911, 69 percent of single women but only 9.6 percent of married women had jobs, most in their husbands' business, running small beer houses or provision shops. Women did what they could to help support their families, in cities, planting vegetable gardens or raising animals, usually pigs and hens, to supplement the family diet and sell the surplus. They opened cafés in their houses or set up outdoor stands to sell prepared food or drink. A knife-maker's wife in Sheffield, England, bottled a fermented drink she called "pop" to sell to city residents in summer.

In the United States the only large group of regularly employed married women besides blacks (valued as domestic servants) were immigrants in New England textile mills. Native-born educated women often looked down on them as ignorant, but immigrants resourcefully adapted their skills to local requirements. Southern Italian women used to picking fruit and vegetables found similar work in Buffalo, New York; those on New York's lower East Side sewed or made paper flowers with their daughters at home, while their husbands dug ditches or swept streets and sometimes kept house and cared for children when their wives found work in factories and sweatshops. Married Irishwomen who knew only farming quickly learned enough to become domestics and cleaned New York office buildings at night so they could tend their children in the days. European married women usually worked in the least industrialized enterprises; with less separation between home and workplace, they were more able to control their own work rhythms.[33] Married women, clustered in poorly paid, episodic, and temporary marginal work, nevertheless contributed 10 percent to 50 percent of family incomes. Recent studies demonstrate what past studies have suggested—that women spend most of their wages on the family, while men spend much of theirs on themselves.

All industrial societies up to the present have treated women as marginal workers for whom work is a secondary priority. Since women everywhere have also been expected to take responsibility for the unpaid maintenance of households and children, employers and governments have viewed them as dependents who wrap work around their primary concerns, wifehood and motherhood. Employers have paid women low wages when they were young, assuming that their fathers supported them and they needed only "pin" money; and they did not train or promote them, or expect them to advance. After marriage, they hired women at need, paying them little, on the assumption that they were merely supplementing their husbands' incomes. Working-class men won the wage war against women: men fought for and got a "family wage" whether or not they had a family, while women in industrial societies worked seasonally, irregularly, part time, at home, for pittances.

The home, which middle-class writers saw as a comfy nest for reproduction and renewal, protected from the brutal aggressive male public world, was for women a site of power struggle and labor. This was true for all classes, but worst for working-class women. Reproduction was a great burden; renewal was not possible. The conditions of work in industrial society made it difficult and sometimes impossible to raise a child and feed it at the same time. When mothers were absent for hours every day, children suffered, especially infants.

Babies whose mothers could not nurse them were bottle-fed animal milk or soup; in the nineteenth century people did not know about sterilization, so such feeding could give them fatal digestive diseases. Infant mortality rates were high in regions where mothers worked long hours away from home: mothers were blamed. Working mothers pressed daughters of seven or eight into tending younger children or left infants with aged women who were not always scrupulous, and might use contaminated milk or not feed nursing babies often enough. They often fed babies unnourishing bread soaked in sugared water. There were accidents—burns, falls, drownings. To make babies sleep, caretakers used alcohol, laudanum, morphine, or opium-based narcotics that could bring on convulsions.

The alternative to bottle-feeding was wet-nursing, widely practiced in France. Louise Tilly and Joan Scott write that if a baby survived the trip to the wet nurse (often a long distance over rough roads), if the nurse had enough milk to nourish it with the other children she cared for, and if it survived the many hazards of infancy when tended by someone likely to be indifferent, then the child was returned to its parents at an age when it could care for itself. Most infants never returned.

For mothers, survival of a family was more important than any one life. French working couples prospered when both partners worked for wages, but with babies their situation deteriorated. Children needed supervision and cost money; pregnancy, nursing, and tending children reduced a wife's earnings. Wives had to maintain the household, husbands to support it, both almost alone. Things improved when children reached about eight and could contribute to the family earnings. But when children left to set up their own households, aging parents again on their own earned less; if illness, injury or "other crises overtook them, misery often ensued again."[34] The longer children lived at home, the better off the family: families whose children found waged work near home were better off; children could stay home longer if a family had enough to live on: it was a vicious cycle. Remaining home strengthened children's ties to their mother, the heart and soul of the family, whose concern and work kept it alive.

In the traditional division of labor, men ran farms or shops and women managed households. When people began to work outside the home, men still expected women to shoulder the entire domestic burden. They tried; they marketed, cooked, sewed, cleaned, and mended clothing and gave the children most of whatever education they received. Because poor women lacked *things*—furniture, dining or kitchen equipment, objects requiring dusting—housework was less onerous than it became, but work in tiny tenement rooms never ended. The poorer the family, the heavier women's work. Women's major task, finding food, fuel, and water, took hours every day, entailing "scores of errands out of the house."[35]

Women and children sacrificed for men. Contemporary autobiographies record Alice Linton's father, for example, eating butter while the rest of the family ate margarine; one father regularly ate bacon as his family watched hungrily.[36] George Acorn's father took "all the meals we had so anxiously provided without the slightest thought or consideration." Wives said nothing about their poor diets. A woman recalls her mother regularly dining on "kettle-bender" (crusts with hot water, pepper, salt, and a bit of margarine), careful to eat her meal "before father came in for his." A husband might help plan a meal and send the children out to buy haddock, say, then feed them the head and tail. Studies of working-class English budgets from 1860 to 1950 show that seven to eight pence a day was spent on men's food, while the rest of the family lived on threepence or less a day; wives' and children's lower nutrition and caloric intake are well documented.[37]

When a major expense like a childbirth approached, women saved by giving children less food and starving themselves. This practice was not rooted in female self-sacrifice; it was strategic: women gave men what they wanted *in order to keep them and their wages*. Denied their desires, men might abandon their families, as many did. A wife's failure to cater to her husband's wishes, even if he did not support her, was a major violation of men's marital rights. Ellen Ross writes that such failures were a primary factor in assault cases tried at Old Bailey, like that of Robert Plampton, who stabbed and killed his wife, Emily Maria, one afternoon for pawning his blankets when he wanted to take a nap. Women needed husbands, who brought potential pregnancies and beatings but also money, unobtainable elsewhere, into the household.

Men blamed pregnancies on women and considered children one of the irritations attendant on taking a wife. A popular song of the time, "Don't Have Anymore, Missus Moore," implied that the mother was solely responsible for the Moores' twenty children. A woman wrote about hearing her father complain to her mother (who bore nineteen children), "I can't hang me trousers on the end of the bed . . . that you're not like that [pregnant]." Fertility rates were high among London's poor. The usual birth control methods of the period, abstinence and *coitus interruptus*, required male cooperation, but men took no responsibility for sex *or* for children, often raping or beating women who refused intercourse. Some did refuse: London mothers were known for assertive opinions. Others may surreptitiously have used sponges, douches, and, later, diaphragms.

Men often concealed the amount they earned from their wives, giving them only a small allowance, while keeping the rest for tobacco and drink.[38] And they had a legal right to their wives' wages, which many drank up, leaving the family to starve. Harriet Robinson often saw American men searching the Lowell mill for their wives.

> The laws relating to women were such that a husband could claim his wife wherever he found her, and also the children she was trying to shield from his influence; and I have seen more than one poor woman skulk behind her loom or her frame when visitors were approaching the end of the aisle where she worked. Some of these were known under

> assumed names, to prevent their husbands from trusteeing their wages. It was a very common thing for a male . . . of a certain kind to do this. . . depriving his wife of all her wages, perhaps month after month.[39]

As a result, many children saw their fathers as enemies. Adult siblings robbed each other and stole from their fathers, but of hundreds of theft cases listed in newspaper and court records for the years 1869 to 1889, not one described a child stealing from a mother. Mothers held families together by caring and taking responsibility. This may be universal but is documented among working-class families in England, working-class and slave families in the Americas, and in most of Africa. The mother-child relation created the loyalty and sense of family obligation that marked the working class. Many observers noted especially strong bonds of affection between working-class mothers and children, who knew that their mothers sacrificed for them and protected them from their fathers. Children gave mothers "affection and gratitude. . . . Should the mother die, her little ones weep. . . their only friend is gone." When education became compulsory, mothers had to maintain families without help from school-aged children—and the age was gradually raised. After the 1870s they had what their husbands gave them and their own pitiful earnings.

While women struggled to maintain families, men maintained solidarity in a strong pub culture. Many popular music-hall ballads about starving children in pubs begging fathers to come home with money for food reflected this situation, as did the popular temperance movement in the United States. Men's indifference to women and children is not a matter of boyish irresponsibility; an ethnographic study of male pub culture shows it arises from hatred of women, sexual objectification of and preoccupation with controlling them.[40] In this sex war, males expressed their contempt for women publicly, verbally and physically, while women, isolated from each other, lacking solidarity and perceiving the taboo on female anger against men, hid their hostility to men.

When men did come home after spending the "family" wage at a pub, many beat their wives and/or children. Ross quotes one woman: "I should say seven out of ten of the wives down my way feel their husbands' fists at times, and lots of 'em are used shocking." It was generally believed that men had the right to beat wives, but women sometimes left men because of violence, or because men threatened to murder them or attacked their children (this is said to have been rare in the period), or refused to support them or insulted them sexually. One woman told a police court missionary, "I would forgive anything but the filthy names he calls me." She was indeed forgiving: at twenty-three, she was deaf in one ear and had a broken nose from her husband's fists. Wives feared debilitating injury and venereal infection transmitted when drunken husbands raped them. The "sympathetic" police court missionary declared wives living with husbands had to submit to rape. Women did not leave husbands from sexual jealousy; Ross notes that in contrast to contemporary French, German, and Spanish popular music, British music-hall lyrics lacked sexual passion. Male violence to women pervaded working-class society.

Husbands and wives had utterly different relations to children and money, the two major components of family life, and little tolerance of each other's needs.[41] Couples "lived together" only by being economically and sometimes sexually interdependent. They even had different neighborhood friends. They shared goods, services, and sites—shops, pubs, streets, doorways—with people of their own sex. Most women valued children, kin, enough money, and intimacy, not with husbands but with their mothers, children, sisters, grandmothers, and neighbors. Men and boys moved further from home than women, and spent time with other males in talk or drinking, sports, politics, and gambling, often in pubs.

London women too hung out in pubs, but always in groups, not alone, often with their babies and children. (After a 1908 law barred children, pubs became male domains.) Every Monday women took their valuables to a pawnshop to get some cash to tide them over the week, redeeming the item on payday so as to have it over the weekend. Afterward, they stopped at the pub to chat. Female neighborhood networks created a community on which women depended; to a large degree, wives' social skills determined their families' well-being. Neighborhood women shared linens, washtubs, clothing, or items to pawn in times of need. Even if they were not friends, woman neighbors helped each other in emergencies like serious illness or eviction, taking in a beaten wife for a night, an evicted family for a longer period. Women neighbors tended the sick, did their laundry, brought fuel and built fires for them, and prepared their meals. They collected money for big expenses like funerals, but rarely asked help from non-kin men.[42]

This behavior was rooted in compassion and goodheartedness, but it was also insurance. No one knew when she might need similar help. Poor neighborhoods had more female-headed households than wealthier neighborhoods (then as now, in all ethnic groups). Middle-class observers were struck by poor women's compassion for needy children; poor as they were, they pitied children. A man with a criminal reputation visiting a very poor South London district met a woman who kept six children in her "wretched room." Two belonged to a widow who had lived above her but was jailed for assaulting a police officer. The woman had taken them in and intended to keep them until the mother was freed—if she could: "It was only neighborly-like and my heart bled to see the poor young'uns a-cryin', and that wretched and neglected and dirty." Woman neighbors often acted as extra parents, feeding neighbors' hungry children, and sometimes even adopting them.

But this honorable taking of responsibility makes life harder for women, who are often blamed for things they cannot control. In the nineteenth century, a woman's dress and sexual, social, and drinking habits largely created a family's—even a street's—reputation for respectability, and mothers were blamed for children's plight. On a winter day in 1856, an agent of the Children's Aid Society of New York saw two barefoot, thinly dressed, but cheerful children gathering bits of wood and coal on the street. They explained they were finding fuel for their mother and agreed to take him to meet her. Their widowed mother earned what she could street peddling, but had had to sell everything for food: their room was bare and unheated. As they spoke, she sat on a pallet with two children younger than the foragers, rubbing their hands. The agent remarked on the sweet tidy children, but blamed the mother in his report: "Though for her pure young children too much could hardly be done, in such a woman there is little confidence to be put. . . . It is probably some cursed vice has thus reduced her and . . . if her children be not separated from her, she will drag them down too."[43]

Urban Life

For centuries Europe's urban poor lived in the streets, working, playing, and resting in marketplaces and squares. Middle-class observers with notions of privacy were fascinated by the public domestic life of the London poor.[44] The same phenomenon occurred in nineteenth-century New York, where the streets teemed with children peddling, huckstering and scavenging, stealing, or selling sex.[45] Adults scavenged too: like today's bag-people, rag pickers lived on cities' detritus. Street kids slept in groups in nooks and crannies, orphans, abandoned children, or runaways from destitute homes. Sexually abused or beaten children sought the streets, which offered a way to survive. Platoons of six- and seven-year-olds sought fuel for their mothers, ransacking docks, lumberyards, demolished buildings, and artisanal districts for chips, ashes, wood, or coal to take home or sell. New York children convicted of theft and jailed in the juvenile house of correction in the 1850s had been convicted of stealing a bar of soap, a copy of the *New York Herald*, lead or wood from demolished houses, and a board worth 3 cents. A New York journalist wrote that along with malefactors, the city jail held young boys and girls "caught asleep on cellar doors or [those] suspected of the horrible crime of stealing junk bottles and old iron!"[46]

Children rarely stole from people, but some were muggers or pickpockets—dangerous work, but easy enough to learn from men who hung around hotels or business districts, and a single theft could reap a month's wages for a domestic servant, a week's for a seamstress, several weeks' for a huckster. Juvenile prostitution was a permanent street feature; not yet a crime, it paid girls more than any other work. In the 1830s John R. McDowall, head of a reform society, complained that "females of thirteen and fourteen" walked on fashionable Broadway "without a protector, until some pretended gentleman gives them a nod and takes their arm and escorts them to houses of assignation." A journalist walked a mile up Broadway one night in 1854 and counted almost fifty girls soliciting.

In formal reports, reformers blamed women more than men for this situation. Women—widows, abandoned wives, orphaned working-class daughters—were poor: female self-support *meant* indigence. Middle-class reformers insisted that women's poverty was caused by negligence. Mothers of street children were bad parents but also subhuman, like prostitutes. Their inability to demonstrate true womanhood by creating a home placed them outside the pale of humanity. Over the century new ideals of domesticity and the proper role of women had created a new image of civilized society. Social arbiters merged gender and class ideologies to sanctify the home as a private (hidden) space presided over by women, inhabited by children, and frequented by men. Dangerous streets indicated a corrupt family life. Early in the century, philanthropists saw the poor as providence's creations; mid-Victorians thought poverty could be abolished by training the poor, mainly the young, to be better workers, citizens, and family members.

People who believed it was possible to change conditions increasingly emphasized control. New York created a police force in 1845, reformers broadened definitions of crime, and "experts" testified that family relations, not industrial capitalism, caused the visible, widespread, and seemingly permanent misery of city life. Promiscuous sociability, the "almost fabulous gregariousness" of the poor, offended the walled-in middle class; perceiving a crisis, they solved it by ending street life. Middle-class reformers forced the poor to stay indoors, to hide their poverty. They won their battle against street life without ameliorating poverty in any way. By destroying the street life of the working poor, reformers annihilated urban communities and a vital way of using urban space.[47] Streets emptied of life became the haunts of predators, especially dangerous for women.

In 1824 the Society for the Reformation of Juvenile Delinquents set up a House of Refuge to train offending children by corporal punishment and solitary confinement. The Children's Aid Society used a gentler strategy, putting poor children in foster homes to be cared for by "loving gentle women" thought to be so by nature. Poor city children were first sent to nearby farms where labor was scarce, but in 1854 the CAS began sending groups by rail to Illinois, Iowa, and Michigan. By 1860 it had "placed out" 5000 children. The CAS ignored the rights of working-class parents, seeing it as a positive good to separate their children from them. They took children without their parents' consent or, sometimes, even their knowledge. Moral reformer Lydia Maria Child wrote in 1843 that the greatest misfortune of "the squalid little wretches" in New York streets was that they were not orphans. The CAS remedied this: it manufactured orphans.[48]

Despite its declared intention to use the "innate" kindness of women to remold poor children, the CAS relocated mainly boys to be overseen by men, who also ran its Newsboys' Lodging House, where newsboys could sleep and eat for a few cents. The female staff of the CAS were not paid (men were), and ran programs for girls aimed at molding them into wives and mothers dedicated to domesticity, who knew middle-class standards and would use them in their homes and families. Such re-education came to dominate reform programs for working-class females. The settlement houses of turn-of-the-century New York offered mothers housekeeping lessons, brainwashing vast numbers into assimilation in the United States.

CHAPTER 3

UTOPIANISM AND SOCIALISM

As the eighteenth century ended, Europe was in crisis. Old regimes were tottering because their economic systems were inadequate to industrial society. Huge inequities in income had created widespread misery. Political agitation flamed into riot as protestors demanded food, rights, autonomy, or secession in the United States, Ireland, Holland, Belgium, France, and Switzerland. Since France dominated Europe and political thought, its groundbreaking revolution profoundly affected the whole continent. By killing their king, the French had flouted all claims of elite divinity. For a time Napoleon's wars occupied Europe, but after his defeat in 1815 waves of French-inspired revolution swept Europe.

The first wave of revolution (1820–24) was centered in the Mediterranean region.[1] The second (1829–34) convulsed all of Europe west of Russia. In 1830 France overthrew its Bourbon kings, and Belgium won independence from Holland. Most other uprisings were put down, but Irish Catholic emancipation (1829) encouraged further agitation against Britain.[2] In 1847–48, a third wave of almost simultaneous revolutions occurred in France, Italy, the German states, most of the Habsburg Empire, and Switzerland.[3]

Revolution was a reaction to the bankruptcy of a traditional morality that considered some humans superior to others, granting great privilege to a divinely appointed elite and relegating most people to rightless misery. New ideas of human rights and equality opened minds to the possibility of creating political structures that would divide power differently and grant a political voice to a larger proportion of the population. Then as now, conflicts focused on how much participation to allow what people. Conservatives advocated constitutional government and an extension of the suffrage to more men (but not to the masses). Radicals advocated a government responsive to the people and universal manhood suffrage—extending the vote to all adult males. If this was radicalism, heaven knows what they would have called any movement that argued for women's suffrage. No problem: no one did. Yet some well-intentioned people did want to ease women's oppression. Their attempts are the subject of this section.

Building "A Heaven in Hell's Despair"

The philosophy called "socialism" (the word first appeared in 1831 in France) emerged in the early decades of the nineteenth century, and was based in a humanist vision of universal emancipation in an ideal communal society with no inequality, including sexual—a utopia. Utopian thinker Charles Fourier believed: "The degree of emancipation of women is the natural measure of general emancipation." An entire generation of socialist thinkers before Marx (followers of Fourier and Saint-Simon in France, Robert Owen in England, American Fourierites, and Transcendentalists) was committed to female freedom as part of their wider struggle for human liberation.[4]

Yet in the twentieth century many socialists scorned feminism in both its suffragist and second-wave manifestations, as a middle-class movement—as if sex struggle for freedom and status were less revolutionary than class struggle. Feminism is often portrayed as a movement of privileged women ambitious for male prerogatives, rather than as a philosophy that challenges prerogative itself, the very basis of patriarchal moral, economic, and political systems. Both socialists and capitalists reject feminism because it advocates the abolition of male privilege and structural changes more radical than either care to contemplate.

To portray feminism solely as a movement of leisured middle-class "ladies," men had to write early socialist feminism out of history—and this is exactly what they did. Histories that even mention women's rights usually begin with the "Rights of Women" debate of the 1790s and then leap to the Victorian period. Capitalist texts dismiss utopianism by associating it with socialism; Marxists scorn utopianism for not being based in "scientific" thinking.

Most utopias hold socialist ideals of cooperation and sharing, but utopianism is a separate trend with a long tradition in philosophical literature. Francis Bacon, Rabelais, Thomas More, and Daniel Defoe created fictional utopias before the nineteenth century; William Morris, Edward Bellamy, Charlotte Perkins Gilman, and Freda Hossain during it. Utopian works all stress equality, but they define the concept in different ways. All utopias are concerned with social justice, harmony, and individual and sexual freedom, but not all are feminist. William Morris, for example, envisioned a society of justice, equality, harmony, and sexual freedom for men, as if women did not require such things; Gilman and Hossain, on the other hand, were unable to envision a utopian world with men present in it.

Utopian socialists wanted to abolish class divisions, money, the state, and the separation between public and private. When feudalism died, the sense of kinship weakened for both sexes. Eighteenth-century ideas of freedom and rights infused political discourse, opening the possibility of new collectivities and classes; industry transformed conditions so that women's liberation became thinkable, and

nineteenth-century utopian thinkers began to see the power differential between men and women (sexual politics) as fundamental to other inequities. The early industrial age was turbulent because industry revolutionized both the nature of work and relations between the elite and the workers; and it changed relations between women and men, women and work, and women and the family. Both capitalism and industrialism are patriarchal, but they are also (unlike feudalism) dynamic and offer the means for destabilizing patriarchy. They made collective action possible.

Nineteenth-century utopian socialists tried to devise social and economic structures to resist the separations imposed by capitalist industry. Envisaging workers as wholes—both ends *and* means—as people who could create wealth for themselves and not just be instruments for creating wealth for others, they wanted to integrate production and reproduction. They saw that women needed economic security *while* they were reproducing and maintaining society, recognizing the hardship women suffered when they were neither paid nor supported in their "natural" (as many still saw it) work. But women were not their primary concern and they did not examine their preconceptions; they did not ask if it was just to require one sex alone to be responsible for reproducing and maintaining all of society. Only a few, mainly women, used utopian ideas as the basis of feminist theories. All nineteenth-century utopian thinkers derived their ideas from Enlightenment thought in France, Scotland, and England.

France

The only important *philosophe* who unswervingly supported women's rights, the Marquis de Condorcet (1743–1794) argued that to deprive women of political rights on the pretext that their pregnancies and indispositions (menstruation) made them unfit was as absurd as to deprive man of the vote because of his attacks of gout. During the Revolution, women had given the King a list of their grievances *as a sex*, asking for equal rights in civil and political status, education, and work. Excluded from men's political clubs, women formed their own: chocolatière Pauline Léon and actress Claire Lacombe founded the Revolutionary Republican Women Citizens Club; Théroigne de Méricourt marched for women's right to bear arms and founded the Club des Amis de la Loi between 1789 and 1792. Olympe de Gouges' "Déclaration des Droits de la Femme et de la Citoyenne" urged women to create their own National Assembly as men's political and social equals and repudiate the privileges granted the "weaker" sex. Among her demands were an end to illegitimacy and more flexibility in marriage.

Frenchwomen's solidarity and awareness that their problems were tied to their sex were almost immediately suppressed: the Jacobins banned their clubs and barred them from public or political activity in 1793. In a final blow, Napoleon's retrogressive Civil Code of 1804 reaffirmed patriarchal values, private property, the absolute authority of men over wives and children, and the double standard. Depriving women of any legal or property rights, it placed them in legal subjection. Not until Napoleon fell did reformers again begin to address social problems.

Claude Henri, comte de Saint-Simon (1760–1825), a believer in Christianity and industry (he coined the word "industrialism"), believed that capital and technical "progress" could remake society. He and his disciples wanted to create a new elite of engineers and scientists who would use the laws of industry to end exploitation of the poor and the subjection of women. Saint-Simonians held the sexes complementary, accepted women in public roles, and valued sentiment over reason. When Saint-Simon died, his disciples built a school (later called a society), run by Barthélemy Prosper Enfantin, a banker with advanced engineering training.

Between 1829 and 1831, 200 women came to Saint-Simonian lectures on religion, finance, and social subjects. Some became missionaries in or near Paris; a hundred worked in Lyon. Most were kin or close friends of male members. One married couple donated their entire fortune to the community. But women did not throng to the sect, as they did to other religions that promised them equality, because the gap between rhetoric and practice was too obvious. With twelve women and sixty-seven men, the ruling clique was male-dominated; in Paris, no woman was ever allowed to act as a priest or preach the doctrine in public. Men had special uniforms to mark their solidarity, the sexes sang different songs, and the calendar commemorated important events related only to men.

Still, Saint-Simon's ideas deeply affected many women, who, for the first time, sought alternative lifestyles. Most Saint-Simonian women were urban working class: a group calling itself "femmes prolétaires" in 1832 founded the first feminist newspaper, *La femme libre* (*The Free Woman*), and published forty issues before running out of money.[5] Suzanne Voilquin (1801–1877), a laundress and embroiderer who co-edited the paper, complained: "At bottom, the male Saint-Simonians are more male than they are Saint-Simonian." Calling women an oppressed caste, the newspaper urged them to unify across class lines, arguing that "the emancipation of woman [would bring] the emancipation of the worker." The paper concentrated on women's rights in marriage and divorce, education, training, and shelter for poor, homeless or unmarried pregnant women and widows. When the Saint-Simonian church collapsed in 1834, some members remained feminist socialists, and resurfaced in 1848. Their sophisticated analysis of class and gender oppression foreshadowed the feminism of the 1848 revolution.

Of all early Utopian thinkers, Charles Fourier (1772–1837) placed the greatest emphasis on women's liberation. His complex theory traced human evolution through historical stages distinguished by the dominant mode of conjugal relations. In 1808 he traced the "progressive liberation" of women in marriage as "the fundamental cause of all social progress." "Social progress and changes from one era to the next are brought about by . . . the progress of women towards liberty, and social retrogression occurs as a result of a diminution in the liberty of women."[6] He considered women equal and similar to men, and the catalysts of change.

Their emancipation was indispensable to universal freedom.

Humans would progress by stages to Harmony, the ultimate goal, living in communities called *phalansteries*. Hating the family, Fourier envisioned couples united by love as long as it lasted. He proposed communal domestic work: communal kitchens, daycare centers, and sewing workshops. But he did not imagine men working in them. Like William Morris in his utopian novel, *News from Nowhere*, he conveniently believed that women enjoyed and wanted to cook, clean, raise children, and serve men. Fourier theorized radical reorganization ending the wage system and sexual inequality. Fourierist communities in France foundered when they were charged with moral turpitude for their unusual sexual practices.

Louis Blanc (1811–1882), a politician and journalist horrified by industrial society's competitiveness and exploitation of workers, campaigned for manhood suffrage. He thought the vote would enable working men to control the state, and fund "Associations of Production," a network of self-governing workshops guaranteeing everyone jobs and security. (Such workshops were established in Paris during the 1848 Revolution.) Before Karl Marx, Blanc predicted private enterprise would wither away with the state. Pierre Proudhon (1809–1865), an anarchist (advocate of self-government), wanted fair wages and prices based on the amount of labor needed to make goods, not whatever the market could bear.

Flora Tristan (1803–1844), influenced by many socialist-utopian thinkers, joined no group or party. The daughter of a rich Peruvian, she worked in a lithographic workshop and was forced to marry her boss, who beat her. When she left him, she lost her property and custody of her three children, regaining them only after he tried to kill her. Her famous assertion that all women were pariahs emerged from these experiences. Envisioning economic development liberating women morally, emotionally, and economically, she devoted herself after 1835 to feminist-socialist activities and writing *Nécessité de faire bon accueil aux femmes étrangères* (1835), *Pérégrinations d'un pariah* (1838), *Promenades dans Londres* (1839), and *L'Union ouvrière* (1843).[7]

Recognizing that a new class had emerged from a particular historical moment, a political/economic/social situation, Tristan urged workers to free themselves five years before Marx produced the *Communist Manifesto*. Workers, pariahs of the earth, had to liberate themselves as a class, but women, "the proletarian of the proletarian," suffered special problems as mothers, workers, and prostitutes. For Tristan as for Fourier, women's emancipation underlay that of workers. She urged workers to use collective action and form inclusive unions or committees.

Tristan's ideas for workers' unions and the "right to work" grew popular in 1840s France. She urged yearly dues of two francs a person to pay missionaries to convert more workers and a workers' representative to the National Assembly, and most important, to build workers' "palaces," homes for 2000–3000 children and old people, with farms and workshops. Children would be educated identically to develop intelligence, love of humanity, and skill with crafts. For Tristan socialism and feminism were one entity. She championed female education, marriage reform with the right to divorce, and women's right to do any work whatever. But seeing women mainly as mothers, she could not imagine them liberating themselves: men had to emancipate women. Harassed by police and misunderstood by workers, she decided in 1844 to tour France and preach her gospel of cooperation and brotherhood directly to workers. While touring, she came to see herself not as a pariah but as a *femme guide* whose mission was to save the world. Exhaustion made her vulnerable to typhoid, and she died in Bordeaux in 1844.

England and Scotland

Edmund Burke supported the American Revolution but vilified the French in *Reflections on the Revolution in France* (1790). The French Revolution inspired Englishmen like scientist Joseph Priestley, minister Richard Price, and James Watt, inventor of the steam engine, to urge the overthrow of privilege and absolutism in England. Thomas Paine urged democracy in *The Rights of Man* (1791–92).

England's old tradition of Christian communitarianism had produced visions of harmonious egalitarian societies like Thomas More's *Utopia* (1516). The pre-nineteenth-century utopians concerned with women's status (seventeenth-century Diggers and eighteenth-century Shakers) had built communities based on sharing, cooperation, and equality and aimed at earthly felicity and spiritual regeneration. Socialist utopians believed that humans could achieve harmony by communal ownership and character transformation. Determined to end sex and class oppression, they focused on women's rights, believing, like the French utopians, that societal regeneration required female liberation.

The eighteenth-century *querelle des femmes* between haters and defenders of women did not produce a distinct consistent feminist political position. The first coherent feminist theoretical statement, Mary Wollstonecraft's *The Vindication of the Rights of Woman*, introduced the idea of "gender," manufactured sex roles. Wollstonecraft argued that womanhood was artificially created to serve male desire: society molded girls into personal slaves for men. Men praised as "sensibility" a compound of slavish traits—servility, cunning, and "infantile imbecility." The social order consigns women to a stultifying, crippling way of life, she wrote, but "virtue can only flourish among equals." Wollstonecraft too believed that human political and social liberation depended on female emancipation, and her regenerative vision inspired both *Enquiry into Political Justice* (1793) by her future husband, philosopher William Godwin, and "Spensonia," a plan for an agrarian communist utopia by Thomas Spence, a working-class pamphleteer.

Godwin, determined to find ways to achieve and maintain both equality and individual liberty, concluded that the two could co-exist only if private property (which bred inequality) and government (which constrained individual freedom even when benevolent) were eliminated and replaced by a global system of small communities, economically maintained by small self-managed farms and workshops governed democratically by local councils. Both Spence and

Godwin advocated marriage reform: in Spensonia, women, married or single, would participate in a communal land economy on the same basis as men and have the same political rights, except that married women's domestic responsibilities kept them from sitting on government councils. Divorce was permitted and women's marital status was equal to their husbands' (if equality is possible when one sex alone is responsible for reproduction and maintenance, and the other for governance). Female suffrage, Wollstonecraft's ideas on female education, Godwin's and Spence's antimarriage arguments, and the poet Shelley's eloquent depiction of a new era of sex equality aroused much discussion in British radical newspapers of the 1790s.

But events in France—the 1792 Terror, the 1793 overthrow and execution of Louis XVI, and the proclamation of a Republic—terrified the British ruling class and appalled the middle class. While preparing for war with France, the government feared British workers across the country who supported it. It suspended the law of habeas corpus, suppressed worker protest, banned radical societies, and arrested their leaders. Landlords, industrialists, magistrates, and churchmen hired vigilante squads to hit suspected reformers. After a "Church and King" mob burned down his house in 1793, a man wrote to a friend: "I cannot give you an idea of the violence with which every friend of liberty is persecuted in this country." The upper class became even more conservative, condemning any questioning of sex roles as revolutionary and reviling Wollstonecraft's *Vindication* (which had earlier been well received) for advocating promiscuity. Wollstonecraft became infamous: Horace Walpole called her a "hyena in petticoats." Feminism was vilified by respectable people: in 1798 a liberal women's journal declared itself "relieved to report" that the champions of female equality, who were as inimical to the happiness and interest of the sex as those who preached the doctrine of liberty and equality to men, were no longer regarded as sincere and politic friends.

By making feminism taboo and identifying women's rights with sexual libertarianism, free thought, and social revolution, conservatives forced feminists to become radical. (When there is no possibility of society absorbing a new doctrine, adherents focus on changing society.) Society hysterically feared that sexual equality would subvert all social institutions—church, marriage, and family. Feminists, responding to the hysteria, began to equate their goals with radical workers' "leveling" goals, linking sex-struggle with class-struggle. This connection and Wollstonecraft's ideas underlay the Owenite movement a quarter-century later.

Robert Owen (1771–1858), a Welsh visionary influenced by Godwin and Jeremy Bentham, believed character was molded, not innate. He married a woman whose father owned a large cotton mill in New Lanark, Scotland, took over the mill, and tried to create a model environment, improving working conditions, building model houses and schools (free to his workers), and establishing social security. He was still a capitalist, if a benevolent one, when in 1820 he attacked capitalist enterprise and proposed creating communities without private property or salaried work, where people shared, living separately but raising children communally. Finding no support for his plan in England, he emigrated to the United States in 1825 with his son, Robert Dale Owen, and built New Harmony, Indiana. But in 1829 he went back to England to found the National Consolidated Trades Union. After it failed, he left the labor movement and became a spiritualist.

But Owen's ideas had extraordinary influence. His text on marriage, *Lectures on the Marriages of the Priesthood in the Old Immoral World*, damned the family, and advocated civil marriage and easy cheap divorce, which liberal Nonconformists also demanded in that period. Like many men, Owen was a feminist in his head, not heart, admiring Wollstonecraft, seeing the justice of women's protest, but still accustomed to female servitude. His major social statements, like *The Book of the New Moral World*, are visions of an egalitarian future. He tried to ease women's lot by having women share "their" work in community kitchens, cooperative nurseries and daycare, but that both parents should do caretaking and raise children never dawned on him. He was authoritarian, at best paternalist, which may be why his experiments in communal living failed. Obsessed with marriage, he blamed it for almost every social ill—prostitution, adultery, syphilitic degeneration of the species, and the destruction of pleasure and sensuality.

But the movement called Owenism derived less from Owen's ideas or activities than from a generation of conscious, organized radicals. Owenism was not a hierarchical movement dominated by one person, but rather, like today's feminism, a swell of autonomous individuals united by their beliefs. Most Owenites were upper working class, many lower middle class, a few wealthy. At first it attracted radical intellectuals, but in the 1830s and 1840s its appeal widened. From 1840 until its demise, hostile commentators wrote contemptuously of "crowds of women" regularly attending Owenite events around the country: hundreds heard Owenite lectures on women's rights, scores wrote to Owenite newspapers on women's issues, usually under pen names. Women, who rarely spoke in public and never for themselves, were speaking on their own behalf. The Owenites, unique among social movements because they wanted to abolish all relations of power and subordination, including sexual inequality, decided to form exemplary societies which would show the world that, as an Owenite woman wrote, "men and women may meet in equal communion, having equal rights and returns for industry . . . and equal attention given to the cultivation of their whole nature, physical, moral, and intellectual."[8]

Many Owenite feminists had middle-class backgrounds. A middle-class woman easily slipped into poverty, even starvation, if she did not marry, if her husband abandoned her, or if her father left her a house but no income. It was nearly impossible for a middle-class woman of the period to support herself. Those with education became socialists and wrote for working-class journals, trying to make a living as journalists, writers, or lecturers. But polemics against middle-class female idleness or marriage for property had no meaning to working women, for whom idleness meant starvation.

Feminists urged "industrial emancipation" on women longing to be free of it. Yet feminists were vital to Owenism.

Whatever their background, Barbara Taylor writes, most Owenite women were like George Gissing's "odd women," daring to think and act in defiance of the social conventions that constricted women. Only their passionate discussions of serious issues marked them as deviant, and their repudiation of the deforming dress of nineteenth-century "ladies" made them outré in ladies' company. The first to assert Owenite feminist ideas publicly, Anna Wheeler and Frances Wright, came from rich families with prestigious male connections—which is why their careers were recorded.

Anna Doyle Wheeler (1785–1848), born in Ireland to a progressive family, married at fifteen and bore six children. She read constantly, especially Wollstonecraft and texts on the French Revolution, and finally fled her home for Guernsey, then France, where she met Tristan and Fourier. She was drawn to Saint-Simonian feminists, whose work she translated for the Owenite journal, *The Crisis*. By the 1820s she was a militant Owenite, organizing trade unions, speaking before radical Unitarians in London, and involved with William Thompson (1775–1833), an Irish landlord who had joined Owen's cooperative movement. Thompson felt that women deserved a better life and advocated they be given financial support during pregnancy, communal child care, and the chance to work for wages outside the home. Such changes would lead to female economic independence and a more perfect society.

In 1825 Thompson and Wheeler produced the *Appeal of One Half of the Human Race, Women, Against the Pretensions of the Other Half, Men, to Retain them in Political and thence in Civil and Domestic Slavery: in Reply to a Paragraph in Mr. Mill's Celebrated Article on Government.* Published in Thompson's name, it was partly Wheeler's work, and was written to refute James Mill's thesis that women were sufficiently represented by their male kin and did not need the vote. (His feminist son John shared this conviction.) The *Appeal* was the first socialist analysis of women's condition in

England: it argued that competitive pursuit of personal wealth was incompatible with democracy and sexual equality, condemned the double standard and hypocrisy of marriage, and urged birth control. Previously, only poets had questioned women's exclusive responsibility for social and biological reproduction, Taylor notes. Even Wollstonecraft accepted this "duty," merely urging that women be allowed other activities too. By questioning it, the *Appeal* offered a new morality.

Wheeler lectured at South Place Chapel in London, where radical Unitarians and women's rights advocates like W.J. Fox, Harriet Taylor, and John Stuart Mill met in the 1820s and 1830s. Fox's *The Monthly Repository* often published pieces on women's position; Harriet Taylor wrote *The Enfranchisement of Women* in 1851; her husband, Mill, a liberal philosopher who supported women's emancipation, wrote *The Subjection of Women* in 1867. The Owenite press published radical or liberal feminists like Mary Leman Grimstone, Harriet Martineau, and Anna Jameson. Margaret Chappell Smith and Eliza Macauley lectured on economic theory; Smith, one of the most popular Owenite lecturers in the 1840s, discussed currency reform and the history of English financial institutions. Other Owenite feminists wrote on mathematics, natural science, and the most advanced thinkers of the period, including Wollstonecraft, Godwin, Shelley (feminists' favorite poet), and Owen. Few other nonsocialist radicals publicly supported women's cause in the first half of the nineteenth century.

Emma Martin (1812–1851) succeeded Wheeler as the movement's leading feminist publicist. Born and raised in a Bristol middle-class family, Martin had little education, yet in 1830 she became proprietor of a ladies' boarding school and editor of *The Bristol Literary Magazine*. An ardent Baptist, she attacked Owenites who denied divine inspiration to the Bible. Somehow, while raising a family, running the school, editing the magazine, and working for her church, Martin learned languages (including Hebrew and Italian), basic medicine, physiology, and enough theology to discomfit the clerics she debated later in her career. Miserable in her marriage, she discovered feminism and in 1839 took her children and left her husband (who took all her property) and joined the Socialists. She began to lecture as a freethinking feminist, at first receiving a small salary from the Owenite Center.

Reversing her earlier religious conviction, she promoted socialism as the only cure for sexual inequality, and wrote antireligious tracts. She was close and loving with her daughters, but had trouble supporting them: she had to pay for child care when on lecture tours or take them with her and expose them to the risks of travel and local animosity (she was sometimes stoned in the streets). The fact that she took a lover and had another child did not make things any easier. Class background was irrelevant to women supporting themselves; any woman who gave up middle-class status was treated as "common." Barbara Taylor believes such experiences led Owenite feminists to identify strongly with working-class people and to see women's oppression as a cross-class phenomenon. Martin taught, kept a shop, and did midwifery, but could not earn enough to support her family, and had to ask for help publicly. She died young and penniless.

Utopian Communities

Owen argued that labor was the source of all society's wealth and that workers' poverty was not natural or inevitable but a result of the unjust appropriation of their work. He urged workers to work for themselves by creating communities that collectively owned the means of production and distribution. Owenites had founded four cooperative societies by 1828; by 1830, there were three hundred. By 1832 five hundred cooperative societies flourished, and Owen set up a National Equitable Labor Exchange, a bazaar where workers could trade their products for "labour-notes" representing the amount of work time invested in them. Receiving "a just reward" for their work, they cut profiteering distributors out of the loop. A London activist wrote: "The Labor Exchanges will make all masters, no servants or slaves."

Owenites drew up models for communities where like-minded people, not kin, could live in justice and felicity. In most models large connected residences had private bedrooms for adults and dormitories for children. A major concern was getting rid of *private* housework, the "unproductive and repulsive drudgery" that William Thompson calculated occupied nine-tenths of a woman's time. Thompson planned a mechanical laundry and scientifically arranged kitchens; the London Co-operative Society suggested that all adults rotate housework. Child care and education too were to be done collectively. Robert Cooper, a Manchester socialist, designed a model in which children under eleven did housework (which he must have imagined required no knowledge or skill); those aged twelve to twenty-one were responsible for "production of wealth," those twenty-two to twenty-five for its preservation and distribution. Between the ages of twenty-five and thirty-five, people would teach—in his words, direct the "formation of the character of the rising generation." At thirty-five, people governed, and at forty-five, freed for artistic or intellectual pursuits, they became community advisers. At each level, women and men would perform exactly the same tasks. This plan was never realized.

In 1821 twenty-one artisanal families formed a community at Spa Fields, Islington. Women shared domestic labor, freeing themselves to teach and sew, and they pooled their wages to pay for children's education which, like child care, was collective. In County Clare, Ireland, in 1831, twenty-four farming families formed the Ralahine Association on communally held land. They set up collective housekeeping, and an infant school to care for children during the twelve hours a day the women worked in the fields. But since women's wages on this commune were half of men's (as in the outside world) and women were still responsible for children after school hours, it hardly altered their hard lives.

Owen's community in Hampshire, Queenwood (or Harmony), was also agricultural. Each woman had to perform one domestic task for a month, and the heaviest work was done by hired labor.

Everyone rose at six and worked in the fields. Women not on cooking duty also went to the fields, returned at eight for breakfast and went back to the fields until supper. At night, there was singing, dancing, or classes—a "female" class was held once a week. To lighten women's workload, Owen in 1842 began a controversial, expensive building program including a kitchen with elaborate machines. Despite their goal of easing women's burden, Owenites never questioned why women alone were responsible for all domestic maintenance. Women resisted or left many communities. Men's refusal to take care of themselves and their children was more powerful than any principles they adopted. It was male chauvinism, not theoretical inadequacy, that destroyed egalitarian communities.

Most Owenites disliked traditional religion and its conventions. Offended by the legal nonexistence of married women, the double standard, and men's right to beat their wives, and wanting to end marriage based on money and private property, they tried to invent alternative forms of marriage. Disputing scripture, Martin, Fanny Wright, and others contended that mutual loving egalitarian unions could emerge only from free thought and love. Owenites sifted through anthropological data for alternatives to traditional marriage, writing on women and marriage in such exotic places as Turkey, in works like "Amazon Women of the Lost Islands," and "Primitive Peoples of the Geenkonki Delta." Some reworked scripture into socialist theology or Christian millenarianism (belief in the Second Coming of Christ), their communism permeated by female mystical and moral preeminence, the "Doctrine of the Woman" or "Woman-Power." Accepting nineteenth-century middle-class ideas of female moral superiority to men, they attributed to women the redemptive power to fulfill "Woman's Mission" to reform the world.

In his community, Owen ruled that a couple wanting to marry should announce their intention three months beforehand, then proclaim their bond before the assembled community. They could declare a wish to divorce any time after a year, but had to wait six months before the union was considered ended. Divorced people could remarry. Thompson felt that each person over a certain age should have a private bedroom, even after marriage. Acknowledging that sexual liaisons would occur, he drew the line only at parenthood: the right to sexual liaison did not mean the right to reproduce. To separate the two required what Thompson called "individual prudence" or "individual measures to limit population" (contraception). Owen was accused of importing condoms into New Lanark (with its largely female workforce) and never denied it.

However, neither sexual puritanism nor an ideology of free love with social and economic independence solved women's problem. What they wanted was a mutual relationship with men, a way to provide for their children, use their abilities and avoid enslavement by domestic maintenance. But no utopian scheme expected men to share responsibility for maintenance and support of children; thus, while women might enjoy sexual freedom, as long as they bore the responsibility for children, they needed husbands legally bound to support them. Therefore, most women did not want to see marriage abolished and pressured the Owenites not to urge it; they chose marriage as a civil contract that included the possibility of divorce. Female lecturers dwelt on the pleasures of faithful marriage and the miseries of sexual exploitation.

Owen was devoted to education and encouraged women to participate in group educational activities and classes in subjects like housewifery, while Owenite women wanted classes in subjects that might free them from the household and train them for other work—reading, writing, history, and arithmetic. But few such classes were given: men's resistance affected everything. It was not Owenism but a patriarchal system that created women's double bind: only women were denied a living wage and political rights, only women were held responsible for children, only women were socially outcast for being unmarried. Twenty years after Wheeler left her husband, she wrote: "I am a woman and without a master: two causes of disgrace in England." All "masterless" women were pariahs; Owenite women were shunned even by broad-minded liberals. Freethinking women were *witches, she-devils, whores.*

Some women chose not to marry, but some could not find husbands. In the 1830s the high ratio of women to men (who tended to marry late) left many women single. Middle-class women who would not become unpaid servants to male kin became destitute; working-class women could find jobs but not a living wage. The Owenite women discovered that in the real world it was hard to find a man and impossible to survive without one.[9] An editorial of the period argued: "A woman's wage is not reckoned at an average more than two-thirds of a male, and we believe in reality it seldom amounts to more than one-third (and wives have no wages at all). Yet, is not the produce of female labour as useful? . . . The industrious female is well entitled to the same amount of remuneration as the industrious male."

In 1844 Owen was expelled from the governorship of Queenwood, and Owenism collapsed as a united movement of radical thought. The Owenite movement matters to us now because it tried to integrate work and private life, men and women, capital and labor more commodiously than any other movement before or since. Its defeat was also the defeat of integrated thinking: no wide-scale movement since has had this goal. The Owenite analysis of class exploitation anticipated Marxism and was even wider, addressing oppression in the workplace, marketplace, school, and home. The utopian socialist movement was the first arena of massive struggle waged by a popular feminist movement and adherents of cooperative production. Both were defeated: nineteenth-century feminism was defeated by men's adamant refusal to take responsibility for maintaining themselves and their children; cooperative production was defeated by capitalism. But utopian socialist thinking helped shape the future and lived on in later feminism and the modern cooperative movement.

Other Political Struggles

Owenism was one strand in the social protest that disquieted England in the first half of the nineteenth century. During the Napoleonic war that began the century and the depression that followed it, rising prices and falling wages sent thousands of working-class men and women onto the streets in food riots, strikes, and protests. The government suppressed them, hiring spies to unearth evidence against them. The hardest-hit area (then as now) was the industrial north where "radicals" agitated for wider franchise. Workers called Luddites (for Ned Ludd, who supposedly led a demonstration in Nottingham with his wife and co-leader "Lady Ludd") smashed machines or attacked workers who refused to join unions. It took repeated clashes between demonstrators and the army or police—shopkeepers who withheld taxes and formed their own national guard, a cholera epidemic, the king (William IV) hearing rumors of "miners, manufacturers, colliers, and labourers" about to rebel—for the government to pass a Reform Bill (1832) extending franchise to men who paid £10 or more yearly in rent on land held on sixty-year leases: a mere 3 percent of the population.

Corn Laws and Poor Laws also aroused general ire. Corn Laws protected English landowners by placing duty on cheap imported grain so as to keep the price of bread high. This hurt the poor, who pressured manufacturers for wages high enough to buy bread, in turn irritating manufacturers. Poor Laws granted paupers help only in their natal parishes. People who moved regularly seeking work were stranded by this rule, but the number of paupers strained local resources. The Poor Law passed in 1832 reflected the self-righteous morality of a tight-mouthed middle class (vividly portrayed in George Crabbe's *The Borough*). Blindly sure that poverty was a moral flaw rooted in poor character, that jobs were available to anyone willing to work, the government ended the dole and ordered the indigent to be confined in workhouses under conditions so grim they would want to get out. But an early 1840s depression forced the government to re-institute the dole. In 1846 *manufacturers'* pressure led parliament to repeal the Corn Laws.

Female and male workers formed Friendly Societies offering mutual aid insurance, and set up cooperative stores. There were about five hundred such societies with over 20,000 members by 1831. After the 1832 Reform Act, women organized politically to fight oppression by the police, the church, and the privileged. Appealing to "natural rights" and the Bible, in 1837 they demonstrated against the Poor Law. Workers organized trade unions: textile workers and miners formed the National Association for the Protection of Labour; 30,000 joined the Operative Builders Union. The Women's Stocking Makers of Leicester joined Robert Owen's Grand National Consolidated Trades Union of Great Britain and Ireland in calling for a general strike in 1834. This led the government to decide to stamp out unions, prosecute Grand National leaders, and transport them to Australia. Thousands of women marched demanding bread in a general strike in Lancaster in 1843. Employers required workers to sign pledges that they would not join unions.

After 1835 socialists, despairing that the union movement would create a foundation for a workers' commonwealth, turned their energies to transforming traditional thinking. Economic cooperation had failed, but universal enlightenment and cultural reconstruction might succeed. Believing the only way to end the treatment of women as property was to end private property itself, Owenites decided that building a New Moral World required not just abolition of private capital but moral and psychological education to transform human competitiveness. Correct "Character Formation" was essential to social re-creation; therefore all institutions responsible for Incorrect Character Formation—authoritarian education, orthodox religion, patriarchal marriage, and familism—must be destroyed or altered. Socialists could not change institutions but could challenge the hold of one, religion, on common people. Declaring socialism the "Rational Religion" that would supersede orthodox Christianity, they decried scripture. The clergy retaliated. Violent debate between Christians and social scientists exploded in working-class meeting halls. In their offensive against socialist "immoralism," the clergy stressed women's sexual behavior, provoking a new breed of propagandist—Owenite feminists struggling to free their minds from patriarchal Christianity. They lectured and wrote, and the work of a few voluble women swept England, Scotland, and Wales between 1838 and 1845, making everyone aware of the Woman Question.

Some Owenites joined a growing male labor reform movement called Chartism, which flourished from 1838 to 1848. Members wrote a "People's Charter" and circulated it across the country; millions signed it. This "Charter" demanded electoral reforms that had been proposed before 1832: universal male suffrage, secret ballots, annual parliamentary elections, the abolition of property qualifications for members of the House of Commons, salaried House members, and equal electoral districts. Chartism was looser and larger than socialism, with a huge militant female membership. It incorporated a wider range of attitudes. During its peak years, tens of thousands of women campaigned for the Six Points, led mass demonstrations, organized campaigns, prayed in Chartist churches, taught in Chartist Sunday schools, and sometimes attacked the military and the police. Chartism was a working-class movement; it rose from the ashes of defeat of socialist women, and its women were militant, but not feminist. William Lovett, a Chartist leader, idealized the home as a private retreat, extolling homemakers (and his own wife) as "Angels in the House," indicating that middle-class women's constriction within domesticity was filtering down to the working class.

A backlash against all this agitation (perhaps orchestrated) insisted on even greater confinement of women. Women who helped support their families felt the growing disapproval. New ideas of female respectability made it even harder for women to act politically than earlier, when political women like Emma Martin were publicly slandered. Women were now barred from pubs, where many political meetings were held, and a burgeoning moral reform movement held alcohol to be anathema to respectable womanhood. Near mid-century, Victorian sentimentalization of the home and the patriarchal family pervaded all classes; even tough working women shrank into "home-centredness and inferiority." Soon, the idea of separate spheres came to be seen as Natural and Right. The domestic, dependent, private female sphere was rigidly segregated from male work, politics, and public life.

Some socialist organizations endured. But the socialist utopian movement, united by one goal—a New Moral World—from 1820 to 1845, splintered into trade unionism, social science, practical cooperation, spiritualism, free thought (called Secularism after 1850) and feminism, with a small left wing. By the 1860s the Trade Union Congress stated that it intended to work for an economic structure in which wives could remain at home, their proper sphere. The British labor movement has strongly opposed women's employment ever since. Socialism, too, buried feminism, labeling it bourgeois and personal. But in Britain and France—and later Russia—the first socialism was feminist and feminism was socialist.

Early feminism, humanistic and revolutionary, challenged all hierarchies at all levels. Its radical ideas and experiments with socialist communities horrified the articulate middle class, which quivered at feminists' desire to transform society utterly, to turn the world "upside down." Public reaction radicalized upper- and middle-class women, for whom feminism was a simple plea for justice. Moderate feminists arguing for extension of the vote to upper-class women had to spend considerable energy proving their loyalty to capitalism and elite privilege. The demise of Owenism eased their problem: once it was forgotten, middle-class women could agitate for feminist reform without being seen as socialist, sexually immoral, or subversive. By 1860 "women's rights" had enough moderate adherents to be respectable. Working-class radical feminism was forgotten entirely—by everyone.

The United States

Egalitarian enlightenment ideas did not take root in working-class nineteenth-century Americans: after a revolution in the name of equality, the state declared it achieved. Since the New Moral World already existed, there was no need to build one. The American ruling class still uses a rhetoric of achieved revolution, ignoring the nation's vast inequities, privilege, poverty, and conspicuous injustice. Because the United States lacked a tradition of utopian socialism, when feminism emerged, it lacked a socialist or utopian agenda. The women's rights movement grew instead from moral reform societies, temperance, and abolitionist movements.

But industrialization transformed American social and economic life too. People hoping for a higher standard of living went to work in industry: disrupted by urbanization, weakened kinship and community bonds, and alienated from their work, they sought comfort in religious movements like evangelical renewals. The Second Great Awakening began in the south in the late eighteenth century, moving east between 1810 and 1825. Intensely emotional thousands professed themselves reborn. Throwing off the burden of Calvinist predestination and obsession with sin, they tingled with optimism and godliness—a huge number of women among them.

Many formed alternative communities and millenarianist sects—from the Revolution to the Civil War nearly a hundred fledgling utopias sprang up across the country, like Economy, Pennsylvania; Fruitlands and Hopedale, Massachusetts; Pleasant Hill, Kentucky; and Nauvoo, Illinois. Religious communities prepared for the Second Coming or a Golden Age—Shakers in Massachusetts and New York, Amana in Iowa, Oneida in New York. Owen's and Fourier's ideas crossed the Atlantic, inspiring secular communities intended to be new societies—Owen's New Harmony, Indiana (1824), North American Phalanx, New Jersey (1843), and Brook Farm, Massachusetts (1841). Fourierist communities tried to alter conceptions of private property and sexual politics, but like their European counterparts, suffered from disparity between theory and practice, rhetoric and action. None realized sexual equality or economic justice.

Some communities tried to free women from the burden of childbearing by requiring celibacy. Rappites, Zoarites, and Shakers saw that conventional marriage kept women from sexual equality, and either wanted to free them from the pain and danger of childbirth, or believed that chastity made people spiritually pure. Women converted to such religions more than men. Celibate societies expected to increase their numbers by conversions and adoptions, not births. The Shakers were founded by Ann Lee, an illiterate young woman from Manchester. Hounded by the Church of England, she and eight followers came to the United States in 1774, settled in New Lebanon, New York, and built the first Shaker (named for a convulsive dance used in their ritual) church in 1787. Lee believed she was the Christ: the Shaker Manifesto reads: "Do we believe in Jesus, the Son of God? Most certainly, and we also believe in Ann, the Daughter of God." Unique among religions with goddesses, the United Society of Believers saw women as equal to men.

As more people joined, Shakers moved across the country, building villages organized by rules governing all areas of life. Each community had its own government and resources. New members had to abandon their biological families and renounce bonds of flesh and kinship in celibate abstinence devoted to "Our Father in Heaven and Mother Ann." Many converts had yearned for relief from bad marriages or financial problems; women especially longed to avoid marriage in a world of legal male dominance and no birth control. Lee passed strict rules of sexual segregation: members lived in segregated buildings or at opposite ends of buildings, shared rooms with those of their own sex, and entered common areas like dining rooms by different doors. Sisters and brothers could not shake hands, pass one another on staircases, or hang their garments together. Married couples were separated.

The sexes worked apart, men in the fields or at carpentry, women at domestic tasks—cleaning, cooking, laundry, and bread-baking on a rota system.[10] Shaker women were equal to men but the traditional division of labor remained. Sisters had to mend the brothers' clothes and clean their rooms when they were absent. The only concession to female "fragility" was that brothers had to help sisters with heavy tasks and do the milking in bad weather.

Stereotypic ideas pervaded the Shaker religion too: although their deity was bisexual, Shakers identified maleness with intellect and femaleness with emotion. But the Shakers seem to have *practiced* the sexual equality and the appointment of women to posts of authority asserted in their Manifesto; witnesses noted two Elders and Eldresses, three Deacons and Deaconesses overseeing an equal number of women and men at meetings. Shakers still endure.

In 1826 Robert Owen and his son established the most famous U.S. utopian socialist community at New Harmony, Indiana. It allowed a variety of living arrangements: one or two families lived in a small two story house, each family with its own chamber and alcove. Toddlers lived in a communal nursery, older children in a school. Single residents lived in communes, visitors in boardinghouses. Common spaces—dining rooms, kitchens, laundries, halls for dancing, music, and meetings—were open to all. Privacy and community existed at work, play, and household tasks.

For Owen, the main culprit in societal disease—private property—was marriage, which turned love into a power relation and fostered social ills by barring divorce. He wanted to eradicate or weaken the family, he announced in *The New Harmony Gazette*, to change "from the individual to the social system: from single families with separate interests to communities of many families with one interest."[11] Education was necessary for this, and he urged that year-old babies go to school. Parents balked and sent them at two: there were three to four hundred pupils in 1826. Geologist-pedagogue William Maclure believed the sexes had equal capacities and that female political power would improve society: education might even enable women someday to vote!

But New Harmony's leaders accepted inherent sexual differences that fostered traditional power relations. Girls and boys both learned mathematics and natural history (among other subjects) but different manual tasks—boys made shoes, did weaving and carpentry; girls washed clothes, cooked, and served. Everyone in New Harmony had to work; in theory, all were equal. But passbooks for use at a communal store were issued only to husbands. Women worked harder than men—for the community and for their own families. Since family work was not *real* work, it had to be done on weekends, when men could play sports or study. Women quarreled about class: middle-class women objected to doing the same work or eating at the same table as lower-class women. Resentment led to defection, and turnover was swift; the community never cohered. The final blow was the failure of the textile mill, its economic mainstay, after Owen let the community manage it. New Harmony lasted only two years, from 1825 to 1827. Its economic failure was rooted in the moral failure of people who could not give up sex and class superiority.

When Owen returned to England in 1829, his son, Robert Dale Owen, remained and edited *The New Harmony Gazette*. In 1830 he wrote the first birth-control tract printed in the United States, *Moral Physiology*. Insisting that women had the right to decide on birth control, he urged smaller, better-educated families. He represented Indiana in Congress in the 1840s and worked in the antislavery and spiritualist movements, but he is mainly remembered for his radical causes and his collaboration with Fanny Wright.

Frances (Fanny) Wright (1795–1852) was born to a prosperous family—her Scots father manufactured linen—but she had to educate herself. Fortunately, she had access to libraries and read Byron (and cut her hair like his), Epicurus, Wollstonecraft, Bentham, Hume, and other Enlightenment thinkers. She became an audacious antichurch intellectual, writing essays on Epicurean philosophy and three-act plays on political themes before she was twenty-one. Yet she doubted herself; impatient of convention, she was also extremely beautiful and anxious about her strangeness in a period that believed "young ladies ought only to have such a general tincture of knowledge as to make them agreeable companions to men of sense." By her mid-twenties, she had published several books and was known as a literary lady. In 1818 she visited the United States and recorded her impressions. Her strong democratic views pleased Americans but were virulently attacked in England. Deeply attached to General Lafayette, the aging hero of the American and French Revolutions, she proposed to him. He affectionately declined, but returned to the United States with her in 1824. She visited New Harmony and was immediately converted.

The next year Wright bought a plantation in Nashoba, Tennessee, spending most of her fortune to build a cooperative community. A staunch abolitionist, she bought black slaves and set them to work to earn back their purchase price while being educated for freedom. Her antichurch feminist principles led her to ban marriage in her community. This outraged the neighbors, who said that Nashoba men, far from honoring the "free and voluntary affection" Wright urged, intimidated or forced women into sex; but Gerda Lerner's interpretation is that it was the liaisons between people of different races that shocked even abolitionists.[12] Whether what occurred was rape or simply interracial sex, the resulting scandal demoralized the Nashobans. Wright was already notorious among her Tennessee neighbors for her positions on religion and feminism and her customary appearance: she cut her hair short and wore a loose tunic over bloomers—the dress originally designed for New Harmony women. In 1828 Nashoba disintegrated: exhausted, Wright went to New Harmony to recuperate and met Robert Dale Owen.

The two moved to New York City, edited *The Free Enquirer*, and organized political groups (nicknamed "Fanny Wright Societies") to lobby state legislatures for universal free education. They founded the first labor party in the United States, the New York Workingmen's Party, which won a major victory in the 1829 election. Wright, who had become famous for a speech at an Indiana Fourth-of-July celebration in 1828, was the first woman in the United States to make lecturing a career. She urged free education in boarding schools for all children over the age of two, to inculcate egalitarianism—she did not mention the liberation it would offer women. Wherever she appeared, midwest or east, her ideas and appearance stimulated controversy. She crusaded for universal education, communitarian economic enterprises, and above all, rights for women, which included birth control, reform of the divorce laws, protection of women's property rights, and sexual mutuality—which was popularized as "free love."

Yet Wright, like most others who opposed conventional monogamous marriage, believed in monogamy and herself married in a traditional ceremony, only omitting vows of obedience. For arguing that sexual intercourse should involve the "unconstrained . . . unrestrained choice of both parties," Wright was attacked as a "decadent and immoral" promoter of "lewd and promiscuous behavior."[13] The popular press labeled her "the Whore of Babylon." The argument that women should have rights over their own bodies and should be able to make love when (and only when) they choose is interpreted by many men to mean they are sexually indiscriminate.

In 1830, feeling damaged by her notoriety, Wright gave up lecturing. The next year, pregnant, she married her lover, Owenite Phiquepal d'Arusmont, and moved to Paris to try conventional family life. In 1844 she divorced her husband and returned to the United States to resume writing and lecturing. He (Owenite only in name) took her inheritance and custody of their daughter, Sylvia, who became entirely estranged from her mother. Fanny Wright ended up a victim of the very abuses she had long attacked. The most famous of contemporary feminist radicals in the United States, she lived vividly ahead of her time, and her writing was nearly as popular as Owen's.

Also in a perfecting spirit, Unitarian minister George Ripley in 1841 founded Brook Farm in West Roxbury, Massachusetts. New England farmers, artisans, and intellectuals were attracted to the cooperative farm, inspired by Ralph Waldo Emerson's transcendentalism to believe they could rise above materialism and find felicity in a communal life providing work, play, and spiritual nourishment. Brook Farm had a hundred members at most, but its writers or teachers (like Nathaniel Hawthorne) and its famous quarterly, *The Dial*, attracted students from outside the community to its school. In 1845 the community organized Fourierist phalanxes, strictly regimented work-living units. As regimentation kills spirit, however, members left. After an 1846 fire, it died.

Massachusetts-born Margaret Fuller (1810–1850) visited Brook Farm with enthusiasm but did not join (Hawthorne disparagingly portrayed her there, in *The Blithedale Romance*). The Transcendentalist elite—Emerson, Bronson Alcott, Henry Thoreau, Orestes Brownson—had high regard for the erudite Fuller, who in 1840 co-edited *The Dial*. She left Boston in 1844 to become the first woman reporter on Horace Greeley's *New York Daily Tribune* and grew famous as a journalist and critic. In 1846 her job took her to Europe, where she met the most famous writers of the time, including George Sand, the Brownings, and Thomas Carlyle. While in Italy to support Italian independence, she fell in love with and married Italian marquis Giovanni Angelo Ossoli. When the Italian revolution collapsed, Fuller sailed back to the United States with her husband and baby; they all drowned in a shipwreck just offshore.

Fuller passionately believed in sexual equality and argued it persuasively and cogently in *Woman in the Nineteenth Century* (1845). Examining women's inferior social status, she attacked the morality of laws that prevented wives from owning property or inheriting from their husbands. With brilliant originality she demonstrated that women's subordination (which she compares with that of slaves) was rooted in men's universal scorn. Laws institutionalized men's unfounded superiority over women by defining marriage as ownership of women rather than as a mutual relationship. Fuller enriched her arguments by allusions to myth, history, contemporary events, and figures like Sand, Germaine Necker (Mme de Staël), salonist Pauline Roland, Wollstonecraft, and abolitionist Angelina Grimké, and she boldly analyzed the attitudes to women of "great" men like Swedenborg and Fourier.

But like her contemporaries—indeed, like many women today—Fuller was impeded by an essentialist view of the sexes. In a world devoted to power, the belief that women are *by nature* more humane and compassionate, less aggressive and acquisitive than men, justifies the status quo and its division of power. Essentialists, ascribing moral superiority to women, can only plead for equality on mystical or religious grounds (as Fuller did), which move the world of *Realpolitik* not at all. Fuller was a major figure ahead of her time and is important today, but she had little influence on the thought of her period.

Socialism and Revolution

The utopian socialist communal experiments were creative responses to the oppressiveness of the power differential between classes and sexes. All failed but, like the communal experiments of the 1960s, they were different enough from each other that it is hard to generalize about the causes of their failure beyond their members' inability to go beyond sex or class superiority. But the ideas behind the experiments inspired other movements. Class-conscious workers, acutely aware that they were exploited by the rich and the governments behind the rich, blamed *them*, not Nature or God, for the misery and destitution blighting every city.

The poor, writes Eric Hobsbawm, "found themselves in the path of bourgeois society" without traditional protections. They had three choices: they could strive to become middle class too, let themselves be ground down, or rebel; but becoming bourgeois was profoundly distasteful to workers, who despised the individualistic ethic of every man for himself.[14] Intellectuals horrified by industrialization used Enlightenment ideas of human rights and equality to build a new economic morality—socialism. As socialist utopians experimented with alternatives to capitalist industrialization, social philosophers wrote, argued, and formed political groups and trade unions. Meantime, mounting human misery erupted in riots, uprisings, and finally, revolutions.

In the early nineteenth century, absolute monarchs ruled all European states except England (whose middle class had rebelled in the seventeenth century); kingless states like Poland were swallowed up. But kings had become absolute only in name; for centuries they had regularly had to compromise with ambitious nobles and reform economic structures to placate their people. Needing middle class money and support, some members of the nobility encouraged the progressives, intimating that the king might "modernize" society. But this was a lure: all kings were steeped in the values of traditional landed aristocracies and were blind to alternatives. Every rational thinker, even princes' advisers, knew serfdom had to end, but no king ended it: that took revolution.[15]

In 1848 most of Europe was still agricultural. Illiteracy, poor communication, and geographical isolation kept most people ignorant of events not conveyed by their priest or a traveler; few could read the handful of newspapers that existed. Eastern Germany, Russia, and the small Danube states were semifeudal; their peasants were serfs. Prussia had freed its serfs, leaving them with little or no land, forced to work as laborers for landowners who controlled local government and police but paid almost no taxes. As industrialization spread, a new class emerged: the landless disfranchised unskilled workers living in permanent insecurity whom Marx called the *Lumpenproletariat*. They thronged to cities, which swiftly became crowded, squalid, unsanitary, and unsafe.

These people rose up everywhere, sometimes dangerously; some were violently suppressed. Radical thinkers discussed ways of curing society's ills. Friedrich Engels (1820–1895), whose German father was a partner in a Manchester cotton factory, went to England in the 1840s and spent two years working in the mill, observing workers' lives. He wrote vividly of slum life, the dehumanization of workers, and their alienation from their work, in *The Condition of the Working Class in England in 1844*. Noting "class-consciousness," he predicted that the workers' awareness of themselves as a group with common interests opposed to owners' interests would lead in time to revolution.

Engels' ideas impressed Karl Marx (1818–1883) and the two became friends and collaborators. Marx, born to a prosperous German family, studied at the University of Berlin and became editor of the *Rhineland Gazette*. From the start he criticized society and used his editorship to advance change, angering his publishers. Dismissed, he went to Paris, and met Engels in 1844. They decided to try to work out a coherent theory of revolutionary change. But Marx was expelled from Paris and went to Brussels, where he founded the German Working Men's Association and the Communist Correspondence Committee, later called the Communist League. These groups had few or no members and were dedicated to study, not revolution. But the Communist League grew. When it met in London in 1847, Marx transfixed the hundred or so members by denouncing their declarations of universal brotherhood and urging class war. They asked him to write a statement of principles for them in the next two months. Drawing on Engels' and his past work, Marx hastily wrote a text (generously sharing authorship with Engels, who repeatedly insisted that Marx alone had written it). As Europe exploded in 1848, *The Communist Manifesto* appeared. Although barely noticed in the turmoil, it changed the world.

Marx challenged George Hegel's idea that history was driven by ideas in conflict. Hegel claimed that when antithetical ideas synthesize (as red and blue synthesize into purple), progress occurs. For Marx, however, conflict and resolution (dialectic) were based in economics, not ideas; history was a record of class struggle, of conflict between owners (bourgeoisie) and workers (proletariat) over material goods (thus, dialectical materialism). Over time, the method by which material goods were distributed had changed from feudal manorialism to capitalism. Capitalism was a necessary stage in human progress, but would be overthrown. A proletarian dictatorship would take over the means of production *and* the distribution of material goods until capitalism and capitalist thought were eradicated. When the bourgeois state withered away, true communism would emerge as a utopia on earth.

Marx's first sentence, "A spectre is haunting Europe—the spectre of Communism," challenged the world.[16] He used the word "communism" rather than "socialism" because so many forms of socialism existed at the time. "Communism," an older, less loaded word, had a stricter meaning: communal ownership of goods. Asserting that "philosophers have only given different *interpretations* of the world; the important thing is to change it," Marx read history to that end. His analysis of the leading edge of capitalism remains pertinent and profound, even if capitalism had only just begun in 1848 and did not become revolutionary until railroads launched the iron and steel industries, producing the internal-combustion engine, Fordism (assembly lines), and our own burgeoning electronics industries.

Before 1848 most radical groups believed political power rested in franchise and focused on demanding universal male suffrage. Marx insisted that property, not the vote, conferred political power. He defined "value" as the labor-time required to produce goods; workers sell their labor-time for *full value*—the wages necessary to "reproduce" them—keep them alive for the next day. But owners price things above workers' wages, so workers produce "surplus value" which is appropriated by capitalists, who own the means of production—the factory, machines, and raw materials. The Communist goal was the abolition of private ownership of capital.

Marx saw that capitalism separated production from reproduction, the sphere in which labor-power is reproduced. He did not develop his thought about reproduction (biological or social); he granted it value, but did not incorporate it into his theory. This set a precedent; later socialist thinkers ignored the work of childbearing and family maintenance. Engels, however, was concerned with women's oppression and wrote a semihistorical account of its emergence, *The Origin of the Family, Private Property and the State,* which remains important to many socialists. In 1883 socialist theorist August Bebel argued that women were the first humans placed in bondage and should be counted as part of the workforce. But Marx, not Bebel, was the father of most modern socialisms. Marx envisioned capitalism as a dynamic system allowing social change so radical that the powerless could become the authors of history, but he did so *after* the defeat of women in socialism and the restoration of patriarchal priorities in organized labor. Patriarchy triumphed in later socialism as it did in later Christianity and later Islam. Once the formative stage of a movement has passed, men move to exclude women.

Nevertheless, socialism was a revolutionary new human discourse; by interpreting social structure in terms of class struggle—the exploitation of labor and collective action challenging it—socialist thinking provided a language and a set of values for a feminist agenda. But it was complicated by three facts: women participate in both sides of the class struggle (are members of the exploiters and the exploited); at the same time, all women are oppressed by men, including men of their own class. Women's loyalties are further fragmented by their primary responsibility for maintaining men and raising children (some male) to take places in society dictated by their fathers' positions.

Based on the principle of equality, socialism has treated women better than capitalism in some ways. Socialist states gave women access to education and jobs with decent wages long before "democratic" states did so. But women in socialist states suffer from the same discrimination found in the utopian communes and capitalist states: patriarchal bias. Women supported socialism ardently, and it affected millions of women. But it failed them. This failure is not unique: no system has yet been devised that acknowledges women's true centrality to reproduction and maintenance.

Revolutions broke out across Europe in 1848. In explanation, historians cite the greater population of Europe: people crowded into towns with no work. The potato crop failed in 1846 and subsequently wheat in 1847. Poor harvests, aggravated by international financial and industrial crises, caused widespread unemployment, business failure, and starvation. Hungry people rioted, but even before these crises they had been politicized, affected by socialist ideas, ideas of democracy. After 1815 groups worked to wrest a share of political power. Secret brotherhoods called Carbonari, headed by army officers, emerged in Italy and spread through Europe in the 1820s, forcing the kings of Naples and Spain to promise constitutions based on the French revolutionary constitution of 1789–1791. A Belgian insurrection overthrew Dutch rule.

While all governments claim concern for the "national interest" and stress nationalism in times of crisis, the events of the mid-nineteenth century show that rulers are more concerned with protecting their own class and its privileges than with the well-being of their citizens.[17] Privileged classes sell out less-privileged citizens of their countries to preserve their privilege—as the Spanish did in this period.[18]

After Napoleon's defeat, Bourbon monarchs returned to rule France. When the reactionary Charles X tried to undo all that remained of the revolution—restoring aristocratic privilege to the detriment of the middle class—France rose in revolution. Workers, artisans, students, writers, and men and women demanding a republic (Republicans) erected barricades in the streets—more barricades in more places than ever before or since. (The 1830 revolution turned the barricade into a symbol of democratic insurrection.) From behind the barricades they fought soldiers and police, who were reluctant to fire on the people. Charles abdicated, raising the revolutionaries' hope for a republic. But Charles was not the only impediment to a wider sharing of power: a powerful group of bankers, merchants, and industrialists put the duc d'Orléans on the throne (calling him Louis Philippe of *the French*—not of *France*), and granted franchise to 100,000 more males. The heroism of the revolutionaries won nothing except a new consciousness, an awareness of common cause with workers which generated a proletarian-socialist revolutionary movement in Paris.

Workers, students, and writers formed secret societies to study socialist theory, publish attacks and satires, and mount riots. In 1834 the government outlawed political associations, and Paris and Lyon became war zones. The army massacred hundreds and arrested 2000 republican leaders. The elite's stubborn rejection of even moderate change drove moderates into the republican camp. Revolutionaries circumvented the law against political meetings by holding "banquets," and in 1847 mounted a nationwide protest that culminated in a mass banquet in Paris in February 1848. The government effort to squelch it ignited revolution.

Marshal Bugeaud, notorious for his brutality during an 1834 uprising, was ordered to crush this one. He sent four columns of troops to clear the streets. Untrained in street fighting, the troops were soon overwhelmed. Bugeaud's withdrawal demoralized Louis Philippe and his advisers: the king abdicated. A provisional government of ten male parliamentarians and journalists was appointed (seven republicans and three socialists, including Louis Blanc), with George Sand as unofficial minister of information. Paris bubbled with activity: republicans from abroad came to observe and enjoy the great event; newly legal political clubs sprang up everywhere; political journals proliferated.

Jeanne Deroin (1810?–1894), who had tried to organize a worker's union and was imprisoned in the 1840s, resurfaced during the 1848 revolutions. With the other Saint-Simonians (Eugénie Niboyet, Suzanne Voilquin, and Désirée Verret) who had co-edited the first feminist newspaper, *La femme libre,* in 1832, Deroin founded a political club and a new journal, *La voix des femmes.* It called for marriage reform, the right to divorce, and economic opportunities for women. The first issue argued that improving men's lot does not necessarily improve women's—a fact that has had to be rediscovered in every new feminist generation.

Blanc tried to set up a system of national workshops to train workers, distribute goods as a cooperative, and offer unemployment benefits, but apart from a midwifery training school for women, they became only a set of traditional charity workshops, offering minimal wages for hard, often pointless labor. In a France racked by unemployment, the project drew over 60,000 people to Paris in a few months, terrifying the middle class. Under pressure from radicals, the government decreed universal male suffrage; but at the next election men elected mainly conservatives. The government closed national workshops to new members, claiming they drained the budget.

Spontaneous mass uprisings at the Pantheon and Bastille cut Paris in two. Barricades went up in the poorer eastern *quartiers*; people seized weapons from gun shops or homes. Without an overall plan, and with only local leaders, 40,000–50,000 people took to the streets. The government later claimed the rebels were rootless vagabonds, but most were small-scale artisans, skilled workers established in their crafts and communities, men and women desperate enough to risk death to express their wishes.[19] They were crushed. This time the government imported rural soldiers willing to shoot city folk. The artist Meissonier, a captain in the National Guard, described a common scene: "When the barricade in the rue de la Mortellerie was taken, I . . . saw the defenders shot down, hurled out of windows, the ground strewn with corpses, the earth red with blood."

After three days of cruel street fighting and 12,000 arrests, the government hunted people down, sending most to Algerian labor-camps, crippling the Parisian left for a decade. The defeat was so total and brutal that it annihilated radicalism not just in France, but throughout Europe. The government immediately held an election, hoping a strong president could silence dissidence. The reactionary favorite, Louis Napoleon Bonaparte, Napoleon's nephew, won overwhelmingly. Conservatives voted for him, hoping he would protect their property from the radicals; workers liked him because his book, *The Extinction of Pauperism*, offered surefire schemes for prosperity, and because he had a relationship with Blanc and anarchist Pierre Proudhon. Louis Napoleon wanted to be dictator. He won Catholic support by immediately returning control over schools to the Church and re-establishing French deference to the Pope. He won over the workers and the bourgeoisie by creating old-age insurance and laws favoring business. Three years later, he was elected dictator by a plebiscite.

News of the revolution flew across Europe, inspiring political actions in many cities; in nearly every European city with over 50,000 inhabitants in Western and Central Europe, the working poor rebelled.[20] They toppled the rulers of the Austrian Empire, rulers of German and Italian petty states, and temporarily discomfited aristocrats across Europe. But the revolutionaries were not united, and after all the killing and suffering new elites replaced the old: stratification did not vanish.

The 1848 revolutions did not produce democratic socialism or unify states. Nor did they much improve conditions for most people. But they changed the political system of Western Europe by replacing the aristocracy with a bourgeois elite. For the rest of the century the "grande bourgeoisie"—industrialists, bankers, and high-ranking civil servants—comprised a ruling class as adamantly opposed to democracy or socialism as any aristocracy. Authoritarian regimes stopped liberal reforms at the Rhine, and eastern European rulers were successful at suppressing their revolutions. Huge estates remained in Central and Eastern Europe, but the serfs were given their freedom, which somewhat eased their condition. In some states, reform governments were succeeded by repressive regimes more sophisticated in repression, although more aware of the potential danger of revolution and also of the necessity of integrating the working classes into larger society through education. French, Prussian, and Austrian governments began to offer primary education to the masses. Western governments permitted protest to be gradually institutionalized in trade unions and political clubs.

Parisians rose up again in March 1871, forming the Paris

Commune and declaring themselves autonomous. Thousands of women participated in this struggle with the Versailles government, literally interposing their bodies between the Versailles troops sent to suppress the revolt and the Paris National Guard defending the Commune on the Montmartre hills.[21] They drove ambulances, sewed uniforms, wrote for the Commune press, taught Commune children in newly reclaimed public schools, and defended the city of Paris on gunboats along the Seine. Women, newly claiming public space as "citoyennes" (women citizens), were creating the Commune as a structure in which women and workers could rule themselves. But to the government and the elite, women's presence in this transformed public space was a transgression and defamation of the sexual geography of public order that supported the French republic itself.[22] They saw women in the public sphere as whores, thieves, she-men with the audacity to carry guns and wear pants.

The Paris Commune fell, but revolutionary ideals continued to be transmitted over generations by artists and writers. Daumier was often imprisoned for his satirical cartoons on Louis Philippe; in 1849, Dostoievsky was condemned to die (and marched to a wall but not shot) for revolutionary activities; Pushkin was punished for involvement with the Decembrists. George Sand influenced the leaders of the 1848 uprising (as well as Marx and Bakunin), and wrote position papers for the provisional government. She went on writing sympathetically about women and the poor.

In 1848 the *revolutionary* government barred women from political activity and closed Jeanne Deroin's feminist journal. But she ran for the legislature in 1849, and then organized a federation of workers' unions with Pauline Roland, another ex-Saint-Simonian. Both were arrested by the republican government in 1850. Roland died in 1851 and Deroin went into exile in England, but their ideas influenced women like Flora Tristan who, with other feminists, placed female exploitation within a broad, coherent context, influencing people like the painter Rosa Bonheur and initiating a tradition of social protest that was resuscitated by the British women who invented the social protest novel.

These two decades of war, and the ideas and new sense of power engendered by revolutions of rights affected institutions in every major European state. However, changes in borders, laws, and institutions were minor compared to the profound transformation of the political atmosphere. Revolution raised consciousness everywhere. Nationalist and socialist agitation continued, workers formed unions, and feminism became broader-based. The tide of *thought* had turned. Hobsbawm interestingly suggests that autocratic governments tended to mistrust all intellectuals, even reactionaries, because once people accepted their right to think rather than the obligation to obey, the end of despotism was in sight. After 1850 all major European states were forced to grant more democracy. But the new elites ruled by more devious methods. What did not change was male domination of women—everywhere.[23]

CHAPTER 4

MIDDLE-CLASS WOMEN IN ENGLAND

A NEW GENDER IDEOLOGY PERVADED the English-speaking world in the mid-nineteenth century. As ideas of rights and social justice spread more widely, ideas about women *narrowed*. In this period, women lost property rights; they also lost legal identity at marriage and were forced into domestic roles as tight as their corsets.

The Cult of Domesticity (or Cult of True Womanhood or Doctrine of Separate Spheres), which was central to nineteenth-century middle-class thinking about gender, slowly filtered down to the working class. It was an unattainable ideal for black Americans: an area of failure for black men who could not support women as the ideal required and for black women, who, even if supported, could never be "ladies." While many today scorn the image of a pious, sexually pure, submissive, domestic woman as false or constricting, it remains powerful in many media. The ideal was invested not just with moral superiority, but with *glamor*: the "lady," with her upswept hair, high-buttoned blouse, tiny waist, flowing skirt, bent neck, and sweet smile, sat on a velvet couch, protected from the harshness of life, an icon to be desired and emulated.

Revolutionary changes in printing made possible national distribution of magazines, the first mass medium. Magazines (often edited by women) and books like Catherine Beecher's *Domestic Economy* and *Godey's Ladies' Book* by Sarah Josepha Hale became the purveyors of woman's new image. It was still purveyed in the 1950s via *Good Housekeeping*, *Ladies' Home Journal*, *Woman's Day*, and romance novels. In this myth, a standard against which real women were measured, Woman was the pivotal figure in a morality upheld by religion, law, and science. Her function was to stand still yet do what was necessary for men to devote their energies to aggressive, acquisitive competition. Woman's moral excellence exemplified virtue; without it, men claimed, society would fall into viciousness. Western morality was split like Chinese yin and yang between a public sphere, ruled by men, and a separate, private domain, ruled by women. The marketplace was distinct from the home. All sexual divisions of experience are said to be complementary, to offer "separate but equal" powers, but all really maintain inequality. Men could enter the private realm—indeed, owned and controlled it—but women were excluded from the public.

The idea of True Womanhood grew partly out of Republican Motherhood, the sop men threw to women who had supported the American Revolution and wanted its promised rewards—liberty and equality. True Womanhood was defined by four virtues: piety, purity, submissiveness, and domesticity. Religion assigned Woman the role of guardian of the family against the moral corruption of the marketplace.[1] To fulfill this role, she had steadfastly to guard her "purity," the source of her power. Purity essentially meant asexuality. Woman's transcendence of sexuality gave her the moral force she was to use to cool or contain male sexual passion, which (presumably) was beyond male control. This concept is staggering. Most previous societies gave men control over women's bodies, but none considered women asexual or would have tolerated women's

thwarting male desire. What was going on here?

Medieval Christian European men had seen Woman as a temptress threatening male godliness. But godliness took on a new character in nineteenth-century England and the United States. Divine traits were apportioned one to a sex. Especially after Darwin, theorists considered selfish aggressiveness a necessary trait in man's battle for survival of the fittest: virtuous men were killers in the struggle that was life. To complement this new definition of Man, Woman was redefined as an incarnation of love, the other divine aspect.

A new class was emerging. Lacking the semidivine ancestry claimed by aristocrats, the middle class (or bourgeoisie) had to fight for the privileges formerly reserved to nobles—the right to make policy and law, to govern. Men who rose to this class had the energy and will for lonely struggle in the service of a new god, success.

They became rich and powerful, but their success required putting power foremost and sacrificing most pleasures. The greatest threat to such dedication was thought to be sexual desire, which leads men to lose control and abandon the goal, or cede it to another who should properly be subordinate.

It was considered self-evident that the sexes were different species with different aptitudes. Man was active, Woman passive; Man was the "architect," Woman "the soul" of the house. Innate male intellectual capacity for creation, invention, and synthesis justified Man's role as doer, creator, and discoverer. Nature denied Woman such abilities: her judgment was fit only for detail and trivialities.

Therefore the role best suited to her, the occupation that most satisfied her dependent nature was, as social historian W.R. Greg wrote, the role of servant. "They [female servants] are attached to others and are connected with other existences, which they embellish, facilitate and serve. In a word they fulfilll both essentials of a woman's being: they are supported by, and minister to, men." In herself Woman was nothing: "[Women] are . . . from their own constitution, and from the station they occupy in the world . . . relative creatures." As real men dedicate themselves to domination, true women dedicate themselves to service.[2]

As objects of male desire, women in patriarchal societies are always held responsible for human sexuality, but now men were demanding that women thwart male sexuality. That women lack desire was an idea that had floated around in the West for centuries—you can find it in Shakespeare—but asexuality never *defined* the female until the nineteenth century. (Indeed, patriarchal societies often see women as sexually ravenous.) A new society needed a new Woman: "In men the sexual desire is inherent and spontaneous. In the other sex, the desire is dormant, if not nonexistent," wrote Greg. Virtue transformed Woman from Eve to Mary, the "angel in the house." Motherhood, which had been one task among many, became women's central task, as the work that women had done for centuries was now performed outside the home. Society blinded women to diminishment by haloing them: Woman was "the natural and therefore divine, guide, purifier, inspirer of the man," wrote Charles Kingsley.[3] Her power derived from submission to Man, but she was the center of the family, the source of all thought, feeling, and influence, with absolute power over the spirit of man, peace, war, and the fate of humanity: "The hand that rocks the cradle/ Is the hand that rules the world."

Of course, not every woman was a True Woman: working-class and black women were barely human. Class was of the essence, and even middle-class women had to prove themselves True by remaining virgins before marriage, faithful after it, and by creating a safe, spiritual domestic environment with every creature comfort. Home—the realm of Woman—existed, like her, as Man's reward, offering relief from a harsh cruel world. By serving as nurse, cook, child-tender, spiritual adviser, midwife, housekeeper, teacher, floral arranger, and producer of needlework, Woman tempered, soothed, and transformed the male, who was hardened by the necessity of acquisitive aggressiveness, into a being capable of virtue.

The actual situation this myth masked was not pretty, and the condition of this paragon far from divine. According to law and the precepts of religion, a husband owned his wife, who might have "no will of her own, no opinions, nor any feelings but in accordance with the will of her lord and master." Both servants and wives were subject to a male master's extensive control, one that reached into all areas of the subordinate's life.[4] Wives and servants did the same work; all but the wealthiest women did manual labor in the household, and all wives were responsible for managing it and any children. Both were physically abused and threatened with beating, a major source of men's control, more often used on wives than servants. Despite much evidence of widespread male violence in the home, not until the twentieth century was it openly admitted that wife-beating is not limited to working-class men. Nevertheless, women, not men, were scrutinized for sin. Wives were supposed to satisfy husbands' desires miraculously on whatever money they were given. The worst sin a working-class wife could commit, Françoise Basch writes, was to envy the privileged classes, to harbor "that sense of injustice which is the seed of social revolt."

Nineteenth-century ladies' clothes (which few working-class women could afford, fortunately for them) emphasized maternity and constriction. At puberty, girls were put into corsets to minimize waistlines, laced in so tightly that their ribs became deformed. Some died from the constriction, but all corseted women had trouble breathing: the "fainting-couch" had a real function. Corsets pushed the breasts up, exaggerating their size; bustles exaggerated the size of buttocks, making women all "T and A." They also wore layers of long skirts, sometimes over hoops, which impeded mobility considerably. Dress reform was an issue in feminist campaigns that urged women to wear bloomers (long full pantaloons) or at least to eschew corsets.

Women and Institutions in England

Science on Women

Scientists based their assertions of women's inferiority in every dimension except the moral on solid "facts": women, for example, were weaker than men physically. And they were: working women had poor, often inadequate diets and were overworked at jobs that ruined their health; "ladies" never exercised and wore deforming clothes. All women lacked the self-esteem vital to good health. Man had so dominated Nature that he had transformed the longer-lived, more enduring sex into "the weaker sex." To be female was to be sick: doctors blamed this on the female procreative system. Women, a different species from men, grew not from a rib but a uterus, "a highly perilous possession" exerting "paramount power" over them. A professor wrote in 1870 that "the Almighty, in creating the female sex, had taken the uterus and built up a woman around it." Male doctors fixated on the uterus, finding it the source of every female disease and the reason women suffered twice as many ailments as men. Tuberculosis in men was caused by environmental factors; in women by reproductive malfunction.[5]

All exclusively female physical functions were considered inherently pathological. Menstruation and menopause endangered life. And if puberty developed all of the *male* body ("the principles of life superabound in his constitution, and he vigorously performs all the noble pursuits assigned him by nature"), it made girls moody, depressed, petulant, capricious, and sometimes sexually promiscuous ("women . . . always preserve some of the infantile constitution").[6] To survive puberty, young ladies (only ladies could afford to consult a physician for this "disease") were ordered to pursue a strict regimen of domestic tasks like cooking, bed-making, cleaning, and child-tending. The cure for menopause was exactly the same; doctors claimed it was aggravated by sex, socializing, gaiety, or any mental activity whatsoever. There is great hostility in the medical literature on menopausal women: male physicians loathed them, calling them physically repulsive, stupid, dull, and jealous of the young.[7]

Despite the powerful uterus, women were *by nature* asexual. William Acton, a doctor in the Royal Medical and Chirurgical Society, wrote on urinary and sexual diseases and prostitution. In 1857 he published *The Functions and Disorders of the Reproductive*

Organs, a work that amazingly ignores completely the anatomy and physiology of *female* reproductive organs. Discussing female sexuality only in relation to male desire and attitudes toward marriage, and anxious to allay male fears of married sex, Acton offers a fascinating view of female sexuality. The mistresses and courtesans a young man frequents before his marriage are unbalanced, nymphomaniacs; the lady he will marry, on the other hand, will certainly be ignorant of sex and without desire: "Love of home, children and domestic duties, are the only passions they feel." Marital consummation will cause her only suffering and distress, but the husband may rest assured that "the act of coition takes place but rarely in the life of the couple."

Indeed, most nineteenth-century ladies *were* ignorant of sex when they married, and perhaps many did lack desire. Doctors did not always invent their perceptions: their writings betray that they, the experts, had not the slightest idea of how to make love to—as opposed to have sex with—a woman. If doctors did not understand female bodies, ordinary men were unlikely to. If a woman had absorbed the fact that sex was sinful, and feared the mysterious act, she may have disliked being banged, especially since she was the one who could get pregnant. Freud was not the only doctor ignorant of the workings of the clitoris, the organ second only to the uterus in destructive power.

The first use of the emerging field of gynecology was the surgical removal of female sexual organs—clitoris, foreskin, or ovaries. Clitoridectomies were said to cure "mental disorders" like "sexual desire or sexual behavior," pathological when they appeared in women. They were performed occasionally in England and often in the United States after the 1860s. The last known case occurred in the United States in 1948, to "cure" a five-year-old girl who masturbated. At the end of the nineteenth century "great surgical operations are performed on girls, veritable tortures: cauterization of the clitoris with red-hot irons was, if not habitual, at least fairly frequent."[8] And women who were too "masculine"—assertive, unruly, or aggressive—were by a strange twist of logic "cured" by losing their ovaries.

Ignorance is forgivable when it is helpless, but poetry shows that people have known about clitoral function for millennia: nineteenth-century physicians could have discovered it if they'd thought twice. That they did not, but high-handedly defined female sexuality without bothering to study female bodies or consult women, demonstrates the psychological ambience of the period. Men simply nullified female reality, refused to deal with it or with contraception. Bearing, feeding, and tending too many children killed women, and men who loved and tried to support families were sometimes swamped by ten or fifteen children. Few wanted so many, yet nineteenth-century society utterly forbade contraception.

Contraceptives existed; Owenites and the Oneidans knew of some. Between 1820 and 1826, clandestine propaganda for contraception was published but little else appeared over the century.[9] Medical literature shows that abortion, the most primitive form of birth control, was widely used after the 1860s, but contraception was taboo until Margaret Sanger: even feminists opposed it. Contraception gives women a degree of control over their lives and bodies, which was not allowed. Yet ironically, as motherhood was being touted as a spiritual and civic duty, white middle-class women's fertility rates steadily dropped. A woman's average number of children fell from 7.04 in 1800 to 6.14 in 1840, 4.24 in 1880, and 3.56 in 1900; presumably "moral superiority" had successfully restrained male sexuality.

Despite their supposed Natural Aptitude for motherhood, women were historically thought to contribute little to the conception of children. Pre-nineteenth-century scientific accounts of reproduction attribute the form or "active" element of embryos to males.[10] Aristotle held that women, "passive" reproducers, merely provided space and material sustenance for the fetus—the oven for the bun. Females were infertile males; menstrual fluid, "stunted semen," generated females when a surplus interfered with development. Aristotle thought both sexes the same species, but saw females as "mutilated males." Galen believed, with Hippocrates, that both sexes produce seed, weak and strong varieties: strong seed from both parents produced males, weak seed females. Both parents make a material contribution but only males provide the active element in forming an embryo. With the male as model, Galen saw ovaries as "testes," drawing them to resemble testicles and the uterus as an inverted penis. Seventeenth-century medical authorities urged couples who wanted male offspring to eat hot or dry meats, avoid intercourse until "the seed was well developed," or arrange their bodies during copulation so the seed fell to the right side of the womb.

There were a few scientists after 1500 who considered the reproductive function of both sexes perfect and distinct, and females not defective versions of males. For Hieronymus Fabricius (1537–1619), semen stimulated female organs to produce eggs; Anton Van Leeuwenhoek (1632–1723) believed female eggs existed only to nourish the sperm, the source of embryonic form. Swiss physiologist Albrecht von Haller (1708–1777) thought the embryo existed in miniature in a prefertilized ovum. Not until German scientist Karl Ernst von Baer (1792–1876) used a microscope were scientists sure that female ova even existed. Observing female dogs, von Baer concluded that embryos originate in ova formed in the ovary *before* fertilization. Males *did not* create female life.

Scientists, who believed in domination and were certain there was only one true parent, began to fear that the female was that one. The argument that the true parent was the one who carried the ova much disturbed the medical profession. Embryology was placed on a modern scientific basis when Oskar Hertwig (1849–1922), observing the actual fusion of male and female nuclei within the egg of a sea urchin, demonstrated in 1879 that only one spermatozoan entered the ovum of a starfish. It had taken nearly 2500 years to "prove" that mothers as well as fathers passed on traits.

Nineteenth-century medical research "proved" that women's

reproductive organs controlled their brains and that males were more intelligent than females. Phrenologists studied bumps on the skull that "proved" women, Jews, and Africans intellectually inferior to white Christian men. Nineteenth-century scientists assumed that large brains took up more space than small ones, that size meant greater intellect and complexity, and that the skull bulged to accommodate a large brain. When they found more bulges on the skulls of white Christian males than others, their assumptions were confirmed. And when evidence did not support the theory (and some phrenological evidence even demonstrated the opposite), researchers simply suppressed the data and manufactured the desired evidence.

Law on Women

Married women were legally nonexistent in nineteenth-century England; they could not enter into contracts, own property, or control children. A woman's husband was the absolute master of her body, property, and children; she was a chattel. *The law did not recognize mothers*, stipulating that children must obey only fathers: "During the father's life, the mother is entitled to no power . . . but only to respect." If a father died, his nearest male relative became his children's guardian. A husband could force a wife to stay with him against her will, even confining her. A woman who committed adultery lost all rights to maintenance and could be legally separated and abandoned, but men were not penalized for adultery. In fact, a man whose wife left because he was unfaithful could pursue her and sue anyone who took her in; she could not get support without a court order establishing need. Only those with £1000 to pay Parliament for a Private Member's Bill could divorce. Few women, but about two hundred men managed this before 1857.[11]

Separated wives had no rights to their children, not even to visitation. Fathers automatically got custody. Yet philosophers insisted that women did not need the vote because husbands adequately represented their interests, because, men claimed, women and men had identical interests, because, in law, man and wife were one flesh. As laws "protecting" working women locked them into more complete dependence on men, other laws restricted their options. The Reform Act of 1832, which extended suffrage to more males, inserted the word "male" into voting qualifications for the first time in British history. Earlier, the few women who owned large pieces of property had been able to vote. But when in this period a female property owner petitioned Parliament to allow single females with the necessary pecuniary qualifications to vote, the reformed democratic, egalitarian House of Commons burst into laughter.[12]

European women were similarly disinherited, as men everywhere legally wrote them out of rights to property and control of their bodies. In terms of rights, the nineteenth century was women's nadir. From the late twelfth century, men had steadily eroded  women's rights, succeeding in the nineteenth in extirpating them entirely—as working-class women's wretched degradation and middle-class women's silent misery attested. But some men were horrified by this situation, and women were down but not out. Their struggle for economic, legal, and social liberation was a major element in the ferment that characterizes this century.

Most British reformers shunned any suggestion of radical change in social structures. Both socialism and feminism were anathema. Reformers of both sexes took for granted that women had a "special" talent for mothering and that their vocation was the family. Few pointed to the contradiction between women's reality and their exalted image. In *Society in America* (1837), political reformer Harriet Martineau mocked the idea of women's influence, their power to sway "the judgment and will of man through the heart. . . . One might as well try to dissect the morning mist." Bessie Rayner Parkes questioned "this mysterious moral fluid"; Marion Reid compared women's "all-powerful so-much-talked-of influence" with their real lack of rights, remarking that instead of "With all my worldly goods I thee endow," a groom should say "What is yours is mine; and what is mine is *my own*."[13]

Most British feminists focused on a specific injustice like divorce law or single women's difficulty supporting themselves. Caroline Norton tirelessly argued that courts—not fathers' whims—automatically grant wives and separated mothers custody of children under seven and the right to visit older ones. The day before John Stuart Mill married Harriet Taylor in 1851, he wrote a solemn denunciation of the "odious powers" conferred on husbands by marriage. In 1855 Barbara Leigh Smith convened some women to pressure Parliament for a bill allowing married women to keep their own property. Anna Jameson illustrated single women's problems by using 1851 census data—there were half a million more women than men in England; three-quarters of single women lived on their own earnings. In 1865 Harriet Martineau showed that a third of women over twenty-one supported themselves.

Their pressure bore some fruit. An 1839 law allowed mothers to petition courts for custody of children under seven and the right to visit older ones. The 1857 Matrimonial Causes Bill eased divorce for the poor by allowing it in cases of adultery, cruelty, or desertion—but only men could sue for divorce on grounds of adultery. Women had to show that a man's adultery had been aggravated by desertion, cruelty, rape, buggery, or bestiality. (This double standard lasted until *1929*.) The bill also allowed women whose husbands had deserted them to petition for protection of their assets, and legally separated women to ask for *feme sole* status in regard to property acquired by inheritance, gifts, or earnings (this status acknowledged a woman the owner of her goods and chattels, able to make and be bound by contracts, take responsibility for debts, sue, and be sued). A *feme sole* had the same legal rights as a man but not the same political rights—all women, of any status, were barred from professions, universities, political office, and the vote.

In 1857 Leigh Smith and other feminists founded the Association for the Promotion of the Employment of Women to ease "the unhappy condition of women who had to earn their bread." It ran training programs, urging employers to hire women in expanding areas like clerical work. In 1858 "the ladies of Langham Place"—Barbara Leigh Smith Bodichon, Parkes, Adelaide Procter, and Jessie Boucherett—launched the first English feminist newspaper to be entirely written and published by women, *The English Women's Journal*,[14] which became the hub of British feminist agitation. As feminist networks expanded, the *Journal* described Emily Davies' campaign to open public exams to girls and found a women's college, suffragists lobbying Parliament, new women's clubs, model housing projects, and unusual jobs that were available.

Historians consider the decade 1867–77 to be a turning point in the Victorian era. The second Reform Act of 1867 extended the vote to men of the lower-middle and better-off working class, another step toward democracy. Mill tried to amend this bill to substitute the word "person" for "man" to open the door to votes for women. His amendment was defeated but seventy-three Parliamentarians voted for it. The same year, a commission inquiring into schools called feminists Emily Davies, Frances Buss, and Mill to testify. Its report led to swift improvements in secondary and higher education for women, enabling Davies two years later to found Girton College, the first English university to admit women.

In 1868 birth control was publicly discussed for the first time; in 1870 the important Married Woman's Property Act was passed under strong unified feminist pressure. This gave wives the right to their own earnings, revenues, inheritances, investments, rents, and cash gifts over £200. An 1873 law granted courts the power (it was not required) to give mothers custody of children up to sixteen, but in 1878 mothers got custody of children under ten only if the father had committed "aggravated assault."

Women's legal status intensified their inclination to live in homosocial worlds and to form strong bonds with female kin; they used female networks to counterbalance their lack of authority in the family.[15] By helping and supporting each other and leaving their property to each other, women exerted collective moral, social, and financial pressure on family men.[16] A disfranchised caste, women created a self-sustaining world: alimony was rare, so female relations helped divorced women; a woman about to give birth, knowing she faced death, relied on her sisters to protect her children from a future stepmother's abuse. Young widows turned to female kin for emotional and economic support, and older ones depended on daughters to tend them in illness.

Religion on Women

Institutions have contradictory effects. Nineteenth-century religion bolstered the imprisoning image of the pure Victorian wife and mother, but it also offered women another identity, embracing them in a community in which they could use other talents and access an authority more powerful than that of their husbands. By the late eighteenth century, women dominated most religious congregations in numbers and activity. But after 1850 many feminists attacked religion as the main bulwark of sexual hierarchy, and the root of female oppression.

Nineteenth-century Christianity sentimentalized the home, with its religion of domesticity under women's moral influence. The clergy denounced women's efforts to expand their role beyond the home as threatening the balance of power in the family and the balance of moral forces in the state. That women had a unique moral mission was an idea popular with both feminists and antifeminists. For male and female antifeminists, it made confinement at home palatable by exalting Woman ruling the world from her home in purity and righteousness. For feminists, it was a basis for legitimacy: if women were morally superior, society should heed them. But many feminists denied there was an essential, innate femininity, a single, universal female character.

Antifeminists were not unaware of the contradiction in the new female role. One woman wrote: "It might seem inconsistent to claim for woman a spiritual role at least equal to that of her husband and at the same time accede to her social subordination [but] the one quality on which woman's value and influence depends is the renunciation of self."[17] The anonymous author of *Domestic Tyranny, or Women in Chains* (1840) disagreed:

> Far be it from my intention to claim or uphold any privilege which would in the least degree militate against the Scriptural injunctions, "Wives submit yourselves to your husbands, as is fit in the Lord." I would at the same time draw attention to the particular terms of this commandment, "as is fit in the Lord," which certainly imply not a degraded or inferior being in the scale of His creation, or one who was unworthy or incompetent to appreciate such an injunction, but on the contrary, it is particularly addressed to them as responsible and self-governing agents, who are also required to search the Scriptures to know the will of the Lord.

The author's scriptural search led her to conclude that wife-beating, male appropriation of female property, and the denial of the vote were not part of a Divine Plan; rather "it . . . seem[ed] implanted in our nature by the Almighty to rebel against oppression."

The nineteenth-century English Christian revival (like that in the twentieth-century United States) was overtly antidemocratic and systematically suppressed ideas tending to female liberation. Women, the mainstay of virtually all nineteenth-century congregations, were allowed only auxiliary roles in revivalist churches. They were caryatids, woman-shaped pillars supporting the roofs of temples owned and controlled by men. Ministers who preached that women were "God's own repositories" refused to let them direct philanthropic activities; only splinter Methodist sects let women preach in the 1830s. British women of the period, feminists or not, shared an evangelical frame of reference.

As the century advanced, the cult of domesticity generated opposing tendencies. Middle-class women used their "moral superiority" to redefine and expand the private sphere; working-class women, especially the better-off, adopted middle-class values. Working-class men became increasingly opposed to their wives' working outside the home. The ideal working-class wife had been an essential, if secondary, provider who also maintained the household; now the ideal working-class wife was a housewife, an unpaid servant. The new ideal was not foisted on working-class women: they chose it. Of their few options, staying home to raise their children was the least onerous form of oppression open to them.

Single Women

It was crucial for women's well-being, integrity, and pride to find a way to feel and act independent. This was difficult for single women—and there were a great many in this period. Biology caused women to outnumber men in most nations; there were not enough men for all women even if all men married. But single women were supposed to devote themselves to serving their families. Women who stayed single in order not to be domestic servants, but to study or make art were thwarted by this demand. Even if their household had servants and they were not consumed by domestic work, propriety required behavior that killed the spirit. Economically dependent, and suffering the servility that doing tedious, unchallenging, repetitive domestic work entails, single women were miserable. They were forbidden to engage in any physical or mental activity and, confined by dress, custom, and law, could do little more than sit at windows gazing out at life. Tennyson in 1852 wrote "The Lady of Shalott" about a young woman for whom life happens in a mirror on her wall.

Single women were guilt-ridden about undone domestic tasks, and most profoundly, their failure to use their abilities, talents, and initiative. Even more than the wife, the spinster, representing purity, goodness, and virginity, was supposed to sacrifice herself to all who needed her. Many succumbed to mysterious debilitating diseases. Brilliant American Alice James, sister of Henry and William, suffered most of her life from strange ailments. Some of her diary entries suggest she was not entirely unaware of the connection between her ill health and her repression of rage: "How sick one gets of being 'good,' how much I should respect myself if I could burst out and make everyone wretched for 24 hours." Trying to be as pliant and submissive as society required, she felt suffocated (like Edith Wharton, born fourteen years later) and died at forty-four in 1892.

Even if single middle-class women came from well-to-do families, many had to make a living. Inheriting a house or some money no more guaranteed survival than working for wages: single women were haunted by money worries. But the nineteenth century was the first period in history in which middle-class women could live on their own wages (however poorly) free from conjugal or clerical authority. The struggle to accomplish this independence transformed some of them into leaders in the battle for women's rights, heroic pioneers who laid a foundation on which later generations built institutions extending far beyond their plans.[18] Realizing the feminist vision—changing society while enjoying themselves—they were bored when not working in their vocations. They did not enter male arenas like politics, but expanded the domestic realm to include workhouse, hospital, and school.

In the eighteenth century, a year or two of "finishing" school became fashionable for middle-class daughters. Despite the poor education that these schools often provided, they broke the isolation that prevented female solidarity: girls of the same age and class formed close friendships with each other at a formative and anxious time of life. Nineteenth-century families still educated their daughters at such schools, and they, too, often developed lifelong friendships even though few lived near or saw each other much after marriage. Many of these friendships were "romantic," youthful lesbian attachments. Since women were supposed to be asexual, such relations were not considered threats to society but rather as preparation for marriage. Indeed, married women used them to release subversive longings: Charlotte Brontë confided her deepest fears to Ellen Nussey, Florence Nightingale to "Clarkey," her friend Mary Clarke in Paris, and Geraldine Jewsbury bolstered Jane Carlyle. What labeled a woman "deviant" was her refusal to marry; only when women's communities offered an alternative to marriage did their friendships come to be seen as a threat. Few working women could afford to live alone, and communal living was cheaper and more pleasant than lodging in a boardinghouse. Women's communities offered companionship and privacy, fostering self-development.

Education and Women

From the 1840s women struggled for female education, opening secondary schools and offering lecture series. In 1848 Queen's College London was founded to educate governesses so they could demand higher wages.[19] Open to girls over twelve, it taught secondary school subjects but, like advanced educational institutions, provided lectures and grades. In 1849 Elizabeth Reid, a firm feminist, founded Bedford College and insisted that women themselves govern it. Queen's and Bedford were nonresidential; they emphasized remedial work to prepare girls for degree-level study. But girls living at home were drained by domestic drudgery.

Female colleges opened in Oxford (Royal Holloway) and Cambridge (Westfield) but, lacking sufficient financial backing, they had inadequate libraries and teachers and so failed to draw students. Many male journalists were outraged at the thought that women might study independently, free from domestic labor; families reluctantly bore the expense of educating daughters, whose education, unlike their brothers', would neither add luster to the family name nor prepare them for a profession or high-level job in the civil service. For women, college was just a time away from home to live and learn together; the only profession open to them was teaching. Still, the major problem for promoters of female higher education was girls' inadequate early training.

In 1867–68, a Commission of Enquiry on Schools found educational institutions deficient and declared in favor of higher education for women—in principle. Women like Davies and Buss, who had been working for this end for some time, moved swiftly: in 1869, Davies (1830–1921) opened Hitchin (later Girton) College. She knew that without rigorous training, women could hardly pass Oxford or Cambridge honors exams, which were geared to boys' preparation, years of classical and mathematical training. Women's failure of such exams would be attributed to intellectual inferiority; if they passed an easier exam, their claim on "men's" jobs would be weakened. Davies determined that her students would study for the Cambridge "Tripos" exams, following exactly the same course as men. But boys' education began at seven, and girls were already behind when they began the compulsory program of Greek, mathematics, and classics; Davies was not even sure Cambridge examiners would grade women's papers.

The examiners did agree to do so, and in 1872 three females passed the Tripos exams with (unofficial) honors. The women felt they had won a major victory and had proven themselves men's intellectual equals despite their erratic training. In 1881, although women were still barred from university lectures, they were officially admitted to university exams by convincing sympathetic dons to repeat their lectures for female audiences. Struggling steadily against the tide, by 1894 women took the same exams as men in all fields except medicine; by 1897 they were accepted marginally in the English university system.

The privileged women who attended residential colleges were probably the only women in England not required to do household labor and account to someone for every moment of their day. They could set their own rhythms and follow their own inclinations, in the company of others who delighted in learning. All college founders stressed the importance of a room of one's own. When Davies was planning Girton, she spent no money on landscaping but made sure each woman had a bed-sitting room—a space completely in her control, often for the first and last time in her life. The luxury of privacy was enhanced by the pleasure of community;

these women retained their college friends and the memory of a female community throughout their lives. Many joined sisterhoods for social work and nursing.[20]

Female educators disagreed over whether education provided personal enrichment or preparation for a career. They were troubled that only a tiny elite could enjoy university education and that men still scorned them as incapable of furthering knowledge. Female teachers and administrators were trapped in a triple bind: despite their erratic schooling, they had to appear intellectually superior to men simply to be accepted as equal. They had to comport themselves rigidly in a respectable and conformist manner, and had the added burden of responsibility for students in an era when doctors declared that learning "unsexed" women and drained their "maternal energy," causing the "decline of the species." Physicians repeatedly attributed infertility, brain damage, or mental breakdown in a female patient to mental work. And female educators had to forfeit politics: Davies stopped supporting women's suffrage for fear of jeopardizing Girton's reputation.

Nevertheless, teaching was single women's most important occupation throughout the nineteenth and into the twentieth century. As democratic movements demanded universal education, more elementary and secondary schools were established in Britain. Educating children was considered appropriate work for women, an extension of their domestic role; it offered them a respected low-paid career, and teachers in boarding schools rediscovered the harmony of work and community of their college years.

Near the end of the century, men began to question their assumptions about women. Scientist Nicholas Cooke's book *Satan in Society* revealed facts, shocking at the time, about young girls' sexual habits. Authorities began to doubt that women were sexless, leading male "experts" to question the warmth and intimacy of women's relations with each other. This distrust arose just as female solidarity was creating a powerful political women's movement: suddenly, student-teacher relations were suspect as homosexual; schoolgirl crushes on teachers were said to cause permanent disturbance; friendship between teachers was labeled abnormal. While writers like D.H. Lawrence in *The Rainbow* (1915) and Clemence Dane in *Regiment of Women* (1917) portrayed lesbians as malevolent, power-hungry, and manipulating, everyone ignored the pervasive male homosexuality in Oxbridge colleges. Now female educators were suspect for both hetero- and homosexuality.

The Foundations of Nursing and Social Work

The middle class of the 1800s could remain unaware of the plight of the poor only by blinding themselves to it. Middle- and upper-class men had the political power to change the situation, but the poor could only agitate, threatening collective action, or attract sympathy by dying visibly in great numbers. They did both, and if most prosperous people averted their gaze, some tried to alleviate the situation. Male legislators passed laws to ease problems; men organized agencies dedicated to social welfare. Women formed organizations to press for legal change and did social work with the poor, usually directly.

Charitable work was permeated with class distinctions. Men and women established Protestant religious orders for women in high church (Anglican) and low (Evangelicals and Dissenters). Most low-church women started simple institutes to train, coordinate, and pay small wages to devout single working-class women who became visiting nurses (who also propagandized for religion). Middle- and upper-class women joined sisterhoods founded and dominated by high- and low-church male clerics, who dominated the public aspect and expected religious women to obey them in all church matters. But deaconesses and sisters carved out areas of expertise and power in male-dominated churches.

Middle-class women, who had been raised by money to a status "above nature," might patronize, despise, or fear lower-class women as an inferior species. But some began to work with them, albeit condescendingly. They helped some poor women, but they were also helping themselves. Their activities constitute the first major example of female solidarity across classes; their interaction forced both to recognize that their problems were often similar. This recognition fueled the first large-scale feminist movement in history. For the first time since the emergence of patriarchy, women broke class and color lines to support each other.

In 1813 Elizabeth Fry (1780–1845), a Quaker minister, wife of a banker and mother of (eventually) ten children, visited Newgate Prison. Three hundred women and their children, confined in two squalid wards, cooked, washed, ate, excreted, and slept on bare floors. The wards and their nearly naked occupants stank with filth. Without guide or precedent, Fry determined to amend these women's conditions and help them earn a living upon their release. She organized middle-class female volunteers to donate supplies and visit the prison every day; with the donated materials, the prisoners made clothes that Fry arranged to sell in a prison shop run by the volunteers. Profits went to the prisoners—half when their work was sold, half at their release. Fry also set up a school to teach children and young women to read, knit, and sew, and had cleaning equipment brought in for prisoners to scrub the wards and do laundry every Saturday. Contemporaries watched Newgate women's wards transformed into a well-run family or workshop.

A known expert on prison reform, Fry was called to testify on the subject, and visited almost every European country as a prison consultant. But British lawmakers favored strict discipline and a "silent system," and did not heed her. In 1833, Fry founded a refuge for women prisoners at Kaiserswerth, near Dusseldorf, with German pastor Theodor Fliedner and his wife. This developed into a medical center with a lunatic asylum, orphanage, infirmary, and hospital to train nurses, teachers, and "poor visitors" (welfare workers). By 1870 forty-two havens modeled on Kaiserswerth had been built and womaned with "sisters." Florence Nightingale, heroine of her age, fought to train there.[21]

Nineteenth-century hospitals were filthy corrupt warehouses full of the dying poor, tended by old or alcoholic women, often ex-prostitutes. Authorities believed women had innate abilities to teach and nurse, yet they did not want ladies trained or paid, and discouraged pioneers who wanted to reform hospitals and nursing, which required recruiting and training a different kind of nurse. Florence Nightingale (1820–1910) transformed nursing from the most menial to the most exalted female job.

Believing no one but a sister would willingly do such work, the educated public identified nursing with religious commitment. Sisterhoods worked the way the public most admired—without pay. English reformers thronged to Kaiserswerth; and French Roman Catholic nuns and German Lutheran deaconesses initiated wide-scale reform movements, setting new standards of sanitation and conscientiousness. During an 1848 cholera epidemic in Devonport, Lydia Sellon set up a sisterhood to help the poor, and St. John's nurse training school opened in London.

Nightingale, of a wealthy pious family, was deeply religious; she heard a "call from God" when she was seventeen, but could not then act on it. Endowed with the energy and intellect of a genius, she found the life of a middle-class woman stifling to the point of death. "The family is . . . too narrow a field for the development of an immortal spirit, be that spirit male or female," she wrote in *Cassandra*. She rejected marriage with young journalist Richard Monckton Milnes because she did not want to live "someone else's life."[22] But she could not break away from her family (and did not until her thirties) or yet know what she wanted to do.

After a despairing youth, at the age of thirty-one she wrote in anguish, "What am I that [other women's] life is not good enough for me? Oh God what am I? . . . Why, oh my God cannot I be satisfied with the life that satisfies so many people? I am told that the conversation of all these good clever men ought to be enough for me. Why am I starving, desperate, diseased on it?" A year later, she had moved from guilt and self-hatred to criticism of society: "Why have women passion, intellect, moral activity—these three—and a place in society where no one of the three can be exercised?"[23]

She found herself when she decided to train as a nurse. Overcoming many obstacles, she studied at Kaiserswerth and Paris. When England went to war with Russia in 1854, she hounded the government to let her nurse the wounded. She took thirty-eight nurses to the Crimea, where they tended 10,000 men. (Of these nurses, twenty-four were Anglican or Roman Catholic.) Although Britain won the war, 118,000 British and allied soldiers died of cholera and other illnesses. Nightingale knew many deaths had been caused by poor sanitary conditions, which she had tried to improve. In 1856, on her return to England, she was celebrated as a national hero. Her fame enabled her to raise money to establish the Nightingale School of Nursing at St. Thomas' Hospital in London. She dedicated the rest of her life to raising standards in nursing and hospital care in the British Army, London slums, and India. Publicly she was self-sacrificing, but it was her adventurousness that inspired young girls of her period to make her their role model.

Nightingale opened her school in 1860 with fifteen pupils. She believed the key to improved medical care was hospital organization and staff training, and she made innovations that are now standard practice (describing them in an 1869 book).[24] Nurses had no rooms at hospitals, but slept in the same wards as male or female patients, or in wooden cages on landings. Nightingale had a wing built in St. Thomas' Hospital as a nurse's residence, and required that night nurses be given rest time during the day. She also demanded hot and cold water throughout the hospital, elevators, and other conveniences. Modeling her staff on the army, she treated trainees like soldiers at war against disease, dirt, and sin.

Nightingale chose St. Thomas' for her school because she trusted its matron, Mrs. Wardroper, who had reformed the nursing staff as soon as she was appointed in 1854. As Nightingale's "general," she helped set up a program requiring each probationer to account minutely for her time and undergo monthly evaluations of progress *and moral character* which entailed harsh punishments for trespasses like "making eyes" or wearing untidy uniforms. Probationers worked a fifteen-hour day, seven days a week, rising at 6:00 a.m., breakfasting, and making fourteen beds and washing each patient between 7:00 and 8:00. The ward sister came on duty at 8:00 and read prayers, then the "pros" washed all ward utensils—dressing bowls, spittoons, bedpans, et al.; at 10:00 they gave out snacks and helped with dressings. At 12:45, as they gobbled dinner to have time for rest, the ward nurse and sister served the patients in the ward.

At 1:30 the doctor made rounds with students. This godly being was waited on by a sister carrying an inkpot and a pro with a basin of water in which the doctor washed his hands after touching patients. Dedicated pros listened carefully to him, hoping to learn something about medicine. After some free time at 3:30 and a tea hour, they returned to the ward to wash patients again and prepare them for the night, applying new dressings, poultices, and liniments. New patients were usually admitted then. At 8:30 a quick supper, at 9:00 prayers, and then they could relax, write letters, read, and study. They also had to attend lectures squeezed in haphazardly, sometimes at 8:30. Study too had to be crammed into the few free hours. Lights went out at 10:30. Pros were assigned to a ward for three months, and then shifted to night duty to learn to serve breakfast, roll bandages, and complete the day nurses' work. They had a rare free afternoon, but the regimen was designed to eliminate all but the most determined candidates.

Although nursing was promoted as sacred, hospitals retained their unsavory aura and nursing its dubious status until the 1880s, when reform changed their reputations. But sheltered middle-class women were not drawn to nursing until Nightingale's model was widely adopted. Then, the profession grew so fast that by the end of the century nursing had become a major female occupation along with teaching, shop sales, and clerking, and the one respectable job open to women that did not offer competition to men. In the 1860s and 1870s nurses were paid more than any other women workers, and trained nurses advanced rapidly because they were in short supply. By the 1890s, however, they earned less than teachers or social workers. And by 1900 nurses everywhere were poorly fed and overworked, treated with utter indifference. Their complaints—execrable living conditions, long hours, and low pay—were dismissed as reflecting a lack of devotion.

Matrons, who made all decisions regarding nurses, tried to give the profession prestige *by eliminating working-class women*! When matrons in London's voluntary hospitals spoke of "raising standards," they meant having only single "ladies" in the field, a longer training period, and more rigorous rules and discipline. Nursing leaders exploited Victorian women's belief in their self-sacrificing nature: they probably shared it. Nurses' poor food, long hours, and low pay fit women's image of commitment, spirituality, and piety. Martha Vicinus argues that of all female occupations, only nursing broke the rule of separate spheres. Nurses worked daily with male professional or social equals, so nursing leaders had to create a place for women in a male world. Yet nursing is a preeminent example of separate and unequal spheres: in hospitals today female doctors are still regularly taken for nurses.

Religious Orders and Prostitution

Women were drawn to religious communities by a longing for spiritual fulfillment or because they had worked informally in philanthropy and wanted to work more effectively in an organization. Some wanted the safety of a uniform: women were not supposed to walk in the streets alone, but a uniformed sister or deaconess, instantly recognized as a nurse, home visitor, or missionary, was protected by her uniform in body and reputation. Thus armored, a woman could venture into the world alone, walk slum streets—experience "life" raw.

In the 1840s William Gladstone (a member of Parliament, later prime minister), seeing sisterhoods as a way to enable women to do good works while controlling them, proposed, along with other laymen and clerics, the foundation of an Anglican sisterhood. The first Anglican order, "Park Village Sisters," was founded in 1845; most women who joined came from rural parishes and market towns across England and had been reared in large, authoritarian families with patriarchal religions. Used to surveillance and obedience, they adapted easily to religious communities, even over family opposition.

Anglican sisterhoods imposed severe rules on their members: rigorous training for one to three years, separation from kin and friends, constant surveillance of their spiritual devotion, behavior, and relations with others. Sisters were not trained in theology: choir sisters (wealthy women) learned a complex set of services; lay sisters (poor women) the correct way to clean and pray. They had little free time and rarely deviated from regulated prayer, work, eating, sleep, and recreation.

Some sisterhoods founded and ran institutions like hospitals, orphanages, schools, and penitentiaries. The Sisters of the People lived together and went to the slums every day to work with the poor. The largest, the Wesleyan Sisters of the People, was founded in 1887 for devout educated Methodist women who wanted to work as teachers, nurses, and missionaries. There were others: Roman Catholic sisters worked alongside sisters from the Salvation Army in the London streets. All female church workers except Anglican sisterhoods were controlled by local ministers; all wore uniforms and followed a regular worship schedule. By 1900 churches had full-time professional women.

But many criticized women who left home for being unwomanly and abandoning their domestic duties. Sisters and deaconesses worked so hard and lived so austerely that no one could say they left home for an easy life. On the contrary, it was apparent that such women *preferred* arduous labor and austerity to home life, which, as Nightingale wrote, was stultifying, boring, and unloving even for her, a favored daughter. This was hard for people who

idealized domesticity to swallow. Not recognizing that women have selves, they could not comprehend their accepting almost any hardship to freely choose their lives, live with some autonomy, and do meaningful work.

In this period syphilis ravaged the population; children were often born with the disease. In major cities 45 percent of men had syphilis and, according to one study, 120 percent had had gonorrhea; in another, one man in five had syphilis and many repeatedly caught gonorrhea. Of course they contaminated their wives.[25] Appalled doctors blamed prostitutes. Agreeing with W.R. Greg that prostitution was ineradicable, they tried to keep disease from spreading by regulating prostitutes' hygiene, as France did. During 1864 to 1869 Parliament passed the Contagious Diseases Acts, which required medical exams for prostitutes in garrison towns and ports. All known or suspected female prostitutes had to be examined periodically or risk up to three months in prison. A doctor wrote: "Prostitution is a transitory state, through which an untold number of British women are ever on their passage"—most later married.

Women in the orders were convinced that their innate moral superiority helped them to work with prostitutes. Low-church women worked with the poor, tended the sick and homeless, and reformed "fallen women." Society assumed that Evangelical women—educated, devout, "pure" Englishwomen—represented the highest form of Christianity, and simply by example could draw out the latent goodness in others. Actually, they were often ineffectual and self-righteously intrusive, although indefatigable, going out night after night to offer streetwalkers food, a place to stay, training, hoping for "rebirth" in Christ.

Sisterhoods set up slum missions and Homes of Refuge to *protect* "repentant" prostitutes. Prostitutes entered these penitentiaries voluntarily, but were prisoners once inside. They could never be "forgiven" and were not allowed to forget their "sin"; they were taught to define themselves by their history. Although the sisters were enacting maternal roles in a culture that glorified motherhood, their program was designed to crush the penitents' maternal feelings, ignoring their need to be mothered and placing their children in adoptive homes. Even if a penitent fully submitted to the discipline, she could never become a full member of the religious community. Penitents lived isolated from each other and from the sisters, who knew the poor were inferior to the upper classes. A measure of these women's privation is that some preferred the sisters' stern attentions to none at all and asked to stay permanently—especially older women who could no longer face the struggle of earning their living outside, or had no loved ones there. They were the sisters' "successes": a special "Magdalen" order was created for them to guard new arrivals.

After the 1870s attitudes toward prostitution began to change: people criticized the Houses' punitive approach and turned more attention to poor neighborhoods and children. Like penitentiaries, orphanages offered moral indoctrination, instead of trying to create a welcoming environment. The sisters physically cared for and disciplined children, to teach them to avoid sin (sex). They maintained class and sex status, teaching girls domestic skills, not job skills, and exhorting slum women to accept their position, not change it. Churches wanted large memberships, not social change.

The Professionalization of Philanthropic Work

By mid-century, women were doing social work outside religious orders. Wealth had increased and women with more leisure time sought useful work. Philanthropy opened life to them, enabling them to cross class lines, meet women of other classes, and observe poor people's private lives. The poor welcomed them into their homes, blaming women less than men for their oppression. Pioneers like Mary Carpenter, Louisa Twining, and Octavia Hill devised new approaches to child welfare, workhouse arrangements, and model housing. By the 1890s a leisure-class woman without volunteer work was a rarity. Charity work gave women a sense of purpose and the profound satisfaction of helping others; it exposed them to "real life" (from which class protected them), and was their only opening to public life. As charity groups and government bureaus offered more services, they needed professionals to guide and train a virtual army of volunteers—by 1893 about 20,000 British women worked full time and half a million part time in philanthropic projects.

Most active female social workers served as poor-law guardians, on school boards, and in low-level government offices, representing the interests of poor women and children. When they began to struggle for suffrage, women cited their experience with working-class women and children, effective leadership at the local level, and public service as proof that they were worthy of the vote (something men did not have to prove).

Mary Carpenter devoted her life to creating separate penal institutions for children; Louisa Twining successfully reformed poorhouses. Perhaps the most respected female reformer was Octavia Hill (1838–1912), who invented an approach to philanthropy that helped the poor through personal contact. With money from John Ruskin, Hill purchased a block of houses and rented them to poor families in 1865. She trained a corps of female volunteers to collect the rent each week and intervene in tenants' lives to help them find jobs and child apprenticeships, or to teach women housewifery and home decorating. Tenants who did not pay rent promptly were evicted; Hill was proud of guaranteeing a 5 percent return on investment in model housing. But most slum landlords earned twice that and were not induced to imitate her.

In the 1860s Hill founded the Charity Organisation Society (COS), a key organization intended to umbrella overlapping London charities. Its approach accorded with Hill's notions of self-help. It investigated all appeals for help: a volunteer visited each applicant with a questionnaire and wrote a case report. A committee determined who deserved aid. Evidence that kin could help an applicant or that a family member drank meant automatic rejection, but the respectable few who were accepted were given full assistance, which was followed up by investigations and reports. The poor hated the attitude of superiority permeating the COS, and asked for aid only when desperate; the COS hated and attacked groups that simply gave money directly to the poor. Hill's approach was adopted by government welfare agencies of that period in the United States.

Other approaches existed. Socialist and pacifist women founded settlement houses on different lines or crusaded for reforms, working alone or with friends. They pioneered school health inspections, kindergartens, open-air schools for sickly children, and clinics for pre- and post-natal care. But all settlements attracted idealists willing to sacrifice their comfort in the belief that middle-class virtues would "improve" the poor. These "settlers"—as they were known—had no idea that the poor had something to offer their "betters." They wanted to do good, but were imbued with contemporary society's values. Their metaphors came from colonial wars: middle-class women "purified" the slums by their mere presence, "purging" evil under the banner of cleanliness. Like colonists, they "civilized" slum "natives" with sanitation and middle-class speech, deportment, and manners. While their brothers emigrated to colonize exotic places, sisters "emigrated" to the wilds of the East End.

But in fact the process *was* mutual: charity work gave women freedom. No other work—teaching, nursing, or mission work—gave them the mobility to move in forbidden districts. Seeing life up close, they touched reality and brushed danger, adventure, in a way not otherwise possible. Also, they could dress and eat simply and use simple manners without losing respectability. Not until after the First World War did "settler" Muriel Lester work up the courage to walk on Regent Street (in London's fashionable West End) without gloves; yet in the East End, settlers had gone without gloves and hats in the summer for decades. In the slums, middle-class women could walk the streets in safety because they were known as ladies: accent, posture, and demeanor marked them as settlers. Settler women got back as much as they gave.

In time, social workers had to acknowledge that their best efforts were inadequate to the problem. Whatever they did, they could not erase the fact that a third of the people in the world's richest city lived in destitution. By 1910 they were seeking other remedies, mainly suffrage, hoping that a voice in the laws of the state might enable women to deal with the hunger and ill health that were rife in slum neighborhoods. Many organizations investigated working-class women's conditions. The Fabian Women's Group, founded in 1908, studied how wives spent the money their husbands gave them, and proved conclusively that they could not feed, clothe, and house their families on their paltry allowances. Other studies of women factory workers, shop clerks, and servants arrived at similar conclusions. Socialist thinkers argued for sweeping change in tax law and government services.

But as government took over philanthropy, it marginalized or drove out the women who had created it. Virtually all settlers were single women with a wish to help women and children; they had instituted child welfare, schools for the handicapped, and mothers' services. Women's settlement leaders tried to make philanthropy a paid profession, opening schools to train social workers. But payment of trained settlers was erratic and very low until after the First World War. Professionalization of work invariably transforms it. Just as professionalization of medicine narrowed its scope and excluded all but Christian males, professionalization of social work narrowed its scope and put men in charge.

Professional social workers saw themselves as experts on poverty, superior to both nonprofessionals and their clients; they were concerned primarily with methods and systems, ignoring community and friendship. Even women who felt that government institutionalization of the work was necessary were unhappy working for the state, doing more bureaucratic work and having less personal contact with clients. The state put women in subordinate positions, preparing cases, managing centers, or staffing offices; women were assigned mundane tasks and had no control over policy, which was entirely in men's hands. The British government's failure to consult settlers with their extensive knowledge about and connections with those it was trying to help transformed philanthropy from a personal expression of middle-class benevolence to an impersonally managed bureaucracy.

CHAPTER 5

MIDDLE-CLASS WOMEN IN THE UNITED STATES BEFORE THE CIVIL WAR

THE VALUES URGED ON AMERICANS were similar to those urged on British women. The cult of domesticity was powerful in the United States, and if class was less important than in England, slavery and racism were more so. In the United States as in England laws were passed to alleviate the woes of industrialization and women's legalized victimization. And in the United States too, women were among the first to point out similarities in the condition of poor people and women.

Women Writers in England and the United States

Writing, especially fiction, was a major means for middle-class women to urge social change. Writers can call attention to a situation, and arouse sympathy or propose solutions for it. Most men who wrote about poverty offered prescriptions—W.R. Greg, for instance, urged women to become servants. Women, on the other

hand, wrote mainly to elicit sympathy for the poor; women pioneered the "social protest" novel. Most of the men who followed them are remembered; the women are not (although a few have recently been resuscitated). Yet women's social protest novels were well written, had great impact, and were primarily responsible for bringing the injustice and inhumanity of social and economic conditions to the attention of a wide audience.

Women invented social protest fiction and dominated the form throughout the nineteenth century.[1] Historians date protest from Thomas Carlyle's 1839 statement: "A feeling very generally exists that the condition and disposition of the Working Classes is a rather ominous matter at present; that something ought to be said, something ought to be done, in regard to it."[2] But long before that, Hannah More had written *The Lancashire Collier Girl* (1795), Maria Edgeworth *Castle Rackrent* (1800) and *The Absentee* (1812), Harriet Martineau *The Rioters* (1827) and *The Turn-out* (1829), and Charlotte Tonna *The System* (1827). As Carlyle's monograph was being printed, Frances Trollope's *Michael Armstrong, the Factory Boy* and Tonna's *Helen Fleetwood* were appearing in serial form in English journals.[3] Middle-class women began writing out of pity for the downtrodden, perhaps identifying with the disenfranchised. But they gradually recognized their shared oppression. Elaine Showalter dates this awareness to around 1880, when women began to depict men's domination of women along with economic oppression, and a new set of feminist writers appeared: Charlotte Brontë, Elizabeth Gaskell, and George Eliot.[4]

Like men, female authors varied in background, religion, and political leaning. Some, like Tonna, stressed female domesticity (she condemned preferential hiring of women over men for demeaning it). Eliot was agnostic, Tonna ardently Low Church Evangelical, Gaskell Unitarian. But all were deeply concerned with human well-being. Trollope and Tonna depicted women with large families, Elizabeth Stone and Geraldine Jewsbury, uneducated women; Stone, Gaskell, and Fanny Mayne portrayed vulnerable working-

and lower-middle-class orphans and motherless girls. All vividly portrayed the futility and tedium of middle-class women's lives, the misery of being confined to domestic labor, and the disaster of being seduced and abandoned. Forced by censorship (unofficial but more severe for women than men) to omit or skim over sex or brutality, they nevertheless presented life in more concrete detail than male novelists working with similar material (Benjamin Disraeli or Charles Kingsley, for example) and far more accurately presented women's friendships and interactions across class lines.

Americans were slower than the British to depict class or sex oppression, but, as in England, women did so before men and were consigned to oblivion. Rebecca Harding Davis (1831–1910) published *Life in the Iron Mills* in 1861. The daughter of a well-to-do mill manager in Wheeling (in West Virginia, a border state), and bound by the constrictions placed on young middle-class women, she spent tedious hours gazing out the front window of the Harding house as "long trains of mules dragged their masses of pig iron and the slow stream of human life crept past, night and morning, year after year, to work their fourteen-hour days six days a week."[5] *Life in the Iron Mills* claustrophobically depicts the stifling of a working-class man with the potential to create art. Tillie Olsen believes that Davis wrote the novel in utter identification with "thwarted, wasted lives . . . mighty hungers [and] unawakened power."

Davis married for love and often supported her family by writing, yet her husband treated her as a subordinate. Her son, a writer too, was more famous but less accomplished. Davis wrote until she died at seventy-nine, but the only literary journal even to mention her passing was *The New York Times*, which noted that the mother of Richard Harding Davis had died. The *Times* obituary recalled that *Life in the Iron Mills* had "attracted attention from all over the country . . . many thought the author must be a man. The stern but artistic realism of the picture she put alive upon paper, suggested a man, and a man of power not unlike Zola's." Olsen's comment: "They did not mention that she had preceded Zola by two

decades."

However, women novelists were gradually excluded from the literary establishment. Before 1840 many women wrote good novels that were financially successful.[6] After their work won respect for fiction as a form, men became attracted to its lucrative rewards and edged women out of the field. A male elite of editors redefined the novel as "Art" and claimed it as men's territory, dismissing women's fiction as fit for "mass audiences, passive entertainment, and flutter." Fewer women were published, and even fewer were successful, after the 1840s; only a few were admitted into the sanctified precinct of art.

The Economic and Political Background

The United States was run by large landowners and capitalist merchants from the time of independence until 1801, when the Democratic-Republican party elected Thomas Jefferson president. Jefferson's party worked to abolish privileges of birth, wealth, and established religion. Wanting rights extended to all citizens, they successfully campaigned to add a Bill of Rights to the Constitution. As the country grew richer, divisions of class and urban and rural populations widened, but there was a safety valve—a new frontier. Jefferson's 1803 purchase of "Louisiana" doubled the size of the country; settlement of the Northwest Territory—western New York and Ohio (and later the southwest, taken from Mexico)—gave the poor and dispossessed a chance at independence in a largely classless society.

In 1829 antiprivilege Democrats made Andrew Jackson president. Declaring all men politically equal (except slaves, Native Americans, and women), they fought for universal white male suffrage and election (not appointment) of government officials. In the first half of the century, the thousands of immigrants thronging to the United States from Scotland and England assimilated easily. But after the 1840s Irish fleeing the famine, Germans, and other

Europeans encountered bias against their religion or language. No law demanded it, but all institutions, schools, and courts used English. People who worked outside the home picked up enough to get by, but homebound women did not and suffered doubly, living in poverty in an alien land, cut off from communication.

American laws denied women any rights, and legal change was painfully slow, state by state. In 1855 Michigan revised its laws to let married women keep and manage their earnings and property; New York passed a similar law in 1860, other states later. These laws created a new class: women with property but not franchised. Qualified by property standards, they were prevented by their sex from voting, serving on juries, or holding public office. Not until 1911 did a Michigan law grant married women the right to choose to work for wages; before that, husbands determined whether or not their wives could do waged work. The first new laws granted married women control over inheritances and gifts, not over the wealth they helped accrue in a farm or business.

Nineteenth-century American women followed the same pattern as British women: accepting men's definition of them as morally superior domestic creatures, they used it as a lever to smash barriers by extending the meaning of "domestic." In the United States too, single women first opened new professions to women and here too, women's dominance of congregations and "Great Awakenings" gave them confidence in their right and ability to speak and act publicly. But American women had another tool. The men who denied them political rights gave them a sop, honoring them as "Republican Mothers" and granting them education. Now women used revolutionary rhetoric to justify reforms like abolition and the franchise.

Women in Protestant sects founded missionary and charitable societies, converting neighbors, kin, and friends and forming tight-knit circles determined to purify the world by ending prostitution, intemperance, or slavery. They challenged male appropriation of church leadership: as early as 1850, Antoinette Blackwell earned a divinity degree from Oberlin College, becoming the first U.S. female minister (but Oberlin Divinity School did not accept another woman for nearly forty years). Still, by 1880, 165 women were accredited ministers—the Universalist Church alone had thirty-five.

Unlike British women, American women leaders rejected religious orthodoxy. Quakerism, the most egalitarian religion, supported liberal causes, raising women's confidence by encouraging them to speak at meetings. In the first half of the nineteenth century, agrarian Quakers strongly advocated Indian rights, communitarianism, abolition, and temperance.[7] Of fifty-one leading feminist abolitionist leaders, twenty-one were raised in Quaker, Universalist, or Unitarian families.[8] Most leaders raised in orthodox or evangelical sects left them for these churches or none. Quakerism had lost its egalitarian edge: men increasingly dominated meetings, relegating women to a separate, subordinate sphere. When these women organized to aid the sick, poor, orphans, homeless women, or slaves, they based their right to speak and act not on religion, but on female moral superiority. Still, when the feminist movement exploded in the United States in 1848, a large percentage of its members were Quakers.[9]

American Women Use Their Education

In Education

Protestants let women learn to read so they could teach children religion, not realizing that women turn any instrument they are given to their own purposes. Literate women wanted their daughters educated, but no institution of higher learning would take them until Emma Willard opened a seminary in Troy, New York, in 1821. She taught her students they were intellectually equal to men, and she traveled tirelessly, lecturing, giving workshops, promoting education.[10] Her graduates founded or taught in schools across the country; over 200 schools founded in this period were modeled on Willard's "Troy ideal."[11] In 1837 Mary Lyons founded Mount Holyoke, in Massachusetts, considered the oldest women's college in the United States, and Oberlin became the first co-educational college in the country (but female students had to clean rooms and do laundry for male students!). Massachusetts opened the first state normal school (teachers'college), Lexington Academy, in 1839.

In the struggle for higher education, women often used the argument of female moral superiority. Even the assertive Willard advocated "true womanhood" as the goal of female education (but more of her graduates had careers and they had fewer children than less-educated women). Sophia Smith founded Smith College in Massachusetts in the hope that "the higher and more thoroughly Christian education of women" would prepare them to purge "the evils of society," especially "the filth" in literature. But some women wanted knowledge, not True Womanhood. The first woman's literary club in the United States was formed in 1837 in Lowell, Massachusetts, that hotbed of female solidarity.

The career of educator Catherine Beecher was a paradox: she spent her life in the public realm *urging other women to stay home*. The sister of novelist Harriet Beecher Stowe, Beecher believed women could influence society by teaching, and she built schools across the country, concentrating on the educationally deprived frontier. She would persuade backwoods communities to fund schools, then staff them with her protegées. Her *Domestic Economy* was the most popular and important housewifery text of the antebellum period.

Women thronged to teaching, the one profession by which single middle-class women could live independently. By 1870 they made up over half the 200,000 primary and secondary school teachers in the country. Of course, they were paid half as much as men, at best 60 percent, and "feminization" had its usual effect (the more women, the lower the status and pay). Women were also kept at the lowest echelons: by 1850 they dominated grammar-school teaching, but were only slowly hired by secondary schools and colleges and almost totally excluded from administrative jobs. White Anglo-Saxon women began to be promoted (in negligible numbers until the mid-twentieth century) only after women from other ethnic backgrounds entered the field. In the 1880s female teachers were dismissed for marrying: working-class women, black and white, were allowed to do backbreaking labor whether married or single, but "ladies" with husbands were not permitted to work for pay.

There were some advantages to living in a country without traditions. The British used tradition to exclude women from schools, but the American educational system was just forming, and many new colleges followed Oberlin in accepting women—Antioch (1852), University of Iowa (1856), Swarthmore (1864), and others out west. By 1880 nearly half of U.S. colleges accepted both sexes. Still, most new land-grant colleges had a "gender-differentiated" curriculum. In 1865 forty-one male and no female students were enrolled in traditional college courses, and sixty-six women and no men in the normal school at the University of Wisconsin. Old prestigious men's colleges opened sister schools with second-class status. In 1874 Harvard opened Radcliffe; although its students were taught by Harvard faculty, they were barred from Harvard College libraries. In 1889 Barnard opened with its own faculty, but students used Columbia University's library and other facilities. In 1887 Tulane opened Sophie Newcomb College, which was emulated in 1891 by Pembroke/Brown.

The career of Graceanna Lewis of Media, Pennsylvania, illustrates the difficulties erudite women faced in this time. An ornithologist and scientific illustrator, Lewis applied for a job on the Swarthmore College science faculty in the early 1860s. When a male naturalist also applied, Lewis withdrew, feeling less competent than he. Maria Mitchell, professor of astronomy at Vassar, urged Lewis to apply for a similar position there. Lewis had to have an income—she supported herself by teaching in a high school—and the Vassar job would give her professional recognition and status. John Cassin, curator of birds at the Academy of Natural Science in Philadelphia, and Spencer Baird, secretary of the Smithsonian, wrote strong letters supporting her, but she was rejected in favor of a male geologist. She went on working and in 1868 published the first of a projected ten-volume *Natural History of Birds*, a catalog and general scientific treatise on ornithological classification. Its critical and popular success led to invitations to present papers at the American Association for the Advancement of Science.[12]

This triumph would have assured a man a prosperous career, and in 1870 Lewis was nominated for the Philadelphia Academy of Natural Science, supported by George Tryon, ornithology curator, and by librarian Edward Nolan. She was rejected, but a week later the board reversed its decision, admitting Lewis and two other women. Important as this was to her status, she had to earn a living. Still unable to get a job in a college, she returned to teaching in a high school. But she was too old and learned for such work: intellectually, emotionally, and physically drained by living at a girls' boarding school, she fell ill in 1871 with "an affection of the brain." For two years she lay in bed, attended by her sister, Dr. Rebecca Fussell, sliding into invalidism.

In succumbing to the overwhelming social pressure against independent women, Lewis became a statistic in a campaign to prove that learning was injurious to females. While women tirelessly strove for learning, male debate raged around them, deprecating their capacities while ignoring what they actually achieved. Marshaling "facts" from biology and neurology, academics and scientists "proved" women to be physiologically and intellectually inferior to men. One authority reported that average male European brains weighed forty-nine grams and female brains only forty-four grams: ergo, women were intellectually inferior to men. The greatest threat was that Woman, formed around a uterus, would damage it with study. Massachusetts-based Edward Clarke argued that women, being creatures of their bodies, must limit other activities to realize their biological destiny, motherhood. His best-selling *Sex in Education* (1873) used Darwin and Spencer to give sexism and misogyny a scientific basis. He cited studies of college women to demonstrate that education had given them dysmenorrhea, acute and chronic ovaritis, *prolapsus uteri*, hysteria, and neuralgia *inter alia.*

In Writing

Yet women built successful careers in journalism and literature in this period. Wide female literacy led to a veritable explosion of periodical literature for women in this century, magazines dealing with motherhood, housekeeping, health, recreation, morality and religion, reform, fashion . . . everything but politics. Editors dictated the style and substance of such journals, and many of their editors and writers were women. Some "female" literature contained progressive ideas, and many female writers openly scorned males, but the progressives were not the scorners. Scorn for males is so pronounced in some pieces that today's critics call them feminist. But just as the women who express most scorn for men today are right-wing women who feel that abortion enables men to evade their responsibilities, the nineteenth-century women who most condemned men and their realm were those who most exalted domesticity and motherhood. Feminist journals were *in competition with* those that exalted mothers and homemakers.

It was in this period that people began to define feminism as a political movement that aimed at equality for women in the public realm and was hostile to traditional "feminine" values and culture. Simultaneously, advocates of domesticity developed value systems hostile to the male world, challenging male hegemony by stressing feminine values and female culture. The conceptual division of women's movements into a "feminist" struggle for political equality and a "feminine" struggle for a protected moral-domestic sphere remains a damaging fissure in female solidarity.

To the chagrin of authors like Nathaniel Hawthorne (who sneered at "scribbling women"), women dominated the literary market in the nineteenth-century United States, outselling Hawthorne and other men. Male critics horrified by women writers' "unfemininely bitter wrath" belittled their work and subject matter, ignoring it when they could. Scholars re-evaluating women's work today discover critical prejudice against both female authors and female form. Male-oriented critics accept only one pattern as fulfillling the conditions of art: a single figure is pitted against his environment, struggles, and wins or tragically loses. Life is a battle waged in lonely exile for a personal goal. This is the pattern adopted by most male writers. Women tend to see life as experience suffered, enjoyed, endured; their protagonists usually live amid a community that eases their struggle or pain.[13] Male novels, like male histories, tend to exemplify male power; female writing tends to describe the quality of experience. Critics decreed only one kind of legitimate, excellent, Art. Emily Dickinson (1830–1886), arguably the greatest U.S. poet, remained virtually unpublished all her life.

It was women who wrote the first social protest novels in the United States as well as in England. While some women writers idealized domesticity and sentimentalized family relationships, others wrote harsh books about women locked in cruel marriages, their arduous manual labor and economic dependence. Their most common image was the villainous husband. Mary Virginia Terhune (Marion Harland), Catharine Maria Sedgwick, Lydia Sigourney, Caroline Gilman, and E.D.E.N. Southworth, as well as other ancestors of the great female writers of the end of the century—Willa Cather, Ellen Glasgow, Harriet Beecher Stowe, and Kate Chopin—produced novels of power and import.

It was hard for Victorian women to see themselves as serious writers. Catharine Sedgwick denied that she cared about her craft or was concerned with style, or that the reception of her work mattered to her emotionally or financially: "My *author* existence has always seemed something accidental, extraneous, independent of my inner self. My books have been a pleasant occupation and excitement in my life . . . but they constitute no portion of my happiness." Edith Wharton lived later, yet never lost a sense of shame about her work. She was famous and supported many people but concealed the act of writing much as Jane Austen concealed her texts with embroidery. Wharton worked in bed mornings, and appeared downstairs beautifully groomed and ready for the day, about eleven. In her autobiography (1934), she made light of her writing. Her disavowal of serious intention eased the way for male critics eager to belittle women writers to dismiss her work after she died. Although important in her time, she was barely remembered by 1950. Only recently has her greatness been recognized.

Critic Ann Douglas claims nineteenth-century American culture was "feminized" by a sentimentalism that diminished our really great (i.e., male) authors and produced modern consumerist culture—ads and sitcoms depicting happy families with happy problems.[14] She does not discuss how politics dictate literary standards (including her own), or consider men's exclusion of women from modern culture. Douglas blames the women who tried to uphold humane standards and a vision of felicity for the victory of the power-seeking makers of modern culture who exploit and degrade such standards in the marketplace.

In the Arts

Writers learn by reading widely and exercising their skill. Graphic artists and musicians, however, must learn technical skills. In the past, most female artists, composers, and musicians were related to men who were trained in an art. Eight American female artists, for example, were related to artists—the nieces, granddaughters, and a daughter-in-law of Charles Wilson Peale, daughters of Gilbert Stuart and Thomas Sully, and Thomas Cole's sister earned their livings as painters.[15] Women were not sent to art school or apprenticed to masters no matter how much talent they showed, so their only possible way of learning was from male kin. Few women were able to study abroad as men did, and in any case, art teachers so disregarded female pupils that they would undermine the confidence needed for a career in art. A woman who overcame all these obstacles still had hardship surviving: over half the women in the New York Historical Society's *Dictionary of American Artists: 1564–1860* were financially dependent on male kin because they were paid so little for their work.

Two art schools that took women opened in 1851–52: the Philadelphia School of Design and Cooper Union Institute School of Design for Women in New York. But women were still barred from life classes—the sex that gives birth was forbidden to look upon the naked human body! Such barriers continued into the twentieth century: Canadian painter Emily Carr, born in 1899, wrote about them in *Growing Pains*.[16] Women continued to challenge this taboo or tried to compensate for the handicap by attending anatomy lectures at medical schools to acquire the detailed anatomical knowledge that they needed. Most accepted what they could not change, and painted flowers, still lifes, portraits, and miniatures.

A few American woman sculptors were successful in the 1850s—an extraordinary accomplishment given the requirements of the field. Since sculptors *had* to study abroad, they needed money; and they needed commissions for work. In short, they needed people of means with confidence in them. Harriet Hosmer, Vinnie Ream, Emma Stebbins, and Edmonia Lewis all became successful sculptors. The government commissioned Ream to design memorials to Abraham Lincoln and Admiral Farragut; New York City commissioned Stebbins' "Angel of the Waters" for Central Park. Lewis, half-black, half-Indian, born on a Chippewa homeland in upstate New York, studied at Oberlin and in Rome, and was the first black artist to become nationally known, especially for a bust of H.W. Longfellow.

Hosmer, the most famous of the four, was supported by her physician father, a teacher and patron. Critics attributed Hosmer's "Zenobia" to a man; she sued, but rumors persisted that she had not created the work. She was charged with indecency for portraying a female naked: a critic wrote, "Her want of modesty is enough to disgust a dog. She has casts for the entire female model made and exhibited in a shockingly indecent manner."

American women expressed their creativity in traditional female arts, embroidery, lacemaking, and quilting, which they made a fine art. A quilter frequently plans her design, chooses her pattern and colors, and collects fabric scraps by herself, but nineteenth-century quilters met in female networks to sew. The quilting bee, popular in the United States, offered companionship to women who were isolated in households, and gave them a chance to use their skills to create useful objects. Quilts traditionally copied set designs but many nineteenth-century quilters illustrated narratives or events. Quilters sometimes signed their work (they were not naïve artists), which then became heirlooms handed down over generations. Not until the late twentieth century were they acknowledged to be works of art.

In Medicine

The profession that attracted American women in the greatest numbers was medicine. As in England, war provided the impetus for women to enter nursing. When the Civil War erupted in 1861, both northern and southern women mobilized. A Cooper Union rally drew more than 3000 New Yorkers, who founded the New York Central Association of Relief, governed by a board of twenty-five, of which twelve were women. They oversaw the collection and distribution of supplies and trained nurses to work in hospitals and on battlefields. This agency, one of 7000 in the Sanitary Commission, was the most important and effective institution created by women during the war. It ran fairs, bazaars, and large two-week fairs in major cities; with the millions it raised, it bought supplies for poor soldiers, widows, and orphans. Southern women made similar efforts, but were less successful.

Women were effective enough that both Confederate president Jefferson Davis and Union president Abraham Lincoln gave them official ranks. In June 1861 Lincoln named Dorothea Dix Superintendent of Nurses for the Union Army. Knowing the social pressure she was up against, Dix stipulated that applicants be at least thirty and "plain." Attractive women (and male patients) protested, but Dix wanted to avert potential attacks on moral grounds. Attacks were still made, but thousands of women (among them author

Louisa May Alcott) volunteered. Some wanted to experience the adventure and danger of war; others wanted work that gave them dignity. Still others, their livelihoods destroyed by a war that took men from marriage and farm, needed the 40 cents a day, food, shelter, and transport that came with the job.

Nurses left their hospital wards to tend men on the battlefields, but had to *fight* to help; military regulations barred them, and doctors preferred to let men die rather than accept female help. Only the wounded welcomed nurses, and despite their great contributions, army nurses were eventually eliminated. Independently of the army, Clara Barton nursed and single-handedly raised thousands of dollars for food and medical help for Union soldiers. Barton, single, thrived on this work; after she was ousted in 1863, she became an invalid. In 1870, when the Franco-Prussian War broke out, Barton seized the chance to organize nursing aid. At its end in 1871, her health failed again, and she lost her eyesight. For ten years she languished—until she conceived the idea of a medical group that crossed national lines in emergencies. Founding the first American Red Cross chapter in Danville, Massachussetts, restored her energy and well-being.

Southerners were even more appalled than northerners at "ladies" tending "ruffians" (their own soldiers): most Confederate enlisted men (and wounded) were lower class. But southern women brushed off all objections, helping all soldiers: one said, "A woman's respectability must be at low ebb if it can be endangered by going into a hospital." Some brought slaves along to help and protect them. The single Sally Tompkins turned a friend's house in Richmond, Virginia, into a twenty-two-room infirmary. It flourished after Davis made her a Confederate Army captain. "Cap'n Sally" treated almost 1300 men over time, of whom only 75 died.

Nursing opened doors to white women only. In the 1890s white nursing leaders followed Britain in upgrading nursing by recruiting only middle-class women. The "professionalization" of nursing excluded blacks. Southern states barred black women from registering for examinations or gave them more difficult examinations. Racism justified whites' hiring black nurses but treating and paying them as servants. Black women could not even train as nurses until black hospitals and nurse training schools opened in the 1890s.[17] (Blacks were also barred from hospitals as patients—the great blues singer Bessie Smith died when no southern hospital would admit her.) When black health-care institutions opened, white professional groups refused their workers membership. White women were as responsible for such policies as men.

This situation continued until war again made men aware of women's skills. Mabel Keaton Staupers, a black nurses' advocate, was executive secretary of the National Association of Colored Graduate Nurses (NACGN) from 1934 to 1946. In 1945 the Surgeon-General of the Army threatened to draft nurses to fill the severe shortage. Staupers publicly confronted him, demanding that the army use black nurses. She generated huge public support for removing American health-care institutions' quotas for blacks (*that kind* of quota was acceptable). In time, once blacks were welcomed into the American Nurses' Association, they dissolved the NACGN. But recognizing that the American Nurses Association (ANA) marginalized and ignored them—very few black women held leadership jobs in the ANA—they founded the National Black Nurses' Association to solidify their voice and their lobby in 1971.

Conditions were worse for women who wanted to be doctors. Few women broke into the profession before the Civil War. The first American woman doctor, Elizabeth Blackwell, earned a medical degree from Geneva Medical College in 1849. She then studied in Europe, and returned in 1851 to New York, where she tried to start a medical practice. But male doctors shut hospital doors to her. With her sister Emily and Maria Zakrzewska (who later taught at New England Medical College for Women), who were also barred from practice, Blackwell founded the New York Infirmary for Women. Not even a desperate need for doctors during the Civil War could break men's prejudice against women, and no women were commissioned as physicians by either side until 1864, when Dr. Mary Walker was sent to the front at Chattanooga, Tennessee. Captured, she was traded for a Confederate physician and made supervisor of the Female Military Prison in Louisville. President Andrew Johnson gave her a medal.

Insurgent feminism provided the impetus for women in medicine. In 1849 the first feminist convention in Seneca Falls, New York, persuaded men to found the Central Medical College, a coeducational medical school in Syracuse, New York. Feminist philanthropists founded medical schools for women. Quaker activist Ann Preston worked tirelessly to raise money for the American Woman's Medical College in Philadelphia, founded in 1850 as the first medical school to offer a medical course and the M.D. to women. For over a decade, the Philadelphia County Medical Society denied it accreditation. Preston raised money from women to send promising young Emmeline Cleveland to study advanced obstetrics at the Paris Maternité Hospital. Preston founded the Woman's Hospital of Philadelphia, and on Cleveland's return she headed obstetrics at the college and became the first female surgeon in the United States at the hospital.

Like many practicing male doctors, Harriot K. Hunt was self-taught. After practicing medicine for fifteen years, she applied to Harvard Medical School in 1850. The faculty allowed her to attend lectures, but male students protested and the administration ousted her. Sexism is stronger even than money: in 1878, twenty-five years after Hunt's expulsion, when hundreds of women were already doctors, Marion Hovey offered Harvard $10,000 to admit women to its medical school. Harvard refused. The first elite institution to accept the carrot was Johns Hopkins, which accepted a large gift from Mary Garrett on condition that it train female physicians.

Medical school was a cruel and undermining harassment for women, and after they completed the academic work they still could not build practices. By barring women from hospitals, men effectively kept them from seriously practicing medicine: men *with-*

out formal training prospered better than formally trained women. Women fought state by state, lobbying legislatures and demanding that women's prisons and asylums (a new development) have woman doctors on staff. They finally prevailed by founding women's hospitals, the New York Infirmary for Women and Children (1854), and the New England Hospital for Women and Children (1862).

The first male-controlled hospital to hire a woman doctor was Mount Sinai, New York, which put Annie Angell, a graduate of the Women's College of New York Infirmary, on its staff in 1874. By the 1880s thousands of women were practicing medicine, but even hospitals that admitted women doctors allowed only one or two. Fearing female encroachment, male doctors urged reforms to improve and standardize medicine. Both sexes practiced medicine without licenses, but the reforms worked only to the exclusion of women.

In 1850 women made up 2 percent of the physicians in Boston. This number soared after they founded their own medical schools and hospitals: by 1890, 18 percent of Boston's doctors were women; at 200, they outnumbered woman lawyers in the whole country. To *professionalize*, Tufts and Boston University medical schools, formerly coeducational, placed a quota on women students. This type of retrenchment spread across the country: Northwestern Medical School simply closed its women's division in 1902. In 1890 women made up *a quarter* of the students in Michigan Medical School; in 1910, about 3 percent. As women swarmed into the public world, men all but closed the entry doors to them. Colleges like Wesleyan, which had been coed for decades, suddenly barred women; others established quotas.

In Social Work

American women turned also to philanthropy. In the colonial period, charity was the obligation of city elites, mainly women. After the Revolution, elite groups created networks of secular organizations modeled on English humanitarian societies to help poor widows, the sick poor, and distressed slaves. Church-sponsored groups aided the poor or ran charity schools for poor children. In New York early philanthropists tried only to alleviate the sharpest pains of poverty: it did not occur to them that they could eliminate it.[18] They gave the poor firewood, food, or used clothing, without trying to alter their lifestyle or attitudes. But as wealth grew, so did destitution. Poverty overran the resources that patricians wished to devote to it, and charity groups buckled. Philanthropists began to seek ways to eliminate poverty.

The well-to-do resented the poor for simply integrating charity into their lifestyles after the Revolution, relying on relief agencies regularly instead of applying to them only in crises. In addition, the grim almshouse, built as a last resort for the elderly, impaired, sick, and mothers of small children, who could not help themselves, was used as a periodic haven by people who, the well-to-do presumed, could. The huge expansion of "outdoor relief" galled those who felt that need was sin and wanted the poor to live under punitive regulation. Contempt for relief recipients, coupled with admiration for English methods, led New Yorkers to found the Society for Prevention of Pauperism (SPP) in 1817.

The gentlemen of the SPP shifted the focus of charity from the *needs* to the *habits* of the poor. British-inspired categories and statistics demonstrated that the causes of poverty were the vices of the urban poor: imprudent hasty marriages, ignorance, intemperance, idleness, thriftlessness, gambling, and promiscuous sex. The SPP's first three reports did not even mention unemployment. They felt that charity to such people only bred indigence, even though New York mayor Cadwallader Colden's 1819 investigation of the almshouse found not one soul "unfit" for charity. Some elite women still held the old view of philanthropy, but SPP men were considered authorities by policy-makers and populace. Their cure was hard work and severity—lifting price controls on bread (a traditional way of preventing starvation), setting stricter licensing laws for taverns, founding savings banks to encourage prudence, and putting treadmills in insitutions to deter laziness. In 1823 they installed a treadmill in the penitentiary.

SPP views dominated American policy toward the poor until after the Civil War, when many women entered philanthropy. Like Englishwomen, American women imbued with belief in female moral superiority but lacking occupation affirmed their sense of worth by weaving the poor into sentimental embroideries of domesticity. Women wanted to improve the family lives of the poor, pointing their male colleagues toward domestic arrangements in tenements. They entered philanthropy through church work. The first large nineteenth-century female organizations had religious goals—they sought moral reform, sending preachers on missions to the frontier and ministers to "uncivilized areas." They entered public spaces to raise money, hand out Bibles, or sell religious tracts. But they had energy and time, and proposed projects to church auxiliaries—collecting food, clothing, and money, as well as visiting the needy or immoral in their neighborhoods to give help or advice.

Women's groups sprang up everywhere. In small communities, women of different religions worked together harmoniously to combat increasingly visible poverty, disease, and social displacement. Over a thirty-year period, the Boston Fragment Society aided more than 10,000 families with gifts of 40,000 pieces of clothing and $20,000. The New York Charity School taught hundreds of students each year. The Female Hospital Society of Philadelphia, organized by the Quakers in 1808, gradually began offering needy women paid work instead of charity, helping many. As in England, women charity workers had closer contact with poor people than did men, and so saw the problems of the poor more clearly. It was middle-class women who first made society aware of poor women.

For the brunt of poverty fell on working-class women. The educational benefits that the Revolution had granted women aided middle-class not poor women. The dignity working-class men derived from a revolution that defined them as citizens and freemen was undermined by industrialization, which prevented their autonomy. Lacking importance in the political and social world, they built a world they could dominate, a fellowship of laborers centered in the workplace and tavern. This male solidarity was bolstered by their power over women in the family. Similar working-class male cultures arose in every industrialized country—France, Germany, and Russia, as well as England and the United States. In all of them, men tormented their families by spending much of their pay on tobacco and drink, and coming home drunk to abuse wives and children.

Many women were hit by drunken husbands, but poor women saw their starving children beaten when the money that the man drank up could have fed them. Temperance became their major priority. Men's consumption of alcohol in the early nineteenth-century United States was staggering. Adults averaged six to seven gallons a year of alcohol in 1810—seven to ten in 1820—and few women drank any. By comparison, in 1986, with women drinking, annual adult consumption was about .84 gallons. In 1826 women founded the American Society for the Promotion of Temperance, a "cold water army." By 1834 it had a million members in more than 5000 local affiliates.

Women's next priority was prostitution. Men too worked to eliminate prostitutes, blaming them for polluting society; most women reformers saw them as depraved, but also as victims. They were certainly the latter: in the United States, too, most prostitutes worked for wages that could not keep them. Of 2000 whores in New York City jails surveyed in 1858, almost half worked as servants, a quarter as seamstresses. Over 60 percent were immigrants, 75 percent under twenty-five years old, most teenagers; *half had children*, of which half were illegitimate; 75 percent were single or widowed; the others had alcoholic husbands or had been deserted. Half had syphilis.

Before the Civil War, in New York City there was one prostitute to every sixty-four adult males; by 1890 the number of prostitutes had multiplied six-fold. Nineteenth-century attitudes toward sex still exist: women are held responsible for all sex performed without a marriage license.[19] A young Presbyterian minister, John McDowall, in 1830 rationalized that women's moral depravity was more threatening than men's because "a few of these courtesans suffice to corrupt whole cities, and there can be no doubt that some insinuating prostitutes have initiated more young men into these destructive ways than the most abandoned rakes have debauched virgins during their whole lives."

Women advocates of moral reform, however, blamed both sexes. In 1834, upon organizing the New York Female Moral Reform Society, they declared: "The licentious man is no less guilty than his victim and ought, therefore, to be excluded from all virtuous female society." They were amazing: bands of ladies stood outside brothels, jotting down the names of men who entered, or went in themselves to get information about runaway daughters or offer help to any woman held hostage. They invaded brothels en masse, praying and singing to discourage business and to try to win over sinners. They printed men's names in their journal, *The Advocate,* and hired the Reverend McDowall and two assistants to visit whores in jails, hospitals, almshouses, and brothels. They sponsored reformatory homes to turn prostitutes into virtuous domestic servants (this regularly failed). They had little effect, but continued angrily to attack "the lascivious and predatory nature of the American male."

In Abolition

In 1830 slavery was a political, not a moral issue: women were its greatest enemies. Men controlled antislavery organizations, but women made up the numbers and did the endless work. They prayed in groups, "memorialized" (petitioned) legislators to abolish slavery, raised funds to support abolitionist journals and agents, and gave "ladies' fairs" to sell handmade articles bearing antislavery messages or emblems. Society considered commerce a male domain, but did not criticize such fundraising activities, which proved extremely lucrative even as they raised consciousness. Yet they also reinforced women's auxiliary role in the movement, for the proceeds supported men's abolitionist work. Women also boycotted produce, cotton, or manufactured goods produced by slave labor. Only gradually did they overcome their fear of male hostility to expand into male terrain—public speaking, writing, editing, and serving as delegates to conventions.

The first women to speak publicly against slavery, the Grimké sisters, Angelina and Sarah, had the daring, courage, and moral commitment to leave their South Carolina slaveholding family to go north, join the abolitionists, and speak before "promiscuous" (mixed sex) audiences. Women who spoke in public were notorious (as Fanny Wright had discovered) and the young Grimkés were savagely attacked more for usurping the male prerogative on public speech than for their position on slavery. This provoked them to address women's rights in their antislavery talks.

At first, women worked state by state to make the nation aware of the evils of slavery by speaking, drafting petitions, and arguing with people they asked to sign. When congressman (and ex-president) John Quincy Adams submitted a petition urging abolition signed by 148 Massachusetts women to the House of Representatives, Virginians "raved incoherently . . . pounded the table with their fists . . . cursed Massachusetts and . . . wished that the women of the state might swing from a lamp-post." As antislavery petitions flooded Congress, hysterical Southern members passed a "gag rule," enabling them to table petitions for abolition without acting on them. This added free speech to antislavery demands, especially for women—as Angelina Grimké said: "The right of petition is the only political right . . . women have." Women intensified their effort, staged prayer vigils, mounted fairs, and converted men (among them the later leaders Wendell Phillips and William H. Seward) to "the Cause." The campaign gave women a taste for militant activity, and opposition radicalized them: antislavery adherents (who had urged patience and peaceful ways to combat the evil) became impatient abolitionists.[20]

The first American women's antislavery society was founded by black women in Salem, Massachusetts, in 1832.[21] That year too Maria Weston Chapman and others tried to organize white women in a Boston Female Antislavery Society. Chapman spent her life on the Cause: she edited *The Liberty Bell*, which advocated abolition, and ran fairs to raise money for the movement. She persuaded writers like Margaret Fuller, Harriet Martineau, Henry Wadsworth Longfellow, and James Russell Lowell to join the Cause, and took over editorship of the *National AntiSlavery Standard* from Lydia Maria Child from 1844 to 1848. (Child had been an extremely popular novelist until she published an antislavery pamphlet, *An Appeal in Favor of that Class of Americans Called Africans,* in 1833.) Chapman, called the "Lady Macbeth" of the movement, was the confidante of black leader Frederick Douglass, who complained of being patronized by white male abolitionists.

Philadelphia female abolitionists gathered around Lucretia and Joseph Mott, active Quakers. Lucretia Mott (1793–1880), who was licensed as a Quaker preacher in 1821, became the best-known woman abolitionist. In 1833, when Philadelphia was hosting the American Anti-Slavery Society (AASS) convention, the convention president in an afterthought invited Quaker women, including Mott. When she rose to speak, however, the men protested: women could attend meetings but not speak. Mott was not one to bow to pressure: she had six children, yet made her home a station on the Underground Railroad and had hidden a fugitive black woman in her carriage under the noses of armed guards. As a minister, she was used to public speaking and was unintimidated by men's presence. She prevailed, making several suggestions that were adopted as resolutions. But none of the women present was allowed to vote on the resolutions or sign the final document. Mott went home and founded the Philadelphia Female Anti-Slavery Society, and acted as its president for the next quarter-century.

But American abolitionism was always a minority movement. Unlike temperance, it never won popular support. Abolitionists annoyed, provoked, and incensed audiences, and were considered dangerous radicals or even lunatics. They were regularly heckled on platforms, and often tarred and feathered. Women's image of pious purity did not exempt them from violence: they may even have been men's main target. On the first day of the second Anti-Slavery Convention of American Women in Philadelphia in 1838, men stoned the delegates; on the second, a mob burned the new Pennsylvania Hall (planned as an abolitionist center), to the ground. Authorities watched, doing nothing.

The major male abolitionist, William Lloyd Garrison, was a radical disciple of "Perfectionist" John Humphrey Noyes; an advocate of immediate emancipation of slaves without compensation, he refused to work with people who urged gradual solutions. He opposed hierarchy, denouncing clerical and political authority, church and state, as bulwarks of slavery. His radicalism made him women reformers' comrade: he repudiated the institutions that barred them from the public realm. This extraordinary man welcomed women as equal partners.

Clergymen who cited scripture to defend slavery now quoted it to silence women, sparking a growing feminist consciousness and reinforcing women's bond to Garrison, whose anticlerical arguments had given the Grimkés ammunition against clerical censure. When clergymen tried to silence them, they and other female pioneers questioned the clergy's role in oppressing blacks and women. Women's rights were problematic for many men in the antislavery movement: Theodore Weld feared that "undue" attention to the "woman question" might distract people from the more "immediate" problem of slavery. Succumbing to unrelenting male pressure, the Grimkés dropped women's rights from their speeches. Sarah published a feminist manifesto, *Letters on the Equality of the Sexes, and the Condition of Women*, in 1838, and then retired with her sister from public life. Angelina married Weld that year.

It is dismaying that a progressive liberal egalitarian movement denied women equality, but it is an even more bitter irony that a movement to eliminate racial oppression was racist. White women called African women the "reason" that drove them to face reality—the arguments and heroism of African women inspired white women to "strike out on their own."[22] Yet when the Grimkés first came to Philadelphia and attended Quaker meetings, Africans were segregated from the congregation. Noticing two black women sitting apart, the Grimkés joined them—Sarah Douglass, a schoolteacher, and her mother Grace. When they became friends, Douglass told the sisters about the discrimination they had endured from Quakers. They wrote a pamphlet about it, but no one in the United States would publish it.

The Philadelphia Society was remarkable for integrating black and white women when even the most liberal Protestant societies were segregated. Among the city's free black women working alongside whites were Charlotte, Sarah, and Marguerite Forten (daughters of prominent black shipbuilder James Forten), Harriet Purvis, and Sarah and Grace Douglass.[23] Enslaved black women fought as they could.

One of these was a woman called Isabella, enslaved to a white man in Kingston, New York. Her owner, who inherited her family, did not want to feed her old father, and freed him with no means of support. He also forbade her to marry a man she loved, flogging her in front of him. She later married a man her owner approved of and had thirteen children, most of whom he sold. In 1817 New York State emancipated slaves over forty, but doomed younger ones to ten more years of bondage. To cut their losses, owners illegally sold their slaves out of state (African Americans were at risk as long as even one state supported slavery). In 1826, believing she would be sold south, Isabella fled to a local abolitionist couple who helped her sue to free her son Peter, who had been sold in Alabama. She won and went to New York City to work as a servant. Illiterate, she worked in the abolition movement under the name Sojourner Truth.

In 1851, at a women's rights convention in Akron, Ohio, a clergyman ridiculed weak helpless women for wanting rights. The audience scornfully heckled the women activists, who sank, defeated. An old black woman stood up in the audience, then came forward to sit on the steps of the pulpit. Some white feminists feared that alliance with abolitionists might injure their cause, and hoped the presider, Frances Dana Gage, would not give the podium to this known abolitionist, Sojourner Truth. As Gage described it, the woman "moved slowly and solemnly to the front, laid her old bonnet at her feet and turned her great speaking eyes to me. There was a hissing sound of disapprobation above and below. I rose and announced 'Sojourner Truth' and begged the audience to keep silent for a few moments." Sojourner faced the clergyman:

> The man over there says women need to be helped into carriages and lifted over ditches, and to have the best place everywhere. Nobody helps me into carriages or over puddles, or gives me the best place—and ain't I a woman?

She raised her strong old bare arm.

> Look at my arm! I have plowed and planted and gathered into barns and no man could head me—and ain't I a woman? I could work as much and eat as much as a man—when I could get it—and bear the lash as well! And ain't I a woman? I have borne thirteen children and seen most of 'em sold into slavery, and when I cried out with my mother's grief, none but Jesus heard me—and ain't I a woman?

Sojourner Truth seized the occasion and turned it around, electrifying the audience. She never stopped working against racism. A decade after the Akron convention, she protested black segregation in "Jim Crow" streetcars, pressuring Congress to ban segregated cars in the district of Columbia. After the ban was imposed, she repeatedly confronted streetcar conductors who refused to pick up blacks, bellowing, "I want to ride!" as they passed her. One day, the conductor of a streetcar she entered tried to shove her off: she pushed back, and he dislocated her shoulder. She took him to court and won: he was dismissed. Before the trial ended, she said, "the inside of the cars looked like pepper and salt."[24]

The clergy's treatment of the Grimké sisters stirred abolitionists like Lucy Stone to shift their efforts to women's rights, and they lectured on the subject throughout the 1840s. The election to AASS office of Abby Kelley, a young Quaker, opened a major rift in the male-dominated group. Male abolitionists who patronized Frederick Douglass and other black male abolitionists, scorned white female support. Calling women's issues an unnecessary distraction from the "real" problem of slavery, they opposed Kelley's election, and seceded to form a separate group (Garrison dubbed them "New Organization Men"). After the split, AASS men mobilized to end the struggle for equality once and for all. The problem came to a head at the 1840 World Anti-Slavery Convention in London.

Garrison's group, endorsing equal standing for women, sent female delegates to the World Anti-Slavery Convention in London that year. The convention refused to seat them. Delegates Mary Grew, Lucretia Mott, and all other women were relegated to a gallery behind a curtain where they could see but not participate in the events. Black abolition leader Charles Redmond, Garrison, and Nathaniel Rogers joined them there, but the women were humiliated and outraged by the cold hostility of the men who blamed them for the split. Elizabeth Cady Stanton (1815–1902) a newlywed there as her husband's guest, was propelled by the experience (and Mott's tutelage) into political feminism. On the sidelines of this convention the two made plans for a women's convention.

In Feminism

Ferment about women's rights had bubbled since early in the century, heated by women like Fanny Wright, the Grimkés, Lydia Maria Child (the self-supporting writer was furious to learn her husband had to sign her will to make it legal), and others. When legal reforms to merge common and equity law began in the United States in the 1830s, feminists lobbied for the inclusion of the women's rights that had been recognized by some courts—to own property, make contracts, sue, and testify in court.

After London, Mott returned to Philadelphia and Stanton to Boston. Stanton's husband moved the family to Waterloo, New York, where, isolated from friends and worn down by the drudgery of tending the six children she bore in eight years, she became depressed and determined to work for women's rights. When the Motts vacationed in upstate New York in summer 1848, Stanton met with Mott, her sister Martha Wright, Mary Ann McClintock, and Jane Hunt (four Quakers) to plan a women's convention. Within a week, they had put a notice in the newspaper, chosen a chapel for the meeting, written a "Womanifesto" based on the Declaration of Independence and an agenda. Stanton insisted on woman suffrage—her husband was so put out that he left town during the meeting.

Despite scant publicity, 200 women turned up at Seneca Falls, New York, on July 19–20, 1848, as well as forty men—which convinced the conveners not to bar males as they had intended. Besides, the organizers, afraid to chair the meeting, asked Joseph Mott to do it. But women did speak. Although nervous in her first public appearance, Stanton announced their purpose: to right woman's wrongs. Frederick Douglass not only attended but was the only man to speak in favor of woman suffrage. Many activist Hicksite Quakers came and a hundred signed the Declaration of Sentiments passed by the convention, which included equality in education, employment, at law, on public platforms, and the vote.

The personal revolt of a small group of women began a revolution that has not ended. Women as a group were protesting the treatment of women as a caste. Women willing to confront overwhelming institutionalized discrimination and men willing to admit its injustice joined to change it. The first feminist revolution explicitly to challenge patriarchy had begun.

The Seneca Falls meeting was followed by a Woman's Rights Convention in Rochester the same year, mainly to discuss suffrage, the most disputed of the eleven Seneca Falls proposals. The women's declaration did not claim a higher moral nature or special talents for women, but asserted it was the "duty of woman, whatever her complexion, to assume, as soon as possible, her true position of equality in the social circle, the Church, and the State." Urging women "no longer to promise obedience in the marriage covenant" but to let "the strongest will or the superior intellect . . . govern the household," they urged women to claim equal authority "on all subjects that interest the human family," especially their economic status. Pointing to the women who "plied the needle by day and by night, to procure a scanty pittance for [their] dependent famil[ies]," they condemned a man's "legal right to hire out his wife for service" and take her wages as a "hideous custom" reducing women "almost to the condition of a slave."

Immediately afterward, Amy Post and Sarah Owen organized the Working Woman's Protective Union, which in the next years found jobs, temporary shelter, and child care for fugitives—female slaves and battered wives. Union women helped each other recast their marriages in egalitarian ways, act independently of their husbands, demand equality in decision-making, travel, speech, and the education of daughters and sons. Two months after Rochester, the Congregational Friends proclaimed: "When we speak of the Rights of Woman, we speak of Human Rights." With "common natures, common rights, and a common destiny . . . [e]very member of the human family, without regard to color or sex, possess[es] potentially the same faculties and powers, capable of like cultivation and development and consequently has the same rights, interests, and destiny." For the next sixty years, Congregational Friends worked in various causes to foster equality for all women.[25] Women of all backgrounds welcomed the movement so warmly that within three years a national convention was possible. The 1851 convention repudiated the doctrine of separate spheres: "We deny the right of any portion of the species to decide for another portion . . . what is and what is not their 'proper sphere': . . . the proper sphere for all human beings is the largest and highest to which they are able to attain."

Then as now, feminism had no central control: women chose to concentrate on grassroots organizing. Women acted as they chose—withholding taxes to protest their lack of representation, challenging institutions that excluded them, protecting women's wages from husbands, publishing journals and tracts urging divorce reform, child custody, temperance, antislavery, and moral reform, or urging women to give up corsets and stays for tunics and loose-fitting pants like Fanny Wright's (called Bloomers because Amelia Bloomer adopted the style). State by state, they pressed for legal change: fourteen states had reformed married women's property laws by 1860, when New York allowed women their own wages. Others followed.

The New York law resulted from a fierce campaign. Feminists targeted certain regions for attention; in 1853–54, under Susan B. Anthony (1820–1906), the greatest feminist leader of this generation, they campaigned to reform New York laws. Anthony, born to an abolitionist family, began her political career working for temperance. When male delegates to a temperance convention in 1852 refused to let her speak, she resigned from the society and with Stanton founded the New York State Women's Temperance Society. She was one of the few women who shared Stanton's priority of suffrage in that period: the two became lasting friends and made a formidable team. In 1854 they devised the strategy of inundating the New York legislature with petitions from women for three demands: control of earnings, suffrage, and child custody after divorce. The reform laws that New York passed in 1860 were the most advanced in the nation—and perhaps the world.[26] They granted women the right to sue in court, keep their own wages, and exercise more control over a husband's property at his death.

The outcry was huge. Some of the new laws were in fact intended not to redress women's wrongs but to assist bankrupt men to keep their property by putting it in their wives' names. Ignoring this, journalists reacted to women's gains by lampooning feminists, harping on superficial issues like dress (as in the 1970s they harped on "bra-burning"). Politicians deplored the "emasculation" of men who "gave in" to women's demands, calling them "husbands in petticoats." Mobs of men with guns and knives menaced women public speakers while police stood by idly. But not all women supported feminism. Women who accepted a "separate sphere" feared male anger or the consequences of independence and disliked feminism, fearing its militance. And feminism seemed a luxury to lower-class women preoccupied with survival—nor did feminists fully understand working-class needs. Only Anthony even tried to ally with them.

The nineteenth-century feminist movement has been faulted for its narrowness. Few feminist groups welcomed black women; only the temperance campaign and those for women's right to keep their wages cut across class lines. Feminism was a white middle-class movement whose successes benefited mainly that class—at the time. Women without any political voice managed to change sexual politics through sheer unremitting effort and dedication, and their achievement benefited *all* women later. What is hardest for late-twentieth-century feminists to accept is the racism so evident in certain feminists—yet our record is only a little better. Without ignoring flaws in the movement, we must acknowledge the difficulty of building female solidarity across the divisions carefully created and stoked by patriarchy over eons.

Despite their revolutionary ideas on one subject, middle-class women, like any people anywhere, had absorbed the beliefs, not to say prejudices, of their period. These not only belittled people of other classes and colors but also themselves. They were often hobbled by a fear of violating social norms when they defied their social role. Single women in public arenas in this period were afraid of public scrutiny of their "femininity," because they lacked the usual "accoutrements of womanhood," husbands and children.[27] The inspired speaker Mary Grew, editor of an abolitionist journal *Pennsylvania Freeman*, declined an invitation to address the American Anti-Slavery Association because she had not "sufficient voice to fill the Tabernacle." Married women like Stanton were too frightened to speak at Seneca Falls.

In Black and White Women's Networks

Carroll Smith-Rosenberg has written about a "female world of love and ritual" that flourished unnoticed by indifferent nineteenth-century men.[28] Networks of female friends sustained women emotionally and gave them a voice. Some of these networks grew into larger groups dedicated to a chosen form of social amelioration, or exclusive clubs with literary leanings (which men mocked). Chicago's Fortnightly Club invited guest lecturers to discuss recent books like George Eliot's *Middlemarch*. Ladies' Clubs sprang up in major cities and in Rockland, Maine; Selma, Alabama; Quincy, Illinois; Cripple Creek, Colorado; and Walla Walla, Washington.

After the Civil War women's clubs grew more thoughtful and feminist. The most famous was founded in protest. Professional women had expected to face barriers when they entered the public sphere, but as more women entered professions, men became more antagonistic and erected new obstacles. When the New York Press Association barred well-known journalist Jane Croly from a banquet for Charles Dickens in 1868, she and her friends founded a club called the Blue Stockings, which attracted many prominent New York women: poets, editors, writers, musicians, professors, artists, teachers, physicians, lecturers, philanthropists, and a historian. The club (later called Sorosis) supported suffrage and other feminist demands, but also focused on working-class women.

The Chicago Women's Club, founded in 1876, contained departments dealing with reform, philanthropy, education, the home, art and literature, philosophy, and science. Within a decade, it had over 200 members; five years later, 400. The majority of women chose to work in the most activist sections—education, philanthropy, and reform. They pressured the Cook County Insane Asylum to hire women physicians and during a severe depression in 1893 provided poor women with money and cheap lodgings. They co-founded useful organizations in Chicago—the Legal Aid Society, the Public Art Association, the Protective Agency for Women and

Children—and raised money for an industrial school for boys. The club improved the condition of the poor in Chicago. Its members were activist and often feminists, but it never officially endorsed women's suffrage. Still growing in 1900, it set a limit of 1000 members.

In 1873 The Ladies' Social Science Association based mainly in the Northeast and Chicago, tried to create a national women's network. This popular club fostered early consciousness-raising—open discussion of marriage and sex. In 1889 Sorosis called a national convention, drawing delegates from over sixty organizations nationwide, to form the General Federation of Women's Clubs (GFWC). GFWC founders planned a network of clubs focused on literature, art, or science, but the federation soon moved into civic reform activism. By the 1890s nearly 100,000 American women were club members; by 1910, 800,000 women were part of a "municipal housecleaning" movement to improve neighborhoods and cities, as well as create kindergartens and libraries across the country.

The YWCA (Young Women's Christian Association), founded in New York in 1858, had at least thirty-six branches by 1873. To help women help themselves, it offered single women newly arrived in cities from abroad or rural areas inexpensive lodging, training in domestic service and other "female" occupations, and a job placement service. The conservative YWCA helped women adapt to, not break barriers. Even so, it was torn by conflict: some members wanted to exclude blacks or accept only Protestants in good standing with their home congregations; some sided with black leaders who saw it as a rich resource for black girls and women. It chartered segregated affiliates in the north but not the south until it became national in 1906. After the First World War, northern branches accepted all classes, creeds, and colors, but southern branches kept blacks in separate branches. Since it did not bar black women, like most national groups (including the GFWC), it was considered liberal and enlightened.

Women's "moral superiority" did not keep them from oppressing others. Knowing how it feels to be excluded for a quality one cannot change, they still excluded black women. As men justified excluding women on grounds of stupidity or emotionality, white women justified barring black women for "moral impurity." Middle-class black women dealt with such insinuations directly. Josephine St. Pierre Ruffin wrote: "Year after year southern women have protested against the admission of colored women into any national organization on the grounds of immorality of these women. . . . The charge has never been crushed, as it could and should have been at first." Fannie Barrier Williams eloquently told a white audience at the 1893 World Columbian Exposition: "I regret the necessity of speaking to the question of the moral progress of our women because the morality of our home life has been commented on so disparagingly and meanly that we are placed in the unfortunate position of being defenders of our name." She shocked them by asserting that white men caused black female "immorality." But nothing changed.

Since the 1790s black middle-class women had formed their own clubs, mutual aid societies based on traditional African female networks to assist mutual survival.[29] Members of the Daughters of Africa, the African Female Band Benevolent Society of Bethel, the African Female Benevolent Society of Newport, Rhode Island, and the Colored Female Religious and Moral Reform Society of Salem paid dues, pooling them to pay women benefits in times of sickness or death, give widows and fatherless children money and visits, and clothe children in African Free Schools. In the 1830s they changed their focus to "mutual improvement." Wives and daughters of ministers, teachers, and businessmen—the African American elite—founded self-educational groups. Members of the African American Female Intelligence Society of Boston, the Minerva Literary Society, and the Colored Ladies' Literary Society met at each other's homes to read their essays and poems.

Abandoning hope for integration, black clubwomen created their own national network through *The Woman's Era*, a paper published in Boston. In 1896 the National Federation of Afro American Women, with branches in sixteen states, merged with the Colored Women's League of Washington (the largest black female organization in the United States) to become the National Association of Colored Women (NACW). Uniting over a hundred women's clubs, it set up a communications network and sponsored publications and conventions to bring women together. A major step for black women, the NACW was neither an auxiliary to a male group nor a minority in a white female group but a group directed by and oriented to black woman. Its first president, Mary Church Terrell, born to slaves during the Civil War, earned a degree from Oberlin College in 1884. A teacher and the first black woman named to the D.C. Board of Education, she expanded the NACW to almost 50,000 members and over a thousand clubs.

Deeply concerned about the health of black women and children, the NACW established social programs. Educator Olivia Davidson wrote: "Three fourths of the colored women are overworked and underfed, and are suffering to a greater or lesser degree from sheer physical exhaustion." White middle-class female social workers addressed themselves to white working-class women in similar conditions but NACW women had a different perspective from whites. They knew that almost all black women bore the burden of raising children yet worked for wages all their lives, and that most black girls could find work only as servants in homes where white men sexually exploited them. Williams wrote in pain about the constant stream of letters she received from southern women "begging [her] to find employment for their daughters . . . to save them from going into the homes of the South as servants as there is nothing to save them from dishonor and degradation."[30]

Leaders felt it urgent to educate girls to help them escape from whites' power and to disprove white myths about black women by personal example and through their works. Their near-religious reverence for their mothers (who deserved it) inspired deep belief in the moral strength of true womanhood. As sexually pure, pious, and domestic as their white counterparts, middle-class black women came to feel their monopoly on virtue obliged them to "better the race," "uplift" the poor. Educated, prosperous, leisured, they saw poor black females as "The Black Woman's Burden."

Despite their class bias, they did much good. Northerners helped southern migrants by creating residences for young working-class women, kindergartens for their children, and mothers' groups with seminars in child care and home economics. In 1896 the Illinois Federation of Colored Women's Clubs opened Phyllis Wheatley Home for Girls, a residence, social club, and employment bureau for young women. Faculty wives and their friends living near Spelman and Morehouse colleges in Atlanta formed the Atlanta Neighborhood Union, which built a park and health center for black children and sponsored homemaking and woodworking classes, mothers'clubs, and scouting troops. Northern urban women founded organizations to help southerners who migrated in answer to ads placed by northern employment agencies. In 1897 Victoria Earle Matthews founded the White Rose Industrial Association and Working Girls' Home in New York City to protect black female servants from exploitation. Black women opened branches of the National League for the Protection of Colored Women in New York, Philadelphia, Memphis, Baltimore, Washington, and Norfolk to give migrants rooms, education, and jobs. Black men supported these groups, even joining them.

White middle-class American women were more willing to work with different classes than with different colors, perhaps because lower-class women did not expect equality. Earlier, we noted the 1848 founding of a Working Woman's Protective Union to help poor women, fugitive women slaves, and beaten wives. In 1863 New York women started a Working Woman's Protective Union to coordinate city relief programs for women, find them jobs, and provide money. Women in Travelers Aid Societies met incoming ships to offer immigrant girls lodging at a YWCA home and protect them from "white" slave traders. They could live in

YWCA boardinghouses for \$3–\$4 a week and once they found work, female-staffed agencies helped them in other ways. Female immigrants' main problem was that employers often capriciously refused to pay them. The Chicago Women's Club set up a protective agency; in its first year, over 156 women filed complaints, a third of whom made charges that their wages were unjustifiably withheld.

Women's clubs in many cities formed Women's Exchanges to help poor women who could not work outside the home. For \$5, a woman could join an exchange that sold items she made at home, giving her 90 percent of the purchase price. The New England Women's Club gave subsidized lunches to middle- and working-class women and offered evening classes to train them in marketable skills. One dedicated woman could make a great difference in a city. Lucretia Longshore Blankenburg, daughter of the first woman doctor in Philadelphia (who named her for Lucretia Mott), made a difference in that city. She co-founded the New Century Club, which ran a night school for working-class women; she taught bookkeeping, started the New Century Guild, a working-women's club, lobbied the police to hire matrons, and persuaded the Philadelphia school board to appoint women. As president of the Philadelphia Women's Suffrage Association, Blankenburg fought for years to get the major white women's club federation to support it, succeeding in 1914.

CHAPTER 6

THE CIVIL WAR AND ITS AFTERMATH

IN 1860 THE SITUATION OF AFRICAN AMERICANS was worse than ever. In 1820, 13 percent of the 2 million blacks in the United States were free; by 1860, the African population had nearly doubled but only 11 percent were free. After independence, free Africans bought land in New York and Pennsylvania, and in the early nineteenth century they moved into southern Ohio and Maryland. Most bought small farms, but a few acquired urban properties in New Orleans and Philadelphia, as well as New York, Cincinnati, Washington, DC, and Baltimore. When slave trade ended in 1807, owners could only replenish their slave holdings through natural increase so they began to coerce women slaves to produce children. Two women owned by a Virginia planter named Cohoon had seventy-three descendants.[1] Before the Civil War, free black men were artisans and mechanics, and 4000 blacks, most in cities, owned slaves. White men's lust gave black women some mobility: once slave trade ended, more black women than men were freed. More free black women lived in the south, and lived better than men. Most black heirs got property from their mothers.

Abraham Lincoln lightly charged Harriet Beecher Stowe with starting the Civil War by writing *Uncle Tom's Cabin*. But while abolitionism contributed to it, the Civil War was not fought primarily over slavery. Northern businessmen who manufactured goods in competition with English imports wanted protective tariffs; southern planters wanted free trade. This conflict, heated by abolitionist pressure, drove the south to secede from the Union in 1861. For the country at large, the Civil War was a struggle for supremacy between national and state law. But it would determine the future of white southerners and African Americans. Many blacks fought for the Union, proving themselves among the most skilled, courageous soldiers despite prejudicial treatment.[2]

Woman Spies, Soldiers, and Workers

Women took many roles in the war. Army nurses acted as scouts and spies; Dr. Mary Walker (see chapter 5) was sent on an intelligence mission.[3] Belle Boyd, a Confederate Army nurse, joined the army in her teens and became famous for courage and expert horsewomanship. Riding thirty miles one night to tell a Confederate officer about a plan for a secret attack, she was betrayed and captured in July 1862. The northern press smeared her as a "village courtesan" who got information by sexual means. Jeanne d'Arc (found a virgin when she was captured) was similarly accused: such smears keep women from acting in the world.

Rose O'Neal Greenhow, a widowed society woman, lived in Washington, DC, with her eight-year-old daughter. In 1861 the north suspected her of spying and placed her under house arrest, forcing her to sleep with her bedroom door open, censoring her mail, and denying her newspapers and contact with friends. They used her house to imprison other suspected spies—it became known as Fort Greenhow. Freed in 1863, she immediately ran the northern blockade to sail to France, placed her daughter in a convent, and embarked on diplomatic work for the Confederacy. She sailed home in 1864, carrying gold and documents in a diplomatic pouch. Outside Wilmington, Greenhow sighted Union patrols who might seize the ship and tried to elude them by rowing to the harbor. She drowned when her boat capsized, a martyr to the Confederacy.

Another southerner, actress Pauline Cushman, sympathized with the North and declared her principles publicly, yet she remained extremely popular in her native New Orleans. Cushman was able to glean information about Confederate plans and transmit it to Union officers when she toured border states with her theater company. In 1864 the south caught her with plans she had stolen from a Confederate engineer. She managed to escape but was recaptured and sentenced to death. Union soldiers rescued her and she resumed her acting career in the north.

Many women disguised themselves as men to join the armies as soldiers—more than four hundred were found out. Sarah Edmonds became Franklin Thompson, a male nurse with the 2nd Michigan Cavalry. In 1865 she published an account of her adventures as nurse, spy, mail courier, and soldier. The government granted her a pension of $12 a month in recognition of her service to her country (but not until 1884). Ellen Goodridge went to the front with her Union fiancé; Franny Wilson of New Jersey fought with Union troops for a year and a half before being wounded—and exposed—at Vicksburg. Most female soldiers were discovered wounded, in hospitals. Southern women were far less likely to adopt this disguise, and those who did had usually accompanied their husbands. But southerner Amy Clark remained a soldier after her husband was killed at Shiloh, and was exposed only after capture by the north.

Southern women were less likely than northerners to abandon traditional roles, but not because they were weaker or less spirited. They had the harder lot, since most of the war was fought on southern territory. They suffered terribly from shortages. After a long siege, when the only food in Vicksburg was rats, women instigated food riots and looted government warehouses. When Union soldiers occupied the south, they took over southern houses, forcing the women in them to cook, clean, serve, and do laundry. As Union troops moved on, they stripped farms bare of food and valuables, and often burned the houses down. Toward the end of the war, they adopted a "scorched earth" policy, burning crops in the fields. When Confederate soldiers arrived, southern women welcomed and fed them, but they consumed whatever the Union men left. Yet southern women were infamous in the north for their spirited hostility toward Union soldiers, so much so that one officer ordered that any woman showing disrespect for Union soldiers was to be treated like "a woman of the town." Neither victory nor defeat eased the lot of women in occupied areas.

A new job area opened to women during the Civil War—white-collar work. Lack of men led storeowners to hire women; female shop clerks were paid as little as $5 a week for long hours—sometimes over a hundred hours a week. Yet it was probably because of the pay that women kept these jobs when the war ended. Before the Civil War, a few women were hired as clerks in the patent office. War opened jobs for women in the civil service. Frances Spinner, appointed Treasurer of the United States in 1861, hired about a hundred women for government service; other government offices did the same: nearly 500 women worked in Washington by 1865. Spinner paid women $600 a year in 1861, and $720 by 1865, which allowed them to live decently. Other government departments, especially the Post Office (an all-male preserve until it hired women to work in the Dead Letter Office), paid women half or a third of what men earned for doing the same work. Still, women earned more than they could elsewhere, doing relatively clean safe work, and they eagerly sought government jobs. They earned excellent work records.

But good work did not prevent them from being fired when the war ended. Officials insisted that "government girls" give way to returning veterans, in some cases arguing the impropriety of men and women working in the same office—even though they had done so harmoniously for several years. The men got rid of women, who made up only 3.3 percent of office workers in 1870. But the precedent for white-collar women workers had been set, and by 1880 the percentage of women working in offices doubled; by 1890, it tripled. By 1900 women filled over 75 percent of the jobs in private and government offices; two-thirds of all typists and stenographers were females aged fifteen to twenty-five. As white-collar work was feminized, however, wages fell and, despite their numbers, women were not promoted but continued in low-level jobs. Most were single and lived with their parents, and they took what they could get.

Once the war was over, men everywhere expected women to return to their prewar status. This was impossible. An estimated 620,000 men had been killed in the conflict, nearly a generation of young men. Women who had struggled to keep the children alive and the farm productive during the war had to pick up the broken pieces of their lives. The situation was worst in the south, where they were left with houses in ashes, scorched fields, and a devastated countryside. Alabama alone had 80,000 destitute widows. Sexual imbalance persisted in the south until the 1880s.

Transcontinental Shift

Men who survived the war sought a better future by heading west or north or south to Latin America. Entire families moved west for a clean start; over 350,000 people made the long trek overland to Oregon, California, and points along the way. In 1879 7000 blacks moved to Kansas, fleeing persecution by southern whites; many fled elsewhere—men to escape violence and find work, women to protect their children. In the spring, homesteaders loaded supplies and valuables into Conestoga wagons for the five- to seven-month journey, covering fifteen to twenty miles a day along the Platte River valley on the north central plains, across the Rocky Mountains into Wyoming.

The journey was easier for men; women were still expected to do all the work of maintaining the family—cooking, mending, laundering, healing, and tending children. They had to gather dry buffalo dung for fuel and cook over an open fire: "From the time we get up in the morning until we are on the road, it is hurry scurry to get breakfast and put away the things . . . pulled out last night," one woman recalled. Every night they had to reverse the process, unpacking utensils, gathering fuel, and cooking—often burning themselves. Afterwards, the men relaxed around the fire while the women cleaned utensils, clothes, and children before they could sleep. But the most unpleasant experience was to be pregnant while traveling over rough terrain and to give birth in a Conestoga wagon. Many died.

These women developed great hardiness and learned to drive wagons and handle weapons. And once the journey was over, homesteaders built one-room sod or log houses miles from the nearest neighbor. Sod houses were always covered with a layer of dust; some had grass floors. Log houses had chinks and were drafty; women stuffed the chinks with rags and mud. Furniture that had not been brought in the wagon was rudely crafted. Roofs leaked so badly that women kept their skillets covered so that mud, rain, and muck would not drip into dinner. The mark of a seasoned pioneer was that she no longer bothered to wear gloves when she collected buffalo dung. One man remembered his mother making biscuits: "Stoke the stove, get out the flour sack, stoke the stove, wash your hands, mix the dough, stoke the stove, wash your hands, cut out the biscuits, stoke the stove, wash your hands, put the pan of biscuits in the oven, keep on stoking the stove until the biscuits are done. Mother had to go through this tedious routine three times a day." And it was only one step in producing meals.

As usual on farms, women worked in barnyard, dairy, and vegetable garden, earning money from butter and eggs, and providing food for the family. Homesteaders spent surplus money on machinery to lighten men's work, or on new barns, rather than on conveniences to ease the drudgery of women. As always, women's huge contributions to their households were simply expected and gave them little voice in financial decisions. Many died of hardship—one walked five miles to find a tree tall enough to hang herself on.[4] One Nebraska homesteader went through four wives: he left a bride behind when he went west, and then married a woman who went mad on his isolated farm. His third wife, a mail-order bride, deserted him after two weeks, so he ordered a wife from Europe. She became pregnant almost immediately and had to remain, but was miserable, her daughter wrote.

The Homestead Act, passed by Congress in 1862, allowed anyone twenty-one or over, or the head of household, to stake a claim to 160 acres for $14 and receive final title if they showed they had lived continually on the land for five years and improved it. The wording of the law enabled women to stake claims and a fair number did. Mary O'Kieffe's husband regularly disappeared; she finally packed up her belongings and her nine children and left the family farm on the Missouri River. With her children, she "hitched the horses, loaded the cultivator, strapped a cage of poultry to the wagon-top and made a fifty-one-day, 500-mile trek," to claim land in Nebraska, build a sod house, and prosper.[5]

Even before the Homestead Act was passed, women went west alone, some when gold was discovered at Sutter's Mill, California, in 1849. When a man named Guerin died in 1857, his destitute widow cut her hair, put on pants, named herself "Mountain Charley," and embarked on a career as a male wagon-train driver to California for thirteen successful years. In towns that were nearly all-male, adventurous single women worked as cowgirls and sharpshooters, or in dance halls, saloons, and brothels. All single women in the west were considered whores; whatever their sexual activities, most eventually married. Some became models of respectability; some grew rich in marginal occupations. Irish-born Mary Josephine Welch migrated to the United States in her teens. In 1867, single and twenty-three, she left Chicago for the mining frontier, settling in Helena, Montana, near Last Chance Gulch. Calling herself "Chicago Joe," she ran the Red Light Saloon, importing women from Chicago to work as dollar-a-dance "hurdy-gurdy girls." She took part of their earnings—as much as $50 a night. When newspaper accounts celebrated Chicago Joe's Valentine's Day ball, moral reformers were outraged. In 1873 they succeeded in making dance halls illegal.

The south had more women than men, the west the opposite—Wyoming had six men to one woman. To lure women west, the Wyoming legislature granted them citizenship—the right to vote and hold office. Feminist activists gained the vote in Washington Territory, Idaho, and Utah—where female suffrage backfired.

Joseph Smith's Church of Jesus Christ of Latter-day Saints was often persecuted. The sect was driven from upstate New York to Illinois and, after Smith was killed in 1844, it followed Brigham Young to the barren salt flats of Utah. Smith, eager to attract women to his sect, supported women's societies, but in the 1830s established polygyny. Some think he hoped to draw older single women and widows unlikely to marry, but it is more likely he wanted to attract men to a sect whose moral code forbade both men and women from extramarital sex. Young had twenty-seven wives. Suffragists, arguing that Utah women needed to outlaw polygyny, won the right to vote in 1870. But female Mormons obeyed their church fathers, and barred women from public office. They used the franchise to give men political control of the state.

Native American Women

In their advance westward, whites trespassed on and appropriated Native American land. In the Northwest Ordinance of 1787 the government pledged: "Utmost good faith shall always be observed toward the Indians; their land and property shall never be taken from them without their consent." But from Washington on, presidents violated the treaty. As Justice John Marshall was defining Native Americans as a "dependent nation" within the United States

(1832), President Andrew Jackson was fomenting war on Indian societies that blocked frontier settlement. The army forced Indians off their land in cruel massacres; they retaliated with raids. By the 1840s, war on the frontier was constant.

Some of our knowledge of Native American customs in this period comes from people kidnapped by Indians. Texan Rachel Plummer, who was held by Comanches for almost two years, was appalled by women's status in Comanche society: "The women do all the work, except killing the meat. They herd the horses, saddle and pack them, build the houses, dress the skins, meat, etc. The men dance every night, during which, the women wait on them with water." She did not note that white women too did most of the work, or that whites also excluded women from their councils.

Like European Americans, Native Americans divided labor by sex, but did not regulate sex the same way. A Moravian minister who spent years with Native Americans, mainly Delawares, wrote: "Marriages among the Indians are not, as with us, contracted for life; it is understood on both sides that the parties are not to live together longer than they shall be pleased with each other. The husband may [leave] his wife whenever he pleases, and the woman may in like manner abandon her husband." A male observer of the Cherokee resented their view of adultery—perhaps seeing it as female usurpation of a male right. The Cherokee, he wrote, "have been a considerable while under a petticoat government, and allow their women full liberty to plant their brows with horns as oft as they please, without fear of punishment."

A woman of the Fox tribe recalled a strict division of labor and training—girls and boys were raised separately and trained differently, but the sexes had complementary status and responsibility. When she left her lazy, abusive first husband, no law stopped her; she alone made the decision to marry a man she loved, who waited until the time she set to approach her. Choosing not to interrupt her active sex life by having children, she drank a potion given her by a wise woman to prevent pregnancy. But when her husband died, she decided to marry a last time to have children and found the wise woman again. "Is there perhaps a medicine whereby one might be able to have a child if one drank it?" There was; she drank it, became pregnant, and later had several children.

After the Civil War, Native Americans were confined to reservations, their numbers severely reduced by war and the disease and famine it brought. Their children were taken away and placed in schools to "Americanize" them, "to kill the Indian and save the man." The Dawes Act (1887) forced white notions of private property on Native Americans, destroying with a stroke of a pen an age-old tradition of communal ownership. When Oklahoma entered the Union in 1906, Indian Territory ceased to exist.

The Situation of African Americans[6]

Emancipation did not make freed slaves citizens. The government passed three amendments to the constitution: the Thirteenth abolished slavery; the Fourteenth made blacks citizens; the Fifteenth forbade discrimination on grounds of race or prior status and granted males suffrage. After passing Congress, however, the amendments had to be ratified by two-thirds of the states. Intense lobbying ensued. Women were in conflict about the Fifteenth Amendment. Some, like abolitionist Sarah Parker Redmond, worked for black male suffrage despite the exclusion of women; others, like Sojourner Truth, predicted that exclusion would lead to the domination of black women by black men. It is noteworthy that she used the future tense.

Slaves lacked all rights—civil, political, economic, or social—so any sexual domination among blacks was situational, not legal. It lacked an institutional base. Any male dominance drew from American culture or African tradition, compounded by women's tendency to bolster pride and confidence in those they love, especially those continually beaten down. African Americans lived in the same overall society as whites, but their position within it required different strategies for survival.

Like whites, African American men wanted dominance, felt that manhood needed continual proof, and associated freedom with manhood. In 1773, when revolutionary fervor swept the colonies, black male slaves petitioned the Massachusetts legislature for freedom on the grounds that as slaves they *lacked authority over their families*. They asked: "How can a husband leave master and work and cleave to his wife? How can the [wives] submit themselves to . . . husbands in all things?"[7] At abolitionist meetings in the 1850s black male leaders complained: "As a people, we have been denied the ownership of our bodies, our wives, home, children and the products of our own labor." They urged black "mothers and sisters" to "use every honorable means to secure employment for their *sons and brothers*." In William Wells Brown's early African American novel, *Clotel* (1861), black women are accused of wanting to become their white masters' lovers.[8]

Knowing that male slaves scorned cooking, sewing, laundry, cleaning, bathing children, or picking lice out of their hair, owners punished them by forcing them to do such tasks. A Louisiana cotton planter made male offenders wash clothes and forced chronic offenders to wear women's dresses. A historian reported that men treated this way were more tormented by what they considered public humiliation than by harsher punishments: "So great was their shame before their fellows that many ran off and suffered the lash on their backs rather than submit to the discipline."[9]

As oppressed women sacrifice solidarity if they accept traditional patriarchal class divisions, oppressed groups lose solidarity if they accept patriarchal sexual divisions. Men who feel they must prove they are men invariably choose to prove it by dominating women rather than by refusing domination by other men. No group or class of men seems immune and African American women's extraordinary resourcefulness and endurance seems only to have intensified African American men's need for superiority.

The burden shouldered by slave women was an extreme form of

that borne by other women.[10] Until the nineteenth century most women were responsible both for reproduction (and the enormous tasks associated with it) *and* for production. Slave women were not uniquely but extremely oppressed. To cement their control, white owners denied slaves any power over their lives, including the right to marry (yet scorned them as sexually unbridled). Family had great meaning for slaves, so keeping a family together was an act of defiance. Since owners regarded slave children as *their* property, an intact family was a triumph and gave people a place of their own in the midst of dispossession and alienation. African mothers had always been the center of the family, struggling to maintain its integrity and welfare.[11]

Owners who gave skilled jobs only to males and never gave slave women authority over men in work, rarely made sexual distinctions on grounds of strength. Owners made women carry very heavy loads and work long hours, barely lightening their burden when they were pregnant or nursing. (Yet they wanted strong healthy babies who fetched high prices.) But slaves helped each other. Jacqueline Jones wrote about the Bell family on a Virginia wheat farm. During the harvest, Frank Bell and his four brothers followed their parents down the long rows of grain so that "one could help the other when dey got behind. All of us would pitch in and help Momma who warn't very strong." The overseer forbade families to work together, believing "dey ain't gonna work as fast as when dey all mixed up," but the driver was Bell's uncle, who "always looked out for his kinfolk, especially my mother."

James Taliaferro recalled that his aunt Rebecca ("a short-talking woman that ole Marsa didn't like") was usually assigned more work than other women. His father one day counted the corn rows she was allotted, and told her she had twice as many as anyone else. Indignant, Rebecca confronted the owner. Only after threatening to sell James' father for meddling did he grudgingly reduce her workload. On another plantation, fieldworkers surreptitiously added handfuls of cotton to the basket of a young woman who "was small and just couldn't get her proper amount." (Slaves had to pick a certain amount each day. Failure meant a whipping.) Even the work of house slaves was hard and endless: only about 5 percent of all adult slaves worked as house servants, and during the harvest season, all slaves, even those in the house, had to go to the fields to pick cotton.[12]

Children too were treated without sexual distinction. All were dressed in a "splittail shirt," a knee-length smock slit up the sides: "They call it a shirt iffen a boy wear it and call it a dress iffen the gal wear it." Children between six and twelve lugged kindling for woodboxes, built fires in bedrooms on chilly mornings and evenings, made beds, polished shoes, washed and ironed clothes, and stoked fires while whites slept at night. They fetched water and milk from the springhouse and meat from the smokehouse, set the table three times a day, helped the cook, served meals, "minded flies" with peacock-feather brushes, "passed the salt and pepper on command," and washed dishes. In the house, they swept, dusted, served drinks, and fanned visitors. White mistresses gave their babies to slave children barely beyond babyhood themselves to bathe, diaper, dress, groom, and entertain. Children on farms "gathered eggs, plucked chickens, drove cows to and from the stable, and 'tended the gaps' (opened and closed gates)." In fields they acted as human scarecrows, toted water to workers, and hauled corn shocks. As an old woman, ex-slave Mary Ella Grandberry said she "disremember[ed] ever playin' lack chilluns do today."[13]

The central irony in slave women's history is that *because* owners ignored physical differences in fieldwork, slaves maintained a strict sexual division of labor in their households and communities. The home, such as it was, was the place where slave men's pride could be rebuilt by women following sex rules traditionally African or copied from whites. For black women, the family was the center of resistance to oppression; for white women, the family was the center of oppression.

Free African Americans lacked property, education, or white

acceptance, and faced a terrible struggle for survival in which it must have seemed essential to pull together, not separately. And they felt strongly that black women's refusal to work in white homes annulled white power over blacks. Women supported by men could pay full attention to their own families. Most stopped working in the fields or worked only at harvest time. Outraged southern men noted that "negro women are now almost wholly withdrawn from field labor"; statistics show that not only did many wives stay home, but those who still did field labor worked like humans, not slaves—shorter hours and fewer days a year.

Production fell drastically in many regions. Aware that "women were as efficient as men in working and picking cotton," landowners enraged at losing their unpaid workforce blamed "female loaferism" and forced black women to work for them. Lucretia Adams of Yorkville, South Carolina, told the Freedmen's Bureau, which negotiated labor contracts between planters and blacks, that eight drunk white men seized and assaulted her, saying, "We heard you wouldn't work. We were sent for . . . to come here and whip you, to make the damned niggers work."[14] Intimidated workers remained silent, fearing complaint might lead to reprisals. Whites seized black children to "apprentice" them, supported by southern courts. In Maryland alone an estimated 10,000 children were bound to labor over their parents' objections.

Discrimination against African Americans continued on every level and the government ignored its promises to give them land. Still, blacks succeeded for a time. After a post-war tour of the south, Frances Harper reported that African Americans "were beginning to get homes for themselves . . . and depositing money in the bank . . . . They have hundreds of homes in Kentucky."[15]

Whites determined to put a stop to this: they paid blacks so little that a man could not earn enough to support a wife and children. In 1867 they resuscitated a sharecropping system used on feudal manors in Europe as feudalism was collapsing. Landowners offered landless men cabins on their plantations, providing tools, seed, and use of the land. In return, sharecroppers paid landlords a share—usually half—of the crop they raised, usually cotton. This form of labor departed radically from the "gang" farming characteristic of plantation slavery and from the wage economy that characterized northern industry. It involved private individuals working land not theirs for a return on their labor—an incentive to hard work. Landlords won a good return on land they could not afford to pay workers to farm. Black sharecropper husbands assumed the main responsibility for agricultural work; their wives assumed the responsibility for maintaining the family and helped the men on the land, especially during planting and harvest. Children too worked in the fields at those times, so the whole family worked in relative safety from intrusion by whites.

Although this arrangement helped landless families, it imposed the traditional division of labor and power; this division was also reinforced by the black church, which, like white churches, exhorted wives to submit to husbands. Female herb doctors and "grannies" were revered in the black community, but men dominated black political and religious organizations, holding all positions of authority. Like white men, they felt they had a right to dominate and to beat their wives, an abuse that greatly increased in this period; what black men needed to bolster egos damaged by white persecution or exploitation was *domination.*

Few African American women could afford the luxury of refusing to work for whites. Women without men or whose men lacked land had to work for wages, often as domestic servants; many were the economic mainstay of their families. Yet black male writers blamed such women, insisting that their husbands were actually able and willing to support them, and that they worked for whites merely to obtain finery and luxuries. African American men chose to emulate the white patriarchal model whenever possible. Some black women welcomed dependency, some were forced to accept it, and some resisted it.[16] The pressures on black women to accept the white middle-class model were great: all women are taught that male pride and ego depend on female dependency, but black male pride had suffered incalculably. But both sexes suffered for their allegiance to a patriarchal family structure.[17]

A small class of middle-class African Americans had thrived in the United States for over a century before the Civil War. They went north: free African-descended Barbadians and other islanders, escaped or freed slaves. They were cautious because they were always in danger. Yet they educated their children and many became teachers. The first known African American teacher, Catherine Ferguson, an ex-slave, in 1793 opened Katy Ferguson's Schools for the Poor in New York City. In 1851 white Myrtilla Miner opened the Miner School for Colored Girls in Washington, DC; in 1852 the Institute for Colored Youth was founded in Philadelphia. After the war, young northern-born middle-class black women ran schools for freed people funded by the American Missionary Society and other philanthropic groups. No schools opened in the south until Josephine Griffin pressured Lincoln to let her collect volunteers to help freed blacks find food, homes, and establish schools.

With Lincoln's sanction, Griffin founded the Freedmen's Bureau, under whose aegis people moved south to teach former slaves: by 1869 it had 9000 teachers, of which half were women. Susie King Taylor, laundress for the first black Union regiment, nursed the wounded, then became a teacher. Charlotte Forten, an educated middle-class black, gave up a comfortable life up north to teach African Americans on the Union-occupied Sea Islands off South Carolina. For the two years that Forten lived and taught in Port Royal, she kept a diary—the first black female diary published in the United States, one that remains inspiring reading today. Black and white northerners who moved south encountered hostility, ridicule, and even violence, yet many remained even after Union troops withdrew in 1877. They prepared the way for the civil rights movement of the future: W.E.B. Du Bois called them the "tenth crusade."

Educated or not, black women could find few jobs after the war. Although the number of female field workers in the south dropped sharply in the 1870s, only women supported by men could afford to reject fieldwork. Most freedwomen did the same work as slaves—stuck in it by their skin color, years after most white women had gone to factories and offices.[18] As late as the 1930s, over a quarter of black working women in the United States did agricultural work; most others were domestic servants or washerwomen. The situation was identical in the north. Between the Civil War and the First World War, black women flocked to northern cities but most could find work only as servants. Women with small children could not live in a white household and could only wash white men's shirts at the going rate of 13 cents a dozen. In 1900, 84 percent of black working women were servants or laundresses; in 1960, almost a third of African American female workers were domestic servants and over half the country's 2 million domestic workers were black women.[19] Until recent decades, black women constituted a permanent service class in the United States.

Since white churches barred or discriminated against African Americans, black congregations built their own churches. But the black clergy who defied Paul's dicta on slaves accepted his position on women and systematically denied them leadership within the church.[20] Like white women in support positions in their churches, black women essentially held the church together, teaching Sunday school, counseling and sponsoring youth groups, singing in the choir and establishing their own missionary societies. Some nineteenth-century black women Baptists created a feminist theology, using Bible stories to justify a more aggressive public role for women within the Church without breaking with orthodoxy. Over male objections, women in the African Methodist Episcopal Church preached, claiming that their call arose from extraordinary visionary and spiritual experiences. Fannie Jackson Coppin and a committee of women at the Mother Bethel African Methodist Episcopal Church opened a home for destitute young black women.[21]

When reconstruction ended in 1877, northern troops were withdrawn and the Freedman's Bureau became, wrote Du Bois, a "dead-letter." White southerners amplified their campaign to re-establish white supremacy and destroy black political power and prosperity, which had been gradually increasing. By 1889 black men were disenfranchised in the south. Each locality had a subterfuge for accomplishing this, like poll taxes, or literacy tests not given to whites. White school administrators diverted funds allocated to black schools to white ones, state governments legalized segregation, and whites began to use terror, subjecting blacks to mob violence and lynchings. Between 1890 and 1915, the white campaign of intimidation was so extreme that few blacks challenged it, and many moved north, preferring its racial discrimination and *de facto* segregation to the south's Jim Crow laws, a rigid system of apartheid enforced by terrorism.[22]

Once African Americans were free, racism intensified. Racism, the claim that one race is superior or inferior *humanly* to another or others, is a strategy like sexism (the assertion that one sex is superior or inferior humanly to the other), devised to justify legal, social, economic, and political subjugation of a group.[23] African American slavery was *always* racist; white indentured servants were all eventually freed. Africans differed from Europeans not only in color but also in culture, and people tend to rank differences. Slavery came to an end in the United States but racism did not. The extremism of southern terrorist organizations was not anomalous; racist hatred of blacks in the United States was and is almost as profound and pervasive as woman-hatred (*almost* because woman-hatred is more pervasive—men of color are also misogynist—and is worldwide). Gradations in skin color are probably the first thing we notice about people after their sex.

In both north and south, whites cooperated in actively or passively impeding blacks, denying them decently paid jobs, residence in their communities, jobs in their workplaces, and places in schools and other institutions. Under persecution, thriving black communities dwindled into dirt-poor ghettos full of neglected children: both parents had to work just to survive, no child-care facilities existed or money to pay for them if they had.

After the industrial revolution, the middle class in England, the United States, and Europe treated the working class similarly and caused them similar suffering. But some middle-class people pitied and worked to ameliorate workers' situation; more important, workers themselves achieved a rough solidarity, a class-consciousness that enabled them to fight for decent lives. Their numbers and solidarity frightened governments and industry into making concessions to them. Whites had far less empathy for blacks; the racist myth assumes that blacks hate whites and are a mortal threat to all whites—although as we have seen, the oppressor always hates the oppressed far more than the opposite. Every black-consciousness movement that has arisen in the United States has been swiftly and brutally suppressed, and black leaders imprisoned or killed. Blacks remain about 15 percent of the population of the United States; they lack the numbers to threaten to shut down society. Under J. Edgar Hoover, the FBI pursued a policy of intimidation even against the nonviolent campaign of Martin Luther King Jr. When blacks frighten industry or government, those bodies do not hesitate to use force. Public outcry is limited to blacks and a few whites because whites, who far outnumber blacks, have been convinced by racist propaganda.

Racism was fostered by intellectuals who taught that blacks were subhuman, morally degenerate, and incapable of education. Their ideas were based in the work of scientists (who "scientifically" defended the enslavement of Africans) like Dr. Cesare Lombroso (who also cast contempt on women and Jews: see chapter 8), whose book, *Criminal Man* (1876), asserted that men with non-Anglo-Saxon features tend to love "idleness and orgies," pursue evil for its own sake, lust to murder, mutilate corpses, and "tear . . . flesh and drink . . . blood." A similar campaign was waged against immigrants who came to the United States in the late nineteenth century. Theodore Roosevelt and Henry Cabot Lodge upheld "eugenic" ideas foreshadowing those of Hitler. Xenophobia spread as the "science" of eugenics taught that certain groups—mainly Latins, Slavs, and Jews—tended to be feeble-minded and must be sterilized so as not to pass on the trait. "Manliness," the great good, required white racial solidarity and a warrior ethic; European anarchists and socialists were "effeminate" and decadent. By 1900 reformers fully believed in hereditary criminal tendencies and "irredeemable deviance." Massive propaganda campaigns in the 1950s and 1960s quieted such views, but they still thrive.

People concerned with True Womanhood were oblivious to black or working-class women. Only "ladies" were human—other women were outside the realm of discourse. The elevation of "ladies" (the word automatically excluded blacks or workers) led to the onus of sexual sin and evil in the world being placed on female "nonladies," especially blacks. Society at large assumed that black women were *inherently* immoral, sexually licentious. The irony that this judgment was the result of their victimization by white men is too cruel to bear.

Southerners justified violence against blacks by claiming they were protecting the virtue of "white womanhood." They were also implicitly warning white women who were asserting themselves in the new climate. The "pursuit of the black rapist represented a trade-off . . . the right of the southern lady to protection presupposed her obligation to obey."[24] White men had always abused white women, belittling them, taking black slave lovers, battering them when they were drunk. Suddenly these same women were "unsullied alabaster icons," so delicate that a black man's glance could pollute them.[25] But a myth of "knights" protecting chastity gave violence a Christian religious basis.

The south's persecution of black men of course harmed black women. A nineteenth-century historian wrote that blacks were so degenerate they could not survive without slavery and white supervision, and that black men raped white women in disgust at the "wantonness" of black women.[26] His view was not extremist; it was mainstream thinking. From the post-Civil War until the civil rights movement, black women in the United States were perceived—and

treated—as sexually available to any man.

Vigilante groups—the White Citizens' Council, The Knights of the White Camelia, The Knights of the White Magnolia, and the Ku Klux Klan—used terror as a weapon. All lynched blacks; the Klan soon became a terrorist gang. Sheets concealed their faces, transforming men considered pillars of the community into outlaws whose trademark was lynching, often in a brazenly public carnival atmosphere. They castrated blacks and fought over body parts as trophies.[27] Black executions increased in time: an average of fifty-seven black men a year were lynched in the 1880s; in the 1890s, 116 blacks every year except 1892, when 162 souls were lynched—four outside the south. The murders were invariably presented as retribution for black men's approaching white women but in the climate of the south at that time, black men did not even dare to look at white women—and five people hanged in 1892 were women.

A woman led the fight against lynching. Ida B. Wells (1862–1931), born six months before the Emancipation Proclamation to slaves in Holly Springs, Mississippi, went to a local Freedman's Aid Bureau school. But when she was fourteen, her parents and three siblings died in a yellow fever epidemic. Claiming she was eighteen, she applied for a teaching job to support her remaining four siblings and taught in Holly Springs until she was twenty-two, when she moved to Memphis. There, she refused to leave the all-white "ladies" car of a train (she had all the attributes of a lady but blacks could not be "ladies"), and was thrown off. Wells' account of this experience for a black-owned newspaper opened a new career for her. When she wrote about Memphis schools providing inferior education for black children, she was fired from her teaching job. She then earned her living by her pen: traveling throughout the south, she wrote about black people. In 1889 she bought into the *Memphis Free Speech*, and became editor.

The peak year of lynchings, 1892, changed Wells' life. Three young black men were lynched for raping a white woman. Wells knew their real crime was running a successful grocery store in competition with a white one. She wrote a powerful condemnation of the lynching, urging blacks to move to Oklahoma Territory. Thousands did. She remained in Memphis to boycott the city trolley system until a mob of whites invaded her newspaper office, destroyed the press, and threatened her life. She took them seriously, moved north, and embarked on a campaign of lecturing and writing about white terrorism against blacks. Her pamphlet, "Southern Horrors," itemizes the extent and acceptance of lynching in the south, stressing that such murders had nothing to do with white women or sex, but were racially motivated executions.

The indefatigable Wells founded women's clubs and antilynching committees in the north; she toured England, lecturing and gaining considerable support for her antilynching movement. In 1895 she married, settled in Chicago with her husband, Ferdinand Barnett, and published *A Red Record* (with an introduction by Frederick Douglass), which recorded the lynchings of the three previous years in brutal detail. Wells was part of an 1898 delegation which demanded that President McKinley act on the lynching of a black South Carolina postmaster. Huge public anger rose against her, but she never stopped. Around 1900 she joined other crusades like the Niagara movement, a campaign for racial equality led by Du Bois, and helped found the National Association for the Advancement of Colored People (NAACP).

A feminist, Wells joined the woman suffrage movement despite southern white suffragist protest; she criticized Susan Anthony for allowing segregation in the movement. In the course of her career, she argued with everyone. She rightly accused WCTU head Frances Willard of racism; she defied the United States Secret Service when it threatened to arrest her for treason if she would not stop publicizing the government's hanging of nineteen black soldiers who defended themselves against an attack by white soldiers. She fought with important black leaders like Booker T. Washington, who did not support equal rights for blacks and was for much of his career an apologist for white supremacy, and with Du Bois and the

NAACP, for the weakness of their antilynching program. Wells was one of a handful of women who, unlike male leaders, refused ever to compromise for the sake of profit, advancement, or obedience to a party. Like Emma Goldman and Rosa Luxemburg, she ended her life in political isolation. Like them, she remained steadfast to the truth as she saw it, and looking backward, we must acknowledge her vision as indeed true.

The Black Middle Class

Black women educated their daughters: an African American woman passed the bar exam in the 1880s. The first female physicians to practice in the south were black. Around 1900 Booker T. Washington's National Business League listed thousands of accomplished black women: journalists, writers, artists, 164 ministers, 160 physicians, 10 lawyers, 7 dentists, 1185 musicians and music teachers, and 13,525 educators.[28] Blacks developed class-consciousness and a new militancy; some joined Marcus Garvey's Universal Negro Improvement Association (UNIA), the only serious African nationalist movement to emerge in the United States.

Marcus Garvey, a charismatic West Indian, declared that European imperialism was dying. Insisting that blacks would never be treated as equal in the United States, he urged they return to Africa to create a new united society. Calling himself Provisional President of Africa, he planned to buy a steamship to transport people to Liberia. Drawing poorer blacks (who had reason to agree with his negative estimate of their future in the United States) partly by disparaging light-skinned blacks, he held huge UNIA rallies with pomp and pageantry—complete with plumed hats, medals, titles, and parades—established an African Orthodox Church with a black Virgin and a white Satan, and supported women's rights.

As soon as the First World War ended, the United States government began a campaign to root out "subversives"—people who dissented on any ground from the capitalist status quo—by creating a division of the Justice Department under J. Edgar Hoover.

One of its targets was Garvey. In 1920 Garvey held the first UNIA convention in Madison Square Garden, and the following year sent the first UNIA mission to Liberia. In 1923, Hoover arrested Garvey for mail fraud, imprisoning him for three months until President Harding ordered him released. Two years later he was convicted and imprisoned, and in 1927 President Coolidge commuted Garvey's sentence and deported him as an undesirable alien.

Many middle-class blacks and black intellectuals opposed Garvey. The intellectuals were creating a brilliant new culture in northern cities, centered in Harlem and called the Harlem Renaissance. It began just after the First World War, and was perhaps rooted in black music, the first characteristically American music and, worldwide, the most influential music of the twentieth century.

Blacks had distinguished themselves in the arts before the twentieth century: we have previously noted New England poet Phillis Wheatley and sculptor Edmonia Lewis (1843–1900?).[29] The first novel by an African American was by a woman. When Harriet E. Wilson published *Our Nig* (1859), whites ignored it because the novel dealt with northern racism in a period when northerners felt self-righteous because they were fighting for abolition. When the novel was rediscovered, it was deemed so good that it was said to have been written by *a white man posing as a black woman*.[30] Many black women wrote in the late nineteenth century: the best known are Frances Ellen Watkins Harper, Alice Dunbar-Nelson, and Anne Perry.[31]

But in the 1920s African American music, art, and literature suddenly flowered magnificently. Harlem was a center of excitement: while exhilarating Garveyite rallies drew huge crowds at Liberty Hall, the 135th Street YMCA presented speakers like Du Bois and plays by Du Bois, Angelina Grimké, or Georgia Douglas Johnson, and a new generation of black poets read at the 135th Street branch of the New York Public Library (now Schomburg Center). Paul Robeson appeared on stage; offered a theatrical career, he turned it down for law school. Artists like Bessie Smith, Josephine Baker, Louis Armstrong, and Duke Ellington performed in Harlem nightclubs, which were in the height of fashion. (Yet clubs like Connie's Inn and the famous Cotton Club accepted blacks as performers only, not as patrons. They were also too expensive for most blacks. Some clubs were mixed and some all-black.) Downtown, all-black musicals and revues were staged for the first time, with huge success; Edna Guy did classical dance; and Marian Anderson sang at Town Hall.

In Europe, where jazz and black music were adored, black singers like coloratura Marie Selika and soprano Caterina Jarboro built operatic careers, and sculptor Meta Vaux Warrick (1877–1968) and portraitist Laura Wheeler Waring studied and exhibited. Warrick studied at the Pennsylvania School of Industrial Arts and the Colarossi Academy in Paris, where she met Saint-Gaudens and Rodin. Returning to the United States, she married Solomon Fuller, a physician, in Framingham, Massachusetts, and over his opposition built a studio with her own hands. Although insufficiently appreciated in its own time, her powerful work inspired later generations. Augusta Savage (1900–62), another inadequately appreciated black woman artist, was born in Florida and was one of the first women to study sculpture at Cooper Union. Sculptor Selma Burke (1900–95) is remembered for the Franklin Delano Roosevelt profile on the dime. The greatest artists of the movement were Warrick and Aaron Douglas (1898–1979), the Harlem painters who broke with academicism to create a brilliant African American style.[32]

In the 1920s Douglas met Du Bois, the Harvard-educated editor of the NAACP magazine *The Crisis*, and did designs and illustrations for *The New Negro* (1925), the literary anthology edited by Alain Locke that first brought widespread attention to Harlem Renaissance male writers like James Weldon Johnson, Countee Cullen, Langston Hughes, and Sterling Brown. Locke, a philosopher, devoted a 1925 issue of *Survey Graphic Magazine* exclusively to Harlem artists; it became the manifesto of the movement. Some intellectuals wanted African American artists to withdraw from

American culture entirely. Locke wanted them to express their Americanism with pride in their history and culture—African heritage, black traditions, and community life.[33]

Jessie Fauset (1885–1961), who published *There Is Confusion* in 1920, was the first woman identified with the Harlem Renaissance to publish a novel. Described as the "most prolific novelist of the Harlem Renaissance," she published four novels between 1924 and 1933 and edited *The Crisis*. An advocate of black pride, she tried to reach all of the United States.[34] Claude McKay, a Jamaican living in Harlem, issued *Harlem Shadows* (1922), the first book of poetry published by a Harlem Renaissance poet, celebrating black beauty. Other black literary figures like poet James Weldon Johnson, who edited an anthology of Black American verse, Jean Toomer, author of *Cane* and other novels, poets Countee Cullen and Langston Hughes, as well as Carl Van Vechten, whose novel *Nigger Heaven* deals with Harlem life, all helped bring a new consciousness, a new language into American culture. Nella Larsen, who had a Danish mother and a black father from the Virgin Islands, published *Quicksand* (1928) and *Passing* (1929). But the most important woman connected with the Harlem movement was Zora Neale Hurston (1901–60).

Black colleges and universities lacked the trust funds that supported white institutions, with portfolios built up over decades by prosperous alumni. Howard University, the largest black college in the United States, depended on Congress for funding, and government funding means government control. In the repressive 1920s it was discovered that the Howard library contained a book promoting socialism. A Congressional reprimand forced the president of Howard to apologize, vowing that the school neither taught nor advocated socialism. Zora Neale Hurston protested in *The Messenger*, the most militant black journal of the period, that the president "should have informed the body that we could teach what we liked and if the money was withheld, we would have the satisfaction of being untrammeled."[35] After a year at Howard, she went to

New York to study anthropology at Barnard with Franz Boas and Ruth Benedict. In 1925, she became editor of a black journal, *The Spokesman*, stressing literature based on black folklore. She published her first book of poems in 1926, and in 1937 produced her masterpiece, *Their Eyes Were Watching God*. She disappeared after the Harlem Renaissance at the end of the 1930s and died penniless and in oblivion in 1950, to be rediscovered by feminists in the early 1970s.

The Harlem movement spread to Washington, DC, Cleveland, and Chicago, strengthening African American confidence and identity. Then the Depression hit and the movement was over. Langston Hughes later wrote: "Between 1919 and 1929, Harlem was in vogue." Economic recessions always wipe out the poor first, and the Depression gradually ravaged Harlem. It was never the same again. During the 1930s many blacks turned to Communism as their only hope. The great majority of blacks were thrust back into poverty and marginality, but the monuments of the Harlem Renaissance remain to inspire future generations of blacks and whites.

White terrorism made normal life impossible for blacks in the south. When the urgencies of the First World War forced northern industry to open jobs to blacks, a mass migration occurred: 2 million blacks moved to northern cities between the two world wars. Whenever possible, black families tried to educate their children, and in periods of prosperity many entered the middle economic class. But black middle-class people were not treated as part of "the middle class"; they were shut out of middle-class and even poor white neighborhoods clear across the United States.

Wealthy, middle class, or poor, blacks lived in segregated communities, attended black churches, and joined black social organizations. Their lives were circumscribed by the black community and they were either ill at ease or outright terrified in the white one. Whites remained ignorant of blacks, if not downright hostile. At first blacks could express themselves or take the lead only in church: the church was their shelter.[36] Black class structure was modeled on that of the master race—the elite were light-skinned—but it accorded people status for education and correct behavior rather than for income.

During the First World War, some African Americans who moved north to take jobs in industry earned decent wages for the first time in their lives; they sent their children to standard integrated schools, voted, held office, and gained confidence in themselves as part of the larger world. As male doctors, teachers, educated ministers, and small businessmen carried their families into the middle class, their wives formed social clubs and reform societies, becoming leaders in antilynching and suffrage campaigns.

The Temperance Movement

The most important nineteenth-century female society was the Women's Christian Temperance Union (WCTU). A temperance society had been formed by men and women earlier in the century, but it was sidetracked by the Civil War. In the depression years of 1873–74, women in the midwest protested male drinking. Imitating itinerant preachers, they invaded town bars singing hymns and reciting scripture, praying and urging temperance. Nearly 25,000 women took to Philadelphia streets in an 1874 "Women's Crusade": they protested at 406 bars, pressured 38 church members to evict saloons from their property, persuaded 80 bartenders to resign, and extracted pledges of temperance from 280.[37] They formally organized as the WCTU.

National officers sent Plans of Work to WCTU locals detailing suggested strategies. In 1874 they recommended holding Gospel Temperance meetings "in the streets, billiard-halls, and churches . . . offering the Gospel cure for intemperance," with women moving among the audience playing the tune of "Jesus, Lover of My Soul" to invest the act with the solemnity of a religious service, urging people to come forward and sign a pledge. When Frances Willard (1839–98) became president of the WCTU, it became a political force. She ran it from 1879 until her death.

Born to educated parents in Wisconsin, Willard was a genius: with only a mediocre education at a female seminary, and after only a few years of teaching, she became president of Evanston College for Ladies. When Northwestern University absorbed Evanston, she became dean. Dealing with an all-male board of trustees and a president who was her ex-fiancé may have radicalized her, because after three years she sought another vocation. Rising equally swiftly in temperance work, she became head of the Illinois chapter, then the national union, in months. Temperance was not a passion but a vehicle for Willard; her goal was always to attract apolitical women into a militant women's rights movement.

Temperance drew women like no other cause. Most WCTU members were middle class, not poor women visibly victimized by husbands who drank their wages and abused their families. We may surmise what went on in middle-class homes. The women of the WCTU were convinced that banning alcohol would purify the world of evil. Soon after her election as president, Willard (called "St. Frances" by her followers) launched a campaign, collecting 180,000 signatures on a petition to prohibit the sale of alcohol. Within a few years, the crusade had spread to every state in the union. Willard then extended her "Home Protection" campaign, arguing that only the vote would enable women to fulfill their True Womanhood and protect their homes from the "demon rum."

By 1880 the WCTU had become the largest female organization ever seen in the United States, international in scope and organization, and the largest reform movement of the century. Over 200,000 dues-paying members and thousands more sympathizers embraced the notion of woman's "separate sphere." They founded their reform philosophy on it, seeing temperance agitation as a natural extension of their roles as wives and mothers protecting the home. Accepting a narrow role at first, they expanded it, storming streets, taverns, and legislatures to "purify" them in the name of the home. More than any other female society in the nineteenth-century United States, WCTU members were conservative, domestic, pious, respectable middle-class married white women who never touched alcohol or tobacco, went to church regularly, and were sexually irreproachable—precisely what society demanded they be. They were pressuring men with the very morality that men insisted they uphold, and temperance literature contains a certain retaliatory aspect. Noting that "in the popular division of responsibility . . . the father may be a moderate drinker [but] the failure of the boy to grow up good and pure is adjudged to be his mother's fault," it stressed mothers' importance and responsibility.

Injustices suffered by other groups mattered less to Willard than her constituency and its aim, "to make the whole world *homelike*." She said this was her goal: maybe it was or maybe this was the only discourse available to her. For it is true that many women who crusaded in the name of domesticity and the Home never married, had children, or managed homes. Willard was single and worked with an exclusively female support network that included single women like Catherine Beecher and Sarah Josepha Hale, who supported themselves by advising women on domestic matters but never ran their own homes. Other female agitators had marriages unconventional by nineteenth-century standards: Elizabeth Cady Stanton discarded her husband; Lucy Stone found a supportive one.

In 1881 Willard succeeded in obtaining WCTU endorsement of woman suffrage. Although some suffragists were uncomfortable with WCTU support, they welcomed the hundreds of thousands of women it added to the movement. When Willard died—before Prohibition became law—her organization reverted to its old form, becoming a single-issue lobby. Her great accomplishment was not banning alcohol, but raising the consciousness of thousands of middle-class women about their importance to society and their right to a voice.

Settlement and Prisons in the United States

Idealistic young college graduates in the United States were inspired by the British settlement movement, and in 1886 Stanton Coit founded the first settlement house in the United States, the Neighborhood Guild in New York City. Settlement swiftly became a female cause as young educated middle-class women seized this outlet for their abilities. In 1889 seven Smith College alumnae rented a tenement on New York's Lower East Side for a settlement house. Other women founded settlements in Boston, Philadelphia, and Pittsburgh; Jane Addams and Ellen Gates Starr founded Hull House in Chicago; and Lillian Wald founded the Nurses' Settlement in New York. In 1894 Susan Chester, a Vassar graduate, built the Log Cabin settlement near Ashville, North Carolina, to adapt urban reforms to a rural area. She started clubs for girls and women, revived the weaving industry, and created a library. Local people regularly walked eleven miles to her cabin to use the cherished library.

Jane Addams, one of those sickly middle-class single women who "proved" men's claim that women were weak, was educated by her wealthy family and then was expected to spend her life at home caring for aging relatives. She understandably collapsed with "nervous prostration" and was treated by Dr. S. Weir Mitchell (who also treated Edith Wharton). His Hospital of Orthopedic and Nervous Diseases specialized in female "nervous complaints." A spinal problem kept her bedridden for six months and in a leather, whalebone, and steel corset for two years. But when she founded Hull House (and, perhaps, acknowledged her sexuality) she recuperated. Her dream was to transform the poor community by helping poor women find work: she later said that helping others helped her even more. Their same-sex relationships sustained Addams and Lillian Wald throughout their lives.[38]

Most settlement workers focused on practical programs like child-care centers, kindergartens, manual training, and industrial education. Hull House collected money to feed striking Chicago textile workers in 1896. In 1910 Addams derided the idea that "the sheltered, educated girl has nothing to do with the bitter poverty and . . . social maladjustment which is all about her, and which, after all, cannot be concealed, for it breaks through poetry and literature in a burning tide which overwhelms her; it peers at her in the form of heavy-laden market women and underpaid street laborers, gibing her with a sense of her uselessness."[39] When she wrote this, over four hundred settlements thrived in the United States.

Most American settlements were nonsectarian; workers lived in the settlement houses, their relations with their poor neighbors uneasily progressing from suspicion to affection. The overwhelming majority of settlers (three-quarters) were women, young, single, and college-educated. A tiny group in the poor masses, they were extremely effective, keeping their organizations flexible and personal. Female "settlers" associated with poverty, prostitution, and criminality.

In 1857 reformers sympathetic to women accused of crimes, especially young ones ("juvenile delinquents") established the first reform school for girls, in Massachusetts. Like sisters in British penitentiaries, women superintendents in reform schools had an exalted notion of their task. One wrote: "It is sublime work to save a woman, for in her bosom generations are embodied, and in her hands, if perverted, the fate of innumerable men is held."[40] Reformers tried to train women in domestic skills; most American reform organizations were not tied to a church, but reform was pervaded with moralistic thinking based in religious notions of purity and taint, especially when it concerned women.

Sex determined what was a crime. Men were jailed for (alleged) violence to property or persons, but women could be confined in reformatories or lunatic asylums for masturbating or sex before marriage—or "wantonness." Some girls were incarcerated for life for such acts. Early reformers kept them from "temptation" by locking them in reformatories and teaching them domestic skills to "redeem" them. Once reformers accepted eugenic theories that viewed criminal tendencies as hereditary and deviance irredeemable, they confined women with no effort at reform.

Many institutions were extremely punitive, using solitary meals, permanent handcuffing, and imprisonment in dungeons to control inmates. In a rare case of organized resistance, women in the New York Hudson House of Refuge rioted to protest the dungeon and extreme corporal punishment in 1899. Late in the century, prison reformers worked for separate prisons for women. Women in mixed prisons were treated very harshly—at Sing Sing Prison, they had their hair cut off, were gagged, locked in straitjackets, and kept in solitary confinement cells without windows or light. Such abuses roused feminists to work for prisoners' rights as "their sisters' keepers." In female prisons, female superintendents used gentler means to keep order.[41]

Utopian Visions after the Civil War

The early socialist agricultural cooperative communities had been forgotten, but some people devised cooperative techniques geared to industrial society. In 1868–69, Melusina Fay Peirce, the wife of a Harvard professor, published a series of articles in *Atlantic Monthly.* She argued that women should do two things "as the conditions not only of the future happiness, progress and elevation of their sex, but of its bare respectability and morality. First: They must earn their own living; Second: They must be organized among themselves." She urged cooperative stores, kitchens, laundries, and bakeries; she suggested that groups of women do housework cooperatively, billing husbands for the service on the same scale as skilled male workers. Men did not want their wives working to "make other men comfortable," but public kitchens and cooperative dining halls became popular late in the century, some supported by the settlements. Single women ran an impressive array of cooked-food delivery services, cooperative dining clubs, and communal bakeries and laundries, and they delivered prepared food by horse-drawn carriage or automobile in towns from Evanston, Illinois, to Palo

Alto, California, from 1869 to 1920.

Edward Bellamy's *Looking Backward*, published in 1888, became one of the century's best sellers. The hero of Bellamy's utopian novel awakes in 2000 to a world in which women have full political and economic equality. The state supports pregnant women and pays for domestic work in public kitchens and dining rooms, day schools and nurseries, freeing women from economic dependence on men. The novel inspired the political Nationalist movement.

Charlotte Perkins Gilman (1860–1935) became spokesperson for the movement. Gilman, grandniece of Harriet Beecher Stowe, was a complex and important figure.[42] Her father deserted the family when she was seven, and her childhood and adolescence were very unhappy. Her brother was sent to MIT and earned a degree, but Charlotte was allowed only a short stay at the Rhode Island School of Design. She married at twenty-four but, after giving birth to a daughter the next year, had an acute breakdown. Despite severe depression, she began to write. When she recovered, she divorced her husband. When he remarried, she gave him custody of her daughter, Katherine, and went off to write and lecture in Europe and the United States. In 1892 she published the powerful "The Yellow Wallpaper," a claustrophobic account of a woman driven mad by the seemingly loving ministrations of her doctor husband.

Gilman went on to publish *Women and Economics* in 1898, a brilliant analysis of modern industrial economy and women's position within it. Society confuses women's sexual and economic functions, in a holdover from the past that is anachronistic in modern industrial society. Gilman urged economic reorganization to give women equal participation in public life and enable them to develop fully into independent human beings who contribute to society, "rather than creatures of sex": men sell labor for survival but women, denied wage-earning jobs, were forced to sell sex to survive. Her next book, *The Home: Its Work and Influence* (1903), accused the single-family home of wasting resources and isolating women. She proposed "French flats" (apartments), in which wives, not domestic servants, would be paid for household maintenance. Mechanized household gadgets only chain women to the house: professional services should launder, wash diapers, prepare food, and do other household tasks. Gilman also wrote utopian novels: *Herland* (1915), the most famous, was serialized in her magazine *The Forerunner*, which for fifteen years published feminist analyses of law, education, fashion, and sports. Gilman was another expert on domesticity who had repudiated it in her life.

CHAPTER 7

WOMAN SUFFRAGE IN THE UNITED STATES AND GREAT BRITAIN

In the United States

THE AMERICAN SUFFRAGE MOVEMENT was an uneasy alliance of women whose main bond beyond their sex and inferior status was work in some area of reform. Few were militant feminists. Some were active abolitionists; most were evangelicals working in moral reform, political conservatives who claimed a right to political action on grounds of moral superiority. Their vision of women as superior collided with the feminist vision of women as like men. Conflicting interpretations of Woman's Nature produced a tension that characterized the suffrage movement (and women's movements into the present) in debates over education, protective legislation, maternity leave, and other issues.

In the early republic, some women had the franchise: in 1783 New Jersey granted the vote to all residents of age worth £50. Only two women voted in 1787, because of confusion about eligibility, but few women had £50. Women's participation in local elections (in large numbers in 1797), aroused male resentment: newspaper articles ridiculed "petticoat politics," warning of a legislature "filled with petticoats." Men opposed to women's voting often claimed that slaves did too; an 1806 election was voided after reports that women, blacks, and white men voted more than once. After John Condict, a Republican representative from Essex County, New Jersey, was nearly defeated by women's vote, he led a campaign to limit eligibility. In 1807 New Jersey limited the franchise to white male adults with property.

In the nineteenth century, women made giant steps toward full citizenship, but won not one victory for woman suffrage. Men feared suffrage more than any other reform as a threat to "the family," that is, to male supremacy. Too cowardly to admit this explicitly, they argued that women who wanted the vote were insulting their husbands, who always voted in the best interests of the entire family. Woman suffrage would generate domestic chaos (two voices instead of one), unsex women, and emasculate men, as women abandoned housekeeping and child-rearing, leaving them to men.[1]

Suffragist-abolitionists were disturbed by the Fifteenth Amendment because, in granting suffrage to freed slaves, it added a word never before used in the constitution—*male.* Introducing sex discrimination into the constitution affronted all women, especially abolitionists. In essence, the drafters of the amendment were rubbing female abolitionists' noses in their victory: women were being made to pay for abolition. Suffragists, outraged that men whose slavery they had fought to end had been granted a right denied them, became racist: patriarchy had triumphed again.

Citizens could work to pass the amendment extending suffrage at least to black men, or work against it. Most male and some female abolitionists lobbied for the amendment, dissociating themselves from the women's movement. In 1865 the charismatic antislavery orator Wendell Phillips told suffragists he was setting aside female suffrage to ensure franchise to newly emancipated black males: "I hope in time to be as bold as Stuart Mill and add to that last clause 'sex.' But this hour belongs to the negro." The *negro* was apparently male. Devastated by the amendment's wording, bitterly disappointed by the desertion of black and white abolitionists whose cause they had championed, women in the suffrage movement split. Elizabeth Stanton, Susan Anthony, and others in the National Woman Suffrage Association (NWSA) rejected the Fifteenth Amendment. Lucy Stone, her husband Henry Blackwell, and Julia Ward Howe accepted it and left the NWSA to found the American Woman Suffrage Association (AWSA).

The adamant opposition to the women's movement, which had originally called for a total makeover of society, had forced it to narrow to a single issue: suffrage. Some contemporary feminists fault the single-minded pursuit of suffrage, a strategy that ignored other needs and relinquished hope for larger change. But men obstructed every proposal that might relax legal and social constrictions on women—even those that would benefit men, like contraception. Given the fierce opposition, it may have been necessary to concentrate on one issue.

In addition, a footnote: the December 1999–January 2000 issue of *Ms. Magazine* featured interviews with a dozen women a hundred years old or older. One of the questions asked them was what event was most important for women during the preceding century. Nine of them said "the vote"; two said feminism (or women's lib); and one, a Chinese woman whose feet had been bound as a child, cited the end of footbinding. People now disenchanted with the political scene dismiss the importance of the vote, but the women who lived through not having it, then having it, know better.[2]

Over the century, middle-class women's birth rate dropped by half. The decrease from an average of 7.04 children for each married woman in 1800, to 3.56 in 1900, suggests that women took control of reproduction somehow. They were given very little information about contraception or their sexual and reproductive organs; doctors authoritatively offered false advice, designating as safe a time of month when we know now conception is most likely, or insisting that women could not get pregnant if they did not reach orgasm. Women often refused sex or made men withdraw before orgasm—which should have made men welcome birth-control devices. Ignorance of birth control was willful. Rubber condoms were advertised and available in the east in the 1850s. A diaphragm-like "womb veil" invented before 1864 was banned in the United States until the 1920s.

A small group of feminists, including the redoubtable Victoria Woodhull, argued for contraception to limit family size. (They did not claim to want to free sex from conception or ease women's burden: such ideas were too radical for the times.) But men opposed "planned parenthood." In the front line against contraception were

religious leaders, backed by a male establishment that feared giving women such freedom. Theodore Roosevelt's denunciation of contraception as "race suicide" (white women must reproduce or the nation would be overrun by "hunger-bitten hordes") was popular with elite southern whites. In 1872 New York's YMCA, to enforce the ban on immoral material (anything mentioning sex), hired investigator Anthony Comstock "to prosecute, in all legal forms, the traffic in bad books, prints and instruments." He later worked in the same job for the United States Post Office so zealously that the ban was called the "Comstock law." His first victim was Victoria Woodhull.

Born in 1838 in Ohio, one of ten children, Woodhull was neglected and uneducated, a vagabond. In her teens, she turned to spiritualism. She married at fifteen but continued to travel, earning her living as a clairvoyant for a decade. Beautiful, intelligent, and enterprising, she divorced, remarried, then met Cornelius Vanderbilt. She persuaded him to back a New York brokerage company that she founded with her sister, Tennessee Claflin. Woodhull, Claflin, & Co., the "Lady Brokers of Wall Street," made a fortune and in 1870 persuaded socialist Stephen Pearl Andrews to publish a weekly paper, *Woodhull and Claflin's Weekly*, which offered radical feminist ideas even about sex: equal rights for women, "free love," ending the double sexual standard and sexual hypocrisy. Woodhull became famous (or infamous); the popular press called her "Mrs. Satan," "Queen of Prostitutes." Yet she appeared in the Congress speaking in favor of woman suffrage.

This extraordinary woman argued that the Fourteenth and Fifteenth Amendments granted citizenship to everyone born or naturalized in the United States; women were citizens, and suffrage was a right of citizens which could be endorsed by a mere Congressional Act. Her 1871 speech won the support of Stanton and Anthony (and of the NWSA), who had been ambivalent about Woodhull. Hundreds of women went to polls in 1871 and 1872. Anthony went to one in Rochester, expecting to be turned away and planning to sue, but was allowed to vote. Two weeks later, federal marshals banged on her door and arrested her for voting illegally. She lost her court case but used it to publicize woman suffrage. Woodhull tried to take over the NWSA; when Anthony thwarted her, she started her own Equal Rights party, which nominated her for president and Frederick Douglass for vice president (without his knowledge). Douglass disclaimed the nomination, and no campaign was launched.

But Woodhull's most scandalous act was her revelation in 1871 of an adulterous love affair between Henry Ward Beecher, a famous reform minister, and Elizabeth Tilton, wife of his best friend, reformer Theodore Tilton, both his parishioners. The affair had long been rumored; Woodhull may have published it to expose sexual hypocrisy in the middle class, but people were less shocked by the affair than by her defying propriety in revealing such behavior in moral leaders. Tilton sued Beecher for misconduct. The sensational trial dragged on for weeks and ended in a hung jury: Elizabeth Tilton could not testify in her own defense. It harmed the women's movement: Beecher had been president of the AWSA;

Stanton and Anthony, who defended Elizabeth Tilton, were tainted. People associated the Beecher-Tilton affair and Woodhull's "free love" with the women's rights movement.

By the 1890s publicly approved laws muzzled contraception advocates and banned birth-control devices and information. The only means to limit family size were abstinence or abortion. From 1800 to 1830 there was (estimated) one abortion for thirty live births; by 1850 the figure was one in six. Since it was illegal, women without sympathetic doctors (fortunately, many doctors were sympathetic) had to resort to riskier practitioners. Two-thirds of the women who sought abortions were married, 60 percent had one child or more. Those too poor to pay for an expensive illegal procedure aborted themselves. Many died rather than bear another child: in the 1920s, one of two pregnancies was aborted.

Sojourner Truth and Stanton predicted that the constitutional amendments would deepen sexual antagonism: "Woman will then know with what power she has to contend. It will be male vs. female, the land over." Both Stanton and Anthony seemed most offended by the right of lower-class men—ex-slaves, indigents, immigrants—to vote, when middle-class women could not. Stanton was outraged at "refined" white women being ruled by men from "the lower orders of Chinese, Africans, Germans and Irish, with their low ideas of womanhood." Anthony fumed: "While the dominant party have with one hand lifted up *two million black men* and crowned them with the honor and dignity of citizenship, with the other they have dethroned *fifteen million white women*—their own mothers and sisters, their own wives and daughters—and cast them under the heel of the lowest orders of manhood." Like the European feminists who tried to offset class fear by urging that only propertied women be granted suffrage, Stanton suggested giving middle-class white women the vote to outweigh "the Freedmen of the South and the millions of foreigners now crowding our shores." Giving black men the vote, she said, was giving them a virtual license to rape. As usual, rage was directed *below* rather than above.

Still, blacks worked for woman suffrage. Sojourner Truth, Frances Harper, Sarah Redmond, Mattie Griffith, and Hattie Purvis—all well-known abolitionists—crisscrossed the country by stagecoach, train, and steamboat, sometimes trudging on foot to carry the crusade to towns in Ohio and upper New York State, Wisconsin and down the Missouri River to Kansas City. Frederick Douglass, the six black men in the Massachusetts House of Representatives, and seven of eight black congressmen from South Carolina supported woman suffrage. Inspired by Victoria Woodhull, Mary Ann Shadd Cary registered to vote in the District of Columbia in 1871.

Their huge effort did not succeed during their lives, but Stanton and Anthony have an importance beyond the movement they founded, despite their racist and classist attitudes. They were first to realize that women would not succeed as long as they linked their demands for themselves to demands for others. Imbued with the female ethic of self-sacrifice, women had always tied their needs, like ribbons, to abolition, temperance, or industrial reform packages. Stanton and Anthony saw that women had to work by themselves for themselves in an independent women's movement. They also saw that organization was vital to success.

In 1887 Alice Stone Blackwell, daughter of Lucy Stone and Henry Blackwell, initiated a merger of the AWSA and NWSA into a National American Woman Suffrage Association (NAWSA) with Stanton as president. Perhaps exhausted by the failure of their forty-year effort, Stanton and Anthony adopted a strategy of "expediency." A movement that had begun by demanding justice in human rights was reduced to arguing that votes for women would offset the "foreign influence" (immigrants and black men) in politics. A new generation of suffragists, led by Carrie Chapman Catt and Alice Blackwell, found Stanton rigid and old-fashioned; they could deal with her only through beloved "Aunt Susan" Anthony, who took over as NAWSA president in 1892. But Catt too argued that the nation was threatened by foreign men's votes and wanted them revoked in favor of middle-class women.

Anthony asked Frederick Douglass to absent himself from the next NAWSA convention—*Douglass*, who had spoken at Seneca Falls! The 1895 convention, the first in the south, was to be held in Atlanta, and she feared he would be an embarrassment. Stanton pleased the southern audience by warning against enfranchising "illiterate" women, but Anthony and Stanton's daughter, Harriet Stanton Blatch, voted against her proposals. Stanton, a prolific writer and the intellectual force of the movement, was dejected by the mean narrow thing her cause had become and turned her attention to religion as a major antagonist to women's rights. From 1895 to 1898, she issued the *Woman's Bible*, a commentary on biblical passages on women. Her brilliant work gained her a host of new enemies; even NAWSA voted 53 to 41 to repudiate it officially.

But Stanton was right about the church: Christian churches worked fiercely, if covertly, against suffrage. The most visible lobby opposing woman suffrage, the liquor industry, feared women would vote for prohibition. (The Eighteenth Amendment prohibiting the sale of alcoholic beverages was passed in 1919 *before* women won the vote, and was later repealed. The industry did not foresee that women would someday drink.) Businessmen fought woman suffrage on economic grounds but, like clergymen, camouflaged their views by declaring that God had not intended women to vote.

The 1899 NAWSA convention refused to back a resolution that black women need not ride, according to the Jim Crow laws, in railway smoking cars: claiming NAWSA could not control railroad company policy, Anthony rejected black women's cause. Fearing defection by white southern women if it supported black women, NAWSA let white men dictate its policy. Blacks outnumbered whites in many of the southern states that barred black men from voting. Southerners feared they could not thwart women too: as W.E.B. Du Bois explained, "You can bribe some pauperized Negro laborers with a few dollars at election time, but you cannot bribe a Negro woman."

Yet white women's rejection did not deter black women from working for suffrage—it spurred them on. Fannie Barrier Williams pointed out: "The exclusion of colored women and girls from nearly all places of respectable employment is due mostly to the meanness of American women, and every way that we can check this unkindness by the force of the franchise should be religiously done." By the 1900s the NAACP had a female-staffed suffrage department, and black women's suffrage clubs thrived in tens of American cities. The indomitable Harriet Tubman, Frances Harper, and Mary Church Terrell addressed suffrage meetings.

NAWSA remained divided over the best way to win the franchise. Anthony wanted to concentrate on a constitutional amendment; others urged working state by state. But local campaigns proved disappointing: of four hundred mounted between 1870 and 1910, only seventeen led to referenda and only two approved suffrage. In 1900, worn out by *fifty years* of meetings, speaking, writing, trudging from door to door begging for signatures on petitions, enduring ridicule and hostility, traveling across the country (shocking for a woman alone), sleeping in carriages, suffering frostbite: exhausted and defeated, Susan Anthony resigned—although she remained the vital force and head of the movement until her death in 1906. Her friend Elizabeth Stanton died in 1902. The Seneca Falls generation died feeling they had failed.

In 1907 suffragists, including Stanton's daughter, Harriet Stanton Blatch, met in New York City to discuss ways to revive the crusade. They founded the Equality League of Self-Supporting Women (later the Women's Political Union—WPU), which by 1909 had 19,000 members including Rose Schneiderman and Charlotte Perkins Gilman. In 1910 the WPU launched a new campaign—large-scale demonstrations and parades showing the movement's broad base. A newpaper account of a 1912 march read: "Women who usually see Fifth Avenue through polished windows of their limousines and touring cars strode steadily side by side with pale-faced thin-bodied girls from the sweltering shops of the East Side. . . . All marched with an intensity and purpose that astonished the crowds that lined the streets."[3]

Younger suffragists Alice Paul, Blatch, and Lucy Burns had worked with British suffragists and urged more militant action. They wanted to adopt the British strategy of holding current administrations accountable and protesting against the party in power. The day before Woodrow Wilson's inauguration as president in 1913, they marched in Washington. Ida Wells tried to join the contingent but whites, insisting that southerners would not accept her, urged her to march with a "colored delegation." She disappeared into the crowd but when the parade was under way, suddenly stepped among the Chicagoans and finished with them.

By June 1916 women had won suffrage in presidential elections in twelve states. Hoping women might bloc-vote in the next election, Paul formed the National Woman's Party (NWP) to campaign for pro-suffrage candidates, but its spirited anti-Democratic campaign did not defeat Wilson. In 1917, with the First World War raging in Europe, the NWP picketed the White House with demands for suffrage. For months, the police remained passive and Wilson courteous, but after the Russian Revolution the Russian Kerensky, whose revolutionary government had granted woman suffrage and other rights, visited the White House. Suffragists held up banners announcing that the United States was not a democracy but the fief of Kaiser Wilson. Male onlookers, some uniformed military men, attacked them violently. Only women were arrested—over five hundred picketers—and nearly a hundred were imprisoned.

Imitating British women, they went on hunger strikes in jail, and American prison officials, like the British, retaliated with forced feeding, martyring the women. Wide publicity roused so much sympathy for them that the government was forced to back down and in March 1918 the District of Columbia Court of Appeals invalidated all prison sentences and illegal arrests of peaceful protesters. Wilson, not personally opposed to woman suffrage, shifted his stance to support it, joining with NAWSA and the NWP to back a federal statute, the Susan B. Anthony Amendment, which passed the House and went to the southern-dominated Senate.

Black women and the NAACP feared an alliance of white suffragists and southern racists, so the NACW's Northeast Federation, representing 6000 black women, applied en masse for membership in NAWSA. NAWSA leaders were appalled: terrified of the south, they were willing to sacrifice black women to gain the vote for whites. They asked black women to defer their aims for the time being for the sake of the *larger cause*—white franchise! While this conflict was hanging, the Senate passed the Anthony Amendment. It still had to be ratified: women faced another fourteen months of lobbying, speechmaking, petitioning, traveling, before the Nineteenth Amendment was finally passed in 1920. The fight for woman suffrage took seventy-two years.

Carrie Chapman Catt wrote that simply to remove the word "male" from the constitution, American women had to conduct "56 campaigns of referenda to male voters; 480 campaigns to get Legislatures to submit suffrage amendments to voters; 47 campaigns to get State constitutional conventions to write women suffrage into State constitutions; 277 campaigns to get State party conventions to include woman suffrage planks; 30 campaigns to get presidential party conventions to adopt woman suffrage planks in party platforms and 19 campaigns with 19 successive Congresses."

Then the official women's movement collapsed, lost cohesion.[4] The strategy of Alice Paul's NWP was concentration on single issues. Believing franchise alone would not change women's status, she urged a constitutional amendment guaranteeing women economic and legal equality. When the Equal Rights Amendment was submitted to Congress in 1923, Crystal Eastman remarked it was worth fighting for even if it took ten years! But focusing on the ERA meant ignoring other matters of vital importance to women—birth

control, *de facto* disfranchisement of black women, peace, and protective legislation. The NWP dismissed these as "diversionary and divisive," the same grounds on which abolitionists sixty years before had renounced the cause of woman suffrage.

But at the moment feminism was falling into disrepute, a host of women's organizations sprang up, many formed by former suffragists.[5] The New League of Women Voters, the National Consumer's Leagues, Business and Professional Women's Clubs, the National Congress of Parents and Teachers, and the American Association of University Women: each had its own specific agenda. They sometimes allied, but solidarity was a thing of the past: the movement had won the only cause that united it.

Analysis of the conflicts between women's organizations in this period shows they defined womanhood differently.[6] They might argue about protective legislation versus equal rights, disarmament versus military preparedness, prohibition versus repeal, but the core of their conflicts concerned the Nature of Woman. Protectionists urged laws forbidding employers to order women seen as "overburdened and vulnerable" to carry heavy weights, do hard labor during pregnancy, work excessive hours, or at night. Stressing woman's difference from man, especially as reproducer, they discussed her *need* to work. The NWP and career women saw women as eager, robust and similar to men. Stressing the social construction of gender, they talked of women's *preference* to work.

Maybe people were so indoctrinated by the age-old division of women into madonnas and whores that they could not see beyond it. No one condemned defining women by one trait—sexuality seen as sinful—which allowed women only asexuality or licentiousness. No one argued that all beings are both vulnerable and strong, or that women's "special" needs were in fact their responsibility for maintaining the human race and supporting their families at the same time. One cannot challenge stereotypes of women without challenging stereotypes of men, received ideas about the nature of nature. The same issues split British women after suffrage.

In Great Britain

For a decade after William Thompson and Anna Wheeler's *Appeal of One Half of the Human Race* in 1825, not one systematic radical analysis of women's status appeared in England.[7] In 1843 Mrs. Hugo Reid's *A Plea For Women* argued that suffrage was women's only recourse from injustice, the only tool that could end the oppression of half of humanity by the other. After the 1857 Divorce Act, some sensational, widely publicized cases of divorce and separation shocked the public into awareness of infidelity and violence in respectable upper-class families. Frances Power Cobbe warned that marriage was a lottery in which any woman could pick "an unfaithful or cruel husband," but no one protested the plight of wives until 1868; even then feminists barely mentioned the areas of greatest suffering: men's rights to women's property, earnings, children, and divorce. They did not address birth control at all.

Because the idea that women were human beings intellectually—or even potentially—equal to men was too radical for Englishmen before the twentieth century, British feminists could not fight for women on that ground. Owenite socialism was long forgotten in society's obsessive pursuit of respectability, and the women in feminist causes were eminently respectable. Many had worked in campaigns to abolish slavery or repeal Corn Laws. They had learned through such campaigns that sustained pressure by organized groups had an effect despite women's lack of political voice, and they brought this knowledge to the emergent women's movement. The antislavery crusade had made them aware of the similarities between slaves and women and that female abolitionists were in the vanguard of feminism in the United States after 1840. British abolitionist Anne Knight wrote the Grimkés after the 1840 London Anti-Slavery Conference refused to seat female delegates: "Yes, dear Angelina dear Sarah, your noble spirits lighted a flame which has warmed [us who] thought not of our bondage."[8]

By 1850 the position of upper middle-class women had

improved enough, especially in education, that they could contemplate achieving political equality with men of their class. Harriet Taylor and John Stuart Mill bolstered this hope. Taylor's "The Enfranchisement of Women," in the *Westminster Review* (1851), asserted that women were equal to men and so were entitled to political equality; Mill's *The Subjection of Women* (1869, written with Taylor), asserted that women were human beings equal to men and should have a political life and realize their natural abilities.

The impetus for the first British women's suffrage society came in 1866 from the great Barbara Leigh Smith (Bodichon) and from prominent woman pioneers in education, medicine, and legislative reform. When the first eminent feminist, John Stuart Mill, was elected to Parliament in 1865, the group was galvanized to collect 1500 signatures on a petition for female householders to vote. In 1867 Mill made the first major public statement on woman suffrage in the House of Commons, generating new suffrage groups and persuading more people to sign petitions, especially in Manchester, where 13,500 signatures were gathered. The first public meeting of Smith's suffrage society was held in London in 1869. After Mill presented a bill for woman suffrage, feminist leaders pursued a policy of regularly presenting private members' bills to the House of Commons. In 1884 Liberal prime minister William Gladstone promised that if women joined a group *he* had set up, they might "earn" the right to vote. He betrayed them, and women abandoned the strategy of pleasing male leaders.

From 1893 to 1906 Manchester textile workers—the best organized female industrial workers in England—joined the suffrage movement by the thousands. A coalition of female trade unionists, socialists, and Women's Cooperative Guild organizers with socialist principles strategized winning the franchise by organizing working-class wives who were more radical than middle-class suffragists.

The lives of working-class wives were hard even if they did not work for wages: "No cause can be won between dinner and tea, and most of us who were married had to work with one hand tied behind us," wrote one. They cooperated: when a woman spoke or went to London on business, another tended her children or prepared her complaining husband's dinner. As political activists in socialist or labor groups or women's trade unions, they well understood the degree of male opposition they faced. No trade union or the Labor Party—or even the radical Independent Labor Party—*ever* supported woman suffrage. Most men wanted women home washing clothes and cooking meals. One man slapped his wife's face publicly on her return from a meeting; others did worse in private. During women's speeches, men heckled them, crying, "Go home and wash the pots!" or "What about the ole man's kippers?" One woman lamented: "Public disapproval can be faced and borne, but domestic unhappiness, the price many of us paid for our opinions and activities, was a very bitter thing."[9]

For two decades, suffragists concentrated on raising the consciousness of educated women, but women of all classes flocked to the movement despite almost universal press hostility. The National Union of Women's Suffrage Societies pressured members of Parliament and the Liberal party, constantly marched, and held fund-raising bazaars, membership drives, and educational meetings. Emmeline Pethick-Lawrence exhorted audiences to work for suffrage not for "the Vote only, but what the Vote means—the moral, the mental, economic, the spiritual enfranchisement of Womanhood; the release of women, the repairing, the rebuilding of that great temple of womanhood, which has been so ruined and defaced." British feminists knew to fight for themselves from the first.

Emmeline Pankhurst, convinced by her experience as a Poor Law guardian that profound change was necessary, joined the suffrage movement in the 1880s, and in 1903, with her daughters Sylvia and Christabel, formed the Women's Social and Political Union (WSPU). In the early 1900s thousands of formerly apolitical middle-class women contributed their time, energy, and money. Fiery, young, impatient women of all classes joined the WSPU, the most militant suffrage group. With the motto "Deeds, Not Words," WSPU members were willing to disrupt or break laws to call attention to the cause.

In 1906 the Pankhursts moved the WSPU to London to be near Parliament and government offices. Emmeline and Frederick Pethick-Lawrence joined Christabel and Emmeline Pankhurst in leading the WSPU. They ruled autocratically, fearing their swiftly growing organization would lose force if it bogged down in democratic decision-making. They sold their journal on street corners, organized thousands of meetings, rallies, and colorful marches throughout the country, and heckled Liberal speakers at by-elections, demanding party support. In under three years, they had seventy-five organizers (they started with one) and an £18,000 income. But in June 1909 Emmeline Pankhurst and eight well-known women were rudely turned away from Parliament. Outraged suffragists smashed government office windows; 108 were arrested. One went on a hunger strike to protest the refusal of the Home Office to grant women political prisoner status—the first use of the device. She was freed, but other women who followed her example were forcibly fed on the orders of King Edward VII.

Midge MacKenzie's *Shoulder to Shoulder*, a great film on the British suffrage movement, portrays the force-feeding. Three or four female guards open the cell door for a doctor carrying a long rubber tube; the prisoner sits up on her cot, protests; is pushed down; two hold her down forcibly, the other gags her. The doctor inserts the tube (often used repeatedly without cleaning) into a nostril or the mouth, pouring a mixture of milk, bread, brandy, and often an anti-vomiting agent down it. The procedure left its victims nauseous, cramped, with headaches and sores in mouth, nasal passages, and stomach. Most also suffered severe indigestion and constipation. But the worst part was the anticipation, waiting in agony, hearing their comrades screaming in pain. Some women broke down under the strain, expecting to die.

Lady Constance Lytton nearly did. Gently reared, she lived with her mother, as a dutiful daughter of the nobility until her late thirties. Sylvia Pankhurst claimed that years of dependency had left her extremely anxious about hurting others or asserting herself. Yet when this "childlike" woman decided to join the suffragists, she chose the militant wing—although her decision deeply distressed her family. Her health was poor, but in 1908 she led a delegation to the House of Commons and in 1909 threw a stone at Lloyd George's car in Newcastle. On both occasions she was arrested and sent to jail, where her rank procured her gentle treatment. So in 1910 she dressed like a worker and gave a false name when she was arrested. Sent to Walton prison, Liverpool, she was forcibly fed eight times despite her weak heart. When the authorities discovered her name, they released her, but she was "more dead than alive," irreparably damaged.

Constance's sacrifice galvanized her brother, Lord Lytton, to back a bill enfranchising a million Englishwomen heads of household. In July 1910, the "Conciliation Bill" passed the House by 139 votes, but contention between Commons and Lords led Parliament to dissolve and Prime Minister Asquith procrastinated. Constance Lytton was jailed again, and suffered minor heart seizures throughout 1910–11, culminating in a stroke in 1912. She survived until 1923, an ardent supporter of suffrage no longer able to act politically. She never stopped hating prison doctors.

The WSPU women continued to destroy property; they chained themselves to the fence around the meeting house of the British cabinet and broke windows in Parliament Square—unthinkable acts for British *ladies*. They were attacked, however, simply for occupying public space. Men pawed, pushed, pinched, or punched them in the breasts, groped under their skirts, spat at them, threw stones, whispered obscenities in their ears, hurled rotten fruit. The police arrested and imprisoned the *women*. On November 18, 1910 ("Black Friday"), a large delegation of suffragists set out for the House of Commons, but they were violently attacked by police and male bystanders. They fought back for six hours, while *four men and 115 women* were arrested. Police officials had called in East End police rather than the usual "A" Division police, who knew and liked the suffragist delegations. East End police regularly dealt with the poor and did not scruple to treat women brutally. The revelation of how far men were willing to go to hold women down shocked middle- and upper-class feminists.

In 1911 the WSPU began systematically to smash windows. Convicted women were sentenced to prison with hard labor. They continued. After they attacked expensive West End shops, the police raided WSPU headquarters. Christabel Pankhurst fled to Paris, broke with the Pethick-Lawrences, and led the WSPU from abroad. Now semilegal, it operated underground, changing headquarters and local leaders regularly to evade raids. For two years, members bombed letter boxes and fuse boxes, smashed street lamps, cut up golf courses, and burned empty houses. The public grew hostile. Memories of violations—forced feeding, blows, violence—in their bodies, memories of betrayals and male contempt in their minds, left the women angry and desperate, martyred. But none died until 1913, when, as the king rode to the Derby, Emily Wilding Davison hurled herself in front of his horse crying "Votes for women!" The WSPU was in disarray, its leaders in jail or being hunted down; Davison's funeral was its last major demonstration.

That year, the home secretary pushed through Parliament a bill allowing the government to free hunger strikers until they recovered their health, then re-arrest them. Called the "Cat and Mouse Act," it gained huge publicity for the WSPU, which was delighted also by its "mice," who adeptly eluded re-arrest, then appeared with stunning drama at meetings. The cycle of arson, imprisonment, hunger strikes, release, and re-arrest continued until the First World War broke out in August 1914. Although Sylvia urged WSPU members not to support the war effort, most of them did. Emmeline Pankhurst worked tirelessly, traveling throughout England rallying women to work in munitions factories and essential services. Although she was acting as a patriot, she had an eye on the war's end, when women would be rewarded by the franchise. Sylvia, more radical, broke with her mother and sister, seeing the war as a patriarchal device to submerge class differences in nationalism. She denounced the government for the war and for exploiting female labor, and worked with some success to gain equal pay for women, and safeguards and decent working conditions in hazardous munitions and airplane factories. Her mother repudiated her. Sylvia continued to work for the rights of East End working-class women. Emmeline Pethick-Lawrence joined Jane Addams' international peace movement. The glory years were over.

After the war, Parliament granted suffrage to all men who had fought in the war, without property or residency restrictions, but did not mention women. When suffragists protested, it granted the vote to single women and wives over thirty of men listed on the Local Government Register. This age limit prevented women from becoming the majority of British voters: 8 million British women were enfranchised in January 1918. Moderate women's suffrage groups redirected their energies to electing women to Parliament and lobbying for bills on "women's issues." Women could not yet claim *all* issues were their issues, as all are men's. For years, feminists pressured Parliament to remove the age limit on women voters, but did not succeed until 1928.

At the end of the campaign, militants looked back at their eight years of battle as an exalted period: women had been central in British political life, making upper-class men shudder under female assault for the first time in their lives. American women used the Cult of True Womanhood to expand the notion and in the process destroy it; Victorian Englishwomen's militancy radically defied their socializing, but was also its epitome. Inculcated with the belief they must spend their lives serving others and sacrificing the self, they used their training in hard work, service to the community, religious faith, discipline, extraordinary idealism, and self-sacrifice to serve *their own* ends. From 1906 to 1914 over a thousand women went to prison and thousands more were arrested. The WSPU's legacy to later generations was a new image of woman as rebels, articulate, visible, and organized.

Women's most striking advances resulted from the war, when they took jobs formerly reserved for men. They worked as skilled engineers (mechanics in the United States) in munitions plants, on farms, as chauffeurs and ambulance drivers. As in the United States, educated women found administrative jobs in the civil service, managing new wartime bureaucracies. That their filling "male" jobs made the men at the front feel emasculated suggests the weak base of the male psyche. When the men returned, male solidarity forced women out of their jobs, but during the recession that followed the war many men could not find work. Men never fully reasserted their former dominance over women, who, once they could support themselves, could reappraise just what men gave and what they cost.

After winning the vote, women did not maintain the strong sisterhood achieved by suffragists. They did not vote as a bloc, but allowed class (in the United States, color) divisions to fragment their voice. Both egalitarians and protectionists concentrated on legislative reform, but in trying to assimilate into the male political world, they cut themselves off from other women. Feminists usually lost political contests, and political parties shunned them as liabilities (it is unclear which caused which). Women made only minor changes in the organization or regulation of industry, the church, military, or the government—to this day they have not been able to influence the policies of such institutions. Male solidarity and prejudice and women's continuing acceptance of responsibility for children combined to perpetuate female inequality in the marketplace. Working-class women were still paid least, and were the least skilled in the least pleasant jobs—they remained marginal, easily dismissed or replaced.

These unwon fights do not diminish what women did accomplish. Middle-class women utterly transformed their position in the nineteenth century. However, the contradictions that pervaded their actions also characterized the results—and contradictions were rife. In a period that idealized motherhood, women halved their family size. Confined within the domestic realm, they embraced the confinement and simply proclaimed their sphere to be the world. Required to be angels devoted only to family, and presiding in isolation at home, they organized. Organization was a necessary condition for their success. For the first time in history, women achieved large-scale solidarity.

Women's reform networks succeeded because their power base—home and church—was considered their legitimate sphere. Adopting a rhetoric of domesticity and purity, they circumvented established male authority structures and institutions, which did not at first perceive them as a threat. Men saw women's networks as auxiliary and separate; women considered them central. Their dynamic conception of their appropriate sphere allowed them continually to expand it. Perhaps some used the rhetoric of True Womanhood cynically, but most believed it. Although powerful when they acted in concert, individual women remained hobbled by belief in female asexuality, moral superiority, and the appropriateness of certain arenas for their sex, not to mention their sense of sex as tainted. Such beliefs, along with biases of class and race, led women to disavow other women. They milked the Cult of Domesticity, which united and fragmented them at the same time.

In a little over a century, women in England, the United States, and other European states altered the course of patriarchy. Every ancient patriarchal state made the confinement of women in the domestic sphere—their exclusion from a voice and civil rights—a primary rule of society. And suppression of the female, once achieved in states like China, India, and Japan, remained immovable for millennia. Capitalism, with its emphasis on rights and individuals and its division of people and experience into rigid spheres, made feminism possible. Nineteenth-century feminism did not overturn patriarchy but damaged it enough to make further gains possible in the twentieth century.

Women fought for suffrage around the world. First to win it

were New Zealanders, in 1893—but no New Zealand woman held a high-level political position until 1947. Women in South Australia won the vote in 1894, and it was the first state to allow them to stand for parliament, but other Australian women had to wait until 1947. Finnish women voted in 1904 after only twenty years of agitation; Russian women in 1917, after the revolution. Sometimes women won suffrage but remained barred from high-level political life. In Norway, women won the vote in 1913, but did not begin to stand for high political office until 1945; Sweden, 1919 and 1947; the Netherlands, 1919 and 1956; Germany, 1919 and 1956; Brazil, 1932 and 1982; and Turkey, 1934 and 1971. In Egypt, men adamantly opposed woman suffrage until 1956.[10] Other countries surrendered even later. But women won. And they won with only themselves—without weapons, political rights, or much wealth, they had only their minds, bodies, spirits, voices, influence, charm, rage, tenderness, and strength to turn the world around. And they did.

CHAPTER 8

LABOR MOVEMENTS

MIDDLE-CLASS WOMEN HAD THE LEISURE TO FIGHT for political and economic rights; working-class women struggled to survive. Reformers tried to ameliorate poverty, not eradicate it, which would require economic and political changes they were unable or unwilling to contemplate. But segregated people develop a group consciousness and come to see that their problems are not individual but collective. Once they realize that not personal failure but the structure of society itself causes their difficulties, that they are the sacrificed in a system designed to benefit another group, they feel empowered to fight to change that structure or win a voice in it.

In the United States

Before the Civil War

Five million immigrants flooded the United States between 1815 and 1865; 80 percent settled in northern industrial cities. Many took low-paying factory jobs. The overwhelming majority of textile workers in the United States were single white women. Working conditions were atrocious. In the 1820s to 1830s, women in Lowell,

Massachusetts, factories worked twelve to sixteen hours a day in huge hot noisy rooms, with no fresh air, running water, or toilets. Meals were provided but the women had to run to a boardinghouse, eat, and return in only a half-hour: many became ill. In 1845 they took a major step and created the Lowell Female Labor Reform Association; the company punished them by ending support for their literary journal. The women went on strike, demanding a reduction in the workday from fourteen to ten hours. They lost, but Sarah Bagley, an association leader, had them sign a petition for a ten-hour day and sent it to the Massachusetts legislature, which opened an inquiry into factory conditions—the first in the United States.

Profits were high but owners wanted more. They bought larger, faster, noisier machines, and had workers tend more machines for less pay. They cut hourly wages, adding hours to make up the difference. In 1825 woman tailors in New York City organized and tried to shame employers by publicly naming those who paid women 10 to 18 cents a day. When this had no effect, they struck. Women struck in Dover, New Hampshire, in 1828; they too failed, but after further pay cuts in 1834, 800 women unionized and struck. The company hired scabs (nonunion workers), forcing them to sign agreements not to join any union, and broke the union. The national press, widely reporting female labor agitation, warned mockingly that government might "have to call out the militia to prevent a gynecocracy."

In 1844 Allegheny and Pittsburgh cotton workers agitated for a ten-hour day; in 1845, with Manchester mill women, they threatened to "declare their independence," to "make war" on the Fourth of July if their demands were not met. Owners blackballed the leaders, locked out any who would not work twelve hours and hired scabs. Workers protested this and in October, a riot erupted in a Pittsburgh mill. The government was completely behind the owners and sent strong-arm men to put it down, but workers outnumbered the thugs, beat them off, and took over the plant. They won a ten-hour day, but their wages were reduced. Although many women wanted to strike again, most settled for reduced hours.

Whatever method they used—strikes, walkouts, or shutdowns—workers did not win permanent improvements. Without coordinated campaigns or sophisticated strategies, they were no match for wealthy owners with government support and an endless supply of scab workers. Owners resourcefully countered workers' efforts—if forced to pay higher wages, they raised rents at company boardinghouses; if forced to grant shorter days, they lowered wages and ordered increased production (speed-ups) that undermined workers' morale and health; and they hired scabs, abundant in an era of massive immigration and poverty. They set worker against worker. Dropping any pretense of common purpose with the farm community, mill owners fired native-born women, hiring easily intimidated destitute illiterate immigrants often unfamiliar with English. But labor protest continued as tailors, shoemakers, and laundresses unionized in cities across the country.

But the greatest obstacle that working women faced was men. Women averaged a quarter of men's wages, yet most male unions refused to support women's strikes (women supported men's—for example, cotton workers at Pawtucket, Rhode Island, joined male co-workers in a strike protesting wage cuts and longer hours in 1824). Husbands or fathers used violence to keep women from attending union meetings or joining strike lines. Men prowled around women's meetings and promised women easier lives, then lured them into prostitution. Men defended *their* turf: the small percentage of men in cotton manufacture were better paid than women, and all supervisors were men. Some argue that women were not promoted because they did not remain long at their jobs—in 1836, only 18 of 233 female employees at one mill had worked there over six years. But women left because they knew they would not be promoted. In the 1860s about 300,000 northern women and 12,000 southerners worked in textile, shoe, and clothing factories, and in printing, keeping their jobs twice as long as the earlier generation—yet men still held all managerial positions.

When it came to women, hostility between male owners and male workers melted. Whatever their struggles with each other, men united in opposing any step that would allow women independence. Both wanted to exploit women—owners to pay them low wages, husbands and fathers to keep them in servitude. Even men whose lives would be easier if their wives earned higher wages fought women's attempts to improve their lot. The interests of men of different classes coincide when the issue is maintaining patriarchal control and dominance over women.[1] Discussion of the sexual division of labor and "woman's place" in production pervaded American journals and newspapers from 1850 to 1880.[2] Writers on the sexual division of labor identified different occupations as "female" or "male," but all believed their ideas were Natural Law.

The American Labor Movement after the Civil War

Still, there are moving examples of men cooperating with women. Collar laundresses in Troy, New York, worked twelve- to fourteen-hour days in 100° temperatures from furnaces heating water for their tubs; they washed, blued, dyed, and rinsed, and lifted heavy hot irons to press the detachable collars and cuffs of men's shirts. For this arduous labor they were paid \$2–\$3 a week. In 1864 they unionized. Troy unions of male puddlers and boilers in the iron industry supported them, and the Troy Collar Union thrived. Its 400 members donated \$500 to striking bricklayers in New York City and \$1000 to Troy iron molders striking in 1866. When the laundresses struck in 1869, the male unions sent them \$500 a week and promised "to continue the same for weeks to come rather than see such a brave set of wenches crushed under the iron heel of these laundry nabobs." But the company starved the women, who had to swear to renounce the union to get their jobs back. The invention of paper collars broke the union in 1870.

Shoe binders formed the first national women's union; it had over forty lodges from Lynn to San Francisco but did not last long. After the Civil War, a few male unions accepted women—in 1867 the National Union of Cigar Makers embraced women and blacks. When the Women's Typographical Union disbanded after nine years, men accepted them in the national union on equal terms with men (but never chartered another women's local). Women supported men, though: during an 1877 railroad strike, 100,000 men and women faced police, militia, and federal troops. The press was horrified not by armed forces being used against citizens in a bitter fight but by an "Amazonian army" of "enraged female rioters," an "unsexed mob of female incendiaries."

However hard life was for white workers, it was worse for blacks. They still had no choice of work and were paid too little to live. They could still resist inhumane employers only by feigning illness or incompetence or failing to show up for work. Until the First World War, 10 percent of African Americans lived in northern cities where men had trouble finding work and women supported the family by domestic and personal service work. Three-fourths of southern African Americans lived on farms or plantations as sharecroppers, unskilled laborers, laundresses, or domestic help. Most unions rejected all women, emphatically black women, who worked only as domestics and laundresses. So black women started their own union in Mississippi, the Washerwomen of Jackson, in 1866. Washerwomen unionized in Galveston, Texas (1877), Atlanta (1881), Greenville, Pennsylvania (1886), and Bibb City, Arkansas (1889). Some struck for higher wages. Few won.

Between 1880 and 1930, when the United States restricted immigration, over 27 million people, most from southern and eastern Europe, emigrated in desperate need. Three million Italians migrated from 1880 to 1910, as well as millions of Poles, Czechs, Slovaks, and other Baltic peoples. Pogroms in the 1880s to 1890s propelled 2 million East European Jews from their ghettos, about three-quarters from Russia. Over 90 percent settled in the United States. Greeks, Portuguese, Armenians, and Syrians risked the journey hoping for a better economic life. Hard as life was in the United States, it was worse elsewhere. Farmhands in Sweden earned $30 a year with room and board in the 1870s; in the United States they earned \$200 a year. Pennsylvania mineworkers earned \$40 a month, railroad workers \$1–\$2 a day. Passage to New York cost \$12–\$15 from England, \$30 from Copenhagen: emigrés could save enough to bring their families to the United States.

It was hard to get to the United States and terrible afterwards. Millions of immigrants packed slum rooms or flats without running water, toilets, or even heat in teeming neighborhoods infested with fleas, bedbugs, and lice. Single men rented sleeping space in a family's kitchen. Arriving with little or nothing, many spoke no English and were grateful for the meanest jobs. They ate poorly, contracted tuberculosis or pneumonia. Women, as always burdened doubly, tried to earn money to help the family while raising the fruit of their repeated pregnancies. They aged quickly, and their poor diet contributed to a staggering rate of infant mortality.

Americans responded to foreigners, with their odd languages and poverty, with virulent xenophobia. In the 1840s–1850s, to guard "white natives'" prerogatives, "nativists" formed the Know-Nothing Party. An anti-Catholic movement began in the 1880s. The two-and-a-half-million-member American Protective Association tried to limit immigration with stricter naturalization laws. Anti-Semitism grew, and clubs and resorts adopted a "Gentiles only" policy. German Jews who had been assimilated for decades suddenly found themselves *persona non grata.* Discrimination in housing and jobs followed. In 1891 the government enforced anti-pauper laws at Ellis Island and other ports of entry. Jews who had been stripped of property by Eastern European governments had to prove they had money or relatives in the United States.

Perhaps the most vicious xenophobia was directed toward the Chinese. Thousands of single men imported to build the Central Pacific railroad during the Civil War stayed on afterward to work in western mines, farms, and canneries, and faced what Florynce Kennedy called "horizontal hostility"—antagonism directed at equals rather than oppressors. White male workers blamed their low wages not on exploitative employers but on the Chinese, who lived on almost nothing. Such hostility reproduces itself: abused exploited men exploited and abused their women in turn.

Most Chinese women who entered the United States between 1840 and 1880 were slave prostitutes. Chinese families often sold girl children into servitude. By 1850 the business of certain Chinese societies was importing girls for west-coast brothels—the secret society Hip-Yee Tong alone imported 6000 females from 1852 to 1873, many just children. Their lives were awful; they aged fast, and died young. Some were promised release from their contract after a fixed term, which never came; many were forcibly addicted to opium. When their plight became known, public outrage prodded the California legislature to investigate prostitution in 1876. A San Francisco pastor explained:

> The women [generally] are held as slaves. They are bought or stolen in China and brought here. They have a sort of agreement to cover up the slavery business, but it is all a sham. . . . After the term of prostitution service is up, the owners so manage as to have the women in debt more than ever, so that their slavery becomes life-long. There is no release from it. . . . Sometimes women take opium to kill themselves. They do not know they have any rights, but think they must keep their contracts and believe themselves under obligations to serve in prostitution. . . . They have come to the asylum all bruises. They are beaten and punished cruely if they fail to make any money. When they become worn out and unable to make anymore money, they are turned out to die.

Tension over hiring and wages between white and Chinese workers culminated in the Sandlot Riot of 1871. The U.S. solution was "Keep orientals out." Legislators hysterical about "the yellow peril" in 1882 passed the Chinese Exclusion Act, the first law barring immigrants in the United States. It banned all females from China (barely affecting brothel keepers, who kidnapped girls within California). Whites hoped that without women, Chinese men would return to China. Some did, but more stayed. In the west, anti-Chinese fury erupted in major riots in Tacoma, Seattle, and Wyoming in 1885. In the 1920s, hysterical waves of paranoia led to the deportation of masses of Chinese.[3]

On the east coast, mill owners hired new immigrants at low wages (lowering wages throughout the industry) and let working conditions deteriorate. During the Civil War, the south stopped sending raw cotton north, closing northern mills. Desperate mill women swarmed to cities seeking work in the needle trades. The invention of the sewing machine revolutionized the garment industry—a man's shirt that took fourteen hours to sew by hand was made in an hour on a machine—and the number of sewing machines doubled during the war. After the war, owners moved their factories south; Irish immigrants began to leave New England textile towns, and impoverished French-Canadians moved in. There was always another wave of poor people to exploit, and conditions in the garment trades grew worse as sweatshops sprang up in most cities.

Garment workers put in fifteen- to sixteen-hour days in stifling, crowded, dimly lit workshops; some slept on fabric piled on the floor to save rent. Most were women: in 1900, 65 percent of New York City seamstresses were single Jewish girls paid so little that many became prostitutes to survive. The top men in a shop earned $10, women $3 to $6 a week. Work was ranked: only native-born white women could work as shop girls for $5 a week or librarians for $3—badly paid, but less injurious occupations. Daughters of immigrants were barred from "genteel trades." Until the Civil War, except for 2 million unpaid slave women, the vast majority of women worked only at home; only about 10 percent earned any money. By 1880, mainly because of immigration, 2 million women worked for wages (the figure doubled in the next decade).

In 1881 the Noble Order of the Knights of Labor chartered the

Working Women's Union. The Knights, a combination of secret fraternal society and reform organization, admitted workers and middle-class men, excluding "parasites"—lawyers, saloon keepers, bankers, stockbrokers, and professional gamblers. It supported equal pay for equal work and equal treatment for women and blacks. When it became open, it admitted women: at its peak its 700,000 members included 50,000 women. Female Knights struck in Yonkers, New York, in 1885: 2500 women picketed the mill. The company called the police, who were so violent to the women that the public pitied and helped them, enabling them to hold out for six months and win their demand: *rescinding a pay cut.*

As strikes grew more frequent and damaging, employers used heavier hands. When steelworkers struck at Andrew Carnegie's steel mill, he hired immigrants, had them shepherded off the boats that brought them from Europe right into sealed locked boxcars, and transported them right *inside* the mills, to live and work at gunpoint. Speaking no English, the men had no idea what was happening. Such repressiveness climaxed in the Chicago Haymarket riot.

On May 1 (May Day), 1886, 80,000 mostly male workers marched down Michigan Avenue, then met with women tailors to plan a general strike for an eight-hour day. On May 2, Lizzie Swank, a brilliant labor organizer, marched with hundreds of women from the garment district, stopping at each shop along the way to urge women workers to join them.[4] Even the *Chicago Tribune*, a hostile newspaper, was moved: "The ranks were composed of women whose exterior denoted incessant toil, their in many instances worn faces and threadbare clothing bearing evidence of a struggle for an uncomfortable existence. As the procession moved along the girls shouted and sang and laughed in a whirlwind of exuberance that did not lessen with the distance traveled."

On May 3, as workers rallied peacefully in Haymarket Square, the police advanced, ordering them to disperse. A bomb exploded, the police fired on the crowd. No one knows how many were killed—200 were injured. On May 4 a police dragnet arrested almost every activist in the Chicago labor movement, charging eight with murdering policemen in the riot (which was probably staged by police killed by their own crossfire). Only one of the accused was even in the square during the riot and he was on stage in public view. Nevertheless, the government executed five men.

As industrial capitalism became more firmly rooted, the Knights' rank and file lost hope for a cooperative commonwealth and focused on practical working problems. The Order's leaders did not respond to this shift, and could not overcome employers' strong attacks after the Haymarket affair. The organization lost two-thirds of its members in two years, from 1886 to 1888.

In the 1890s, 1 percent of Americans had more income than the bottom 50 percent: the top 1 percent earned 25 percent of the national income, the bottom half less than 20 percent. People starved: women abandoned babies on doorsteps; children, at least ten thousand, lived on the streets and slept in areaways. (Jacob Riis photographed them in his 1890 study of the tenements of New York, *How the Other Half Lives.*) The Chicago Women's Alliance launched a campaign for compulsory education for children in 1889, eventually forcing passage of a bill establishing a twelve- to twenty-four week school year for children aged seven to fourteen, with half-days off to work.

The gains won by female organizers' efforts seemed impermanent in these years, but they lasted: in 1878 few women had the courage even to attend a union meeting, but in 1886 hundreds of women marched for an eight-hour day and in 1903, 35,000 marched in Chicago on Labor Day.[5] Early organizers raised working women's class-consciousness and taught them that they had the right to a decent wage and decent working conditions, and the right to fight when they were denied—which was news to these uneducated women.

The women's local that marched before the Haymarket massacre disintegrated after it, but organizer Elizabeth Morgan persuaded Samuel Gompers of the American Federation of Labor

(AFL) to charter women in a union of mixed occupations—a "federal" union—a catch-all to unionize men in different trades when there were not enough to found a trade union, or to organize women or blacks separately. Male locals rejected women and blacks but Gompers himself chartered federal unions to bypass locals. Federal unions brought together large numbers of working women from different trades, as well as housewives. A women's union meeting could be a social function (men met in saloons). The disadvantage of having separate unions was that male and female locals in the same shop bargained separately, sometimes against each other, and women usually lost; or men bargained for both, trading women's raises for their own.

The AFL claimed to be egalitarian, to support women and equal pay. But it really tried to keep women disorganized, slotting them into the Union Label League, whose only function was to propagandize for goods with union labels. Leaders claimed the AFL could not organize women because they were unskilled and the AFL charter was for skilled workers—but they would not let women apprentice to learn skills. Groups of women workers who applied for admission to the international in a craft were rejected. If they appealed this, AFL leaders said they had no control over the decisions of an international; if they asked for a charter as an independent local, they were refused because that would violate the jurisdiction of the international in that craft. Thwarted at every juncture, women were demoralized. The AFL stand harmed not just women but the entire labor movement.

WTUL and Triangle

There were only four women delegates at the 1903 AFL convention at which William English Walling and Mary Kenney first set up a national Women's Trade Union League (WTUL) modeled on the English WTUL. In an effort to organize *all* workers in trade unions and gain equal pay for equal work, an eight-hour day, a minimum wage scale, and woman suffrage, the founders set up locals in

Chicago, Boston, and New York. Lacking male union support, the New York local turned to middle-class women—professionals and wealthy women drawn to the WTUL by sex solidarity. But few understood labor problems, and class and ethnic divisions generated argument in the League, for example, debate over whether the New York WTUL should focus on organizing downtown Jewish or uptown "American" girls. Constant debate about whether to concentrate on organizing or legislation split along class lines, with workers supporting the former. The AFL was now conservative (it voted to exclude Chinese from the United States); the WTUL was split between conservative and socialist policies.

In November 1909 a small waistmakers' local in the International Ladies' Garment Workers Union called for a general strike against New York shirtwaist manufacturers. Thirty thousand workers spontaneously answered the call—the strike was called the Uprising of the Thirty Thousand, or "the women's movement strike," because the WTUL led the entire women's movement from the Fifth Avenue elite to Lower East Side socialists to support the strikers, mainly teenaged girls. It rented Cooper Union for the meeting. Workers from three shops (Leiserson's, Rosen Brothers, and the Triangle Waist Company) had already struck; the meeting was to exhort others to join. The hall overflowed; union leaders frantically searched for others. Beethoven Hall, the Manhattan Lyceum, and Astoria Hall also filled and overflowed. At Cooper Union, the stage was full—of *men*. Gompers, other union officials, a woman from the WTUL—none of whom worked in a shirtwaist shop—spoke.

Suddenly a young woman from the audience stood up and asked for the floor. Despite rumblings of disapproval, the chairman held that as a striker she had as much right to speak as he did, and she walked to the platform. Clara Lemlich had helped found the shirtwaist local, had led the walkout at Leiserson's, which sent thugs to beat her up on the picket line. She knew precisely what the women were up against and how profound their anger and anguish were. She spoke rousingly in Yiddish, then put the motion for a general strike. The entire hall rose to endorse it.

The women, many only girls, starved as they picketed through a cold winter. Leiserson's thugs regularly beat them up, especially Lemlich, who had six ribs broken. Police arrested the women and sent them to the workhouse. Leiserson hired scabs; they themselves were so disgusted by the owners' tactics that they joined the strikers! The heroic women held out for thirteen weeks, up to a thousand women joining them every day. Three hundred and thirty-nine shops settled, but each separately, consequently without major gains. One of the two biggest makers, Triangle, refused to recognize the union and settled partially, rejecting (among other demands) open doors and adequate fire escapes (foremen locked the doors to keep the women from sneaking out for air): all garment factories were firetraps. The next year, Triangle went up in flames. When the alarm went off, one exit was aflame, the other locked: workers had no way out. The shop went up in minutes: piles of fabric lay everywhere and so much lint hovered that the very air burned. Women leaped from the fire escape in burning clothes to be impaled on a spiked iron fence below it. A hundred and forty-six died, hundreds were injured.

Triangle's two owners were tried for negligence, but were acquitted. One was later fined $20. The press claimed the fire was started by a smoking worker. Rose Schneiderman of the WTUL spoke at a memorial meeting after the fire: "This is not the first time girls have been burned alive in this city. Every week I must learn of the untimely death of one of my sister workers. Every year thousands of us are maimed. The life of men and women is so cheap and property is sacred. There are so many of us for one job it matters little if 143 of us are burned to death." Public outrage eventually forced the passage of fire safety laws in factories.

A depression from 1907 to 1909 devastated the labor movement; marginal workers (women) lost their jobs or accepted lower-paid ones and dropped out of unions. In Chicago, women's union membership fell from 37,000 to 10,000; not one female local remained in 1910. About 8 million women worked for wages, most in factories where they earned $2 to $6 a week, a third as much as men doing comparable work. Associations of working and middle-class women fell apart too when groups like San Francisco women concerned primarily with suffrage refused to support a strike of streetcar conductors; the workers felt betrayed and abandoned the group.

The IWW

In 1905, revolutionaries from the Western Federation of Miners and the Socialist Party founded a new union, Industrial Workers of the World (IWW)—the "Wobblies." Mother Jones was one of the founders. The IWW wanted to destroy capitalism through class solidarity and uncompromising class war, and to create a base for working-class production after capitalism disappeared. Their goal was visionary but their practices were geared to achieve realistic working-class solidarity. Trying to avoid the exclusionary practices of the AFL, they organized by industry, not craft, welcoming everyone in an industry—migrant and unskilled workers, immigrants, Asians, women, men, whites, and blacks in a south still dominated by the Klan and its lynch mobs. The IWW analyzed oppression in socialist terms, dividing the world into workers and capitalists. It mobilized blacks and women as workers who would be liberated when wage slavery and the class system ended, but it ignored their special experience.

Socialist groups arose in the United States late in the century, usually at times of economic hardship. The collectivist aspect of socialism drew great numbers of women; women helped shape it, but its narrow analysis always bothered them. At the first socialist International in The Hague in 1872, an American delegate defied the party to announce: "The labour question is also a woman's question, and the emancipation of woman must precede that of the workers." The party held that "universal suffrage cannot free humanity from slavery. . . . The gaining of the vote by women is not in the best interests of the workers." Marx had implied that women's condition was a gauge of society's progress, but American socialism was created mainly by German immigrants imbued with patriarchism. Annoyed by suffragists and bourgeois reformers, they demanded that women reject suffrage for socialism, and then relegated them to ladies' auxiliaries. When the Socialist Party of America was founded in 1901, only 8 of its 128 delegates were women.

The IWW also opposed woman suffrage, but was the only labor organization to discuss birth control; it also made good use of women during strikes. While the AFL slotted women into "union label leagues," and the socialists kept them in auxiliaries, IWW organizers enrolled workers' wives in locals, especially in the west (wives too were oppressed by employers). For example, bosses in the Mesabi iron mine traded men safe jobs in the mines for sexual use of their wives or daughters. The families of workers who lived in company-owned houses were evicted during strikes. As workers or wives, women proved more militant than men; they stood in the front ranks wielding rolling pins, brooms, and pokers to battle scabs; they were beaten, fire-hosed, and arrested—everywhere. When fish dealers reneged on an agreement with striking fishermen, their wives hurled rocks at them. An IWW organizer ordered them to go home quietly. "Who are you?" they roared. It was their fight.[6]

But because it never saw women's problems as distinct, the IWW could not address them. Since it considered women's locals and support for women's rights disruptive of class solidarity, despite repeated suggestions by feminists like Sophie Beldner, Elizabeth Gurley Flynn, Joe Hill, and Frank Little (the latter two killed for their politics), it never recruited large numbers of women, and hired only three female organizers in its history.

IWW men were reluctant to treat women as equals and scorned them, saying they resisted organization, and would probably marry soon. Men did not see that unions did not guarantee women equality in marriage or help them produce and raise children.

Nothing did. Women's only hope for decent lives lay in finding decent men who would support them. A fertile woman's well-being depended on her personal relation with one man; joining a union would impede, not help that.

The 1912 Lawrence Strike

The IWW tried to organize workers in Lawrence, Massachusetts, in 1905, with little success until 1911, when the Atlantic Cotton Mill, wanting to lay off 40 percent of its weavers, ordered workers to tend twelve looms at a piece rate of 49 cents rather than seven at 79 cents. The weavers mounted a small strike: strong IWW support brought it public notice. The IWW issued frequent bulletins and imported major speakers like the young socialist "rebel" Elizabeth Gurley Flynn and IWW agitator James P. Thompson. After Thompson spoke, the IWW intensified its campaign with mass meetings indoors and outdoors, leaflets, and stickers.

On January 1, 1912, a law reforming labor practices in Massachusetts went into effect, barring women and children from working over fifty-four hours a week. Not foreseeing this would lead to a pay cut, reformers did not lobby against it. The Italian IWW local held a meeting and voted to strike if pay were cut. Other groups agreed. On January 12, they anxiously opened their envelopes: the company had deducted two hours' pay. Two hours' pay was 30 cents; this bought five loaves of bread. Five loaves a week meant the difference between surviving and starving.

Deciding "Better to starve fighting than to starve working," 20,000 people struck that day. Owners and journalists were dumbstruck: Lawrence was barely unionized—only a few hundred men were in the AFL, a few hundred in the IWW. Half the mill workers were women and children too worn down to protest: women could not even take time off for childbirth, squatting between looms to give birth. In an age when the average lawyer or clergyman lived to sixty-five, spinners died at thirty-six; 172 of 1000 of their children were born dead, *all* children were malnourished. IWW leader Bill

Haywood explained: "It was a chronic condition. These children had been starving from birth. They had been starved in their mothers' wombs. And their mothers had been starving before the children were born."

They struck in subzero weather in falling snow, swarming out of the mills to throng the streets; groups went into factories to pull workers out. Owners placed men on the bridge leading to some factories to turn hoses on workers who approached. Enraged strikers entered a mill and broke machinery and windows and tore fabric from the looms. Owners demanded the mayor call in troops; the mayor called the governor, who called the National Guard, including Harvard students freed from class to "have their fling at these people"; they roamed the town, itchy. IWW knew what the strikers were up against. An organizer warned: "You can hope for no success on any policy of violence. . . . Remember the property of the bosses is protected first by the police, then by the militia. If these are not sufficient, by an entire army. Remember, you are also armed . . . with your labor power which you can withhold and stop production." They encouraged strikers to restrain rage and preserve organization. They brought in outside contacts who publicized the strike and raised money for the strikers. But the spirit of struggle really rose from the strikers' desperation: it "existed before the IWW came and after it left."[7]

When the company called in scabs, thousands of women spontaneously picketed. An army of women surrounded the mill district and took control of the streets. Firing into the crowd, police killed a young striker, Anna Lopezza, but charged two IWW leaders with her murder. Police harassed strikers, arrested them, and jailed some for a year for obstructing the sidewalk! (At least they ate in jail.) Major IWW leaders like Haywood and Flynn stayed on, helping, working, and later testifying to the courage and resourcefulness of the workers, who maintained soup kitchens and commissaries, investigated cases needing special relief, and kept their own books.

The strikers carried banners announcing what they wanted—

"Bread and Roses"—which gave the strike its name. Women, half the strikers, were violent too. Some met a policeman on the bridge, grabbed his gun, club, and star and were removing his pants when he was rescued. Arrested, they were sentenced to jail terms by a judge who informed them "in awful tones that the body of a policeman was sacred." As the strike wore on, women grew more active, making street confrontations, dismaying owners, the police and the press, who whined, "One policeman can handle ten men, while it takes ten policemen to handle one woman." Husbands and priests tried to keep women out of it; Haywood and Flynn held meetings to heighten the women's confidence.[8]

Strikers began to send their children to sympathizers in other cities, where they would be fed and kept safe from the soldiers (who were assaulting them). But once the children were photographed in the press, their visible emaciation and illness drew national attention to the Lawrence workers' plight. Angrily, the owners sent police to assault the next batch of women and children who went to the railroad station. News reports of "cossacks" beating women and children got even more coverage, but the act outraged women. Announcing that even soldiers with bayonets had mothers and would not attack a pregnant woman, a tiny Italian woman and another woman, both pregnant, led women picketers. The soldiers beat and arrested all of them; the pregnant ones miscarried. This was reported in a Congressional committee.

Public opinion and Congress pressured the owners to settle, and they began negotiations in March. They accepted a 25 percent raise for the lowest-paid workers (earning 9 cents an hour), lesser raises along a sliding scale, time and a half for overtime, and no retribution against strikers. The success of the Lawrence strike led to other strikes across New England, which were all quickly settled. Twenty-five thousand textile workers gained by the Lawrence strike.

American Socialism

At its founding in 1901, the American Socialist Party endorsed equal political and civil rights for women, including suffrage. A large party with a broad political base before the First World War, it won some mayoral and congressional seats and almost 700,000 votes for socialist presidential candidate Eugene Debs in 1912. Party members were active in the AFL and the WTUL. But its most important role was providing political discourse. No other political body did this: the two major political parties disagreed on some points, but no one—not they or suffragists or trade unionists—wanted or dared to challenge capitalism itself. Only socialism offered an alternative to a capitalist organization of society; only socialism had a different political perspective. It drew women who could not accept the limitations of other movements.

Socialist women's groups arose in many American cities to discuss issues the major parties ignored and to give women a forum where they would not be overshadowed by men. Female membership grew tenfold in a year, and the party published a huge body of literature aimed at working-class women. But once a substantial percentage (10 percent) of the party was female, there were rifts over suffrage strategy. At this time, some European suffragists were demanding the vote as property owners on the same terms as men. Many middle-class women's organizations opposed protective legislation for female factory workers, which socialists favored. At a convention of women socialists, Clara Zetkin and other German socialists decided to work for suffrage independently of suffragist groups because of such differences.

But in the United States, the main opponent of protective legislation was the AFL, and no suffragist group supported limited franchise. Socialist women were already working with suffragists to support the shirtwaist-makers' strike. American socialist women bowed to the party decision because they felt they needed to seed the ground for class struggle by urging socialism along with suffrage.

Moreover, suffragists had never acknowledged the socialists' huge contribution to the shirtwaist-makers' protest, and barred them from certain public platforms, fearing public identification with them. *Everyone* assumed the vote would make women fully equal to men in society and end female oppression and male hostility overnight. Socialist *men's* opposition to woman suffrage subverted American socialism. In 1912 radicals sympathetic to the IWW left and conservatives (who gave nothing to the WNC) abolished the Women's National Committee as too expensive and ended publication of the newspaper. Many women left the party or lapsed into inactivity.

When the First World War erupted, nationalist "patriots" fervently supported it. The Socialist Party (SP) opposed it as an imperialist struggle forcing working-class men to kill each other, deflecting their attention from their real enemies, capitalists. No one foresaw that a pointless war would eradicate an entire generation of young European men (and many women and children), and mark the end of the leisure class along with the old European social/economic structure. NAWSA suffragists and WTUL members supported the war, hoping for a post-war reward of franchise; many took government jobs. Alice Paul's NWP protested despite the war, picketing the White House asking how Woodrow Wilson could make the world safe for democracy he did not have at home. The AFL pledged not to strike for the duration. Some feminists (like Jane Addams) were pacifists; the IWW and most socialists opposed the war.

Then as now, people who opposed wars were called traitors and persecuted: NWP picketers were mauled by soldiers, arrested, sent to the workhouse, and went on hunger strikes. They were forcibly fed. Socialists were hounded, jailed, and murdered. At the end of the war, the government used it to justify suppression of dissent (a similar "Red Scare" followed the Second World War and the attack on the World Trade Center in New York in 2001). It targeted labor groups for elimination despite their support for the war, showing that capitalism, not war, was the issue. Unions that were inactive during the war were vulnerable to a massive government union-busting campaign that destroyed steel, meatpacking, dock-worker, and lumber unions and shook many others: the AFL lost over a million members. Organized labor suffered a serious decline, losing about half its members between 1920 and 1933.[9] Socialist groups were fragmented by raids, persecution, deportations, and quarrels over strategy after the Russian Revolution. Dissent from capitalism had become a crime, a heresy.

In this climate arose a heroine.[10] Rose Pastor, born in Poland in 1879, immigrated with her family to Cleveland to work making cigars. At twenty-four, she became a journalist for a Yiddish newspaper in New York City and in 1905 married J.G. Phelps Stokes, a millionaire reformer of one of the oldest richest U.S. families. Labelled "Cinderella of the Sweatshops" by the press, Rose led her prince into the Socialist Party to organize hotel and garment workers, mounting a legal defense of strikers in Paterson in 1913. With her husband, she left the Socialist Party because most members opposed American entry into the First World War; a year later, she left him to return to the party. Speaking against the government for war profiteering got her indicted for antiwar activity in 1918 and sentenced to ten years in prison under the Espionage Act. Eugene Debs, head of the Socialist Party, spoke in her defense at her trial. Her sentence was overturned on appeal, but Debs' speech was used to convict him for "espionage." Her experience with the United States government persuaded her that only revolution would alter it. Scorning feminism as "bourgeois and elitist," accepting separate women's committees only to aid the spread of socialism, she left the Socialist Party in 1919 to help found the American Communist Party.

Prosecuted for founding the Communist Party (and other "crimes"), she did not go to jail, probably because of Stokes' wealth. Her marriage faltered on its political and class differences. Divorce thrust her into poverty; she lived by writing and speaking. In 1927, she married V.J. Jerome, a Communist eighteen years younger than she, with whom she lived happily, if in poverty. In 1929, demonstrating at a rally demanding withdrawal of United States troops from Haiti, she was clubbed by the police, after which her health declined. Rose Pastor Stokes died of breast cancer in 1933, true to her principles unto death.

African Americans in the Early Twentieth Century

The First World War was a turning point for African Americans. Before it, northern mills did not hire black women, although a larger percentage of black women than white did waged work. Few unions accepted women, even fewer blacks until the Committee for Industrial Organization (CIO) was formed in 1935. (Yet in 1920 the AFL Hotel and Restaurant Employees' Union had ten black locals in the south; the CIO-affiliated United Domestic Workers' Local Industrial Union in Baltimore had one in 1942.) After black women could join, the white male leaders of industrial unions bartered the interests of blacks and women to protect or consolidate their own gains; their strategies often led to the complete exclusion of blacks from workplaces. Scarce in industry, unwelcome in unions, isolated in white households, black women could only protest individually, informally.

In 1900 less than 3 percent of wage-earning black women worked in manufacture. In 1910 more than 700,000 black women in the south worked for pay, most in tobacco plants as stemmers, the lowest job in the industry hierarchy. They did the "dirty" jobs—sorting, cleaning, stemming tobacco—working apart from white women (who did "cleaner" jobs, inspecting and packing tobacco). White men presided over the entire workforce, supervising black and white women and black men who hauled hogsheads of tobacco from "dirty" prefabrication departments of the factory to "clean" manufacturing and packaging departments. Chicago meatpackers, too, relegated black women to "dirty" sectors, the most disagreeable jobs—hog-killing and beef-casing—"under repulsive conditions."[11]

Amalgamated Meat Cutters and Butcher Workmen locals never organized black women and wanted them eliminated from the labor force.

Linked by the physical and verbal abuse they endured from white foremen, by shared racial, sexual, and class oppression, black female tobacco workers became race, class, and sex conscious. Aware of black female power, if not feminism, they formed factory networks that extended into communities, overlapping with church groups and women's clubs. Network support gave individual women courage to protest their working conditions and treatment.[12]

Black club women founded a Women Wage-Earners Association in Washington, DC, to teach black working-class women how to organize to demand better wages, housing, and working conditions. In 1917 a branch in Norfolk, Virginia—600 domestics, waitresses, nurses, and tobacco-stemmers—protested. They were ignored and the stemmers (about half the organization) struck. Domestic servants followed (hitting whites at home), then stemmers' husbands and most oyster-shuckers. Since the country was at war, the government had extreme powers and threatened to arrest as subversive those who refused to work. But 3000 white male navy-yard workers who had recently struck for higher wages were not arrested. Black workers were, breaking the strike and the Norfolk branch.

Persecution in the south drove black workers north when jobs opened up to them during the First World War. Northern domestic servants earned $8 a week, twice or more what a black woman earned in Mississippi. But the south that persecuted them did not want them to leave: police seized blacks from northbound trains and arrested labor recruiters. For a time, southern employers raised wages and improved conditions. But 500,000 blacks went north in this period, a million and a half more before the next world war.

By 1920, *100 percent* more black women worked in manufacturing and mechanical industries than a decade earlier. For the first time they could use machines in laundries and garment factories and were hired as clerks, stenographers, and bookkeepers, as social workers, counselors in schools and courts, public health workers, pharmacists, bacteriologists, and chiropodists. For the first time, they were accepted in the same jobs as white women, but only because whites left them. As white immigrants left factories for higher-paid work in munitions plants, blacks took their places.

But the situation in the north was not much better. Black women remained the most oppressed group in the country: of the 2 million who worked for wages in 1920, almost half were servants, almost half were in agriculture. They made up only 6.7 percent of industrial workers. Yet this tiny gain incited the worst antiblack violence ever seen in the United States: after the First World War, they were attacked by mobs, lynched, and caught in sudden outbursts. In 1917 blacks marched silently down Fifth Avenue in protest. So many blacks were lynched in 1918–19 that the NAACP held a conference on the subject and published *Thirty Years of Lynching in the United States*. The government tried but failed to suppress it. In 1919, as the black 369th Infantry Regiment returned from France and marched up Fifth Avenue to huge cheering crowds, Attorney General Palmer launched the "Red Scare" by creating a special division of the Justice Department headed by J. Edgar Hoover to spy on, raid, and eliminate radicals and blacks, including Marcus Garvey. That year, twenty-five race riots exploded in cities across the country. A nationwide steel strike in 1920 caused a major defeat for organized labor. The United States was growing increasingly repressive.

The white backlash succeeded: industry cut back black hiring and fired black women as 4 million soldiers returned to the workforce. Industry slowed down, immigration resumed, and the KKK reorganized, spreading from Maine to California. In 1921 Missouri Representative L.C. Dyer sponsored a bill supported by Garvey's UNIA, the NAACP, and the YMCA, making lynching a federal crime, but the KKK and Nativism had the political clout to force passage of the National Origins (or Immigration Restriction) Act in 1924. It excluded all Asian immigrants and limited Europeans by nationality to 2 percent of those who had immigrated in 1890.

Thousands of black women were out of work and those with jobs had their wages reduced. Tradeswomen could work only in black-owned businesses (even in Harlem, only a fifth of businesses were owned by blacks). Unions, always hostile to blacks, again excluded them, virtually shutting them out of industries they had been working in, like garments and furs. The civil service had begun hiring black women, but President Wilson blocked this practice, and discrimination spread to municipal civil services. The telephone company, department stores, insurance companies, and restaurants refused to hire blacks or gave them only the most menial jobs.

Oddly, black women could work in the professions, where competition was lighter. By 1920 two of ten black university graduates were female; in 1921 three black women earned PhDs from prestigious schools. But in fields requiring college or post-graduate degrees, black female legal, medical, educational, and social workers earned paltry incomes compared to their white counterparts. Huge numbers of black women were forced back into the jobs reserved for women—domestic service and prostitution.

Heroines

Despite the Red Scare, some feminists with strong socialist views, like Jane Addams and Lillian Wald, opposed the United States's entering the First World War and were able to continue their work. Crystal Eastman, Margaret Sanger, and Emma Goldman, reformists dedicated to female sexual freedom, were a generation younger than Wald and Addams. Eastman, a journalist and attorney specializing in labor conditions and injuries, drafted the first New York worker-compensation law, the model for such laws across the country. An early supporter of female athletics, she toured the United States with champion swimmer Annette Kellerman, promoting "women's right to physical equality with men."

Eastman founded the New York branch of the American Union Against Militarism, the "mother" of the American Civil Liberties Union, and served as executive director with Wald as president.[13] In 1914 Eastman, Addams, and Emmeline Pethick-Lawrence created the Woman's Peace Party to try to keep the United States neutral in the First World War and stop it from invading Mexico in 1916. Eastman, Wald, and Addams dined with Wilson and his advisers at the White House and lobbied Congress, trying to influence events. After the United States entered the war in 1917, Eastman and Roger Baldwin worked in the Civil Liberties Bureau (renamed ACLU) to protect the rights of conscientious objectors and dissenters. The government used the war to justify domination and technology and to stifle dissent.

The Espionage Act and Sedition Acts of May 1918 made certain wartime acts retroactively illegal, and legalized removing radical publications from the post (in line with Comstock's focus on mail in an earlier wave of enforced conformity). Dissenters were imprisoned (including Eastman's brother Max) as well as thousands of anarchists, socialists, labor leaders, and conscientious objectors. Some were deported in the Red Scare following the war. These acts radicalized Eastman, who came to believe that capitalism had to be (peacefully) destroyed if liberty was to be possible. With Max, she started a protest magazine, *The Liberator*. Believing socialism stood for democracy, equality, and liberty but not for women's rights, she created a women's rights program around sex and reproduction, accepting birth control and "free love." Addams disavowed her. Blacklisted in the United States, she moved to England but failed to find work and died at forty-seven in 1928.

Margaret Sanger, a visiting nurse on Manhattan's Lower East Side and socialist IWW supporter, had helped strikers in Lawrence and Paterson. Daily exposure to poor women convinced her that birth control was necessary. In 1913, in France to study birth-control methods, she found that despite the Catholic Church and government allowances to mothers of large families, the French working-class birth rate was declining. Returning to the United States, she started a magazine, *The Woman Rebel*, devoted to female sexual freedom, and was indicted by the U.S. Post Office for "a philosophical defense of assassination" for writing:

> A woman's body belongs to herself alone. It is her body. It does not belong to the Church. It does not belong to the United States of America. . . . The first step toward getting life, liberty and the pursuit of happiness for any woman is her decision whether or not she shall become a mother. Enforced motherhood is the most complete denial of a woman's right to life and liberty. . . . Once the women of the United States are awakened to the value of birth control, these institutions—Church, State, Big Business—will be struck such a blow that they will be able only to beg for mercy from the workers.

Sanger thought birth control would ease poor women's lot and free them sexually but also strengthen the working class. She fled the country until her trial (which she wanted to turn into a public forum), but before leaving she published a pamphlet, "Family Limitation," a digest of her knowledge of contraceptive techniques (douches, condoms, sponges, diaphragms, and suppositories) that contested claims that *coitus interruptus* harmed women's health. She urged that sex be mutually fulfillling, not an imposition of men's conjugal rights. The pamphlet was printed clandestinely but 10 million copies were issued and many more mimeographed, hand-copied, or typed over the years. Thousands of grateful readers of both sexes sent small sums for Sanger's trial.

Throughout Sanger's career, the IWW had been her strongest ally, despite its reluctance to espouse birth control. But the government had destroyed the IWW. The IWW did not seem to understand the repressive potential of class rule: it never acted secretly, keeping open membership lists and a loose organization with no mode of communication but the mail.[14] When the government decided to eradicate the IWW during the First World War, it was able to seize all its publications and members in a few raids, and then prosecute and jail people on flimsy charges. Sanger had to look elsewhere for help. She found it in Emma Goldman.

Emma Goldman (1869–1940), arguably the greatest American political figure of her era, disappointed her Russian Jewish family by being a girl. With three female children by a first husband who died, Emma's mother felt it urgent to remedy her failure and have a son. Both parents cared only for sons. Emma's father suffered from repeated business failures and brutal Russian anti-Semitism, and took out his rage on Emma and her sister Helena, beating them continually, especially after their brother died. He sent Emma to live with an uncle who took her out of school and used her as a servant, treating her as cruelly as her father (kicking her down a flight of stairs). Two kindly woman neighbors rescued Emma from him and restored her to her family. She went to work as a seamstress and was raped: her angry father tried to force her to marry. After threatening to jump into the Neva River, she and Helena decided to go to the United States and live with their sister Lena.

They settled with Lena in Rochester, where Goldman worked as a seamstress, less happily than in Russia: the American factory was modern but regimented. St. Petersburg seamstresses talked and sang while they worked; in Rochester, conversation was utterly forbidden—foremen stood over the women working at their machines. Not only were workers isolated but Goldman's ideal of Jewish solidarity crumbled—the factory was owned by a wealthy German Jew who exploited Russian Jewish immigrants. With little formal education, Goldman educated herself with political novels like Chernyshevsky's great *What Is to Be Done?* whose heroine Vera Pavlovna escapes from an exploitative family, starts a flourishing communal female workshop, and lives in sexual freedom.

She moved to New Haven, Connecticut, to work in a unionized corset factory with decent working conditions. She also found comrades, Russian immigrants who gathered after work to discuss socialist and anarchist theory. She was fascinated by the level of discussion and by anarchy. Through her friends she met German anarchist Johann Most, an eloquent speaker despite an apparent facial deformity. Once a member of the Reichstag and German Social Democratic Party (SDP), he edited the *Berliner Freie Presse* and wrote a popular summary of *Das Kapital*. Expelled from Germany, he went to London where he published *Die Freiheit*, an anarchist journal. Most, impressed with Goldman's eloquence, trained her in public speaking. But she noticed he lost interest whenever she expressed her own ideas. Another ideal collapsed as she saw that even a man committed to individual freedom, opposed to all inequities and hierarchies, expected to dominate women.

Goldman became politically and sexually involved with Alexander (Sasha) Berkman, an anarchist. In 1892, workers at the Carnegie Steel plant in Homestead, Pennsylvania, struck for higher wages. Henry Clay Frick, chairman of Carnegie, replaced them with scabs, and locked them out of their company-owned houses. The strikers stood firm; he sent 300 Pinkerton men to attack them, and three Pinkertons and ten workers were killed. Outraged, the twenty-two-year-old Berkman decided to kill Frick with Emma's help. She planned and financed the assassination attempt: Berkman managed to get into Frick's office and fire three shots, seriously wounding Frick, but he was captured. The act that Emma expected to trigger workers nationwide to take over factories instead sent Sasha to prison and Emma underground, and provoked a new wave of repression. Workers' organizations were fractured by arguments over tactics. Emma began privately to question the wisdom of violent acts like Berkman's.[15]

Goldman later defined anarchy as liberation of the human mind from the dominion of religion, liberation of the human body from the dominion of property, and liberation from the shackles and restraints of government. For her, anarchy meant a "release and freedom from conventions and prejudice" without denying life and joy: "I want freedom, the right to self-expression, everybody's right to beautiful, radiant things," she wrote. All her acts bespoke an unwavering commitment to all people's right to live free from oppression. Anarchy offered no political program but a morality no political group was prepared to realize.

Goldman surfaced at an 1893 rally in Union Square, New York, to speak and march with a red banner alongside unemployed women and girls. The next day she was arrested, charged with "inciting a riot and . . . disbelief in God and government," and sentenced to a year at Blackwell's Prison. Her brilliance in court won her wide press coverage and on her release she found herself a national celebrity. In the next years, she visited Vienna (learning about Freud) and London, meeting major European radicals like Louise Michel, heroine of the Paris Commune, and anarchist Peter Kropotkin, who believed modern technology could maintain a cooperative communist society and that revolution was a natural process, not a violent overthrow. In 1900, Goldman returned to the United States, worked as a midwife-nurse (having trained in jail), and lectured on contraception, which she felt integrated her life. She thought that contraception abetted sexual revolution, helped free women, and subverted government efforts to leash personal freedom.

In 1906 Goldman founded an anarchist journal, *Mother Earth*, as an alternative to *Masses*, the socialist journal. Aimed at a less intellectual but more radical readership, it presented political messages from literary figures and Goldman's mix of politics and art. She found the suffrage movement hostile to labor and never worked for women's suffrage. But she spoke on an even more provocative subject, female sexual freedom, as well as birth control. At every talk she gave in every city, she sold Margaret Sanger's magazine, *The Woman Rebel*, which had been banned from the mail for "obscenity"—birth-control information. When Sanger's husband William was arrested for giving a visitor to his home a copy of her pamphlet "Family Limitation" in 1915, Goldman wrote an editorial in

Mother Earth condemning legal censorship. Her eye was always on principle—not advantage, influence or power, or the power, influence, or status of a party. This was true of no male leader.

As the possibility quickened that the United States would enter the war, Goldman's speeches linked war and birth control, warning that the increasingly repressive atmosphere in the United States was related to war preparations: a country at war subordinates all needs and dissent to the State's desire for unity. After the United States declared war on Germany, she continued to speak against conscription. Attendance at her speeches was huge: once, 5000 filled the hall and 30,000 massed outside as she urged workers to copy the revolutionaries who overthrew the Czar in February. After one speech the government arrested hundreds of draft resisters. Since the government was using her talks to entrap prospective war resisters, she chose not to speak again but only write. But she was arrested the next day, along with Berkman, who was now out of jail. The arresting officer carried not a warrant but the June issue of *Mother Earth*, which, he said, held enough treasonable matter to send them to jail for years. They were found guilty of "conspiracy against the draft," and after declaring Goldman "probably the greatest woman of her time," the judge imposed the maximum penalty for conspiracy against the draft—two years in prison and a $10,000 fine.

Under the Espionage Act, the government arrested thousands, especially foreign antiwar agitators and radicals, giving the longest sentences to Bill Haywood of the IWW, Eugene Debs, Socialist Party head, and Kate Richards O'Hare, major socialist activist and reformer. Mail censorship increased. The postmaster banned a book of essays by Voltairine de Cleyre for pieces on Goldman and sexual slavery; her linking of sexual freedom and antimilitarism threw him into virtual hysterics.[16] Most dangerous, the government felt, was "Justice for the Negro," a Wobbly leaflet pointing out that while black soldiers were asked to fight for democracy abroad, ninety-one blacks had been lynched at home.

The Alien Immigration Act of 1917 gave the government power

to deport foreign-born anarchists. Arrests became arbitrary when the war ended in 1919: paranoia generated "Palmer raids" on groups connected in any way with foreign, antiwar, or radical activity. When Joseph Kershner, whom Goldman had married and left years before, died in January 1919, she was no longer a citizen by marriage and the government sought a way to deport "Red Emma" as it had long wanted to do. It hired a woman to infiltrate the anarchist network as Goldman's secretary and report on the activities of "those damned kikes." Early on December 21, 1919, a bitterly cold day, Emma Goldman, Sasha Berkman, and 247 others guarded by 250 soldiers each with a rifle and two pistols, were marched onto a dilapidated military ship, and expelled from American soil. The United States had cast out its greatest moralist.

With Berkman, Goldman went first to Russia to observe the revolution. She spoke Russian, knew many radicals visiting there, and was a figure of considerable stature, so she could observe widely. And what she saw was misery. Goldman complained to Lenin, who received her graciously, persuading her and Berkman to help build the revolution. For a year they toured the country, seeing poverty everywhere, hearing about people's disillusion, and their terror of the Party and of the secret police, the Cheka. She learned of the ghastly conditions in prisons, discrimination against intellectuals, and pervasive anti-Semitism. With Berkman, she decided to tell the world what she had seen.

Her criticism of the revolution lost her what friends she had left; in the next months, Goldman and Berkman were imprisoned in Latvia on Bolshevik orders, while American officials hysterically mounted defenses against her possible return. Two years after their deportation, the pair left Soviet space, sailing into a void, friendless, without destination. Because her loyalty lay with humanity, not any cause, Goldman was abandoned. In the next years, she wrote her autobiography and lectured in England, Holland, Denmark, and Germany, continuing to warn the human race of threats to its freedom, arguing that Hitler's fascism showed the same disregard for the individual as Lenin's Soviet Union and American capitalism. Hope gone, Goldman died in May 1940.

Women in American Labor after 1930

Millions of American working women who strategized, organized, and protested were also defeated. During the first phase of labor struggle, they were beaten mainly by capital, as employers succeeded in "hungering" them out. Men and male unions helped some women's unions during this period, but in most cases, men impeded or cut women out entirely. White men used trade unions, which could have united all workers to stand fast against employers, as a weapon to defend relative privilege against other workers.

When the Committee for Industrial Organization (CIO: later called the Congress of Industrial Organizations) was formed in 1935, women were more accepted by organized labor, and by the end of the Second World War, neither AFL nor CIO unions barred women from membership; only the International Brotherhood of Bookbinders had separate women's locals (common in prewar years). More women had staff positions too, if mainly on the local level, but only one, the United Federal Workers, had a woman president. Few women sat on national executive boards. The most impressive (but atypical) was the United Electrical Workers, whose organizing staff was over a third female in 1944—almost matching its 40 percent female UEW membership.[17]

Some women union leaders developed and promoted special programs to meet the needs of women, despite male leaders' opposition to their advanced ideas. Their efforts led many unions to provide child care and other community services for women workers and to negotiate contracts providing maternity leave without loss of seniority. By the war's end most unions had endorsed the idea of "the rate for the job," or equal pay for equal work. Unions rarely confronted the real inequalities by trying to eliminate differential wages for "men's" and "women's" jobs, but in 1942, the UEW negotiated a contract with Westinghouse that raised only women's wages. The system of job classification by sex was almost never challenged. A 1944 study of twenty-five industries found that men's hourly earnings were 50 percent higher than women's, and 20 percent higher on unskilled jobs.[18]

According to a United States Women's Bureau survey of 13,000 women workers in war industries in 1944–45, 75 percent wanted to keep their jobs when the war ended. While they expected to be laid off disproportionately because of lower seniority, and neither demanded nor expected preferential treatment, they felt they deserved the same protection as men. They thought that returning veterans should displace workers of either sex only if they had more seniority. Their effort to establish nondiscriminatory seniority systems was quite successful—four-fifths of the union contracts covering 75,000 women workers in a Midwestern war industry area in 1945 demanded plant-wide rather than departmental seniority; only a fifth stipulated separate seniority lists for women.[19]

Thus, while women expected to bear the brunt of initial layoffs, if they were recalled according to seniority, post-war industrial expansion should have reincorporated them into the labor force of the industries where they had done "war work." But often they were not recalled. The UAW affirmed unequivocal support for "Protection of Women's Rights in the Auto Industry," laying out a detailed model policy on equal pay, seniority, and other rights, but did not specify penalties for violating them. Many locals continued to negotiate contracts that openly discriminated against women, and locals had to enforce contracts with formal protections against discrimination. Many shop stewards simply ignored inequities or failed to pursue women's grievances.

The single most important change in the make-up of the labor force after the Second World War was the dramatic rise in female participation; the recent stagnation of the labor movement resulted from its failure to deal with that. Indeed the extent to which industries are unionized is strongly inversely related to the representation of women workers in their labor forces. AFL unions' successful exclusion of women (and people of color) from craft occupations helped to rigidify the sexual division of paid work.

No matter how large their female membership, mixed unions remain male-dominated. When the WTUL merged with the Amalgamated Clothing Workers of America it became 75 percent female, but it has never had a woman director or high officer at the international level and has a tiny female presence on its executive board. No woman held high office in the IWW, despite the importance of women members like Elizabeth Gurley Flynn. Rose Pesotta complained in 1944 that despite its 85 percent female membership the International Ladies Garment Workers Union (ILGWU) reserved only one seat on its executive board for a woman; in the 1980s, the ILGWU sometimes had two women on its board of twenty to twenty-three members. A few small AFL unions had women presidents, but no woman ever sat on the AFL-CIO Executive Council. No woman had ever been president of the AFL-CIO and, as of 1986, none had been regional director. After John Sweeney, a reformer, was elected head of the AFL-CIO in 1995, however, things changed. Sweeney doubled the representation of women and people of color in high-level posts; women, once 6 percent of department heads, now comprise 50 percent. Women head the two largest departments, international affairs and field mobilization. He also created a working-women's department, and a program open to any working woman, unionized or not. Now, 13 percent of the Executive Council, and 15 percent of the Central Labor Council are women.

A female onslaught in the 1970s and 1980s forced skilled trade unions such as electricians and plumbers to accept female members. But the men harassed women; they ganged up against those hired singly or by twos verbally abusing them or refusing to speak to them at all, hung obscene pictures in the workplace, endangered them or used physical violence. However they could, they drove women out. Yet reluctance to make common cause with women and minority workers still undermines organized labor as a whole.

Governments, still elitist, continue to want to destroy organized labor. Three miners' strikes occurred in 1989—in the (then) Soviet Union and Poland (socialist states that prohibited strikes), and in the United States, where miners in three states struck against the Pittston Coal Group. Only in the United States were strike leaders imprisoned. The American press, which gave wide coverage to the strikes in socialist countries barely noted the American one. Since Ronald Reagan successfully broke the air controllers' union in 1981, companies have been hiring "replacement workers" (euphemism for scabs), and firing strikers. Since unions excluded so many people, "replacement workers" are easy to find. Unions' failure to organize workers worldwide has contributed to allowing multinational corporations to arrange to have goods produced where production is cheapest. Clothing manufacturers avoid paying union scale by transferring production to Korea or China or southeast Asia, where they can pay workers too little to survive.

Owners are power-hungry and greedy, but so was labor: the history of white men in the American labor movement is ignoble. They called themselves *the workers* as if only they labored to survive. Cutting out all women and men of color, they seized their piece of the pie. Men who once guarded their privileges in massive steel and automobile industries now pound the sidewalks of Houston and Dallas seeking work or live homeless in New York. The American labor movement turned its back on its own early standards—to create a just and felicitous society—and made its own destruction possible. All workers lost as a result.

At present, union leaders are trying to reform the movement and revive the organizations' past unity and moral force. They have opened their ranks to women and people of color. But labor unions, which in the 1950s boasted a membership of 38 percent of the workforce, now have only 9 percent. This defeat was caused not by labor, but by owners, who moved their factories to other countries in the world—to nations that do not have laws demanding healthful safe environments or wages sufficient to maintain life—to avoid having to abide by labor laws in the United States. Other owners have shifted to staffs largely made up of part-time or contract workers, to avoid having to pay for medical care, pensions, and other benefits. Few workers nowadays earn enough to support families, which must have two working members to survive. The labor organizations that sixty or seventy years ago urged the unionization of the world's workers were on the right track. But that has not occurred yet.

In England

It was the class-ridden English who devised a strategy with the potential to create an industrial society with a democratic, non-exploitative shape. Nineteenth- and twentieth-century labor history is a series of attempts by owners to wrest control from workers' organizations to restructure labor to suit their ends, and workers' attempts to resist this usurpation. Labor lost.

Laws passed in England in 1824–25 gave male organizations (descended from guilds) the right to bargain collectively, allowing them to become full-fledged trade unions and preserve the guild hierarchy of apprentice, journeyman, and master. From the start, male trade-unionists wanted women—"wives and daughters"—to be "in their proper sphere at home, instead of being dragged into competition for livelihood against the great and strong men of the world," as a labor leader said in 1875.[20] Men who felt their jobs threatened by women earning half their rate challenged not the wage rate but women's right to the jobs. Textile unions adamantly excluded women, striking when owners hired them, yet they could not prevent the hiring of skilled women at half wages. Cotton spinners urged women to form their own unions, and many did in the 1830s and 1840s: female and male Glasgow spinners and power-loom weavers joined to raise money to fight for equal pay.

Spinners' unions accepted only men who could afford high entry fees and dues. High dues enabled unions to pay their members during strikes, but strikes also affected workers without an organization or strike fund—like women. Without wages, they starved, so were available as strikebreakers, "knobsticks," scabs. To prevent this, spinners finally accepted a separate organization of piecers and cardroom workers. The Bolton Association of Cotton Spinners admitted women to its piecers' section in 1837. Other unions or union sections were soon organizing piecers and cardroom workers. It was ludicrous to exclude women from unions in an industry in which they predominated, but spinners and cotton weavers admitted them only slowly over years.[21]

In the winter of 1833, the Derby silk industry locked out all workers, initiating a struggle that generated such anger and solidarity among workers nationwide that they created the Consolidated Union. During this strike, women founded union lodges, networking with neighboring women in other industries, who supported them. They joined cooperative workshops and led large demonstrations, fighting with—even stoning—the police. A union man wrote: "From the determined heroism [of these women] I could scarcely believe but that I was surrounded by the descendants of the 'Maid of Orleans,' and are these, I ask . . . to be subdued by the fancied power of the monied capitalists? No, gentlemen of Derby . . . retire from the contest with these Amazonian females; defeat will be yours."

Seeing radical action as an extension of their family duties encouraged women's militancy, but limited its forms. Workers' groups adopted the traditional family sexual division of labor and power. Before 1830 no woman led a sexually mixed union; the Consolidated Union had members in mixed trades, yet women were usually organized in separate lodges, and men's lodges took the initiative in all ventures. Women seem not to have protested or suggested other ways: the old ways were just transferred to the new system. In virtually all industries women worked on different elements or phases of production from men and were paid less. They often organized alongside men, but many mixed organizations collapsed and were replaced by segregated ones. Tension between the sexes grew as owners retooled and debased or eliminated the need for craft skills, hiring unskilled workers—usually women—for less pay. Female labor threatened skilled male workers, who formed sex-segregated unions with men who wanted women out of their industries and unions entirely.

Nineteenth-century industry exploited women almost as cruelly as it did children, but male colleagues did not step in: government did. Government, however, did not regulate industry but its victims, forbidding women and children to work underground in mines. This gratified male miners, whose organizations had been trying to bar women from underground work because they kept "lads and men from getting their proper wages." Many male trade unionists lobbied Parliament to limit the hours women could work, hoping further restrictions on women would limit men's hours "behind the women's petticoats." One union lobbied for hour limitations and proportional quotas on women, and a ban on married women.

After women textile workers unionized, no drive to organize women workers occurred until 1874, when Emma Paterson founded the Women's Protective and Provident League. Paterson intended the league to be a central body that helped set up individual unions, hoping that once women knew how to run a self-reliant, self-supporting organization, the league could withdraw but stand ready to help a union in trouble. At first, it helped unionize women bookbinders, milliners, mantle-makers, and other needlewomen in London, all very small groups in areas traditionally regarded as skilled or semiskilled "women's work." It soon became controversial for its opposition to protective legislation. Its middle-class leaders felt that women had the right to any job and hours they wanted, and that if hours were to be limited, collective bargaining, not legislation should negotiate them.

A few years after Paterson died in 1886, the league responded to changes in trade unionism by changing its policies, financial base, and name; it became the Women's Trade Union League (WTUL). Lady Dilke, who led the league after Paterson's death, wanted to shift from middle-class donations and subscriptions to a firm financial base in the trade union movement and devised a plan allowing any bona fide trade union admitting women to affiliate with the WTUL for a halfpenny a year per female member, for which WTUL would help organize women and raise strike funds. By the 1890s sixty unions, including thirty local cotton worker groups, had done so.

Changing its policy on protective laws, the WTUL now championed them. Female factory inspectors, the first women in responsible government jobs, were few in number but enormously important to women in factories and trade unions. They traveled extensively around Great Britain to factories, back-street workshops, even to wild Donegal; they had detailed knowledge of the laws governing factories and the ability to argue a case in court—thirty years before British women were admitted to the bar. Courageous outspoken women devoted to their work, they went far beyond their assignments to investigate areas where improvement was needed, suggesting new laws or extensions of existing acts. Their annual reports provided an authoritative foundation for campaigns for further laws to protect women workers.

Unlike cotton unions, heavy woolens workers' unions, most in Yorkshire, were often started or virtually run by women. The industry was not organized until 1875, when owners in the Dewsbury area (over fifty manufacturers, two or three finishers, and twelve dyers) colluded in cutting wages. Hannah Wood, Ann Ellis, and Kate Conran founded a Heavy Woolen Weavers' Strike and Lockout Committee and struck, raising a strike fund of £1200 in six weeks. These women had no inhibitions against speaking in public and at one meeting spoke to 9000 people. Throughout the strike, they pleaded for unity of male and female workers. The strike was settled and their union became the first branch of a General Union of Textile Workers.

A government report on strikes and lockouts in the textile industry listed ninety-nine labor disputes in 1898 (fewer than in the five previous years) involving 24,978 workers, directly or indirectly. Of a labor force 42 percent women, 32 percent men, and 26 percent youths, proportionately more women than men were involved in lockouts and strikes. Nonunionized women relied on local trades councils to help organize, support, and negotiate for them after they struck. Unions were reluctant to organize women otherwise.

Trade unions closed to skilled women did not even consider organizing the most gravely exploited workers—unskilled factory women. When radical WTUL women urged such organizing, they were criticized by people like journalist Annie Besant for advocating unworkable schemes. If workers (like the match workers she had mentioned in a recent column) went on strike, hundreds of others would beg for their jobs, she wrote. The column, headed "White Slavery in London," described conditions at Bryant and May, whose female employees worked ten to eleven and a half hours a day, earning from 4 to 9 shillings a week, burdened by innumerable fines: "If the feet are dirty, or the ground under the bench is left untidy, a fine of 3 pence is inflicted; for putting 'burnts'—matches that have caught fire during work—on the bench" they were fined 1 shilling (a quarter of the wages of some). If they were late for work, they were shut out all morning and docked 5 pence from their day's pay of 8 pence.

When Bryant and May told the press that they were suing Besant for libel, she announced she would stand by the statements in her article. The company dismissed three women known to have talked to Besant and asked workers to sign a statement swearing Besant's claims were false. They refused, and the company fired a woman they believed to be a ringleader. All the women in her department left with her; soon, all 1400 women at Bryant and May walked out. They held public meetings, demonstrated, and sent a deputation to ask the home secretary to prosecute Bryant and May for imposing illegal fines and deductions. Still calling Besant's article a "tissue of lies," the company dropped its libel suit. A delegation of "match girls" went to the London Trades Council (LTC) for help; they received £20 for the strike fund and an offer to mediate. The LTC helped them draw up a grievance list and arrange a meeting among the strike committee, trades council members, and Bryant and May directors. The company acceded to almost all the women's demands. All fines and most deductions were abolished, the "pennies" restored, and no retribution was exacted. Most important, the company acknowledged the union. The Match Girls' strike inspired other unskilled workers' unions.

During this period, women began to infiltrate white-collar work, entering civil service by a circuitous route. In 1870 the government took over the telegraph system, placing it under control of the Post Office, which was obliged to retain female telegraph operators who had worked for the private companies. A postal official saw advantages to hiring women, and his brief became the basis for female employment in civil service. He preferred women to men in clerical work because they were quick, accurate, and happier at sedentary occupations. The wages offered would draw a better class of women than men, with the added benefit of superior education—they wrote and spelled better and "where the staff is mixed, the female clerks will raise the tone of the staff." In addition, he wrote:

> Women are less disposed than men to combine for the purpose of extorting higher wages. . . . Permanently established civil servants invariably expect their remuneration to increase with their years of service. . . . Women, however, will solve these difficulties for the Department by retiring for the purpose of getting married as soon as they get the chance. On the whole, it may be stated without fear of contradiction that, if we place an equal number of females and males on the same ascending scale of pay, the aggregate pay to the females will always be less than the aggregate pay to

> the males; . . . and further, that there will always be fewer females than males on the pension list.

The government hired forty women in the savings bank in 1875. Appalled, the men in the office threatened an "indignation meeting" to protest employment of women as causing "grievous dangers, moral and official." Beyond that, they said, women would not be strong enough to write cross-entry acknowledgments, which required "heavy pressure by means of very hard pens and carbonic paper"[!] But the advantage of cheap labor outweighed male prejudice: women became a significant presence in government offices.

In 1906 Mary Macarthur founded the National Federation of Women Workers (NFWW), which lasted only until 1920 but organized more women, mounted more strikes, and did more to establish women's unions than any other group, largely because of her leadership. A freelance journalist, she kept books for her father, a successful Ayr draper. Covering a shop assistants' union meeting for a conservative Scottish newspaper changed her life: "I went to a meeting in Ayr to write a skit on the proceedings; going to scoff, I remained to pray." Impressed with the "truth and meaning of the Labour movement," she joined the union. In 1902 she was elected branch president (the only female president in Scotland), and president of the Scottish National District Council. Involved with the Independent Labour Party, at a 1902 conference, she met Margaret Bondfield, an organizer of shop assistants in the south, who gave Macarthur the confidence to move to London. At twenty-three she was secretary of the WTUL and threw her considerable energy into organizing it and its finances properly. Macarthur stayed connected to WTUL; she created the NFWW as a militant union for women in unorganized trades or trades with unions that rejected women. Workers' only weapon in this period was the strike and between 1906 and 1914 the federation mainly led strikes. The first league leader with experience in trade unionism and the labor movement, Macarthur died in 1921, only forty-one years old.

Tailoring

In the eighteenth century, tailoring was men's work. With the strongest union in England, tailors controlled prices, hours, and labor recruitment through apprenticeship. They strictly limited female employment to dressmaking and millinery, which were lower paid and unorganized. Tailors' wives, unlike those of weavers, did not help them, so only masters could support a wife and family. Tailors' wives earned money by embroidering, making necklaces and mantuas, and selling milk. A journeyman with a working wife could live decently: the family could afford a servant, a few amenities (some books or a piano) and he could enjoy local cultural and political life. Men needed wives to work but felt disgraced if their wives worked away from home, so wives kept shops, did homework and laundry, or took in lodgers. Whatever a wife did, she earned little.

Capitalists reorganized industry in the early nineteenth century and hired "puffers and sweaters" who subcontracted jobs to home workers. Aiming for maximum profit, they sought workers who would take low wages. They found women. The tailors' union, trying to prevent production outside workshops, which they controlled, struck and won. Francis Place, a master tailor in 1824, wrote: "It will be found universally . . . where men have opposed the employment of women and children . . . their own wages are kept up to a point equal to the maintenance of a family. . . . Tailors of London have not only kept up, but forced up their wages in this way."

During the Napoleonic Wars, the government needed cheap military uniforms, and developed a system in which wholesale fabric producers contracted with small masters or unemployed journeymen. They in turn hired cheap labor, often women, to make ready-to-wear—"slop" clothing—in their homes or sweatshops. Slop clothing, cheaper than "bespoke" (made to order), became very popular. New quality clothiers opened "show-shops" of clothes made to standard measurements, driving master tailors out of business. The union protested: "Have not women been unfairly driven from their proper sphere in the social scale, unfeelingly torn from the maternal duties of a parent, and unjustly encouraged to compete with men in ruining the money value of labor?"

In 1834, 9000 London tailors struck for higher wages, a reduction in hours, and the abolition of piece- and home-work. All concerned knew they wanted to put an end once and for all to female tailoring; they threatened women's outwork and show-shop employment, declaring, an editor wrote, a "war against the female tailors." Owners used editorials in their mouthpiece, *The Times*, to lament "dictatorial" union treatment of "honest and industrious females" and hired women scabs. Union men assaulted women and seized their materials. But the men were divided: some supported women's right to work but condemned the shops that hired them. The union accused owners of lying to "turn our mothers and sisters against us"; some wanted to set up a (separate) women's union. Socialists, favoring equality, opened a cooperative workshop during the strike. John Doherty, head of the Lancashire cotton spinners union, said the problem of women was serious, but its solution obvious: men, he exhorted, should "acknowledge the natural equality of women . . . include them in all [their] schemes of improvement." An editorial in *The Pioneer*, an Owenite newspaper, urged equal pay and women's inclusion in unions. In the end, however, the tailors lost.[22]

The Pioneer editorial laid out the options for male unionists who wanted to move beyond defensive sectional militancy toward egalitarian class organization: "Women have always been worse paid for their labor than men and thus, they have been taught to regard this inequality as justice." Since they were "content with merely a portion of man's wage, even when their work is equally valuable," they could be used to undercut men's wages. To prevent lower wages, tailors organized against female employment.

It is not right, the editorial continued, for male workers to undercut the wages of other men; it would not be right for female workers to do this either, if women were equal to men, with the same rights and privileges. "But since man has doomed her to inferiority, and stamped an inferior value upon all the productions of her industry, the low wages of woman are not so much the voluntary price she sets upon her labor, as the price which is fixed by the tyrannical influence of male supremacy. To make the two sexes equal, and to reward them equally, would settle the matter amicably; but any attempt to settle it otherwise will prove an act of gross tyranny."[23]

Women wrote of their male antagonists, "It is clear enough from this whispering spirit of jealousy . . . that the men are as bad as their masters." If the idea of women meeting and organizing outside the home, beyond the direct control of husbands or fathers terrified some men, the idea of women organizing, earning the same wages, and cooperating in work, appalled them. But by refusing to recognize women, excluding them from their unions, and retreating from a demand for equal pay and decent working conditions, the craft unions injured women and destroyed themselves.

Men's loss of domination of crafts led to a breakdown in their sexual authority. They equated losing the power that seemed inherent in their craft, and losing the feeling of strength they derived from status in all-male industries and unions, with a loss of manhood. Losing the powers of purse and status weakened their sense of superiority over women, which had been constructed by customary and legal prerogatives. But men's loss did not liberate women, who were forced into deeper poverty. A study of wife-beating in London in the 1840s found that when women replaced men as the major breadwinners in artisan households, men responded violently, asserting physically an authority that had lost its material foundation. Men's already strong opposition to married women's employment was heightened: a wage-earning wife symbolized male degradation. They believed that a "real man" kept a dependent wife at home.

Women too supported the family wage and bought the ideology of domesticity; it was oppressive and imposed from the outside, but it was the best choice then open to working-class women, given the hideous working conditions and low wages of the time. In the end, though, men's loss of dominance in the family liberated women as they challenged other forms of male dominance.

Printing

Male printers staved women off for a little longer. Printers' organizations were rooted in medieval guilds; the many female printers of the fifteenth and sixteenth centuries probably took over their dead husbands' shops—girls were never allowed into the hierarchy of apprentice, journeyman, master.[24] Printers derived great self-importance from an exclusive craft that barred all women and most men and which required literacy, a mark of status. Few applicants were accepted as apprentices, and printers' sons got precedence. On finishing their training, they were ritually initiated; journeymen became part of an elite group of artisans—citizens, Freemen of the City. Union shops were called "chapels," suggesting printers' awed sense of themselves.

Manufacturers, who constantly seek new production methods requiring less skill, developed Linotype, a mechanized typesetter that needed only one semiskilled operator. The Typographical Association (TA) informed owners that its members would run the machines and share the profits; shorter hours and training it made possible. The TA and the London Society of Compositors (LSC) were strong enough to enforce this (a commentator called the TA "an army of guerrilla bands," the LSC "a panzer division"). British compositors even did unskilled jobs in the trade to retain exclusive control of the composing room. Publishing grew wildly over the century and employers' profits were high enough to satisfy them. As hand-compositors retired or died, younger printers found work in the growing market. By 1900 socialist ideas had penetrated the TA, which allied with what became the Labor Party to unionize the unskilled, and helped form a national Federation of Printing and Kindred Trades to unite all male printers' unions in Britain.

In the world of printing, women were complete outsiders. Few women did printing—300 in 1851, 700 in 1871, and 4500 in 1891—and almost none were compositors. Neither the TA, the Scottish Typographical Association (STA), nor the LSC needed explicitly to bar women, because unions controlled apprenticeship. The unions showed their true colors in an unusual conference held in London in 1886 to deal with the "threat" of women compositors in Edinburgh.

When male compositors in Edinburgh went on strike in 1872, owners hired women and trained them to fill the men's jobs. By 1900 Edinburgh had 750 female compositors. Owners in other Scottish cities began to hire them, and during a depression men bitterly blamed women for male unemployment. Paying women less than men, Scottish firms could undercut London firms, and they began taking their business. The three typographical societies met to deal with this. Wanting to keep women out of the craft altogether, but also to ensure that if women got in, they could not undercut men's wages, they passed a seemingly illogical resolution: "That while strongly of the opinion that women are not physically capable of performing the duties of a compositor, this Conference recommends their admission to membership of the various typographical unions, upon the same conditions as journeymen, provided always the females are paid strictly in accordance with the scale." They knew no employer would hire women at the same wage rate as men, given men's hostility and the limitations of the Factory Act (the protective law that curtailed women's work hours at night).

Men claimed women could not physically do work they were already doing because it involved too much standing and lifting heavy weights. They simply ignored women's work in mines, laundries, and similar industries. They warned that handling type could "destroy the powers of maternity in women." British union histories still dismiss men's antagonism toward women as incidental fallout from the class struggle, given employers' exploitation of cheap female labor. "Had nothing but class interest been at stake, the men would have found women acceptable as apprentices, would have fought wholeheartedly for equal pay for women and the right of women to keep their jobs at equal pay."[25] Instead, they tried to eliminate women from their trade.

What was at stake for men was, as one man wrote, the male need for women to be men's servants, "housekeeper, cook, and several other single domestics rolled into one."[26] This ideal, presented as fact, won union men a "family wage" and kept women out of work. Yet many union men did not marry, many of those who did were negligent toward their families: many women and children were destitute. Men received a "family wage" whether they had families or not; and women did not receive decent wages whether they had families or not. In the period of the First World War, a family wage was paid on behalf of 3 million fictitious wives and 16 million fictitious children—the supposed dependents of bachelors—while real women and children starved.[27] Men claimed that status was an emotional necessity, ignoring women's physical needs: "I felt degraded following the footsteps of generations of compositor-forefathers before me, at having to descend to such vile practices" as working alongside women; if women did the work, "some of the shine would go out of the job for me. Prestige might not be exactly the right word, but it carries what is known as a macho bit, composing. It's man's work." Composing was men's work; "it has always been regarded as men's work . . . a large number of men are attracted to the trade because it is a man's employment." The presence of even one woman transforms it into "women's work."

Unthinkable as it was that women should join the all-male trade society that gave men self-respect as artisans and as men, it was equally unthinkable that employers would hire women at the same wages as men. The printers' societies tactic succeeded. A few bold employers went on using women at low rates, but no women were admitted to the English TA; Jane Payne, accepted by the LSC, resigned in 1898. Feminists tried to organize women compositors in Edinburgh, but the STA was unwilling to accept them.[28]

Male hostility toward women became hatred in 1904 when Glasgow printers asked owners for a wage raise. When the arbitrator denied the request on the grounds that by excluding women, compositors hobbled Glasgow firms in competing with Edinburgh firms, union branches in other Scottish cities rose up against women. Solidarity brought victory; after a fifteen-week strike, Aberdeen printers won a promise that no more women would be hired at case (hand-typesetting) or on machines. The Dundee branch had all women compositors fired but two; Perth got all its females fired.

Edinburgh compositors delayed until 1909 the crusade against women that the trade had been anticipating. In the interim, the monotype machine was introduced. It separated the two parts of printing, setting type and casting. Typesetting could now be done like typewriting, on a keyboard like other female jobs. Now the Edinburgh men were threatened by women in both hand and machine composing. Late in 1909, the Edinburgh branch of the STA sent a "memorial" to printing masters: get rid of women. As printers agitated, employers vaguely agreed to reduce the number of "girls" at case. This was a ploy—female keyboard workers threatened compositors at case. The men asked for backing by the local Federation of Printing and Kindred Trades, unskilled men in the Warehousemen and Cutters' Union, and the National Society of Operative Printers' Assistants. In return, they promised to help their drive for recognition by employers.

Three hundred women compositors signed a petition and sent it to the masters and their association. Temperate and reasonable, they argued the unfairness of firing them: they were competent, they had been doing the job for forty years, and they too were part of the labor movement. They begged the men at least to listen to them before acting further. The STA exploded, saying their petition had been produced by a small coterie of outside feminists "engaged in political warfare. . . . The vast majority of girls knew absolutely nothing either of the memorial or its authors." Any women compositors involved were surely the better paid. "The bitterest opponents to this funny little game . . . are . . . the ranks of the girls themselves," who did not want "the sympathetic help of a class political body, or My Lady's tea parties." The men, strong in "conscious righteousness," knew they had "the moral backing and financial support of the entire trade in the UK. . . . We are going into battle. Let us stand together like comrades and brothers."

Brothers indeed. The largest group of men ever to attend a union meeting in Edinburgh turned out to hear the employers' response to "The Woman Question," breaking all records "for size and solidarity of feeling." Employers promised not to hire any new women compositors for seven years. That was not enough: the men held out until employers agreed not to hire any new women at any job for six years (until June 1916) and to have men run all future keyboards of composing machines. As older women compositors eventually died off, the agreement became a ban on women in the industry that was still in force in 1953.

In no industry did sexual segregation change from 1901 to 1971. Women workers remained clustered horizontally in certain types of work, and vertically in the lower ranks of seniority and pay. They predominated in clerical and secretarial work (80 percent), occupying a few low-level managerial jobs, usually supervising women's work. They were 11 percent of workers on national newspapers, 28 percent on local and provincial newspapers, and 5 percent of newspaper managers. On newspapers, women held mainly clerical, canteen, and cleaning jobs. In 1977 not one woman compositor worked on a national newspaper, and only 300 (with over 11,000 men) worked on regional papers. Then came the computer.

In the second half of the nineteenth century, British working-class men organized against women. To keep women economically, socially, and politically dependent, working-class men denied them jobs and a living wage; to accomplish this goal, labor historically colluded with its class enemy, and British labor politics became centered on the single issue of the male wage, and male economic power: no egalitarian wage politics existed. This struggle also reinforced men's belief that they had no responsibility for—were exempt from—concern about "women's" realm: reproduction and renewal. Finally, working men's economic struggle affected theories of social change in Britain: the main impetus to Owenism, and its most profound challenge to capitalism—to ward off the division of experience into categories of production versus reproduction and renewal—was sacrificed to the male ego.

The suffrage movement was dominated by middle-class women with (often) little comprehension of the plight of their working-class sisters, but some middle-class women were sympathetic and many working-class women worked in the suffrage movement. Indeed, feminists struggled to be heard within every socialist organization. But feminist ideals were disregarded by Marxist groups like the Social Democratic Federation and by larger, non-Marxist bodies like the Independent Labor Party. Labor politics became a mirror image of capitalist politics, obsessed with power, profit, and male ego at the cost of all other concerns. In the late nineteenth century, British socialism revived within labor and reflected its values. Politics became a nightmare like a Russian doll: each constituency replicated the others on a different scale. There were no alternatives: the nature of socialism was transformed. Capitalism had the potential to challenge patriarchy by creating a free labor market; people freed from the old bonds of blood and feudal kinship could have transformed the patriarchal family into an egalitarian relation. But labor politics thwarted that challenge as socialists ignored the brilliant socialist insight that the worst evil of capitalism was its sundering of integrated life.

By the time Marx's work was translated into English, British socialism was already firmly patriarchal. Marx's perspective and terminology, his couching of problem and solution, stressed strategy more than ideals. It gave socialists a more acute awareness of the obstacles impeding a revolutionary movement, and as they systematically adopted a Marxist approach, as communism acquired clearer direction and focus, it was masculinized (in the sense in which the word is used in this study), filed to a sharper but narrower point. At the same time, it was transformed from a possible alternative to patriarchy into a variation of it.[29]

CHAPTER 9

THE WAR AGAINST WOMEN

BY THE NINETEENTH CENTURY, women in much of the world seemed subdued by the combined forces of religion, law, and male will, which did not shrink from physical coercion. Some women were destroyed by subjugation; others found ways to survive within it; some grew stronger because of it. But however effectively it inhibited women's bodies and acts, it never tamed their powers of thought. Women can behave within the boundaries allotted them and yet not be defeated. However constricted and oppressed, women have always fought for power over their own lives using psychological, emotional, and sexual strategies. Men deeply resent this. Having defined women as submissive and obedient, having appropriated women's sexuality and taught them that virtue—even the right to life—lay in accepting male ownership; having denied women any political and most economic rights and, to differing degrees, education, they still had to *think* about them, guard against them, deal with opposition often of the subtlest variety. Men who believed male definitions and saw women as inferior, slavish, stupid, and incompetent *by nature* were outraged when women protested or demanded rights.

This contradiction between orthodox definitions of femaleness and women's actual willful behavior leads men to divide women into categories of madonna or whore, a division that has always reflected not actual women but men's sense of the hostility and personal will that lie beneath women's compliant surfaces. The propaganda campaigns waged by dominators always convince *them* that their rule is necessary, deserved, good. But dominators are shocked and outraged when the dominated suggest, however subtly, that they have minds and purposes of their own. Since the orthodox definition of Woman does not grant her the selfhood to possess a purpose, men interpreted female willfulness to be aimed at undermining *them*, as malign, evil.

In the industrial west, as women rose up to demand rights, they had to argue that they were part of the human species, with the same needs and desires and therefore the same rights as other (that is, male) humans. Barriers of law and custom cannot be blown down with a huff and a puff: even the moderate reforms described in this book took decades, lifetimes to effect. But during the struggle, both sexes continued to live in traditional relationships; even women who tried to change traditional expectations, however, remained subject to them. Working-class women who had freed their minds of received ideas enough to walk a picket line were married to men unwilling to cook their own dinners. Leisure-class women might have felt free as they hurled a rock at a window but could not for more than that moment forget that they were dependent on a father or husband for their very food. However active women might have been in unions or demonstrations, whatever their class, *all* women were subordinate to men, whom they had to pacify, placate, or disarm. Men who believed in the rightness of their rule quite correctly felt manipulated.

There have been many revolutions in history, uprisings of classes, ethnic groups, races, and struggles by discrete groups to throw off the domination of other discrete groups. But before such groups can revolt, they must forge self-consciousness. Slaves cannot rebel when they live isolated in separate households; they require community, consciousness of themselves as an oppressed group. Women are oppressed *as a caste:* that is, *all* women are oppressed because they are women, regardless of class, color, or religion. But women live in isolated units *with* their oppressors, and—except for the women's communities found among the aboriginal Australians—have nowhere on earth to flee (with their children) where they can be free. Female oppression was legitimated by abstract external forces—law, religion, and custom—but those who enforced that oppression were women's most intimate kin—fathers, husbands, brothers, and sons. Civil war is the cruelest kind because it sets members of the same nation against each other, sometimes even brothers. But women's rebellion invariably sets women against their families, the very men on whom they must depend.

Painful as this is for women, it is not without pain for men, some of whom are aware of the justice of women's cause. Some nineteenth-century men tried to redress injustices in the world or their own families, but most were convinced of male superiority. When they saw women acting in the world, they presumably felt, like Dr. Johnson, that they were seeing a dog walking on its hind legs. They blustered in Parliament, pubs, and at home; wrote scurrilous articles, beat their wives, and did scientific or philosophic work that bolstered their stance.

Since most cultures define the sexes as opposites (at best, complementary opposites) rather than as members of the same race, change in the definition of one necessarily alters the definition of the other. If women changed role, men would have to as well (the change men feared above all in the late nineteenth century was the subject of innumerable cartoons showing men pushing baby carriages). Whether women accepted the role of domestic angel, stretching it to cover the world, or rejected the role to demand fulfillment, men dealt with their fear, discomfort, and rage not by examining themselves or their institutions, but by blaming women.

These attitudes inform the scientific disquisitions, novels, poetry, and art of the period—the most remarkable fact about which is their obsession with Woman.[1]

While artists obsessively focused on the naked female, continually redefining Woman, they rarely depicted active healthy forward-looking working-class women. A.J. Munby was one artist who did sketch some working-class women. In comparing his sketch of himself and a colliery woman with a photograph of them, we see that in the sketch Munby is drawn far thinner and more bodiless than he is, and much taller than the woman; her sex is indeterminable, her bearing somewhat menacing, and she is filthy. The photograph, on the other hand, shows Munby under his hat only a fraction taller than a strapping young girl, who is more erect and vigorous and less menacing than in the sketch.

This chapter focuses on male attitudes toward women as shown in cultural artifacts. I have drawn largely on two analyses: Bram Dijkstra's *Idols of Perversity: Fantasies of Feminine Evil in Fin-de-Siècle Culture*, and Klaus Theweleit's *Male Fantasies: Women, Floods, Bodies, History*,[2] both of which acknowledge considerable interpretive help from feminists. Dijkstra concentrates on the years 1880 to 1920 and Theweleit on Germany from 1918 to 1923, from the end of the First World War to the emergence of Hitler.

After 1850 Western painters suddenly produced hundreds of images of Woman as Dying Swan, reflecting a reality of the era: idle, repressed middle-class women like Clara Barton, Jane Addams, Charlotte Perkins Gilman, Florence Nightingale, and hosts of others who did not recover from their malaise, who, like Alice James, languished because they were forced into inactivity and purposelessness. No one painted active, starved, exhausted sick working-class women. Science in this period defined Woman as sick by nature, but art romanticized, eroticized, this condition. Artists' depictions of spiritually luminous beautiful women, white, dying, or dead, ignored totally women's misery and rage, transforming pain into glamor. Languid beauties expire orgasmically and seem to cry out for a firm clasp by strong male arms. Such paintings often bore the names of literary figures—the most popular were Shakespeare's Ophelia (who had the advantage of going mad), George du Maurier's Trilby (a passive creature controlled by an evil Jew, Svengali), Zola's Albine (who needs a male for completion), and Tennyson's virgins, Elaine and the Lady of Shalott, doomed to die without having lived. That Tennyson may have been projecting his own sense of life does not alter the fact that he projected it onto females.

Anthony Ludovici wrote popular advice books on the "woman question" in this period. He criticized men who exalt women, writing that a man who remains faithful to a wife who fails "to stimulate him adequately" places himself disastrously "under the empire of women."[3] Dying erotic women seem to need men but make no demands on them, giving them the pleasure of feeling desired without having to fulfill "virile" responsibilities.[4] It is unthinkable that these beautiful weak females in need of "saviors" would ever stand up to demand rights or decide to get jobs.

By the 1860s and 1870s, feminism terrified men, who portrayed it as a kind of madness, female delusion, regression to a primitive stage of human existence. Men had a more intellectual moral sense; women, with intuition and a *natural* need to be absorbed by men, required male guidance. In 1869 one male writer warned that if women won the vote, they would destroy American society, wreck public virtue, and end "our new-born, more beneficent civilization."[5] Another cautioned that the idea of rights could profoundly injure the fragile feminine mind, exciting it to "feelings of indignation and dissatisfaction with [her] present condition," and leading her to "cease to be the gentle mother, and become the Amazonian brawler."[6] Certain that the absence of sexual desire in women was the foundation of a healthy society, he warned that newfangled notions of education were leading Woman to abandon purity. This man had earlier written a book praising female friendship, but now he cited research by French scientists showing that female masturbation was widespread, fostered mainly by female boarding schools where masturbation "is . . . acquired and practiced." Female friendship can even lead to the depths of degradation, for "the same bed often receives the two friends."[7]

The hostility to femaleness implicit in the desire to control them (because only what constitutes a threat needs to be controlled) became evident as the virtuous domesticity of earlier portrayals of groups of women gave way to portrayals of ugly and voluptuously sexual females. In 1886, in *Psychopathia Sexualis*, Richard von Krafft-Ebing described a condition he named "masochism" after Leopold von Sacher-Masoch, a popular author of soft porn whose heroes are sexually aroused by humiliation and pain. Krafft-Ebing thought masochism, "the wish to suffer pain and be subjected to force," was a perversion when it *appeared* in men, but was *built into* women. *Nature* gave Woman "an instinctive inclination to subordination to man," an "instinct" for "servitude." This was not a new idea. In 1858, P.-J. Proudhon wrote: "Woman does not at all dislike to be treated a bit violently, or even to be raped."[8] Male authors usually plant masochism in female, not male, figures, but it is men who are obsessed with it and have written most of the sado-masochistic literature. (Emotionally honest James Joyce alludes to Sacher-Masoch's *Venus in Furs* in *Ulysses* to suggest the masochism of his *male* hero, Leopold Bloom.) The French, who first discussed arousal by punishment, called it "the English disease," believing it infected British boys from frequent beatings in public school.

Female masochism intoxicated artists. The end of the century is crowded with characters like Zola's *Nana* (1880), Trina in *McTeague* (1899) by Frank Norris (whose theory of women was drawn from Schopenhauer), Concha in Pierre Louis' *Woman and Puppet* (1898), and Franz Wedekind's Lulu, who inspired an opera and a movie with Louise Brooks.[9] Oscar Wilde and Mark Twain testify to women's love of abuse;[10] Thomas Hardy makes a *female* character (Sue Bridehead in *Jude the Obscure*) say: "No average man—no man short of a sensual savage—will molest a woman by day or night, at home or abroad, unless she invites him." Coventry Patmore, who invented the phrase "angel in the house," had his finger on the pulse of his time, for he also wrote a stanza that inspired generations of painters and cartoonists:

> Lo, how the woman once was woo'd;
> Forth leapt the savage from his lair,
> And fell'd her, and to nuptials rude
> He dragged her, bleeding, by the hair.

Eugene Delacroix and a host of lesser-known artists painted harems thronged with naked women, bodies posed like "pin-up" girls in the grasp of or awaiting male ravagers. Masochistic, women were shown to *crave* rape and suppression, literally.

Experts sanctioned rape. Theories popular in the 1890s asserted that evolutionary progress in women was accompanied by diminished sexual drive: Harry Campbell, a London pathologist, believed the sexual instinct of civilized women was atrophying. This, they said, made rape *necessary*: men must take responsibility for reproduction if the human race is to continue. The newest thinking countered the theory that women did not become pregnant without orgasm.[11] "The female must lend herself to the sexual act" but the example of "primitive" men, who regularly took women by force shows that female sexual drive is not essential to successful coitus: "woman need not be a willing agent" in sex.[12]

Indeed, rape was *better* than mutual sex. Cesare Lombroso and Guglielmo Ferrero, in *The Female Offender* (1899), warned against unleashing female sexuality because the sexual impulse was male. When awakened in women, it roused the inherent "criminal instinct" and made them "excessively erotic, weak in maternal feeling, inclined to dissipation, astute and audacious." They start to dominate, subtly or by force, and take up violent exercise. Such behavior, "vices," and dress make them resemble the "sterner sex"—a cardinal offense. "Normal" women are monotonous, look alike, and are impervious to suggestion. They are intuitive and *imitative*—their best efforts can produce only copies of men's. Charles Darwin said so, and a host of authors followed him, creating female characters who reflected the world without "ever really understanding it."[13] That women were inherently imitators, not originators, was a cliché in the 1870s.

Woman-hating attitudes became pervasive around 1900, as late nineteenth-century biologists, sociologists, and anthropologists wrote on sexual differences. Charles Darwin's *The Origin of Species* (1859) and *The Descent of Man* (1871) are important because they help us understand the evolution of the cosmos and humanity; but they also contain elements that were used politically. Many men used Darwin's notion of the survival of the fittest to justify predatory *male* (not female) behavior. An 1866 essay, "The Darwinian Theory," claimed that the largest, strongest males get the best food and are most attractive to females, and transmit their powers to their offspring.[14] Differences in aggressiveness explain inequities among classes and races, why "the Negro, the Malay, the Mongolian, are almost precisely what they were five thousand years ago." Auguste Comte used Darwin's theory of natural selection to build a *System of Positive Polity* (1851–54), a "science of society" later used to justify domination as necessary for the survival of the fittest.

After Darwin's *Origin*, Herbert Spencer put huge amounts of energy into trying to prove that predatory individualism was an evolutionary force. Using complex, seemingly logical arguments, he showed that the widest inequalities existed in the most advanced societies and that the *natural* rulers of a society were its most "individual," intellectually advanced, financially successful men. Defining evil as "non-adaptation of constitution to conditions" (whatever conditions might be), Spencer traced a human "progress" from "barbarous lower" races to white Europeans, the acme of evolution, proving it by citing craniological evidence according Europeans larger brains than "the savage."[15] Carl Vogt "proved" in 1864 that non-Germanic peoples belonged "to the lowest races of man," citing craniologists who had shown that "the female skull is smaller" than the male's: "the skulls of man and woman are to be separated as if they belonged to two different species." The conclusions these men extracted from their false data are remarkable: not only did smaller skulls mean lower intelligence, but the skulls of European men were larger, compared to European women's, than African men's skulls were to African women's.[16]

Vogt called the German male the pinnacle of evolution and the African woman the nadir. But all women were said to be frozen at an early evolutionary phase: "We may be sure that, whenever we perceive an approach to the animal type, the female is nearer to it than the male." To find the "missing link" between humans and apes, science should focus on the female. Quoting Vogt, Darwin agreed in *The Descent of Man* that "the female somewhat resembles her young offspring throughout life." Spencer saw women and men as utterly different mentally and bodily, especially in powers of abstract reasoning and "the sentiment of justice—the sentiment which regulates conduct irrespective of personal attachments."[17]

The "brainless" woman (the dumb blonde) was a scientific fact. Since Woman did not need intelligence to be a mother, nature had not given her any, proving that maternity should be her only activity, and intelligent men should marry "healthy women, not brain-ladies." Education was not only wasted on women but made them "nervous and weak," said Paul Möbius, brilliant pathologist and inventor of the Möbius strip. Reflecting these ideas, Degas, Renoir, and a host of others painted zombie-like women, expressionless, sleepy, passive, empty, stuporous. One male critic noted a "fixed stupor of expression" on Degas' women; another gushed over Renoir's female "playthings," with their "beautiful, deep, azure, enameled eyes of dolls, of adorable dolls, with flesh molded of roseate porcelain. . . . [In an] original and perhaps very wise conception of the famous 'eternal' feminine . . . the artist has suppressed virtually completely any elements of intellect his models might have possessed [and] compensated for this by including in his work a lavish display of his own."[18]

These ideas influenced men's view of women and women's self-image, and contributed to cruel predation by contemporary Europeans in Africa and Asia; they also inspired twentieth-century experiments with social control like eugenics, lobotomy, mass imprisonments, and murder, culminating (but not ending, for this way of thinking is not dead) in genocide, the holocaust. The immediate effect on Europeans was less dramatic but calamitous—an obsession with children, girls and boys, who were erotic but ignorant and could demand nothing, and a fierce terrified loathing of mature females who were not passive lumps of flesh.

Erotic portrayals of children begin to appear just as Freud was suggesting (to Europe's shock) that children had sexual feelings. But if Freud's observations triggered such art, they did not supply its content. Whatever children's sexuality, only molested children see themselves as sexual commodities. Painters of this period did not depict childhood sexuality, but projected their sense of commoditized sex (the body as goods for sale) onto children. Emile Zola and the Reverend Charles Dodgson (Lewis Carroll), among many who were obsessed with young girls, eroticized their "innocence."[19] Paul Chabas, a hugely popular painter of the era, produced endless images of adolescent girls in sexually suggestive poses, like the girl in "September Morn." Males and females portrayed little girls as miniature courtesans appraising their wares. Even Carl Larsson, the great idealizer and sentimentalizer of domestic life who inspired a generation of children's book illustrators, was not immune. The appeal of the girl child lay in her paradoxical combining of malleability, sexual innocence, and knowingness, her precocious sense of herself as an object for men's gaze.

Even babies and little girls were tainted with depravity.[20] For some reason, young men were free of it. The true aesthetic and moral ideal was the sensitive adolescent, the grown boyish male, who could be heroic (girls could not) and as provocative as a girl without overtones of wily calculation.[21] He might be James Barrie's

Peter Pan (Barrie was enamored of young boys as Dodgson was of little girls), or a "blond God." Artists and thinkers used the young god-figure to personify the aggressive, evolving mind of man.[22] An emblem in philosophies like Oscar Wilde's, a familiar intellectual world view at the time—Platonic idealism with Darwinian overtones—the androgynous boy-god linked virulent hostility for the petty bourgeoisie with adoration of a Nietzschean ideal of power and transcendence. Transcendence of the material world means transcendence of nature; thus women (nature incarnate) cannot attain it. The ideal body suggested physical power without flesh, aspiration without materialism; his "rippling muscles and steel blue eyes" symbolized aspirations toward transcendence for many intellectuals then—and forty years later.[23]

Fin-de-siècle male intellectuals hated the bourgeoisie mainly for its materialism, its obsession with money, and its lumpish entrenchment in domestic comfort. And no one was more associated with domestic comfort than Woman, who maintained it, whose duty was to devote her life to it. Although women were not responsible for bourgeois enterprises or aggression, as upholders of its standards they incarnated the class for many men. Symbolic association occurs on a deeper level of sentience than logic; by association, all women were tainted. The rising chorus of speculation that Woman was sexual after all compounded her menace. Many sensitive men in this time had a horror of Woman, terrified by her encompassing body as if it would swallow them up, her mindless offering of domestic comfort as if it answered all need, and her clamor as she entered public space with other women to raise her voice and even her arm to overthrow the rule of Man. Artists from Edvard Münch to James Thurber and the later Willem de Kooning portrayed women as vampires, demons, and enveloping monsters.

Fin-de-siècle artists' view of Woman is extraordinary: passive, asleep, a zombie with inert flesh, an absinthe-dulled or syphilitic woman of the town, a "clinging vine" draining the life out of men, or a seductress practiced in bestiality. Walter Pater called daughters in families "serpents" tempting the men in the household; other writers call Woman feline, "catlike," sinuous, serpentine, snake-like.[24] Women were connected with snakes: a Baudelaire poem describes a prostitute "coiling like a snake/ across hot embers." Her "fluid lips" promise unheard-of pleasures but "once she'd sucked the very marrow from my bones," she becomes "a slime-flanked mollusc full of pus," then a "cadaver taut with force/ Having gorged itself on blood," and finally, "scattered pieces of skeletal remains."[25]

Animals that Darwin thought were wildly promiscuous appear with women in many paintings—an antelope ("the most inordinate polygamist in the world") has nude women riding it; gorgeous naked women entwine with or fondle lions, wild boars, elephants, seals, huge dogs, and extremely long-beaked fowl.[26] Sometimes the connection between Man and Woman-animal is explicit. Sirens cavort in water, luring men to their death. Physically powerful, bestial Woman, driven by lust, threatens the male Knight of the faith.

Literature showing women as man-killers was immensely popular. Sacher-Masoch and his cruel heroines were highly regarded by intellectuals, especially the French, who translated his complete works and made him a member of the Legion of Honor in 1883. Among his admirers were Zola, Victor Hugo, and Camille Saint-Saëns, whose opera *Samson and Delilah* portrays a woman who subverts a hero. Richard Strauss used Wilde's *Salome* as a libretto, and made his *Elektra* a madwoman, and his *Die Frau ohne Schatten* (with Hugo von Hofmannsthal) was barren. Alban Berg's *Lulu*, Antonin Dvorak's *Rusalka*, Paul Hindemith's *Mörder, Hoffnung der Frauen*, and Massenet's *Thaïs*, on similar themes, all date from this period. Ferrucci Busoni and Giacomo Puccini wrote operas based on Carlo Gozzi's *Turandot*, a man-killer.

Judith, the Jewish heroine who saves her town from Assyria by cutting off the head of the Assyrian captain, Holofernes, while he sleeps, was extremely attractive to male thinkers in this period. An extremely popular figure for woman painters in earlier eras, Judith had suggested their anger and desire for vengeance against men. As men became aware of women's anger, she became representative of all women. Salome was the "true centerpiece of male masochistic fantasies": a "virginal adolescent," a gorgeous exotic dancer with a virago mother and "a hunger for man's holy head," she epitomized the period's "libidinous fetishes."[27] As war approached, men painted Woman as its spirit.

Definitions of the sexes are interdetermined, and these convulsive redefinitions of Woman affected men's self-image. The same authorities who defined Woman defined Man. Women, stuck in an early phase of evolution, were virtually a different species from men; people of color, too, exemplified a primitive stage of evolution. Cultures that find so much that is human repugnant, basically hate humanness itself. They are suicidal. Having declared most of the human race subhuman, men scoured the male sex for traces of contamination: any taint of effeminacy was damning (as a drop of Jewish blood would be forty years later). An 1895 article anatomizing "The Psychology of the Weakling" declared that men who were cautious, tolerant, respectful of others, and scorned violence were "unmanly."[28]

In 1903 Otto Weininger's *Sex and Character* electrified European intellectuals. Weininger was a twenty-three-year-old Viennese; his ideas were neither logical nor new, being derived from Plato, Schopenhauer, Kant, Darwin, Spencer, the social Darwinists, the woman-haters of *Mercure de France*, and Freud, who liked the manuscript. Weininger organized a "scientific" system, conflating ideas related at a deep psychological level. He produced his theory at a moment when Europe's intellectual climate was open to such things, and it became very popular. Ford Madox Ford lamented that the book "had spread through the serious male society of England as if it had been an epidemic." Wilhelm Fliess angrily accused Freud of leaking his ideas to Weininger, letting him steal Fliess's intellectual "property."

Weininger holds that the human race was originally bisexual; sex differentiation was its first step toward a higher form. The further the race evolved, the closer people came to pure maleness and femaleness. But since sex differentiation is never complete, human advance is retarded. Woman's body, the site of physical reproduction, is a negative pole; man's brain, spiritual understanding, is a positive pole. The more completely male Man becomes, the more spiritual; the more completely female Woman becomes, the more materialistic and brainless. Intellectual women are sexually intermediate: absolute females lack logic, morality, and souls. Association with such benighted beings hinders male progress to spirituality, so "homosexuality is a higher form than heterosexuality." Intermediate states notwithstanding, human beings are always either male or female. Men still have a sex drive, a vestige of femaleness, but if "man possesses sexual organs, her sexual organs possess woman. . . . Sexual excitement is the supreme moment of a woman's life." Women are parasites and cannot live without men or each other; man needs only himself.

Here Weininger touched a major strand in Western thought, one that runs like a barely visible deep stream feeding surface soil all the way from Aristotle: Man is defined by volition. Weininger projects Kant: "I am responsible only to myself; I must follow none other; I must not forget myself even in my work; I am alone; I am free; I am lord of myself." So pervasive, universal, and ancient is the definition of manhood as isolated heroism that we do not perceive its insanity. Men live—and writers create male characters who live—as if isolation led to triumph, utter transcendence. In fact, it leads only to death: isolation is desolation; all humans are responsible to each other, no one is free of the human condition, and no one totally controls even himself. Weininger accurately perceived the ultimate end to which his principles led. Since the major impediment to human progress is effeminacy, defined as men allowing themselves to be enticed by and come under the power of women, the only way to achieve transcendence was for men to free themselves of sex, forcing women to do the same: "The rejection of sexuality is merely the death of the physical life, to put in its place the full development of the spiritual life. . . . That the human race should persist is of no interest whatever to reason."

Like Vogt, Weininger linked women and "degenerate races"—Jews, blacks, "orientals." By inbreeding or failure to evolve, these groups had become effeminate and degenerate. Judaism in particular "is saturated with femininity." Jews, like Woman, did not see that property is indissolubly connected with the self, "thus they were "readily disposed to communism. . . . Greatness is absent from the nature of the woman and the Jew, the greatness of morality, or the greatness of evil." Opposed to the Jew and woman is the Aryan man, in whom good and evil are "ever in strife." True to his principles, the Jewish Weininger committed suicide a few months after his book was published. But his ideas lived on: his book was important to Hitler, who echoes the ideas in *Mein Kampf.*

Some writers linked transcendence with homosexuality, as distinguished from effeminacy, traditionally ascribed to homosexual men. André Gide's *Corydon*, which advocates male homosexuality, links "masculine idealism" and male aggression: "Periods of martial exaltation are essentially homosexual periods, in the same way that belligerent peoples are particularly inclined to homosexuality" (as both D. H. Lawrence and Yukio Mishima suggested). Stylistic innovation in the arts in this period had to be macho to stifle accusations of effeminacy: "to be original was to be masculine," tough.[29] Critics' most vicious attacks were reserved for women artists, all "imitative" of men. Writers, marginal to the world's power centers, were verbally belligerent, ruthlessly belittling the imbecile masses, "the infantile inferiority of nonwhite races, and the brainless inanity of women." The "gratuitous act" became their badge of power.

The ideological roots of Nazism and other horrors of our century are evident in this material. Moreover, men who failed in True Manhood were lower-class: the intelligentsia had contempt for the masses. One thinker wrote that a proletarian might gain enough intellectual dignity through self-denial and hard work to be included in the lower ranks of evolved manhood, but:

> pauperism, prostitution and crime [are] the attendants of a state of society in which science, art and literature reach their highest developments. . . . If we should try, by any measure of arbitrary interference and assistance to relieve the victims of social pressure from the calamity of their position, we should only offer premiums to folly and vice and extend them further. . . . The sociologist is often asked if he wants to kill off certain classes of troublesome and burdensome persons. No such inference follows from any sound sociological doctrine, but it is allowed to infer, as to a great many persons and classes, that it would have been better for society, and would have involved no pain to them, if they had never been born.[30]

Even Karl Marx, whose work represents the point of view of the intelligentsia to what they would consider "lower" beings, workers, also regularly referred to lower-class men as "beasts" and "asses."

Marx expected the socialist revolution to occur in Germany, with its strong popular socialist party. After Germany lost the First World War, Chancellor Ebert, over socialist protest, tried to build a government with strong ties to the old ruling class. He created the Freikorps, a volunteer secret army. Ebert, a socialist, did not trust working-class soldiers from the regular army, which was in any case limited by peace treaty to 100,000 men. So he recruited demobilized officers, mainly from semicommando units trained to penetrate enemy lines in sudden daring attacks. These men did not return their weapons as required but took them home, buried them in oilskin, and dug them up afterward.[31]

Most Freikorps leaders came from a rural petty bourgeoisie with semifeudal traditions—a class usually considered conservative, honest, and decent, the backbone of a country. Their fathers owned small estates, were ministers, military officers, civil servants, tradesmen, small farmers. From 1918 to 1923, the Freikorps, a set of "largely autonomous armies each commanded by its own charismatic leader," roamed Europe attacking "enemies"—Polish communists and nationalists, Latvians, Estonians, the Russian Red Army, and the *German* working class. A free-ranging gang of marauders, government-appointed but not government-controlled, it killed those it *chose* to kill. Some members were imprisoned or exiled, but most survived the relatively quiet years from 1923 to 1933 to follow a man who spoke for their values and attitudes. Becoming the nucleus of Hitler's SA, they reached high positions in the Third Reich; one was kommandant of Auschwitz.

The Freikorps was most active between 1918 and 1923, but literature about it does not appear until after 1933, when a spate of novels depicts politically aware soldier-heroes trying to build a national socialist (Nazi) movement. These works contain striking, strongly held, shared attitudes. The Freikorps was strongly anticommunist, but *communism* was code for nature, the body, and women. They loathed the same elements that intellectuals and artists scorned but with a major and devastating difference: the art of these men was killing. They *loved* killing.[32]

Freikorps writing is a literature of sons: its perspective is always that of a son trying to deal with mothers and sisters. Fathers do not have a voice in Freikorps books. Even authority figures write as sons, rebels who survived their father's disgrace (Wilhelm II's abdication) and intend to correct his errors. Even Hitler writes as a son: "The kaiser should have died at the head of his capitulating army." The father's surrender was an abdication of legitimacy; now it was the turn of sons.[33]

They are also brothers to each other and to women. The only positive relation men can have with women is as son or brother. A number of the Freikorps soldiers married each other's sisters or sister surrogates, women they considered pure, pious, domestic, and above all, virgins: "white" as opposed to "red" women. In letters to comrades, the men note their marriage but do not mention their bride's name, or mention it once and not again for the rest of their lives. They emphatically did not marry for love, but to avert lust;

they marry nurses (Germans call trained nurses *sister*) who nourish and comfort men, but are asexual—pale, cold as marble, unapproachable, the idealized cool white nurses on war posters, comforting wounded soldiers; the dead or dying women in paintings of heroes.

There were other nurses, "Red" nurses. Whenever the Freikorps attacked a working-class enclave, women were on or near the front lines, fighting alone or alongside men. The departure of men to war meant that working-class women had to support their families by working in factories. Food shortages during the war forced them to stand in long queues, and they had confrontations with the police in every German city. For the first time, German women demonstrated for higher wages and decent food rations; they even looted display windows. They learned how to operate in the world, to deal with male officials about wages or the rent on factory-owned housing, becoming in the process confident and authoritative. They changed, and their men were dismayed when they returned. These women supported their men in the socialist conflict after the war but, even when men seem to be praising their efforts, they have a "peculiar note of irritation," as in this report on miners' wives (emphasis mine):

> The spatial confinement in mining districts promotes a solidarity among women and men who are on strike or locked out. The same thing is difficult to muster in occupational groups living in a more scattered community. It isn't rare for women to take an active role in men's battles, where they often accomplish more than the men through picketing and related assignments. Once a woman has gotten fired up about the legitimacy of her demands, she almost amasses such enormous energy that *it puts most men to shame*. In the process she may often give free rein to her *temperament*, but at the same time she *calmly* takes the consequences into account. During the general lockout of the Ruhr miners in

> May 1924, whole companies of female pickets assembled. Armed with sticks and moving along *secret paths,* they intercepted those men prepared to give in and go back to work, and drove them back to their homes. When the night shift changed, *it was a strange thing to see* the women marching out of their villages with burning lanterns, ready to surround every mine within a large radius.[34]

These fighting women called themselves "nurses." To the Freikorps, they were all prostitutes. Their leaders believed the women carried arms, and offered false evidence to prove it. One claimed that communist bands were entrenched in the hills: "In any camp . . . wild scenes could be witnessed of Red bandits strutting back and forth . . . surrounded by those most repulsive of characters, the Red 'nurses.' These women indulged even unwounded warriors with prophylactic attentions; and as for the men, the spring season was in their blood. They did it right there in the fields and forests." The Freikorps lusted to deal with Red nurses. A soldier who spied a couple making love later boasted that "a grenade had caught her off guard in the practice of her true profession." The terror these women inspired in Freikorps men is incomprehensible, even considering the woman-hatred and fear pervading men's associations with female sexuality in this period.

Indeed, it pervaded the opposition culture too. Socalists did not elect women to their executive councils, and paid women less than men even when workers' organizations themselves set wage scales. So did the Red Army in 1920: "Remuneration . . . is in accordance with the terms of the March 22nd bulletin: 165 marks for front-line troops; 40 marks for local service; 30 marks for female personnel." Demobilized men demanded that women be ousted from any job with status. Marx's values were similar: in a letter to Engels, he announced: "Yesterday morning, between six and seven, my wife [Jenny von Westphalen] was delivered of a bona fide traveler—unfortunately of the 'sex' par excellence." (That "the sex" was a common term for females in this period implies maleness was asexual.)[35] So-called proletarian literature of the 1920s never describes women acting politically or in the public sphere. In it too, men marry sisters or sister-surrogates who are spotless maidens, come from their own homeland, and belong to a category for whom they previously had "no time at all"—nonprostitutes. Hardworking, with clean houses, dutiful, pious, and devoted to the workers' movement, Red women too are "white."

Both sides blame women for failures. Fascist men blame women for communism; socialist men hold them responsible for communist defeats. Women were responsible for the failure of a putsch, a Freikorps officer explained, because they had the task of typing out appeals to the people. Men of all classes had similar attitudes. Educated writers, artists, and thinkers, and those who wrote German "proletarian" novels in the 1920s, all depicted the women of the opposite class as sexually depraved.[36]

Women are killed off in novels from both camps; the only important difference is that women in "proletarian" novels die for the good of the party, and not as gruesomely as in fascist works. The threat women embodied for fascist men was so great that it was not enough to divide women into good (asexual and nurturing) and evil (erotic and threatening): they annihilated both, beating or killing "evil" women and rendering the nutritive, "good" women lifeless. Attack on any woman not categorized as mother/sister is "essentially self-defense," so any act is acceptable. It is hard to say which was more brutal, Freikorps men's *acts* or the *language* in which they are described.

A recurring image in right-wing fiction and reportage is of women hiding weapons under skirts or aprons, grenades between their legs; women often attack men astride horses (which actual women did not have) and kill by cutting bits off them—ears, noses, heads, anything protruding, sometimes the genitals proper. The hidden weapons symbolize concealed penises; removal of body parts symbolizes castration—Freikorps soldiers "experience communism as a direct assault on their genitals."[37] Red women look ordinary, so men cannot wait to be attacked but must take the offensive, as a general urged in a pep-talk before a putsch:

> "It's a well-known fact that women are always at the head of these kinds of riots. And if one of our leaders gives the order to shoot and a few old girls get blown up, the whole world starts screaming about bloodthirsty soldiers shooting down innocent women and children. As if women were always innocent."
>
> We all laugh.
>
> "Gentlemen, there's only one thing to do in cases like that. Shoot off a few flares under the women's skirts, then watch how they start running. It won't really do much. The magnesium in the flares will singe their calves or behinds, and the blast flame may burn a few of their skirts. It's the most harmless device you can think of! So, gentlemen, no more warning shots! Flares between the legs will do the job best."

In reality Freikorps men bend women over, strip their buttocks naked, and whip them with riding crops; hurl grenades at their field kitchen trucks, shoot them as they weep over their children's bodies, club or beat them to death with whips if possible, rather than shoot them. Shooting showed respect; beating did not. The Freikorps planned to beat Rosa Luxemburg to death with a rifle butt; they shot Karl Liebknecht, German and male, but beat Jewish Leo Jogiches to death (see Volume 4 of *From Eve to Dawn*, Chapter 1). The actions are hideous, but the glee, the exaltation of their descriptions is worse. A contemporary novel urges: "With their screams and filthy giggling, vulgar women excite men's urges. Let our revulsion flow into a single river of destruction. A destruction which will be incomplete if it does not also trample their hearts and souls." Whether women block soldiers' paths, call out derisively, or offer to inform, they are the ultimate enemy. A living woman is a "stinking carcass"; the body of the woman whipped to death is "a bloody mass, a lump of flesh that appears to have been completely lacerated with whips." Prurient loathing pervades descriptions of specific parts of female bodies; mouth, buttocks, and genitals—beneath their skirts.

"Mouth" symbolizes vagina, "spittle," its secretions. A female mouth is nauseatingly evil, a "venomous hole" spouting "a rain of spittle." Soldiers punch a woman in the mouth, club one in the teeth with a rifle butt, shoot one's open mouth. Punishment on the buttocks humiliates; soldiers kick women in the rear, lash them with riding crops. They make a working-class woman "snort" from her "bare cheeks" and a redhead "with a loud screech, show . . . her behind." Freikorps men attack women from horseback, with whips, bullets, rifle butts, and boots—all phallic surrogates. They rarely touch them with their bare hands—only one slap is recorded in the texts.

When the sexual woman dies, order is restored to the world. Descriptions of murders of women often end with a sigh of relief, a "peculiar note of satisfaction ('and there was peace again in the land')" that distances the narrator from the horror and shame he must also somewhere feel.[38] Men's major emotion—"passionate rage"—cannot end until its object lies silent. But it can in fact never end, rooted as it is in loathing for the flux and substance of nature and body, the uncontrollability of *emotion.*

A new man emerged in the eighteenth and nineteenth centuries. His major activity was expansion. At home, he fought kin for territory, enclosed land, expanded cities. He extended his hold on the globe. The European assault on non-Western civilizations was symbolically a penetration of the female body; male domination of female in the patriarchal family and white male conquest of people of color were two forms of the same drive. In all of this, women's bodies provided the "raw material" for the new man's images: they symbolize what he was trying to vanquish: desire, need, vulnerability, and his subjection to uncontrollable nature and emotion. Western art suggests men are obsessed with women after the eighteenth century. Even abstract sculpture focuses obsessively on female body forms, breast, and buttocks.

In the eighteenth century, having appropriated women's sexuality and reproductive powers, and limited their mobility and activity, men had tried to transform women's bodies to make them more sexually attractive to men: ideal women should alter their shape with corsets, learn "correct" posture, grace, elocution, and change their hair and eyebrows to achieve "beauty."[39] Manuals offered what gentlemen preferred: a 1715 *Frauenzimmerlexikon* (Ladies' Lexicon) listed thirty "required" components of complete beauty: women should be "in correct proportion"—not too fat or thin, with small, reddish ears which did not protrude much from the head. They should wear a gracious smile. Besides "lovely, agreeable speech" uttered with "pure and gentle breath," they needed "delicate skin, underlaid with tiny blue veins," a "long alabaster neck," and "tiny, narrow feet, well-proportioned and facing outward." Another manual prescribed the desired shape, size, and coloring of calves, knees, thighs, buttocks, and especially breasts. Women, who needed a man to survive, complied.

Eighteenth-century women were urged to feel (or show) passion but only if it was centered on men. The first books asserting that masturbation led to insanity appeared in 1716; it was later labeled deviant and punished by clitoridectomy.[40] Nursing one's baby was considered disgraceful and some marriage contracts stipulated the wife was to be relieved of the task (powders dried up breast milk in forty-eight hours). The breast was reserved for sexual use only. Women were also expected to be cultivated, to dance, sing, or play instruments, not for their own pleasure but as an adornment appealing to men. Literature praised specific female body parts, mainly breasts and vagina; poems were written to *die Schooss* (the womb or lap). Johann Besser's enormously popular *Die Schooss* (1700) pleased even the electoress Sophie and her court ladies. In such poems, the vagina of a high-born beauty is a sea of delights, a utopia. Geographies and ethnologies of this time contained physical portraits of women from the countries discussed.

A century later, however, society required women to renounce both the appearance and reality of sexuality. The middle-class revolution repudiated aristocratic eighteenth-century norms. In the nineteenth century, German industrial society, like the American and English variety, made "a contract for dominance that bases male production on the division of the sexes ('separate spheres') and the subjugation of woman-nature."[41]

The values of the Freikorps are not unique to it or to the Nazis. If they were, we would not only know who our enemies are, but they would be—blessedly—outside us and defeated. But even the well-meaning progressive German physicians and psychiatrists who tried to understand and deal with the war by writing a *Moral History of the World War* discuss "dark, vengeful feelings of degenerate femininity" and rape being "lustfully received by the woman who is defeated in love." Good liberal authors who distance themselves from gung-ho soldiers share the woman-hatred that is the foundation for machismo, fascism, and inhumanity. The Freikorps' values are not unique to any class, or unfamiliar to any of us. They are the values of men *and women* throughout the world.

My purpose in including this segment is not to analyze fascism, although it shows that fascism, rooted in fear and hatred of women, is an extreme, overt, and recent example of the bases of patriarchal systems. Fascism differs from other systems in its degree of hatred for humanness (seen as vulnerability and need); it locates transcendence in individual male power in the world, not beyond it, as religions do, or in a community, as socialists do. Nor is my point to demonstrate that ideas we call "fascist" derive from a foundation of "humane" arts and letters created by the most eminent men of their age—although this is also true. My purpose is to give texture to women's environment, to show what they were up against, and to contrast their actuality with men's images of them. The contrast is shocking.

NOTES

Introduction

1 It is often the mother-in-law who actually performs the murder.

2 Frans de Waal is the leading expert on chimpanzee society. See *Chimpanzee Politics* (New York: Harper & Row, 1982); *Good Natured* (Cambridge, Mass.: Harvard University Press, 1996); *Our Inner Ape* (New York, N.Y.: Riverhead Books, 2006).

3 This information comes from Jane Goodall. See *In The Shadow of Man* (Boston: Houghton Mifflin, 1971), *The Chimpanzees of Gombò Cambridge* (Mass.: Belknap Press of the Harvard University Press, 1986); *Through a Window* (London: Weidenfeld & Nicolson, 1990).

4 Frans de Waal, *Primates and Philosophers* (Princeton, N.J: Princeon University Press, 2006).

5 For descriptions of these cultures, see Richard B. Lee and Irven deVore, ed., *Kalahari Hunter Gatherers* (Cambridge, Mass; Harvard University Press, 1981), Colin Turnbull, *The Forest People* (New York: Simon & Schuster, 1961); and Richard A. Gould, *Yiwara* (New York: Scribner, 1969).

6 Some of their marvelous sculptures are on exhibit in the Archaeological Museum in Konya.

7 Catal Hüyük was discovered and described by James Mellaart. See his Catal Hüyük, *A Neolithic Toiwn in Anatolia* (New York: McGraw-Hill, 1967)

8 Even as late as the composition of the Jacob cycle of stories in Genesis, the writer did not understand how young were conceived, and imagines conception in sheep is influenced by what the ewe sees as it drinks.

9 For the political ramifications of religious prejudice against women, see my *The War Against Women.*

10 Ann Jones, *Winter in Kabul* (New York: Picador, 2006).

CHAPTER 1

1 George Dorsey, *Man's Own Show: Civilization* (New York: Harper and Bros., 1931).

2 For the political difference between wife- and sister-status, see Karen Sachs, *Sisters and Wives: The Past and Future of Sexual Equality* (Westport, Conn.: *Contributions in Women's Studies,* 10, 1979). For an analysis of Kongo in these terms, see Susan Herlin Broadhead, "Slave Wives, Free Sisters: Bakongo Women and Slavery c. 1700–1850," in *Women and Slavery in Africa,* eds. Claire Robertson and Martin Klein (Madison, Wisc.: University of Wisconsin Press, 1983).

3 For more information on women in this empire, see Margaret Strobel, *Muslim Women in Mombasa,* 1890–1975 (New Haven: Yale University Press, 1979).

4 Basil Davidson, *The Story of Africa* (London: Mitchell Beazley, 1984).

5 Howard Zinn, *A People's History of the United States* (New York: Harper & Row, 1980).

6 Frederick Cooper, "Islam and Cultural Hegemony: The Ideology of Slaveowners on the East African Coast," in *The Ideology of Slavery in Africa,* ed. P. Lovejoy (Beverly Hills: Sage Publications, 1981).

7 Mtoro bin Mwinyi Bakari, *Desturi za Waswahili,* ed. and trans. by J.W.J. Allen as *The Customs of the Swahili People* (Berkeley: University of California Press, c. 1981).

8 Cooper, *Ideology of Slavery in Africa.*

9 Marcia Wright, "Women in Peril," *African Social Research* 20 (1975): 800–19.

10 Julian Cobbing, "The Mfecane as Alibi: Thoughts on Dithakong and Mbolompo," *Journal of African History* 29 (1988): 487–519.

11 George E. Brooks, Jr. "The Signares of Saint-Louis and Gore: Women Entrepreneurs in Eighteenth-Century Senegal," *Women in Africa: Studies in Social and Economic Change,* ed. Nancy J. Hafkin and Edna G. Bay (Stanford, Calif.: Stanford University Press, 1976).

12 E. Frances White, "Creole Women Traders in the Nineteenth Century," Working Papers No. 27, African Studies Centre, Boston University; and *Sierra Leone's Settler Women Traders: Women on the Afro-European Frontier* (Ann Arbor: University of Michigan Press, 1987).

13 Babatunde Agiri, "Slavery in Yoruba Society in the 19th Century," in *The Ideology of Slavery in Africa.* ed. P. Lovejoy (Berkeley: Sage Publications, 1981).

14 Anna Hinderer, *Seventeen Years in the Yoruba Country: Memorials of Anna Hinderer*, edited by her friends (London: Seeley, Jackson & Holliday, 1852).

15 Citations in this sections come from Christine Qunta, who is herself quoting Tendai Mutunhu, "Nehanda of Zimbabwe," *Ufahamu*; and from Terence O. Ranger, *Revolt in Southern Rhodesia 1867–70* (London: Heinemann, 1967).

16 David Sweetman, *Women Leaders in African History* (London: Heinemann, 1984).

17 R.S. Baden-Powell (founder of the Boy Scouts), a guest at the ceremony at which Prempeh was forced to bow to the British governor, wrote about her: "the only man among them was the Queen."

18 Iris Berger, "Rebels or Status-Seekers? Women as Spirit Mediums in East Africa," Hafkin and Bay, *Women in Africa.*

19 For some examples, see M.J. Bessell, "Nyabingi," *Uganda Journal* 6, 2 (1938), cited by Berger in "Rebels or Status-Seekers?"

20 The section on Africa could not have been written without the help of Marcia Wright and Susan Hall, who worked tirelessly to help protect me from mistakes. Marjorie Mbilinyi also consulted on this section, and Christine Gailey was a consultant on Dahomey. Sources not noted in the text are M. Kwamena-Poh, *African History in Maps*; *African Women South of the Sahara,* ed. Margaret Jean Hay and Sharon Stichter (New York: Longman, 1984); Marjorie Mbilinyi, "'Women in Development': Ideology and the Marketplace," in *Competition: A Feminist Taboo?,* ed. Valerie Miner and Helen E. Longino (New York: Feminist Press, 1987), and "Wife, Slave and Subject of the King: The Oppression of Women in the Shambala Kingdom," *Tanzania Notes and Records* 88–89 (1982): 1–13; Claire Robertson, "Ga Women and Socioeconomic Change in Accra, Ghana," in Hafkin and Bay; *Slavery in Africa; Historical and Anthropological Perspectives,* ed. Suzanne Miers and Igor Kopytoff (Madison: University of Wisconsin Press, 1977); Rosalyn Terborg-Penn, "Women and Slavery in the African Diaspora: A Cross-Cultural Approach to Historical Analysis," *Sage* 3, 2 (fall, 1986): 11–15; Marcia Wright, "Justice, Women, and the Social Order in Abercorn, Northeastern Rhodesia, 1897–1903," in *African Women and the Law: Historical Perspectives*, ed. Margaret Jean Hay and Marcia Wright; and Marcia Wright, "Technology, Marriage and Women's Work in the History of Maize-Growers in Mazabuka, Zambia: a Reconnaissance," *Journal of African Studies* 10, 1 (October 1983): 71–85.

Chapter 2

1 Alice Kessler-Harris, *Women Have Always Worked: A Historical Overview* (New York: The Feminist Press, 1981).

2 Carroll Smith-Rosenberg, "The Female World of Love and Ritual: Relations Between Women in Nineteenth-Century America," *Signs* 1, 1 (autumn 1975): 1–29.

3 Françoise Basch, *Relative Creatures: Victorian Women in Society and the Novel,* 1837–67 (London: Allan Lane, 1974); and *Rebelles Américaines au XIXième Siècle: mariage, amour libre, et politique* (Paris: Meridiens Klincksieck, 1990).

4 For concrete examples of women's experience, see Diane Balser, *Sisterhood and Solidarity: Feminism and Labor in Modern Times* (Boston: South End Press, 1987). For direct quotations from women factory workers of the period, see *Victorian Women,* ed. Erna Olafson Hellerstein, Leslie Parker Hume, and Karen M. Offen (Stanford, Calif.: Stanford University Press, 1981).

5 Joan W. Scott and Louise A. Tilly, *Comparative Studies in Society and History,* Vol. 17 (Cambridge: Cambridge University Press, 1975); and Louise A. Tilly and Joan W. Scott, *Women, Work and Family* (New York: Holt, Rinehart and Winston, 1978).

6 For a moving account of women in the Lowell mills, see Harriet Robinson, *Loom and Spindle or Life Among the Early Mill Girls* (1898: reprint. Kailua Hawaii: Press Pacifica, 1976).

7 Jacqueline Dowd Hall, Robert Korstad, James Leloudis, "Cotton Mill People," *American Historical Review* 91, 2 (April 1986): 245–85.

8 Christine Stansell, *City of Women: Sex and Class in New York, 1789–1860* (New York: Alfred A. Knopf, 1986) and "Women, Children, and the Uses of the Streets: Class and Gender Conflict in New York City, 1850–1860," *Feminist Studies* 8, 2 (summer 1982): 309–32.

9 Cited in Diane Balser, *Sisterhood and Solidarity,* 34.

10 Joan W. Scott and Louise A. Tilly, *Comparative Studies in Society and History,* Vol. 17 (Cambridge: Cambridge University Press, 1975).

11 Dolores Janiewski, "Making Common Cause: The Needlewomen of New York, 1831–69," *Signs* 3, 1 (1976).

12 Rosalyn Baxandall, Linda Gordon, Susan Reverby, "Boston Working Women Protest, 1869," *Signs* 3, 1 (1976).

13 Ibid.

14 Munby's portraits can be found in Michael Hiley, *Victorian Working Women: Portraits from Life* (Boston: David R. Godine, 1979).

15 Visiting the Wigan pits, intrigued by the dress and demeanor of the Pit Brow girls, Munby called Wigan "the picturesque headquarters of rough female labour." George Orwell visited Wigan fifty years later, and noticed only men; Beatrix Campbell corrected his oversight, on a visit to Wigan fifty years later, when the pits were closed and the town was dying. Beatrix Campbell, *Wigan Pier Revisited: Poverty and Politics in the Eighties* (London: Virago, 1984).

16 Cited by Tilly and Scott in *Women, Work and Family.*

17 Leonore Davidoff, "Mastered for Life: Servant and Wife in Victorian and Edwardian England," *Journal of Social History* VII, 3 (spring 1974).

18 Theresa McBride, "The Long Road Home: Women's Work and Industrialization," *Becoming Visible: Women in European History*, ed. Renate Bridenthal, Claudia Koonz and Susan Stuard (Boston: Houghton Mifflin, 1987).

19 Christine Stansell, *City of Women: Sex and Class in New York, 1789–1860* (New York: Alfred A. Knopf, 1986).

20 William Blackstone, *Commentaries,* 1893, cited in Davidoff, "Mastered for Life."

21 Katherine Schlegel, "Mistress and Servant in Nineteenth-Century Hamburg: Employer/Employee Relationships in Domestic Service, 1880–1914," *History Workshop Journal* 15 (spring 1983): 60–77.

22 Lee Holcombe, *Victorian Ladies at Work*, ed. Lee Holcombe (Hamden, Conn.: Anchor Books, 1973).

23 Ruth Rosen and Sue Davidson, "Introduction," *The Maimie Papers*, ed. Ruth Rosen and Sue Davidson (Old Westbury, NY: Feminist Press, 1977).

24 Mary Gibson, *Prostitution and the State in Italy*, 1860–1915 (New Brunswick, NJ: Rutgers University Press, 1986).

25 For a description of the living conditions of a group of British prostitutes, see Frances Finnegan, *Poverty and Prostitution: A Study of Victorian Prostitutes in York* (Cambridge: Cambridge University Press, 1979).

26 W.R. Greg, "Prostitution," *Westminster Review* (1850).

27 This information comes from Rosen and Davidson, *The Maimie Papers.*

28 Judy Walkowitz, *Prostitution and Victorian Society: Women, Class, and the State* (Cambridge: Cambridge University Press, 1980).

29 For a description of the life of an early twentieth-century prostitute in her own words and from her own perspective, see Rosen and Davidson, *The Maimie Papers.*

30 Friedrich Engels, *The Condition of the Working Class,* (1844: Harmondsworth: Penguin, 1987).

31 Basch, *Relative Creatures.*

32 Tilly and Scott, *Women, Work and Family.*

33 Ibid.

34 Louis Reybaud, cited by Tilly and Scott, *Women, Work and Family.*

35 Stansell, *City of Women.*

36 Cited by Ellen Ross, in "Survival Networks: Women's Neighbourhood Sharing in London Before World War I," *History Workshop Journal* 15 (Spring 1983): 4–27.

37 In the 1980s, the women in Wigan lived on beans on toast and tea, giving any real food they could afford, like a steak and kidney pie, to their men. The men, who ate better, spend much of their wages at the pub. Campbell, *Wigan Pier Revisited.*

38 Ellen Ross, "'Fierce questions and taunts': Married life in working-class London, 1870–1914," *Feminist Studies* 8, no. 3 (Fall 1982).

39 Robinson, *Loom and Spindle.*

40 Ann Whitehead, "Sexual Antagonism in Herefordshire," *Dependence and Exploitation in Work and Marriage,* ed. D. L. Barker and S. Allen (London: Longman, 1976).

41 Ross, "Fierce Questions and Taunts."

42 Ross, "Survival Networks."

43 Stansell, "Women, Children, and the Uses of the Streets."

44 Ross, "Survival Networks."

45 Stansell, *City of Women.*

46 Stansell, "Women, Children, and the Uses of the Streets."

47 Stansell, *City of Women.*

48 Ibid.

CHAPTER 3

1 Spain (1820), Naples (1820), and Greece (1821). The Greek uprising succeeded; revolutions in Naples and Spain were crushed, but the latter quickened a liberation movement in Latin America.

2 Popular uprisings in Modena, Bologna, and Parma gained neither reform nor national unification. With heavy military force and difficulty, Russia put down a Polish uprising (1830–31). Uprisings erupted in Switzerland and parts of Germany and Italy, civil war in Portugal and Spain.

3 Less serious disruptions troubled Spain, Denmark, Rumania, Ireland, Greece, and Britain.

4 Barbara Taylor, *Eve and the New Jerusalem: Socialism and Feminism in the Nineteenth Century* (New York: Pantheon Books, 1983).

5 Its name changed several times, ending as *La tribune des femmes*.

6 Charles Fourier, "Théorie des Quatre Mouvements," in *The Utopian Vision of Charles Fourier*, ed. Jonathan Beecher and Richard Bienvenue, (Boston: Beacon Press, 1971), 194–96.

7 *The Need to Welcome Female Strangers Kindly*; *Travels of a Pariah*; *Walks through London*; *A Worker's Union*.

8 *The Liverpool Standard*, 1839: Barbara Taylor, "The Men Are as Bad as Their Masters . . .": "Socialism, Feminism and Sexual Antagonism in the London Tailoring Trade in the 1830s," in *Sex And Class in Women's History*, ed. Judith L. Newton, Mary P. Ryan, and Judith R. Walkowitz (London: Routledge and Kegan Paul, 1983).

9 Françoise Basch, *Relative Creatures: Victorian Women in Society and the Novel, 1837–67* (London: Allan Lane, 1974).

10 Fredericka Bremer, a Swedish visitor, was highly impressed by a knitting machine. She described it in *The House of the New World: Impressions of America* (1853).

11 *The New Harmony Gazette*, October 1, 1825.

12 Gerda Lerner, *The Majority Finds Its Past* (New York: Oxford University Press, 1979).

13 Catherine Clinton, *The Other Civil War* (New York: Hill and Wang, 1984).

14 E.J. Hobsbawm, *The Age of Revolution: Europe 1789–1848* (London: Cardinal l988).

15 Ibid.

16 Karl Marx and Friederich Engels, *The Communist Manifesto* (1848: reprint, London: Penguin, 1985), trans. Samuel Moore (1888), ed. A.J.P. Taylor (1967).

17 In our own time we have seen rulers rob their countries of their wealth and flee, or murder large numbers of citizens. Elected officials start wars that kill their own citizens to benefit an elite. In the mid-nineteenth century, Austrian, Prussian, and Russian rulers cooperated in brutally suppressing their people.

18 Ferdinand VII, the authoritarian king of Spain, quashed democratic agitation with help from France, which sent him 200,000 soldiers in 1823. When Ferdinand died, his widow Maria Christina allied with middle-class liberals to get the throne for her daughter Isabella. In return for their help in defeating Ferdinand's reactionary brother Don Carlos, she granted them a constitution that gave them—but not the lower and working classes—a voice in the legislature. Eventually, their fear of this silent majority led the middle class to welcome an authoritarian dictator.

After Napoleon's defeat, Louis XVIII, Louis XVI's brother, was given the French throne. He also mollified the middle class with a constitutional charter establishing legal equality and a bicameral parliament, but limiting the vote by age and property ownership to about 100,000 men. He died in 1824, succeeded by his brother, the reactionary Charles X, who immediately indemnified nobles whose property had been seized during the revolution, and restored exclusive control of education to the Church. Wealthy middle-class deputies rebelled, passing a vote of no confidence in the government. Charles dissolved the chamber and called for new elections, which defeated his candidates. He dissolved the chamber again, issuing laws repressing the press and suffrage.

The 1848 revolution in France sparked uprisings across Europe. In Vienna as in Paris, students massed the barricades; the Austrian government took the same action as the French, but its soldiers would not fire. The Austrian Emperor abdicated in favor of his nephew, and Metternich's government fell, replaced by one that promised a liberal constitution. The collapse of Austria's government heartened leaders in its subject states—Hungary, Bohemia, Czechoslovakia, and the Italian city-states. People everywhere clamored not just for bread and work but for a new society. As French rebels were demanding universal (male) suffrage and a republic, central Europeans were calling for constitutional systems. Rebels in Germany and Italy, still divided into petty states ruled by absolute princes, demanded some form of national unity. Even the Slavs, forgotten by history, rose up demanding nationhood: to Marx's dismayed disapproval, nationalism proved stronger than class in most of the 1848 revolutions.

In Milan, Naples and Sicily, Venice, Lombardy, and Tuscany, working-class armies successfully fought Austria for national unity and reform. Three hundred and fifty people were killed in the Milan insurrection: a few were students, clerks, or from landowning families; the rest were workers, 74 of them women. But ruling aristocrats in these principalities feared and detested workers (a "mortal menace") more than they feared Austria. Their fears of the lower classes and quarrels with each other precluded Italian unity; the cities were soon reconquered by Austria. The Czechs also squabbled once they had power: being anti-German, they refused to ally with German-speaking Austrians who wanted a united Germany. Their quarrels weakened them enough for Austria to reassert its control.

In Prussia, uprisings forced King Friedrich Wilhelm to concede a popular elected assembly. But the assembly proved hostile to Russia and granted self-government to Poles in the section of partitioned Poland under Prussian rule. Then the Germans in Prussian Poland rebelled against the Polish government and the Prussian army crushed the Poles. Other German states and principalities tried to quiet unrest by expanding relief programs or encouraging emigration. Hungary presented the Austrian emperor with a set of laws decreeing equality before the law, abolishing peasant corvée, tithes, and tax exemptions for aristocrats, and demanding a liberal constitution with a property-based franchise giving the vote to about a quarter of all adult males. Austria was at war in Italy and accepted these reforms, but as it gradually subdued the Italians and improved its military situation, it sent troops into Hungary and defeated it. Thus ended the revolutions of 1848.

19 Roger Price, *The Revolutions of 1848* (London: Macmillan, 1988).

20 Hobsbawm, *Age of Revolution.*

21 Kathleen B. Jones, "Citizenship in a Woman-Friendly Polity," *Signs*, 15, 4 (summer 1990): 781–812.

22 Ibid.

23 Françoise Basch was consultant for this section. Also consulted was Dolores Hayden, *Seven American Utopias: The Architecture of Communitarian Socialism* (Cambridge, Mass.: MIT Press, 1975).

Chapter 4

1 Lee Virginia Chambers, *Schiller, Liberty, a Better Husband: Single Women in America: The Generations of 1780–1840* (New Haven: Yale University Press, 1984.)

2 Greg is quoted in Françoise Basch, *Relative Creatures* (London: Allan Lane, 1974).

3 Cited in Basch, *Relative Creatures.*

4 Leonore Davidoff, "Mastered For Life: Servant and Wife in Victorian and Edwardian England," *Journal of Social History* VII, 3 (spring 1974).

5 Ann Douglas Wood, "The Fashionable Diseases," in *Clio's Consciousness Raised,* ed. Mary S. Hartman and Lois Banner (New York: Harper & Row, 1974).

6 Carroll Smith-Rosenberg, "Puberty," in Hartman and Banner, *Clio's Consciousness Raised,* quoting a nineteenth-century physician describing puberty in women and men.

7 Smith-Rosenberg, "Puberty."

8 Michel Foucault, *Power/Knowledge,* ed. Colin Gordon (New York: Pantheon, 1980), 217.

9 The propaganda was produced by Francis Place and Richard Carlile.

10 Maryanne Cline Horowitz, "The 'Science' of Embryology Before the Discovery of the Ovum," in *Connecting Spheres: Women in the Western World, 1500 to the Present,* ed. Marilyn J. Boxer and Jean H. Quataert (New York: Oxford University Press, 1987).

11 Basch, *Relative Creatures,* 23.

12 Bonnie S. Anderson and Judith P. Zinsser, *A History of Their Own* (vol. II) (New York: Harper & Row, 1988).

13 Parkes, cited by Basch, *Relative Creatures,* 11; and Marion Reid, *A Plea for Woman Being a Vindication of the Importance and Extent of Her Natural Sphere of Action* (London and Edinburgh: 1843).

14 Later called *The Englishwoman's Review.*

15 Linda K. Kerber, "Separate Spheres, Female Worlds, Woman's Place: The Rhetoric of Women's History," *Journal of American History* 75, 1 (1988): 9–39.

16 Marilyn Ferris Motz, *True Sisterhood: Michigan Women and Their Kin, 1820–1920* (Albany, NY: State University of New York Press, 1983).

17 Sarah Lewis, *Woman's Mission* (1839).

18 Martha Vicinus, *Independent Women: Work and Community for Single Women, 1850–1920* (Chicago: University of Chicago Press, 1985). The discussion of single women throughout is indebted to this work.

19 American readers may be unaware that in Britain, "college" can mean a secondary school as well as one of university level.

20 Vicinus, *Independent Women.*

21 Information about Elizabeth Fry comes from Anderson and Zinsser.

22 It is still expected of women that when they marry they will adapt to their husbands' economic and social level, live his life rather than their own. This is the problem of Isabel Archer in Henry James' *A Portrait of a Lady.* She rejects suitors whose lives are fixed in order to marry, disastrously, a man who seems to promise that she can create her own.

23 Cited by Anderson and Zinsser.

24 Florence Nightingale, "Method of Improving the Nursing Service of Hospitals," (1869).

25 Maria Ramas, "Freud's Dora, Dora's Hysteria," in *Sex and Class in Women's History,* ed. Judith L. Newton, Mary P. Ryan, and Judith R. Walkowitz (London: Routledge and Kegan Paul, 1983).

Chapter 5

1 Ellen Moers, *Literary Women* (New York: Doubleday, 1977); Joseph Kestner, *Protest and Reform, 1827–1867* (Madison: University of Wisconsin Press, 1985).

2 The quotation from Thomas Carlyle is from his *Chartism* (1840).

3 Moers, *Literary Women.*

4 Elaine Showalter, *A Literature of Their Own* (Princeton: Princeton University Press, 1977). In addition to the writers listed above, Elizabeth Stone, Eliza Meteyard, Geraldine Jewsbury, Camilla Toulmin, Julia Kavanagh, Fanny Mayne, and Dinah Craik were part of the earlier generation mentioned by Showalter.

5 Tillie Olsen, "Introduction," Rebecca Harding Davis, *Life in the Iron Mills*, ed. Tillie Olsen (1861: reprint, New York: Feminist Press, 1972).

6 Gaye Tuchman and Nina E. Fortin, *Edging Women Out: Victorian Novelists, Publishers, and Social Change* (New Haven: Yale University Press, 1989).

7 Nancy A. Hewitt. "Friends: Agrarian Quakers and the Emergence of Women's Rights in America," *Feminist Studies* 12, no. 1 (spring 1986): 28–49.

8 Blanche Glassman Hersh, *The Slavery of Sex: Feminist-Abolitionists in America* (Chicago: University of Illinois Press, 1978).

9 Ibid.

10 Catherine Clinton, *The Other Civil War* (New York: Hill and Wang, 1984).

11 Ibid.

12 The discussion of Graceanna Lewis comes from Lee Virginia Chambers-Schiller, *Liberty, a Better Husband: Single Women in America: The Generations of 1780–1840* (New Haven: Yale University Press, 1984).

13 See Sidney Bremer, "Lost Continuities: Alternative Urban Visions in Chicago Novels, 1890–1915," *Soundings* 64, 1 (spring 1981): 29–51.

14 Ann Douglas, *The Feminization of American Culture* (New York: Alfred A. Knopf, 1977).

15 Clinton, *The Other Civil War.*

16 Carr managed to study abroad, but suffered from exclusion from life classes, the stigma of seriousness in a woman painter, and from constrictions on middle-class women's conduct—obstacles that despite her early assertiveness kept this stubborn forceful woman from painting for fifteen years.

17 Darlene Clark Hine, *Black Women in White: Racial Conflict and Cooperation in the Nursing Profession, 1890 –1950* (Bloomington: Indiana University Press, 1989).

18 Christine Stansell, *City of Women: Sex and Class in New York, 1789–1860* (New York: Alfred A. Knopf, 1986). The discussion of charity organizations in New York is drawn from Stansell's book.

19 On November 2, 1989, a Texas judge was cleared of charges of bias for granting a light sentence to a man found guilty of murdering two gay men. Judge Jack Hampton explained: "These homosexuals, by running around on weekends picking up teen-age boys, they're asking for trouble. . . . I put prostitutes and gays at about the same level. And I'd be hard put to give somebody life for killing a prostitute." (*The New York Times*, November 2, 1989), 25.

20 Clinton, *The Other Civil War.*

21 Angela Y. Davis, *Women, Race, and Class* (New York: Random House, 1981).

22 Raya Dunayevskaya, "The Black Dimension in Women's Liberation," in *Women's Liberation and the Dialectics of Revolution* (Atlantic Highlands, NJ: Humanities Press International, 1985).

23 Eleanor Flexner, *Century of Struggle: The Woman's Rights Movement in the United States* (Cambridge, Mass.: Harvard University Press, 1959; reprint, 1996).

24 Gloria I. Joseph, "Sojourner Truth: Archetypal Black Feminist," in *Wild Women in the Whirlwind: Afra-American Culture and the Contemporary Literary Renaissance* (New Brunswick, NJ: Rutgers University Press, 1990).

25 Hewitt, "Friends."

26 Clinton, *The Other Civil War.*

27 Chambers-Schiller, *Liberty, a Better Husband.*

28 Carroll Smith-Rosenberg, "The Female World of Love and Ritual: Relations Between Women in Nineteenth-Century America," *Signs* 1,1 (autumn 1975). See also her *Disorderly Conduct* (New York: Alfred A. Knopf, 1985).

29 Material on black women's clubs has been drawn mainly from Paula Giddings, *When and Where I Enter* (New York: William Morrow, 1984).

30 Giddings, *When and Where.*

Chapter 6

1 Herbert Gutman, *The Black Family in Slavery and Freedom, 1750–1925* (New York: Pantheon, 1976).

2 Over 180,000 African Americans fought for the Union; several thousand spied for it, although they were at greater risk than whites. Almost half a million deserted southern plantations, helping to cripple the economy of the south.

3 Catherine Clinton, *The Other Civil War* (New York: Hill and Wang, 1984).

4 Ibid.

5 Ibid.

6 Tracey Weis did research for this segment.

7 Paula Giddings, *When and Where I Enter: The Impact of Black Women on Race and Sex in America* (New York: William Morrow, 1984). The emphasis is Giddings'.

8 Ibid.

9 The historian was Leslie Howard Owens, *This Species of Property: Slave Life and Culture in the Old South* (New York: Oxford University Press, 1976), 195.

10 Jacqueline Jones, "'My Mother Was Much of a Woman'": Black Women, Work, and the Family Under Slavery," *Feminist Studies* 8, 2 (summer 1982): 235–269.

11 Ibid.; and Jacqueline Jones, *Labor of Love, Labor of Sorrow: Black Women, Work, and the Family from Slavery to the Present* (New York: Basic Books, 1985).

12 Eugene Genovese, *Roll, Jordan, Roll: The World the Slaves Made* (New York: Random House, 1974).

13 Jones, *Labor of Love, Labor of Sorrow.*

14 Dorothy Sterling, *We Are Your Sisters: Black Women in the Nineteenth Century* (New York: Norton, 1984).

15 Quoted by Giddings, *When and Where.*

16 Ibid.

17 Jones, *Labor of Love, Labor of Sorrow.*

18 Ibid.

19 David Katzman, *Seven Days a Week: Women and Domestic Service in Industrializing America* (Chicago: University of Illinois Press, 1981).

20 Jacqueline Grant, "Black Women and the Church," *Some of Us Are Brave,* ed. Gloria T. Hull, Patricia Bell Scott, Barbara Smith (Old Westbury, NY: The Feminist Press, 1982).

21 Linda Perkins, "Heed Life's Demands: The Educational Philosophy of Fanny Jackson Coppin," *Journal of Negro Education* (summer 1982).

22 E. Franklin Frazier, *Black Bourgeoisie* (New York: The Free Press, 1957).

23 East African Islamic slaveholders in Africa were not at first racist, but justified slavery by asserting the superiority of Islam to other religions. Only after huge numbers of African slaves adopted Islam, which forbids the enslavement of Muslims, did owners resort to racism to vindicate their practice. Ancient slaveholding states—Mesopotamia, Greece, Rome, Islamic states or the later Ottoman Empire—were not racist. Slaves and owners often shared color and even ethnic background. Aristotle justified Athenian slavery by arguing that anyone so craven as to accept slavery was humanly inferior, deserving of enslavement.

24 Jacquelyn Down Hall, *Revolt Against Chivalry: Jessie Daniel Ames and the Women's Campaign Against Lynching* (New York: Columbia University Press, 1979).

25 Clinton, *The Other Civil War.*

26 Philip Bruce, *The Plantation Negro as a Freeman: Observations on His Character, Condition, and Prospects in Virginia* (New York: G.P. Putnam's Sons, 1889).

27 This atmosphere is illustrated by a case cited by Giddings. Henry Smith, a black man in Paris, Texas, accused in 1893 of raping a five-year-old white girl, was tortured with red-hot irons and condemned to be burned

alive. The town made the day of his burning a holiday so schoolchildren could attend it, and the railroads ran excursion cars for rural people. After Smith was ashes, the mob attacked each other in greed for souvenirs—the man's bones, teeth, and buttons.

28 Giddings, *When and Where.*

29 Some other early black artists were Robert M. Douglass Jr. (1809–1887), the brother of abolitionist Sarah Douglass, an abolitionist painter who became an expatriate; and May Howard Jackson (1877–1931), one of the first black sculptors to reject European conventions and use racial problems as a theme. She studied at the Pennsylvania Academy of Fine Arts, and despite the high quality of her work, remained unsuccessful.

30 Wilson's authorship was established only a few years ago by Henry Louis Gates. See David Ames Curtis and Henry Louis Gates, "Establishing the Identity of the Author of *Our Nig*," in *Wild Women in the Whirlwind: Afra-American Culture and the Contemporary Literary Renaissance*, ed. Joanne M. Braxton and Andrée Nicola McLaughlin (New Brunswick, NJ: Rutgers University Press, 1990).

31 Giddings, *When and Where*, mentions Emma Dunham Kelly, *Megda* (1891); Frances Ellen Watkins Harper, *Iola Leroy* (1892); and Victoria Earl Matthews "Aunt Lindy" (1893). Alice Dunbar Nelson, who was part of the Harlem Renaissance, had been publishing poetry and short stories long before it began: *Violets and Other Tales* (1895) and *The Goodness of St. Rocque* (1898). In 1965 Pauline Hopkins' *Contending Forces* (1900) was called "the most powerful protest novel authored by a Black woman with the exception of Anne Perry's *The Street.*"

32 Samella Lewis, *Art: African-American* (New York: Harcourt Brace Jovanovich, Inc., 1978).

33 Mary Schmidt Campbell, *Harlem Renaissance: Art of Black America*, Introduction (New York: Harry N. Abrams, 1987).

34 Giddings, *When and Where.*

35 Ibid.

36 Frazier, *Black Bourgeoisie.*

37 Ruth Bordin, *Woman and Temperance: The Quest for Power and Liberty, 1873–1900* (Philadelphia: Temple University Press, 1981).

38 Blanche Wiesen Cook, "Female Support Networks and Political Activism: Lillian Wald, Crystal Eastman, Jane Addams, and Emma Goldman," *Chrysalis* 3 (autumn 1977); and "Feminism, Socialism, and Sexual Freedom: The Work and Legacy of Crystal Eastman and

Alexandra Kollontai," *Stratégies Féminines/ Stratégies Féministes*, eds. Françoise Basch et al. (Paris); English edition, ed. Judith Friedlander et al. (Bloomington: Indiana University Press, 1986).

39 Jane Addams, *Twenty Years at Hull House* (New York: 1910; reprint, Princeton: 1981), 65.

40 Cited by Clinton, *The Other Civil War.*

41 Ibid.

42 Ibid.

Chapter 7

1 Kathi Kern, *Mrs. Stanton's Bible* (Ithaca: Cornell University Press, 2001), 34.

2 "Twentieth-Century Foxes," *Ms. Magazine*, X, 1 (December 1999–January 2000).

3 Cited in Catherine Clinton, *The Other Civil War* (New York: Hill and Wang, 1984).

4 Nancy Cott, *The Grounding of Modern Feminism* (New Haven: Yale University Press, 1987). The discussion of the split in the women's movement after suffrage was won is indebted to Cott's book and to a review of it by Ruth Rosen, "A Serious Case of Déjà-vu," *The Women's Review of Books* V, 3 (December, 1987).

5 Ruth Rosen and Sue Davidson, Introduction, *The Maimie Papers*, ed. Ruth Rosen and Sue Davidson (Old Westbury, NY: Feminist Press, 1977).

6 Nancy Cott, "Eighteenth-Century Family and Social Life Revealed in Massachusetts Divorce Records," *The Journal of Social History* 10 (fall 1976): 20–43.

7 Françoise Basch, *Relative Creatures: Victorian Women in Society and the Novel, 1837–67* (London: Allan Lane, 1974).

8 Barbara Taylor, *Eve and the New Jerusalem: Socialism and Feminism in the Nineteenth Century* (New York: Pantheon Books, 1983).

9 All quotations in this paragraph come from Jill Liddington and Jill Norris, *One Hand Tied Behind Us: The Rise of the Women's Suffrage Movement* (London: Virago, 1978).

10 Joni Seager and Ann Olson, *Women in the World: An International Atlas* (Simon and Schuster: New York, 1986).

CHAPTER 8

1 Heidi Hartmann, "Capitalism, Patriarchy, and Job Segregation by Sex," *Signs*, I (spring 1976), 137–69; "The Unhappy Marriage of Marxism and Feminism: Toward a More Progressive Union," *Capital and Class*, 8 (summer 1979) 1–33.

2 Ava Baron, "Women and the Making of the American Working Class: A Study of the Proletarianization of Printers," *Review of Radical Political Economics* 14, 3 (fall 1982): 23–42.

3 But fear of Asians peaked during the Second World War, when thousands of Japanese Americans, some of whose forebears had been in the United States longer than those of many European immigrants, had their property confiscated, were placed in concentration camps, and were deprived of all civil rights.

4 Meredith Tax, *The Rising of the Women* (New York: Monthly Review Press, 1989).

5 Ibid.

6 Ibid.

7 Ibid.

8 Ibid.

9 Ruth Milkman, "Organizing the Sexual Division of Labor: Historical Perspectives on 'Women's Work' and the American Labor Movement," *Socialist Review* 49: 95–150.

10 The discussion of Rose Pastor Stokes derives from Catherine Clinton, *The Other Civil War* (New York: Hill and Wang, 1984) and from Arthur and Pearl Zipser, *Fire and Grace: The Life of Rose Pastor Stokes* (Athens, Ga.: University of Georgia Press, 1990).

11 Alma Herbst, *The Negro in the Slaughtering and Meatpacking Industry in Chicago* (Boston: Houghton Mifflin, 1932).

12 Rosalyn Terborg-Penn, "Survival Strategies among Afro-American Women Workers: A Continuing Process," *Women, Work, and Protest: A Century of U.S. Women's Labor History*, ed. Ruth Milkman (Boston: Routledge & Kegan Paul, 1985).

13 Blanche Wiesen Cook, "Female Support Networks and Political Activism: Lillian Wald, Crystal Eastman, Jane Addams, and Emma Goldman," *Chrysalis* 3 (autumn 1977); and "Feminism, Socialism, and Sexual Freedom: The Work and Legacy of Crystal Eastman and Alexandra Kollontai," *Stratégies Féminines/ Stratégies Féministes*, ed.

Françoise Basch et al. (Paris); English edition, ed. Judith Friedlander et al. (Bloomington: Indiana University Press, 1986).

14 Tax, *The Rising of the Women.*

15 Candace Falk, *Love, Anarchy, and Emma Goldman* (New York: Holt, Rinehart and Winston, 1984).

16 Ibid.

17 Milkman, "Organizing The Sexual Division of Labor."

18 Ibid.

19 Ibid.

20 Sarah Boston, *Women Workers and the Trade Union Movement* (London: Davis-Poynter, 1980).

21 Ibid.

22 Barbara Taylor, "'The Men Are as Bad as Their Masters . . .': Socialism, Feminism and Sexual Antagonism in the London Tailoring Trade in the 1830s," in *Sex and Class in Women's History*, ed. Judith L. Newton, Mary P. Ryan, and Judith R. Walkowitz (London: Routledge & Kegan Paul, 1983).

23 Ibid.

24 Cynthia Cockburn, *Brothers: Male Dominance and Technological Change* (London: Pluto Press, 1983).

25 Ibid.

26 Engineer Thomas Wright, in 1868. Cited in Cockburn, *Brothers.*

27 Eleanor Rathbone, *The Disinherited Family*, republished as *Family Allowance* (London: Allen and Unwin, 1949).

28 Cockburn, *Brothers.*

29 Other sources used in this chapter are Mary Stevenson, "Women's Wages and Job Segregation," *Labor Market Segmentation*, ed. Richard C. Edwards, Michael Reich, and David M. Gordon (Lexington, Mass.: D. C. Heath, 1975); and Sidney and Beatrice Webb, *History of Trade Unionism* (London: Longmans, Green Christian Co., 1920).

CHAPTER 9

1 In 1871 Tennie Claflin (Victoria Woodhull's sister) published *Constitutional Equality* (New York: Woodhull, Claflin & Co.). and pointed out that "where five years ago one paper in a hundred only, contained something about the progress of the Woman Question, now only one in a hundred can be found that has not a very considerable space devoted to it." She linked this to the Civil War and women's "bold advance . . . into the heat and strife of active business life."

2 Bram Dijkstra, *Idols of Perversity: Fantasies of Feminine Evil in Fin-de-Siècle Culture* (New York, Oxford: Oxford University Press, 1986); Klaus Theweleit, *Male Fantasies* vol I. Minneapolis: University of Minnesota Press, 1987). I have also drawn from Reinhold Heller, the catalog for an exhibit of fin-de-siècle paintings of this sort shown at the David and Alfred Smart Gallery of the University of Chicago in 1981, *The Earthly Chimera and the Femme Fatale: Fear of Woman in Nineteenth-Century Art.*

3 Anthony Ludovici, *Enemies of Women: The Origins in Outline of Anglo-Saxon Feminism* (London: Carroll and Nicholson, 1948). Ludovici cites this characteristic as specific to late nineteenth-century men, and "almost endemic in England" during this time.

4 Dykstra, *Idols of Perversity.*

5 Horace Bushnell, "Women's Suffrage: The Reform Against Nature," *The New Englander,* 28, 109 (October 1869).

6 Nicholas Francis Cooke, *Satan in Society* (1870; New York: Edward F. Hovey, 1881).

7 Ibid.

8 Pierre-Joseph Proudhon, *On Pornocracy, or Women in Modern Times* (1875).

9 Franz Wedekind, *Earth Spirit* and *Pandora's Box.*

10 See Mark Twain's *Eve's Diary* (1906) and Oscar Wilde's *The Picture of Dorian Gray* (1891) and *Salome* (1893).

11 For a scholarly study of theories of impregnation, see Thomas Lacquer, *Making Sex: Body and Gender from the Greeks to Freud* (Cambridge, Mass.: Harvard University Press, 1990). Norman Mailer resuscitated the old-husband's tale that orgasm is necessary to conception in *Prisoner of Sex.*

12 Harry Campbell, *Differences in the Nervous Organization of Man and Woman* (1891).

13 Dykstra, *Idols of Perversity*; Charles Darwin, *The Descent of Man*. "It is generally admitted that with woman the powers of intuition, of rapid perception, and perhaps of imitation, are more strongly marked than in man."

14 *The Atlantic Monthly* (1866).

15 Herbert Spencer, *Social Statics* (1850); *First Principles* (1862).

16 Carl C. Vogt, *Lectures on Man*.

17 Herbert Spencer, *The Study of Sociology* (1873).

18 Maurice Hamel, *Salon de 1890* (Paris, 1890); Albert Aurier, *Mercure de France* (August 1891).

19 See Emile Zola, *The Sin of Father Mouret*.

20 For instance, Paul Adam, "On Children," *La Revue Blanche* (1895), wrote that girls between eight and thirteen "found a perverse pleasure in watching sedentary middle-aged men expose themselves to them for a few pennies," and concludes "virtually all vices fester in the mind of the child. . . . Evil in adults is a sign of their not having grown up." Lombroso and Ferrero agreed, writing in *The Female Offender*: "What terrific criminals would children be if they had strong passions, muscular strength, and sufficient intelligence; and if, moreover, their evil tendencies were exasperated by a morbid psychical activity! And women are big children; their evil tendencies are more numerous and more varied than men's, but generally remain latent. When they are awakened and excited they produce results proportionately greater." (New York: D. Appleton, 1986).

21 This figure is exalted also by Camille Paglia, *Sexual Personae* (New Haven: Yale University Press, 1990).

22 Dykstra, *Idols of Perversity*.

23 Ibid.

24 Walter Pater, *Marius the Epicurean* (New York: Macmillan, 1907).

25 Charles Baudelaire, "Metamorphoses of the Vampire" (1852). This poem was deleted from the first edition of *Flowers of Evil* (1857).

26 Charles Darwin, *The Descent of Man*. The animal is the Asiatic Antilope saiga.

27 Dykstra, *Idols of Perversity*.

28 Emile Tardieu, in *La Revue Blanche* (1895).

29 Dykstra, *Idols of Perversity*.

30 William Graham Sumner, "Sociology," in *War and Other Essays* (1881).

31 Barbara Ehrenreich, Foreword to Theweleit, *Male Fantasies.*

32 Theweleit, *Male Fantasies.*

33 Ibid.

34 Heinrich Teuber, *Bergmannsfrauen* (1927).

35 Theweleit, *Male Fantasies.*

36 Michael Rohrwasser, *Saubere Mädel, Starke Genossen* [*Spotless Maidens, Sturdy Comrades*] (Frankfurt, 1975).

37 Theweleit, *Male Fantasies.*

38 Ibid.

39 Edward Fuchs, *The Gallant Age, History of Manners* [*Sittengeschichte*], 6 vols. (Munich, 1909–12).

40 Thomas Stephen Szasz, *The Manufacture of Madness* (New York: Harper & Row, 1977).

41 Theweleit, *Male Fantasies*, 358.

SELECTED BIBLIOGRAPHY

Addams, Jane. *Twenty Years at Hull House.* First published 1910. New York: Macmillan, 1981.

Anderson, Bonnie S., and Judith P. Zinsser. *A History of Their Own.* New York: Harper & Row, 1988.

Babatunde Agiri. "Slavery in Yoruba Society in the 19th Century." *The Ideology of Slavery in Africa*, ed. P. Lovejoy. Berkeley, Cal.: Sage Publications, 1981.

Bakan, David. *And They Took Themselves Wives.* San Francisco: Harper & Row, 1979.

Bakari, Mtoro bin Mwinyi. *The Customs of the Swahili People*, ed. and trans. J.W.T. Allen. Berkeley: University of California Press, c.1981.

Balser, Diane. *Sisterhood and Solidarity: Feminism and Labor in Modern Times.* Boston: South End Press, 1987.

Baron, Ava. "Women and the Making of the American Working Class: A Study of the Proletarianization of Printers." *Review of Radical Political Economics* (1982): 23–42.

Basch, Françoise. *Rebelles Americaines au XIXeme Siecle: Mariage, Amour Libre, et Politique.* Paris: Meridiens Klincksieck, 1990.

—. *Relative Creatures: Victorian Women in Society and the Novel, 1837–67.* New York: Schocken, 1974.

Baxandall, Rosalyn, Linda Gordon, and Susan Reverby. Archives: "Boston Working Women Protest, 1869." *Signs* 3, 1 (1976).

Berger, Iris. "Women of Eastern and Southern Africa." In *Restoring Women to History*, ed. Renata Bridenthal, Claudia Koonz, and Susan Stuard. Bloomington, Ind.: Organization of American Historians, 1988.

Bessell, M.J. "Nyabingi." *Uganda Journal* 6, 2 (1938).

Bordin, Ruth. *Woman and Temperance.* Philadelphia: Temple University Press, 1981.

Boston, Sarah. *Women Workers and the Trade Union Movement.* London: Davis-Poynter, 1980.

Bremer, Fredericka. *The Homes of the New World: Impressions of America.* New York: Harper & Brothers, 1853.

Bremer, Sidney. "Lost Continuities: Alternative Urban Visions in Chicago Novels, 1890–1915." *Soundings* 64, 1 (1981): 29–51.

Broadhead, Susan Herlin. "Slave Wives, Free Sisters: Bakongo Women and Slavery c. 1700–1850." In *Women and Slavery in Africa*, ed. Claire Robertson and Martin Klein. Madison, Wis.: University of Wisconsin Press, 1983.

Bruce, Philip. *The Plantation Negro as a Freeman: Observations on His Character, Condition, and Prospects in Virginia.* New York: G.P. Putnam's Sons, 1889.

Bushnell, Horace. "Women's Suffrage: The Reform Against Nature." *The New Englander*, 28, 109, October 1869.

Campbell, Beatrix. *Wigan Pier Revisited: Poverty and Politics in the Eighties.* London: Virago, 1984.

Campbell, Harry. *Differences in the Nervous Organization of Man and Woman: Physiological and Pathological.* London, H.K. Lewis, 1891.

Chambers-Schiller, Lee Virginia. *Liberty, a Better Husband–Single Women in America: The Generations of 1780–1840.* New Haven: Yale University Press, 1984.

Claflin, Tennessee. *Constitutional Authority.* New York: Woodhull, Claflin & Co, 1871.

Clinton, Catherine. *The Other Civil War.* New York: Hill and Wang, 1984.

Cockburn, Cynthia. *Brothers: Male Dominance and Technological Change.* London: Pluto Press, 1983.

Cobbing, Julian. "The Mfecane as Alibi: Thoughts on Dithakong and Mbolompo." *Journal of African History* 29 (1988): 487–519.

Cook, Blanche Wiesen. "Female Support Networks and Political Activism: Lillian Wald, Crystal Eastman, Jane Addams, and Emma Goldman." *Chrysalis* 3 (autumn 1977).

—. "Feminism, Socialism, and Sexual Freedom: The Work and Legacy of Crystal Eastman and Alexandra Kollontai." In *Stratégies Féminines/Stratégies Féministes*, ed. Francois Basch et al. English edition, ed. Judith Friedlander et al. Bloomington: Indiana University Press, 1986.

Cooke, Nicholas Francis. *Satan in Society.* New York: Edward F. Hovey, 1881.

Proudhon, Pierre Joseph. *On Pornocracy, or Women in Modern Times*. Paris: Lacroix, 1875.

Cooper, Frederick. "Islam and Cultural Hegemony: The Ideology of Slaveowners on the East African Coast." In *The Ideology of Slavery in Africa*, ed. P. Lovejoy. Beverly Hills: Sage Publications, 1981.

Cott, Nancy, "Eighteenth-Century Family and Social Life revealed in Massachusetts Divorce Records," *The Journal of Social History* 10, Fall 1976: 20–43.

—. "Feminist Theory and Feminist Movements: The Past before Us." In *What Is Feminism: A Re-examination*, ed. Juliet Mitchell and Ann Oakley. New York: Pantheon Books, 1986.

Curtis, David Ames, and Henry Louis Gates. "Establishing the Identity of the Author of *Our Nig*." In *Wild Women in the Whirlwind: Afra-American Culture and the Contemporary Literary Renaissance*, ed. Joanne M. Braxton and Andrée Nicola McLaughlin. New Brunswick, NJ: Rutgers University Press, 1990.

Davidoff, Leonore. "Mastered for Life: Servant and Wife in Victorian and Edwardian England." *Journal of Social History* 7, 3 (1974).

Davidson, Basil. *The Story of Africa*. London: Mitchell Beazley, 1984.

Davis, Angela Y. *Women, Race, and Class*. New York: Random House, 1981.

Dijkstra, Bram. *Idols of Perversity: Fantasies of Feminine Evil in Fin-de-Siècle Culture*. New York: Oxford University Press, 1986.

Dorsey, George. *Man's Own Show: Civilization*. New York: Harper & Brothers, 1931.

Douglas, Ann. *The Feminization of American Culture*. New York: Alfred A. Knopf, 1977.

Dunayevskaya, Raya. "The Black Dimension in Women's Liberation." In *Women's Liberation and the Dialectics of Revolution*. Atlantic Highlands, NJ: Humanities Press International, 1985.

Ehrenreich, Barbara. *Blood Rites*. New York: Henry Holt, 1997.

Engels, Frederich, and Karl Marx. *The Communist Manifesto*. London: Penguin, 1985.

Engels, Friedrich. *The Condition of the Working Class*. Harmondsworth: Penguin, 1987.

Falk, Candace. *Love, Anarchy, and Emma Goldman*. New York: Holt, Rinehart and Winston, 1984.

Finnegan, Frances. *Poverty and Prostitution: A Study of Victorian Prostitutes in York*. Cambridge: Cambridge University Press, 1979.

Flexner, Eleanor. *Century of Struggle*. Cambridge, Mass.: Harvard University Press, 1980.

Foucault, Michel. *Power/Knowledge*, ed. Colin Gordon. New York: Pantheon, 1980.

Fortin, Nina E. and Tuchman, Gaye. *Edging Women Out: Victorian Novelists, Publishers, and Social Change*. New Haven: Yale University Press, 1989.

Fourier, Charles, "Théorie de Quatre Mouvements." In *The Utopian Vision of Charles Fourier*, ed. Jonathon Beecher and Richard Bienvenue. Boston: Beacon Press, 1971.

Franklin, Frazier, E. *Black Bourgeoisie*. New York: The Free Press, 1957.

Fuchs, Edward. *The Gallant Age: A History of Manners*. Munich: Sittengechichte, 1909–12.

Genovese, Eugene. *Roll, Jordan, Roll: The World the Slaves Made*. New York: Random House, 1974.

Gibson, Mary. *Prostitution and the State in Italy, 1860–1915*. New Brunswick, NJ: Rutgers University Press, 1986.

Giddings, Paula. *When and Where I Enter*. New York: William Morrow, 1984.

Grant, Jacqueline. "Black Women and the Church." In *Some of Us Are Brave*, ed. Gloria T. Hull, Patricia Bell Scott, and Barbara Smith. Old Westbury, NY: The Feminist Press, 1982.

Greg, W.R. "Prostitution," *Westminster Review*, 1850.

Gutman, Herbert. *The Black Family in Slavery and Freedom, 1750–1925*. New York: Pantheon, 1976.

Hafkin, Nancy J., and Edna G. Bay, eds. *Women in Africa: Studies in Social and Economic Change*. Stanford, Cal.: Stanford University Press, 1976.

Hall, Jacqueline Dowd. *Revolt Against Chivalry: Jessie Daniel Ames and the Women's Campaign Against Lynching*. New York: Columbia University Press, 1979.

Hall, Jacqueline Dowd, Robert Korstad, and James Leloudis. "Cotton Mill People." *American Historical Review* 91, 2 (1986): 245–285.

Hartmann, Heidi. "Capitalism, Patriarchy, and Job Segregation by Sex." *Signs* 1 (spring 1976): 137–69.

Hayden, Dolores. *Seven American Utopias: The Architecture of Communitarian Socialism*. Cambridge, Mass.: MIT Press, 1975.

Herbst, Alma. *The Negro in the Slaughtering and Meatpacking Industry in Chicago*. Boston: Houghton Mifflin, 1932.

Hersh, Blanche Glassman. *The Slavery of Sex: Feminist-Abolitionists in America*. Chicago: University of Illinois Press, 1978.

Hewitt, Nancy A. "Friends: Agrarian Quakers and the Emergence of Woman's Rights in America." *Feminist Studies* 12, 1 (1986): 28–49.

Hiley, Michael. *Victorian Working Women: Portraits from Life*. London: Gordon Fraser, 1979.

Hinderer, Anna. *Seventeen Years in the Yoruba Country: Memorials of Anna Hinderer*, edited by her friends. London: Seeley, Jackson & Holliday, 1852.

Hine, Darlene Clark. *Black Women in White: Racial Conflict and Cooperation in the Nursing Profession, 1890–1950*. Bloomington: Indiana University Press, 1989.

Hobsbawm, E.J. *The Age of Revolution: Europe 1789–1848*. London: Cardinal, 1988.

Holcombe, Lee. *Victorian Ladies at Work*, ed. Lee Holcombe. Hamden, Conn.: Anchor Books, 1973.

Horowitz, Maryanne Cline. "The 'Science' of Embryology before the Discovery of the Ovum." In *Connecting Spheres: Women in the Western World, 1500 to the Present*, ed. Marilyn J. Boxer and Jean H. Quataert. New York: Oxford University Press, 1987.

Hunt, James, and Charles C. Vogt. *Lectures on Man, His Place in Creation, and the History of the Earth*. Publisher: London, Longman, Green, Longman, and Roberts, 1864.

Janiewski, Dolores. "Making Common Cause: The Needlewomen of New York, 1831–69." *Signs* 1, 3 (1976).

Jones, Jacqueline. *Labor of Love, Labor of Sorrow: Black Women, Work, and the Family from Slavery to the Present*. New York: Basic Books, 1985.

—. "'My Mother Was Much of a Woman': Black Women, Work, and the Family under Slavery." *Feminist Studies* 8, 2 (1982): 235–69.

Jones, Kathleen B. "Citizenship in a Woman-Friendly Polity." *Signs* 15, 4 (1990): 781–812.

Joseph, Gloria I. "Sojourner Truth: Archetypal Black Feminists." In *Wild Women in the Whirlwind: Afra-American Culture and the Contemporary Literary Renaissance*, ed. Joanne M. Braxton and Andrée Nicola McLaughlin. New Brunswick, NJ: Rutgers University Press, 1990.

Katzman, David. *Seven Days a Week: Women and Domestic Service in Industrializing America.* Chicago: University of Illinois Press, 1981.

Kerber, Linda K. "Separate Spheres, Female Worlds, Woman's Place: The Rhetoric of Women's History." *Journal of American History* 75, 1 (1988): 9–39.

Kern, Kathi. *Mrs Stanton's Bible.* Ithica: Cornell University press, 2001.

Dobosz, Ann Marie. "Twentieth Century Foxes," *Ms Magazine*, 1, December 1999–January 2000.

Kessler-Harris, Alice. *Women Have Always Worked: A Historical Overview.* New York: The Feminist Press, 1981.

Kestner, Joseph. *Protest and Reform, 1827–1867.* Madison: University of Wisconsin Press, 1985.

Kwamena-Poh, M. "African History in Maps." In *African Women South of the Sahara*, ed. Margaret Jean Hay and Sharon Stichter. New York: Longman, 1984.

Lacquer, Thomas. *Making Sex: Body and Gender from the Greeks to Freud.* Cambridge, Mass.: Harvard University Press, 1990.

Lerner, Gerda. *The Majority Finds Its Past: Placing Women in History.* Oxford: Oxford University Press, 1979.

Lewis, Samella. *Art: African American.* New York: Harcourt Brace Jovanovich, 1978.

Campbell, Mary Schmidt. Introduction, *Harlem Renaissance: Art of Black America.* New York: Harry N. Abrams, 1987.

Lewis, Sarah. *Women's Mission.* London: J.W. Parker, 1839.

Liddington, Jill, and Jill Norris. *One Hand Tied Behind Us: The Rise of the Women's Suffrage Movement.* London: Virago, 1978.

Ludovici, Anthony. *Enemies of Women: The Origins in Outline of Anglo-Saxon Feminism.* London: Carroll and Nicholson, 1948.

Mbilinyi, Marjorie. "Wife, Slave and Subject of the King: The Oppression of Women in the Shambala Kingdom." *Tanzania Notes and Records* 88–89 (1982).

—. "'Women in Development': Ideology and the Marketplace." In *Competition: A Feminist Taboo?* ed. Valerie Miner and Helen E. Longino. New York: The Feminist Press, 1987.

McBride, Theresa. "The Long Road Home: Women's Work and Industrialization." In *Becoming Visible: Women in European History*, ed. Renate Bridenthal and Claudia Koonz. Boston: Houghton Mifflin, 1977.

Milkman, Ruth. "Organizing the Sexual Division of Labor: Historical Perspectives on 'Women's Work' and the American Labor Movement." *The Socialist Review* 10 (January/February 1980): 95–150.

Moers, Ellen. *Literary Women*. New York: Doubleday, 1977.

Motz, Marilyn Ferris. *True Sisterhood: Michigan Women and Their Kin, 1820–1920*. Albany: State University of New York Press, 1983.

Mutunhu, Tendai. "Nehanda of Zimbabwe," *Ufahamu*.

Ranger, Terence O. *Revolt in Southern Rhodesia, 1867–70*. London: Heinemann, 1967.

Nightingale, Florence. *Method of Improving the Nursing Service of Hospitals*. London, 1869.

Olafson, Erna Hellerstein, Leslie Parker Hume, and Karen M. Offen, eds. *Victorian Women*. Stanford, Calif.: Stanford University Press, 1981.

Olsen, Tillie. Introduction to Rebecca Harding Davis, *Life in the Iron Mills*, ed. Tillie Olsen. First published 1861. New York: The Feminist Press, 1972.

Owens, Leslie Howard. *This Species of Property: Slave Life and Culture in the Old South*. New York: Oxford University Press, 1976.

Perkins, Linda. "'Heed Life's Demands': The Educational Philosophy of Fanny Jackson." *Journal of Negro Education* (summer 1982).

Price, Roger. *The Revolutions of 1848*. London: Macmillan, 1988.

Ramas, Maria. *"Freud's Dora, Dora's Hysteria."* In *Sex and Class in Women's History*, ed. Judith L. Newton, Mary P. Ryan, and Judith R. Walkowitz. London: Routledge and Kegan Paul, 1983.

Rathbone, Eleanor. *The Disinherited Family*, republished as *Family Allowance*. London: Allen and Unwin, 1949.

Reid, Marion. *A Plea for Women Being a Vindication of the Importance and Extent of Her Natural Sphere of Action*. London: 1843.

Robertson, Claire. "Ga Women and Socioeconomic Change in Accra, Ghana." In *Women in Africa: Studies in Social and Economic Change*, ed. Nancy J. Hafkin and Edna G. Bay. Stanford, Cal.: Stanford University Press, 1976.

Robinson, Harriet. *Loom and Spindle or Life among the Early Mill Girls.* First published 1898. Kailua: Press Pacifica, 1976.

Rosen, Ruth, and Sue Davidson. Introduction to *The Maimie Papers*, ed. Ruth Rosen and Sue Davidson. Old Westbury, NY: Feminist Press, 1977.

Ross, Ellen. "Fierce Questions and Taunts: Married Life in Working-Class London, 1870–1914." *Feminist Studies* 8, 3 (1982): 575–602.

—. "Survival Networks: Women's Neighbourhood Sharing in London before World War I." *History Workshop Journal* 15 (spring 1983): 4–27.

Sachs, Karen. *Sisters and Wives: The Past and Future of Sexual Equality.* Westport, Conn.: Contributions in Women's Studies 10, 1979.

Schlegel, Katherine. "Mistress and Servant in Nineteenth-Century Hamburg: Employer/Employee Relationships in Domestic Service, 1880–1914." *History Workshop Journal* 15 (spring 1983): 60–77.

Scott, Joan W., and Louise A. Tilly. *Comparative Studies in Society and History*, vol. 17. Cambridge: Cambridge University Press, 1975.

—. *Women, Work and Family*. New York: Holt, Rinehart and Winston, 1978.

Seager, Joni, and Ann Olson. *Women in the World: International Atlas*. New York: Simon & Schuster, 1986.

Showalter, Elaine. *A Literature of Their Own*. Princeton, NJ: Princeton University Press, 1977.

Smith-Rosenberg, Carroll. "The Female World of Love and Ritual: Relations between Women in Nineteenth-Century America." *Signs* 1, 1 (1975): 1–29.

Spencer, Herbert. *First Principles*. New York, De Witt Revolving Fund, 1958.

—. *Social Statistics*. London: Questions Publishing, 1910.

—. *The Study of Sociology*. Ann Arbor: University of Michigan Press, 1961.

Stansell, Christine. *City of Women: Sex and Class in New York, 1789–1860*. New York: Alfred A. Knopf, 1986.

—. "Women, Children and the Uses of the Streets: Class and Gender Conflict in New York City, 1850-1860." *Feminist Studies* 1982 8(2): 309–335.

Sterling, Dorothy. *We Are Your Sisters: Black Women in the Nineteenth Century*. New York: Norton, 1984.

Stevenson, Mary. *Labor Market Segmentation*, ed. Richard C. Edwards, Michael Reich, and David M. Gordon. Lexington Mass.: D. C. Heath, 1975.

Strobel, Margaret. *Muslim Women in Mombasa, 1890–1975*. New Haven: Yale University Press, 1979.

Sumner, William. *War and Other Essays*. New Haven: Yale University Press, 1911.

Sweetman, David. *Women Leaders in African History*. London: Heinemann, 1984.

Tax, Meredith. *The Rising of the Women*. New York: Monthly Review Press, 1989.

Szasz, Thomas Stephen. *The Manufacture of Madness*. New York: Harper & Row, 1977.

Taylor, Barbara. *Eve and the New Jerusalem: Socialism and Feminism in the Nineteenth Century*. New York: Pantheon Books, 1983.

Terborg-Penn, Rosalyn. "Survival Strategies among Afro-American Women Workers: A Continuing Process." In *Women, Work, and Protest: A Century of U.S. Women's Labor History*, ed. Ruth Milkman. Boston: Routledge, Kegan Paul, 1985.

—. "Women and Slavery in the African Diaspora: A Cross-Cultural Approach to Historical Analysis." *Sage* 3, 2 (1986): 11–15.

Theweleit, Klaus. *Male Fantasies*, vol. 1: *Women, Floods, Bodies, History*. Minneapolis: University of Minnesota Press, 1987.

Vicinus, Martha. *Independent Women: Work and Community for Single Women, 1850–1920*. Chicago: University of Chicago Press, 1985.

Walkowitz, Judith. *Prostitution and Victorian Society: Women, Class, and the State*. Cambridge: Cambridge University Press, 1980.

Webb, Sidney and Beatrice. *History of Trade Unionism*. London: Longmans, Green Christian Co., 1920.

White, E. Frances. "Creole Women Traders in the Nineteenth Century." Working Papers No. 27, African Studies Center, Boston University.

—. *Sierra Leone's Settler Women Traders: Women on the Afro-European Frontier*. Ann Arbor: University of Michigan Press, 1987.

Whitehead, Ann. "Sexual Antagonism in Herefordshire." In *Dependence and Exploitation in Work and Marriage*, ed. D.L. Barker and S. Allen. London: Longman, 1976.

Wood, Ann Douglas. "The Fashionable Diseases." In *Clio's Consciousness Raised*, ed. Mary S. Hartman and Lois Banner. New York: Harper & Row, 1974.

Wright, Marcia. "Justice, Women, and the Social Order in Abercorn, Northeastern Rhodesia, 1897–1903." In *African Women and the Law: Historical Perspectives*, ed. Margaret Jean Hay and Marcia Wright. Boston: Boston University Papers on Africa VII, 1982.

—. "Technology, Marriage and Women's Work in the History of Maize-Growers in Mazabuka, Zambia: A Reconnaissance." *Journal of African Studies* 10, 1 (1983): 71–85.

—. "Women in Peril." *African Social Research* 20 (1975): 800–19.

Zinn, Howard. *A People's History of the United States*. New York: Harper & Row, 1980.

Zipser, Arthur and Pearl. *Fire and Grace: The Life of Rose Pastor Stokes*. Athens: University of Georgia Press, 1990.

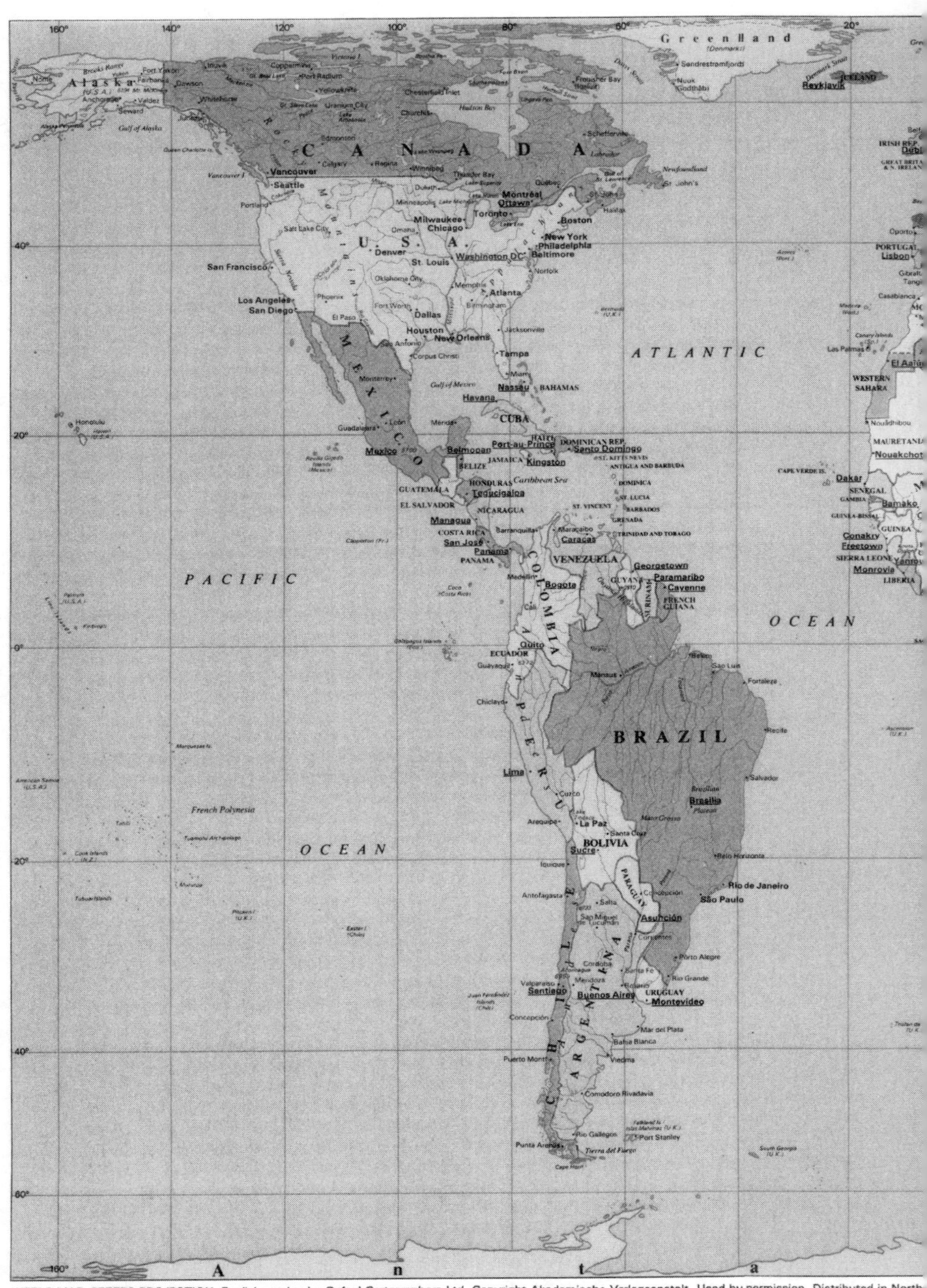

WORLD MAP: PETERS PROJECTION. English version by Oxford Cartographers Ltd. Copyright Akademische Verlagsanstalt. Used by permission. Distributed in North

iverside IDrive, New York, NY 10115.

INDEX

Q

R

The Feminist Press at The City University of New York is a nonprofit institution dedicated to publishing literary and educational works by and about women. We are the oldest continuing feminist publisher in the world; our existence is grounded in the knowledge that mainstream publishers seeking mass audiences often ignore important, pathbreaking works by women from the United States and throughout the world.

The Feminist Press was founded in 1970. In its early decades the Press launched the contemporary rediscovery of "lost" American women writers, and went on to diversify its list by publishing significant works by American women writers of color. More recently, the Press has added to its roster international women writers who are still far less likely to be translated than male writers. We also seek out nonfiction that explores contemporary issues affecting the lives of women around the world.

The Feminist Press has initiated two important long-term projects. Women Writing Africa is an unprecedented four-volume series that documents women's writing in Africa over thousands of years. The Women Writing Science project, funded by the National Science Foundation, celebrates the achievements of women scientists while frankly analyzing obstacles in their career paths. The series also promotes scientific literacy among the public at large, and encourages young women to choose careers in science.

Founded in an activist spirit, The Feminist Press is currently undertaking initiatives that will bring its books and educational resources to underserved populations, including community colleges, public high schools, literacy and ESL programs, and international libraries. As we move forward into the twenty-first century, we continue to expand our work to respond to women's silences wherever they are found.

For information about events and for a complete catalog of the Press's more than 300 books, please refer to our website: www.feministpress.org or call (212) 817-7915.